CONTEMPORARY
NATIVE AMERICAN
POLITICAL ISSUES

CONTEMPORARY NATIVE AMERICAN COMMUNITIES
Stepping Stones to the Seventh Generation

Native American communities and people have survived through the twentieth century and are poised to embark on the twenty-first century. The survival and continuity of Native American cultures and communities has been a varied and complex path. Hundreds of communities continue to preserve many features of their religion, government, kinship organization, values, art, ceremony, and belief systems, and to maintain political relations with the United States. The series is intended to fill an existing void in the literature on Native American contemporary world experiences. While providing a historical background, the series will focus on an interpretation of contemporary life and cultures, interpreted in their broadest contexts. The series will draw from the disciplines of Native American Studies, History, Sociology, Political Science, Religion, and Social Work, and solicit treatments of treaty interpretation, sovereign rights, incorporation into global and national economic, political, and cultural relations, land rights, subsistence rights, health and medicine, cultural preservation, contemporary spirituality, multiple genders, policy, and other issues that confront tribal communities and affect their possibilities for survival. New and culturally creative possibilities have emerged in film, theater, literature, dance, art, and other fields as a result and reflection of the challenges that have confronted Native American communities over the past centuries and will again in the coming century. We believe it is essential to examine contemporary Native American life from the point of view of Native concerns and values. Manuscripts that examine any significant aspect of Native American contemporary life and future trends are welcome.

BOOKS IN THE SERIES

CONTEMPORARY

NATIVE AMERICAN

POLITICAL ISSUES

Edited by
Troy R. Johnson

ALTAMIRA PRESS
A Division of
ROWMAN & LITTLEFIELD PUBLISHERS, INC.
Walnut Creek • Lanham • New York • Oxford

ALTAMIRA PRESS
A Division of Rowman & Littlefield Publishers, Inc.
1630 North Main Street, Suite 367
Walnut Creek, CA 94596
http://www.altamirapress.com

Rowman & Littlefield Publishers, Inc.
4720 Boston Way
Lanham, MD 20706

12 Hid's Copse Road
Cumnor Hill, Oxford OX2 9JJ, England

British Library Cataloguing in Publication Information Available
Library of Congress Cataloging-in-Publication Data
    Contemporary Native American political issues / edited by Troy Johnson
      p. cm.— (Contemporary Native American communities; v. 2)
    Includes bibliographical references (p.) and index.
    ISBN 0-7619-9060-7 (cloth : acid-free paper). — ISBN 0-7619-9061-5
(pbk. : acid-free paper)
    1. Indians of North America—Politics and government. 2. Indians of north America—Civil
rights. 3. Indians of North America—Legal status, laws, etc. 4. Self-determination, National—
United States. I. Johnson, Troy R. II. Series.
E98.P76 C66 1999
323.1'197-dc21   98-40188
                                        CIP

Printed in the United States of America
♾ The paper used in this publication meets the minimum requirements of American
National Standard for Information Sciences—Permanence of Paper for Printed Library
Materials, ANSI/NISO Z39.48–1992.

CONTENTS

PART IV
LAW AND JUSTICE

PART V
REPATRIATION

PART VI
ACTIVISM

INTRODUCTION

Troy R. Johnson

THIS BOOK BRINGS together a collection of articles written by scholars of Native American studies under the title of *Contemporary Native American Political Issues*. The impetus for compiling this collection grew out of discussions that took place over a number of years with numerous colleagues who teach the Native American experience in the contemporary period and a shared frustration that no single volume brings together the myriad issues that need to be addressed. This book and its companion *Contemporary Native American Cultural Issues*, edited by Duane Champagne and also published by AltaMira Press, are the results of such conversations. Together, the two books provide thirty articles that give the reader broad coverage of the many issues facing Native American nations and individuals as they prepare to move into the twenty-first century.

As Dr. Champagne and I began to compile material and place the contributions in what seemed to be logical, topical discussions, we were struck by another issue confronting professors and students of Native American studies. That is: How does one make a clear distinction between issues such as tribal sovereignty, indigenous rights, and law and justice? How do these topics differ, and can they be separated from issues such as identity, health, and the environment? The answer, of course, lies in the interconnectedness of all aspects of Native American life, culture, religion, and politics. In truth, as the reader will find, it is extremely difficult, if not impossible, to discuss one aspect without including the other. And that is as it should be. Still, to provide a readable text and a teachable format, we have selected logical discussion topics which present a variety of specific sites of Native political activity. This format encourages the consideration of Native politics both in terms of unifying themes and contexts and with regard to local situations, needs, and struggles. Themes within each section include this interconnectedness of Native life; the development of and status of the institutional forms in which Native people associate to build communities and assert their rights; the negotiation of philosophical, cultural, and political terms and concepts which form the underpinnings of Native life; the terms on which Native peoples negotiate with state and federal governments, and the formulation of strategies at this interface of culture and power.

NATIONALISM AND SOVEREIGNTY

As Native people and Indian Nations prepare to move into the twenty-first century, no issues are more critical to understanding the challenges to the modern tribal structure and the relationship of Natives to their indigenous heritage than the issues of nationalism and sovereignty. In fact, it can be stated that nationalism and sovereignty are two of the unifying threads that Native American people have retained despite U. S. government assaults upon their very foundations—foundations that are rooted in the U. S. Constitution and reinforced by U. S. Supreme Court cases beginning with the John Marshall Court in *Johnson v. McIntosh*, 1823 and continuing, although in a diminished state, into the close of the twentieth century.

Native nationalism and sovereignty are the linchpins upon which the relationship between the federal government and Native people hinge. In this regard, it should be remembered that the understanding of what constitutes these two concepts has changed over time, and, much to the distress of Native Americans, it has more often changed for the worse than for the better. It is the terms of these agreements—how they are understood historically, how they are interpreted and defined, what constitutes their parameters and jurisdiction—that directly or indirectly informs every aspect of Native politics to the present day. One needs only to review the various federal government policies toward Indian people to see great vacillation in approaches to the recognition or whittling away of the concepts of nationalism and sovereignty: the formative years (1789–1871), allotments and assimilation (1871–1928), the period of Indian reorganization (1928–1945), the termination period (1945–1961), and the era of self-determination (1961–present.) Each period represents a shift in the U.S. government's historical, cultural, and political understanding of Indian Nations and Indian people.

Indian people have been proactive from the time of first European contact in an effort to comprehend and adjust to the non-Indian, Western governing process. Because of the federal government's constantly changing approach, the results have been, at best, frustration, and, at worse, a loss of traditional homelands and an imposed cultural crisis forced upon the indigenous people. The ability of Native Americans to empower their communities and successfully address the spectrum of political issues raised in this volume depends on the recognition of sovereignty and the attainment of the means for integrated self-governance. In their contributions to this section, Ward Churchill and Arif Dirlik discuss the bases of past and future claims to sovereignty and provide hemispheric perspectives on struggles for self-determination by indigenous peoples.

INTERNATIONAL INDIGENOUS RIGHTS

Native Americans struggle for their national sovereignty with a dominant U.S. government that constantly imposes the subordinate status of tribes. Because of this relationship of subordination and dependency, Native politics largely take place on local levels and under the auspices of the Bureau of Indian Affairs (BIA), an internal branch of the federal government created specifically to address the "Indian Problem." However, as the Native peoples assert the centrality of national sovereignty, Native American politics become, really, a matter of international politics. Because U.S. treaties have recognized (in theory, if not in practice) the independent nationhood of tribes, Native people can make strategic use of international law. Despite the fact that United States courts have ruled tribes subordinate rather than equal nations, Native Americans have taken some initiatives in supranational arenas to gain voice and garner support, and to use the ideological and political resources of international organizations and movements. In this context, claims can be brought to a third party in opposition to U.S. policy that would not be actionable under the jurisdiction of domestic courts.

The United Nations (U.N.) has provided the most visible institutional setting for international collaboration among indigenous groups, and many more regional coalitions have been formed as well. One of the major goals of this alliance building is to influence the development of universally recognized legal standards that govern conduct between sovereign nations and monitor human rights within national boundaries. International bodies may apply a degree of pressure on powerful nations such as the United States that American Indian tribes alone would be unable to leverage.

Clearly, while indigenous groups may derive great benefits from political action in international arenas, such alliances must also negotiate the large-scale economic and ideological interests of powerful nations with complex agendas. Thus, the terms on which international policy is developed, its underlying motivations and power relations, and the specific contexts of its implementation, must be rigorously examined if Native Americans are to develop successful strategies. In this section, Stephen Quesenberry examines recent U.N. initiatives concerning indigenous and human rights, and advocates Native Americans' active engagement in international politics. Fae L. Korsmo, through a case study of the Gitksan and Wet'suwet'en in British Columbia, examines the interface between indigenous groups and national and international governmental bodies. Specifically, international politics requires a universalization of concepts and terms according to which standards and legislation are developed, and of crucial concern for the assertion of indigenous rights is the form in which testimony for these purposes is considered legitimate. For example, the status and admissibility of oral history into courts is a source of great debate. In this respect, indigenous groups around the world stand to gain a great deal from sharing experiences of, and strategies for, engaging in political struggles and asserting their voices and rights.

ECONOMIC DEVELOPMENT

The issue of economic development is truly one of the hot topics among Native American people and Native American political issues today, and it will continue to be so well into the foreseeable future. Some may find it strange to find a chapter on economic development in a book on contemporary political issues; however, economic development has become so intrinsically connected with politics on the local, state, and federal levels in this country that it is difficult to speak about one without the other. Further, economic struggles are grounded in issues of sovereignty, tribal status, and jurisdiction, as well as resource use, culture, and world view. Discussions of economic development on Indian reservations, and also in urban settings, necessarily unite questions of political power with the cultures and traditions of Native people.

Unfortunately, the first picture that comes to mind for most people when they hear the words "Indian," and "economic development," is a stereotypical Las Vegas, high-stakes gaming facility. It is true that at latest count there were some 125 tribes with gaming facilities located in twenty-four states, and many such as the Mashantucket Pequot Tribe's Foxwoods Resort Casino, and the Cherokee Smokey Mountains Casino rival most Las Vegas and Atlantic City casinos in beauty, size, and profitability. It is also true that many Native American gaming facilities are only marginally successful and many, such as the 40 gaming tribes in California face strong political opposition and government strong-arm tactics in an attempt to diminish tribal sovereignty and exert more state controls on Indian land. This includes an infusion of funding from Nevada gaming establishments into the California political system to ensure that people from California continue to travel to Nevada to gamble rather than having a comparable Indian owned and run facility within the state.

Gaming is only the most publicized approach to economic development. The articles by Trosper and Anders provide a more in-depth look at traditional American Indian policy, the current issue of Indian gaming, and perhaps more importantly, the goal of a secure economic future for Native American Nations and Native American people. In planning for this future, tribes face many difficult questions and decisions. Under impoverished and subordinate conditions, and under the close scrutiny of the federal government, and often at the mercy of federal budgetary appropriations and regulations, options for development are limited. In many cases, economic development is pitted against traditional values and environmental or health concerns. Tribes have come to a variety of decisions on this front, from accommodating development that may be at odds with their values, to refusing such development, or finding innovative solutions and economic alternatives which attempt to reconcile the two.

LAW AND JUSTICE

The law is both a site and a medium of Native politics. In other words, the continuing contests over sovereignty and tribal jurisdiction make legal status a key political issue in and of itself; meanwhile, Native people have increasingly used the law as a means with which to struggle for other political, economic, and cultural interests more broadly.

Native American individuals and tribes have had very particular, and particularly extensive, experiences with the U.S. legal and criminal justice systems. Throughout the post-contact period, the spectrum of Native life has been subjected to legal scrutiny: from land claims, economic activities, political institutions, citizenship, and tribal membership, to religious practices, cultural and racial identity, and interpersonal relationships. As colonized peoples, American Indians have faced dual realities of indiscriminate, lawless oppression, and the intrusive mechanisms of highly detailed, foreign institutions of law.

Because sovereignty and legal status of tribes are continually challenged, the implementation of many social and economic initiatives within tribes requires engagement with U.S. law. The prosecution of capital crimes, resource use, or development of casinos and gaming are just a few examples of cases in which federal and state governments have pushed for increased control over tribal activities. Deeply resonant in these issues of jurisdiction and sovereignty is the concept of "guardianship," a political and ideological relationship in which the federal government assumes, explicitly or implicitly, that Native peoples and tribes are incapable of governing themselves and thus rationalize increased intervention into tribal affairs. The question of jurisdiction also dictates which U.S. government agency has the authority to negotiate with tribal bodies. At times, as in the case of gaming, tribes are forced to negotiate with or submit to state governments, whereas treaty rights and court rulings have clearly positioned reservations outside the jurisdiction of individual states.

Additionally, American Indian individuals on reservations and in urban settings, like other minority or impoverished groups, disproportionately inhabit prisons and are otherwise engaged with the criminal justice system. This situation must also be seen in the context of centuries of colonial domination, the delegitimization or decimation of traditional institutions, and social problems such as poverty and health. Unfortunately, federal approaches to law and criminality have not taken sufficient account of this context. Social problems are too often met with an increased police presence on Indian lands, and a decrease in tribal jurisdiction and decision-making powers. This is reflected in a shift of federal funding from social programs to criminal justice, and this is of particular concern given the financial dependency of many tribes on the U.S. government.

Articles by in this section by Donald Green and Carole Goldberg work toward fostering new understandings of law and criminality. Their analyses provide greater complexity and context for Native peoples' experiences and orients us toward approaches to law and criminality which prioritize the empowerment and self-sufficiency of Native people and communities.

REPATRIATION

Of equal importance with the issues of gaming and law enforcement on Indian reservations is the issue of the repatriation of Native American human remains, funerary objects, and objects of cultural patrimony. Perhaps no more insulting and insensitive scene can be imagined than the desecration of Native American burial sites by researchers or grave robbers who disregard the law and cultural sensitivities of the Native American Indian people. Equally alarming is the number of Native American human remains and funerary objects held in museums and universities under the guise of research.

On November 16, 1990, Congress enacted the Native American Graves Protection and Repatriation Act (NAGPRA) in an attempt to stop these violations of the human rights of tribal people. This legislation represents a significant shift in power and jurisdiction over cultural objects, though in any particular institutional, tribal, or research setting the implementation and legal details of NAGPRA are constantly contested. A further complication are the terms and types of evidence with which a tribe may "prove" its cultural heritage and claim to particular objects.

A cultural issue rooted in political concepts of sovereignty and human rights, repatriation represents the fundamental connection between culture and politics. As we have seen in a spectrum of Native political issues, competing positions on repatriation reflect the different historical narratives, world views, and economic interests of the parties involved. It is often argued that the interests of Western science are universal, and that "pure research" should not be subject to the identity or history of a particular tribe. In this way, the material culture of Native people is appropriated by "experts" who are believed to have more to say to the world about Indians than do Indians themselves. Further, the standards of "hard science," rather than other forms of evidence such as oral history, form the basis upon which legislation and court decisions regarding repatriation are formed. Our discussions of sovereignty, power, and historicity are thus integral in the case of repatriation as well: the material culture of Native Americans is a political issue of self determination and concerns the ability of tribes and Native people to retain, restore, and create their communities and identities.

ACTIVISM

It is difficult and perhaps incorrect to isolate Native American activism to the contemporary era and to term it strictly as a political issue. In fact, Native American activism can be traced to the earliest periods of this country's history when Indian people first encountered European conquistadors in the Caribbean or on Roanoke Island when the first of the English colonists attempted to settle in the "new world." Native American people rose up in groups and Indian prophets rose up individually to promote active resistance against the new invaders. Tribal groups organized into confederacies, leagues, and nations to protect their lands and their traditional ways of life. European contact was an agency of attack on the political, social, and cultural integrity of these people. Prophets such as Handsome Lake, Tecumseh, Tenskwatawa, Neolin, Deganawida, and Wovoka led activism movements intended to repel or lessen the impact of the European onslaught. Over the centuries, the Indian people have developed a huge variety of mechanisms for surviving and resisting the destruction of their cultures and lifeways, and each issue explored in this volume presents particular contexts and sets of considerations within which such strategies are formulated.

In the contemporary period covered in this book, we focus on organizations such as United Native Americans (UNA), Indians of All Tribes (IoAT), and the American Indian Movement (AIM) to continue the discussion of activism and resistance. Troy Johnson, Duane Champagne, and Joane Nagel present an in-depth analysis of the legacy of Native American activism and address the issues of religious revitalization, social revitalization, and the secular Indian movements that have characterized much of the activism of the twentieth century. The authors place these activism movements within the larger ethos of change and protest that was occurring in American society and state that to understand both the causes and consequences of American Indian activism, it is important to recall the atmosphere of the 1960s and the changes underway in larger U.S. social and political life.

The authors give credit to earlier organizations such as the Society of American Indians, the National Congress of American Indians, and the National Indian Youth Council that provided the leadership training and political awareness for the formation of UNA, IOAT, and AIM. Early events such as the fishing rights struggle in Washington State and the confrontation between Canada, the United States, and members of the Mohawk Nation are also presented to provide the background for the activism of the 1960s.

The authors give the year 1969 as the starting point that begins a unique nine year-period of Red Power protest that included in the 1969–1971 occupation of Alcatraz Island, the 1970 Mount Rushmore occupation, the 1972 week-long occupation of BIA headquarters in Washington, D.C. and the 1973 occupation of Wounded Knee. The last major event of this activism period occurred in July 1978 when several hundred Native Americans marched into Washington, D.C. at the end of the Longest Walk.

Many people have asked and debated the question; What was the impact of this period of activism? The authors believe that perhaps the most profound effect was to educate and change the political and social consciousness of people in the United States and around the world. As a result of the publicity of these acts of protest, by the 1980s, more people were familiar with Indian issues and were supportive of issues of treaty rights, tribal sovereignty, and preservation of Native American culture, traditions, and history. The importance of this support continues to benefit Native Americans as they prepare to move into the twenty-first century and are forced to continue to fight for protections that other groups take for granted. These include tribal sovereignty, religious freedom, self-determination, protection of sacred remains, and the ongoing struggle to protect economic development on Indian reservations.

PART I

NATIONALISM AND SOVEREIGNTY

Sovereignty is an issue that exemplifies the interconnectedness of Native politics, economics, culture, and world view. Today, competing understandings of tribal status are rooted in historical narratives that affirm the legitimacy of particular political institutions, land claims, property rights, individual and human rights, and many other cultural and political concepts. For example, private property and the doctrine of discovery are legal, cultural, and ideological concepts, recognized by the United States government, by which the colonial settling of North America is legitimated. On the other hand, the histories of Native people recognize very different power relations in which cultural practices and tribal institutions which long predated European settlers were conquered by force. From within this complex arena of political power, and in a variety of new institutional and traditional tribal forms, Native people recognize that the assertion of sovereignty is crucial to the survival and development of the economic, cultural, and political life of tribes.

In this section, Ward Churchill and Arif Dirlik provide us with two thought-provoking essays that highlight the ramifications and destructiveness of cultural conflict, colonial imperialism, attacks on cultural identity and power, and ultimately nationalism and sovereignty. In addition to the Native American people of the continental United States, the authors discuss North, South, and Central America and the indigenous people of Hawai'i.

Ward Churchill's essay "The Tragedy and the Travesty" critiques fundamental assumptions underlying the history of relations between tribes and the U.S. government and provides a counterhistory of the treaty-making process and subsequent U.S. Indian policy. Declaring the binding, irrevocable status of the treaties as recognizant of the inherent sovereignty of Indian nations, he interrogates the right of discovery, manifest destiny, expansionism, assimilation, citizenship, and other concepts which have provided the philosophical grounding of much U.S. law, legislation, and politics concerning Indian Nations. This critique reframes the status of tribes such that sovereignty becomes an inalienable basis of Native political struggles.

Arif Dirlik, in "The Past as Project and Legacy," also recognizes the centrality of historical narrative to indigenous politics. Today, Native Americans struggle not only with colonial histories but also with postmodern and cultural critics who take for granted that "nations are 'imagined,' traditions are 'invented,' subjectivities are slippery (if they exist at all), and cultural identities are myths." The problem of political immobilization in the face of postmodern critique has been much noted. Yet at the same time, observers argue that political claims to cultural authenticity— rather than disappearing—are proliferating, and that cultural nationalism, ethnicism and indigenism have emerged as the markers of cultural politics. Thus we have a paradoxical disjuncture between cultural criticism and cultural politics. At the heart of these debates over identity and cultural authenticity lie the questions: What is the relationship of identity formations to power? Are the pasts out of which identities are formed reified or recognized in their historicity? And, what relationship do identity formations establish between the past as legacy and the past as project?

When framed in terms of relations of power, the centrality of identity and historicity to sovereignty and indigenous politics are clear. By exploring the work on concepts of indigenism and identity by diverse critics, artists, and writers in North America and around the Pacific, Dirlik shifts the polarizing debate between "essentialists" and "postmodernists" by claiming that both the timeless and temporal are crucial to indigenous identity. He explores the concepts of cultural identity, (nationalism) as a condition of cultural survival and power using the preface to Leslie Marmon Silko's novel Ceremony as a theme for restoring an indigenous identity for Native Americans, Australian aborigines, Hawai'ians, and Indians of Chiapas. Dirlik compares the writing of Silko to the works of Chinese-American author Frank Chin to show that change is necessary but that the essence of change is contained within the history of the ceremony. Change is not a negative event but is a natural evolution. Silko's narrative, Dirlik states, "is a confirmation of the coexistence of the timeless and the temporal; a sensibility of timeless validity and the changes that are necessary to sustain that sensibility." Thus change becomes an important and natural part of validating and restoring the indigenous identity.

By viewing the ongoing assaults on nationalism and sovereignty through the prism of legacy, tragedy, and travesty, the authors provide us with a better understanding of the paradox that Native American people face today in their struggle to guard against attacks on the Indian individual and the tribal structure while attempting to maintain a meaningful cultural connectedness with the historical past. Sovereignty is fundamental to this ability to both realize and retain indigenous identities and cultures.

1

The Tragedy and the Travesty:
The Subversion of Indigenous Sovereignty
in North America

Ward Churchill

Much ink has been spilled during the late twentieth century explaining that the rights of indigenous peoples are a matter of internal, "domestic" consideration on the part of the various States in which we reside, as if our status was merely that of "ethnic minorities" integral and subordinate to these larger politicoeconomic entities. Such an interpretation is inaccurate, invalid, and in fact illegal under international law. We are nations, and, at least in North America, we have the treaties to prove it. We are thus entitled—morally, ethically and legally entitled—to exercise the same sovereign and self-determining rights as the States themselves. This cannot be lawfully taken from us. Our entitlement to conduct our affairs as sovereigns will remain in effect until such time as we ourselves voluntarily modify or relinquish it.

—GLENN T. MORRIS
1997

 QUESTIONS CONCERNING THE RIGHTS and legal and political standing of indigenous peoples have assumed a peculiar prominence in the world's juridical debates over the past quarter-century.[1] Nowhere is this more pronounced than in North America, a continent presided over by a pair of Anglo-European settler powers, the United States and Canada,[2] both of which purport to have resolved such issues—or to being very close to resolving them—in a manner which is not only legally consistent, but so intrinsically just as to serve as a "humanitarian" model deserving of emulation on a planetary basis.[3] Indeed, the United States in particular has long been prone to asserting that it has already implemented the programs necessary to guarantee self-determination, including genuine self-governance, to the Native peoples residing within its borders.[4] Most

Ward Churchill, enrolled Keetoowah Cherokee, is associate chair of the Department of Ethnic Studies and professor of American Indian Studies at the University of Colorado, Boulder. His most recent book is *A Little Matter of Genocide: Holocaust and Denial in the Americas, 1492 to the Present.*

recently, its representatives to the United Nations announced that it would therefore act to prevent the promulgation of an international convention on the rights of indigenous peoples if the proposed instrument contradicted U.S. domestic law in any significant way.[5]

While it is true that the treatment presently accorded Native North Americans is far less harsh than that visited upon our counterparts in many other regions—by the government of Guatemala upon Mayans, for instance, or of Indonesia upon East Timorese—it is equally true that this has not always been the case, and that the material conditions to which indigenous peoples in the United States and Canada are subjected remain abysmal.[6] Moreover, there are firm indications that whatever relative physical advantages may be enjoyed by North America's Native peoples vis-à-vis those in Third World nation-states accrue simply and directly from the extent to which we are seen as being more thoroughly pacified than they. The governments of both North American settler states have recently demonstrated a marked willingness to engage in low intensity warfare against us whenever this impression has proven, however tentatively, to be erroneous.[7]

Such circumstances hardly bespeak the realization, by any reasonable definition, of indigenous self-determination. Rather, they are more immediately suggestive of internal colonial structures along the lines of those effected in England and Spain during the final phases of their consolidation.[8] It is thus necessary to separate fact from fable in this respect, before the latter is foisted off and codified as an element of international law supposedly assuring the former.[9] The present essay attempts to accomplish this, briefly but clearly, by advancing a historical overview of the process predicating the contemporary situation in which North America's Native peoples find ourselves and, thus, determining with some degree of precision what this situation actually is. From there, it will be possible to offer an assessment of what must be changed, and the basis on which such change might be approached, if indigenous self-determination is ever to be (re)attained on this continent.[10]

Along the way, we will be at pains to explain the nature and origin of the customary and conventional international legal entitlements possessed by North American Indians, and the manner in which these have been systematically abridged by the United States and Canada. We emphasize U.S. practice throughout this essay, if only because Canada has become something of a junior partner in the enterprise at issue, implicitly—yet sometimes with remarkable explicitness—resorting to an outright mimicry of the doctrinal innovations by which its more substantial southern neighbor has sought to rationalize and justify its Indian policies.[11]

THE QUESTION OF INHERENT SOVEREIGNTY

Bear in mind that there is a distinction between nations and states. There is a rough consensus among analysts of virtually all ideological persuasions that a nation consists of any body of people, independent of its size, who are bound together by a common language and set of cultural beliefs, possessed of a defined or definable land base sufficient to provide an economy, and evidencing the capacity to govern themselves.[12] A state, on the other hand, is a particular form of centralized and authoritarian sociopolitical organization.[13] Many or perhaps most nations are not and have never been organized in accordance with the statist model. Conversely, only a handful of the world's states are or have ever really been nations in their own right (most came into being and are maintained through the coerced amalgamation of several nations).[14] Hence, although the term *state* has come to be employed as a virtual synonym for *nation* in popular usage—the membership of the United Nations, for example, is composed entirely of states—the two are not interchangeable.[15]

Regardless of the manner in which they are organized, all nations are legally construed as being imbued with a sovereignty which is inherent and consequently inalienable.[16] While the sovereign rights of any nation can be violated—its territory can be occupied through encroachment or military conquest, its government usurped or deposed altogether, its laws deformed or supplanted, and so forth—it is never extinguished by such actions.[17] Just as a woman retains an absolute right not to be raped even as she is subjected to it, a nation continues to possess its full range of sovereign rights even as their violation occurs. The only means by which the sovereignty of any nation can be legitimately diminished is in cases where the nation itself *voluntarily* relinquishes it.[18]

There can be no question but that the indigenous peoples of North America existed as fully self-sufficient, self-governing, and independent nations prior to commencement of the European invasions.[19] Nor can there be any real doubt as to whether the European powers were aware of this from the outset. Beginning almost the moment Columbus set foot in this hemisphere, Spanish jurists like Franciscus de Vitoria were set to hammering out theories describing the status of those peoples encountered in the course of Iberian expeditions to the "New World," the upshot being a conclusion that "the aborigines undoubtedly had dominion in both public and private matters, just like Christians."[20] The diplomats and legal scholars of England, France, Portugal, and the Netherlands shortly followed suit in acknowledging that Native peoples constituted inherent sovereigns.[21]

In 1793, Thomas Jefferson, author of the American Declaration of Independence and a leading official of the newly founded republic, summed up his own country's position by observing that "the Indians [have] full, undivided and independent sovereignty as long as they choose to keep it, and . . . this might be forever."[22] Henry Knox, the first U.S. secretary of war, echoed this understanding by reflecting that indigenous peoples "ought to be considered as foreign nations, not as the subjects of any particular State."[23] And again, in 1832 John Marshall, fourth chief justice of the U.S. Supreme Court, reflected on how the "Indian nations have always been considered as distinct, independent political communities, retaining their original natural rights, as the undisputed possessors of the soil since time immemorial."[24]

Among other things, such acknowledgments mean that the laws by which indigenous nations governed themselves and/or regulated their relationships to others—"aboriginal law," as it is often called—was and is possessed of a jurisdictional standing equivalent to that of the nation-states of Europe (or anywhere else).[25] This is to say that, within their respective domains, the legal system of each Native people carried preeminent force, and was binding on all parties, including the citizens of other countries. Whether or not something was "legitimate" was entirely contingent upon whether it conformed to the requirements of relevant international and aboriginal law, *not* the domestic statutory codes of one or another interloping state.[26]

Perhaps above all indigenous nations, no less than any others, have always held the inherent right to be free of coerced alterations in these circumstances.[27] For any country to set out unilaterally to impose its own internal system of legality upon another is to adopt a course of action which is not just utterly presumptuous but invalid under international custom and convention (and, undoubtedly, under the laws of the country intended for statutory subordination).[28] To do so by armed force, a pattern which is especially prominent in the history of U.S.-Indian relations, is to enter into the realm of "waging aggressive war," probably the most substantial crime delineated by international law.[29]

While given countries may obviously wield the raw power to engage in such conduct—witness the example of Nazi Germany—they never possess a legal right to do so. Thus, whatever benefits or advantages they may obtain through such behavior are perpetually illegitimate and subject to repeal.[30] Conversely, those nations whose inherent rights are impaired or denied in such fashion retain an open-ended prerogative—indeed, a legal responsibility—to recover them by all available means.[31] It is, moreover, the obligation of all other nations, and the citizens of the offending power itself, to assist them in doing so at the earliest possible date.[32] Although the matter has been subject to almost continuous obfuscation, usually by offenders, there are no exceptions to this principle within the laws of nations.[33]

ON THE MATTER OF TREATIES

While the innate sovereignty evidenced by Native peoples should be sufficient in itself to anchor our exercise of the full range of self-determining rights, there are other even less ambiguous indicators of our rightful status. It is, for instance, a fundamental tenet of international affairs that treaties are instruments reserved exclusively for the defining of relationships between nations. Governments enter into treaties only with one another, not with subparts of their own or any other polity.[34] Hence, it has long been understood as a matter of conventional, as well as customary, law that for a government to enter into a treaty with another entity is concomitantly to convey formal recognition that the other party is a peer, constituting a fully sovereign nation in its own right.[35]

In the United States, this principle is incorporated into domestic law under

Article I, Section 10 of the Constitution, and in Article VI, Clause 2, which makes any treaty, once ratified, "the Supreme Law of the Land."[36] Assorted elements of British Crown and Canadian law go in very much the same direction.[37] All told, the U.S. Senate ratified some four hundred treaties with North America's indigenous peoples between 1778 and 1871 (about eight hundred more had by that point been negotiated by the federal executive, but failed to achieve ratification for one reason or another).[38] In Canada, as part of a process extending well into the twentieth century, a further 138 had been confirmed by roughly the same point.[39] As U.S. Attorney General William Wirt put it in 1821:

> The purpose, then once conceded, that the Indians are independent to the purpose of treating, their independence is to that purpose as absolute as any other nation. . . . Nor can it be conceded that their independence as a nation is a limited independence. Like all other nations, they have the absolute power of war and peace. Like any other nation, their territories are inviolable by any other sovereignty. . . . They are entirely self-governed, self-directed. They treat, or refuse to treat, at their pleasure; and there is no human power that can rightly control their discretion in this respect.[40]

So clear were such pronouncements that more than 150 years later, even such habitual unapologetic Euro-American triumphalists as the late historian Wilcomb Washburn have been forced to concede that the "treaty system, which governed American Indian relations [with the United States and Canada], explicitly recognizes the fact that [both] governments . . . acknowledged the independent and national character of the Indian peoples with whom [they] dealt."[41] Insofar as "recognition once given is irrevocable unless the recognized [nation] ceases to exist or ceases to have the elements of nationhood," it is accurate to observe that the effect of the treaties is as forceful and binding now as when they were signed.[42] Legally speaking, it is the treaties rather than settler-state statutory codes which continue to define the nature of the relationship between most American Indian peoples, Canada, and the United States.[43]

This is and will remain unequivocally the case, absent an ability on the part of the United States and/or Canada to demonstrate that the indigenous nations with which they entered into treaties have either undergone some legitimate diminishment in their status or gone out of existence altogether. To quote Attorney General Wirt again:

> So long as a tribe exists and remains in possession of its lands, its title and possession are sovereign and exclusive. We treat with them as separate sovereignties, and while an Indian nation continues to exist within its acknowledged limits, we have no more right to enter upon their territory than we have to enter upon the territory of [any] foreign prince.[44]

There are of course arguments, typically advanced by officials and other advocates of settler-state hegemony, that literal extinction applies in certain cases, and that the requisite sorts of diminishment in standing has in any event occurred across the board through processes ranging from discovery and conquest to the voluntarily sociopolitical and economic merger of once distinct indigenous polities with the "broader" settler societies which now engulf us.[45] Since any of these contentions, if true, would serve to erode Native claims to inherent sovereignty as well as treaty rights, it is worth examining each of them in turn.

Discovery Doctrine

It has been considered something of a truism in the United States since its inception that America's vestiture of title in and jurisdiction over its pretended land base accrues "by right of discovery."[46] This is a rather curious proposition since, unlike Canada, which has always maintained a certain fealty to the British Crown, the United States can make no pretense that its own citizenry ever "discovered" any portion of North America. Nor, the claims of several of the country's "founding fathers" and many of their descendants notwithstanding, did Great Britain transfer its own discovery rights to the insurgent Continental Congress at the conclusion of America's decolonization struggle.[47] Rather, under the 1783 Treaty of Paris, England simply quit-claimed its interest in what is now the United States portion of the continent lying eastward of the Mississippi River.[48]

Moreover, even had the American republic somehow inherited its former colonizer's standing as a bona fide discovering power, this would not in itself have conveyed title to the territory in question. Contrary to much popular—and preposterous—contemporary mythology, the medieval Doctrine of Discovery, originating in a series of interpretations of earlier papal bulls advanced by Innocent IV during the mid-thirteenth century and perfected by Vitoria and others three hundred years later, did nothing to bestow ownership of newfound territory upon Europeans other than in cases where it was found to be *territorium res nullius* (genuinely uninhabited).[49] In all other instances, the doctrine confirmed the collective title of indigenous peoples to their land—in essence, their sovereignty over it—and, thus, the right to retain it.[50]

> [N]otwithstanding whatever may have been or may be said to the contrary, the said Indians and all other peoples who may later be discovered by Christians, are by no means to be deprived of their liberty or the possession of their property, even though they may be outside the faith of Jesus Christ; and that they may and should, freely and legitimately, enjoy their liberty and the possession of their property; nor should they be in any way enslaved; should the contrary happen, it shall be null and of no effect.[51]

What the discovering power actually obtained was a monopolistic right vis-à-vis other European powers to acquire the property in question, should its Native owners ever willingly consent to its alienation.[52] As John Marshall correctly observed in 1832, discovery "could not affect the rights of those already in possession, either as aboriginal occupants, or by virtue of a discovery made before the memory of man. It gave the exclusive right to purchase, but did not found that right on a denial of the right of the possessor to sell."[53] In substance, the doctrine was little more than an expedient to regulate relations among the European powers, intended to prevent them from squandering the Old World's limited assets by engaging in bidding wars—or, worse, outright military conflicts among themselves—over New World territories. As Marshall noted:

> [Since the Crowns of Europe] were all in pursuit of nearly the same object, it was necessary, in order to avoid conflicting settlements, and consequent war with each other, to establish a principle, which all should acknowledge as the law by which the right of acquisition, which they all asserted, should be regulated, as between themselves. This principle was, that discovery gave title to the government by whose subjects, or by whose authority, it was made, against other governments, which title might be consummated by possession. The exclusion of all other Europeans, necessarily gave to the nation making the discovery the sole right of acquiring the soil from the natives, and establishing settlements upon it. It was a right with which no Europeans could interfere.[54]

That such understandings were hardly unique to John Marshall is witnessed in a 1792 missive from then Secretary of State Thomas Jefferson to the British foreign ministry, in which he acknowledged that the Treaty of Paris had left the United States, not with clear title to lands west of the Appalachian Mountains, but rather with an ability to replace England in asserting what he called a "right of preemption."[55]

> [T]hat is to say, the sole and exclusive right of purchasing from [indigenous peoples] whenever they should be willing to sell. . . . We consider it as established by the usage of different nations into a kind of *Jus gentium* for America, that a white nation settling down and declaring such and such are their limits, makes an invasion of those limits by any other white nation an act of war, but gives no right of soil against the native possessors."[56]

So plain was the pattern of law and historical precedent in Marshall's mind that he openly scoffed at notions, prevalent among his countrymen, that the Doctrine of Discovery did, or could have done, more:

> The extravagant and absurd idea, that feeble settlements made along the seacoast . . . acquired legitimate power to govern [Native] people, or occupy the lands from sea to sea, did not enter into the mind of any man. [Crown charters] were well understood to convey the title which, according to the common law of European sovereigns respecting America, they might rightly convey, and no more. This was the exclusive right of purchasing such lands as the natives were willing to sell. The crown could not undertake to grant what the crown could not affect to claim; nor was it so understood.[57]

The same problems afflicting arguments that title to unceded Indian land which advocates claim was passed to the United States via the Treaty of Paris also beset other acquisitions from European and Euro-American powers. This is most notably true with respect to the 1803 Louisiana Purchase and the 1848 cession of the northern half of Mexico under the Treaty of Guadalupe Hidalgo, but also pertains to the 1845 admission of Texas to the Union, the 1846 purchase of Oregon Territory from Russia, and so on.[58] As concerns the largest single annexation ever made by the United States, encompassing the entire trans-Mississippi West:

> What [the United States] acquired from Napoleon in the Louisiana Purchase was not real estate, for practically all of the ceded territory that was not privately owned by Spanish and French settlers was still owned by the Indians, and the property rights of all the inhabitants were safeguarded by the terms of the treaty of cession. What we did acquire from Napoleon was not the land, which was not his to sell, but simply the right [to purchase the land].[59]

Similarly, the Treaty of Guadalupe Hidalgo, by which the U.S. war against Mexico was concluded, made express provision that already existing property rights, including those of the region's indigenous peoples, be respected within the vast area ceded by the Mexican government.[60] In no instance is there evidence to support assertions that the United States obtained anything resembling valid title to its presently claimed continental territoriality through interaction with nonindigenous governments, whether European or Euro-American. Less can such contentions be sustained with regard to Hawai'i.[61] The matter is confirmed by the 1928 *Island of Palmas* case, in which the International Court of Justice (ICJ, or World Court) found that title supposedly deriving from discovery cannot prevail over a title based in a prior and continuing display of sovereignty.[62]

TERRITORIUM RES NULLIUS

Although John Marshall himself, while readily conceding many of its implications, would ultimately pervert the doctrine of discovery in a relatively sophisticated fashion while attempting to rationalize and legitimate his country's territorial ambitions (this will be taken up below), many of his successors operated in a much cruder fashion. Hence, in the 1842 *Martin* v. *Waddell* case, decided only seven years after Marshall's death, the Supreme Court set down the following opinion (despite the clear exposition of the doctrine's actual contents the late chief justice had so recently bequeathed):

> The English possessions in America were not claimed by right of conquest, but by right of discovery. For, according to the principles of international law, as understood by the then civilized powers of Europe, the Indian tribes in the new world were regarded as mere temporary occupants of the soil, and the absolute rights of property and dominion were held to belong to the European nation by which any particular portion of the country was first discovered. Whatever forbearance may have been practiced towards

the unfortunate aborigines, either from humanity or policy, yet the territory they occupied was disposed of by the governments of Europe, at their pleasure, as if it had been found without inhabitants.[63]

In so thoroughly misconstruing extant law, rewriting history in the process, what the good justices were about was devising a legal loophole. Through it, they intended to pour a veneer of false legitimacy over U.S. plans, by now openly and officially announced as the country's "manifest destiny," of rapidly extending its reach from the Mississippi to the Pacific and beyond, ignoring indigenous rights, not only to land but to liberty and often life itself, at every step along the way.[64] The mechanism they seized upon for this purpose was the principle of *territorium res nullius*, the element of discovery doctrine providing that uninhabited territory might be claimed outright by whomever first found it.[65]

It's not that the Supreme Court of the United States or anyone else ever really argued that North America was completely unoccupied at the time of the initial European arrivals. Instead, they fell back on the concept of the "Norman Yoke," an ancient doctrine particularly well developed in English legal philosophy, stipulating that to be truly owned it was necessary that land be "improved."[66] Whoever failed within some "reasonable" period to build upon, cultivate, or otherwise transform their property from its natural "state of wilderness" forfeited title to it. The land was then simply declared to be "vacant" and open to claim by anyone professing a willingness to "put it to use."[67]

The Puritans of Plymouth Plantation and Massachusetts Bay Colony had experimented with the idea during the 1620s—arguing that while Native property rights might well be vested in town sites and fields, the remainder of the territories, since it was uncultivated, should be considered *terra nullius* and thus unowned—but their precedent never evolved into a more generalized English practice.[68] Indeed, the Puritans themselves abandoned such presumption in 1629.[69]

> Whatever theoretical disagreements existed concerning the nature of the respective ownership rights of Indians and Europeans to land in America, practical realities shaped legal relations between the Indians and colonists. The necessity of getting along with powerful Indian [peoples], who outnumbered the European settlers for several decades, dictated that as a matter of prudence, the settlers buy lands that the Indians were willing to sell, rather than displace them by other methods. The result was that the English and Dutch colonial governments obtained most of their lands by purchase. For all practical purposes, the Indians were treated as sovereigns possessing full ownership of [all] the lands of America.[70]

By the early nineteenth century, the demographic/military balance had shifted dramatically in favor of settler populations.[71] One result was that the potential of invoking the Norman Yoke in combination with the broader principle of *res Nullius* began to be rethought. In terms of international law, the principle eventually found expression in the observation of jurist Emmerich de Vattel that no nation holds a right to "exclusively appropriate to themselves more land than they have occasion for, or more than they are able to settle and cultivate."[72] For all practical intents and purposes, John Marshall himself employed such reasoning in an 1810 opinion holding that portions of Indian Country not literally occupied or cultivated by indigenous peoples might, at least in certain instances, be construed as unowned and therefore open to claims by settlers.[73]

During the next seventy-five years, the principle was brought to bear in the continuously evolving formation of U.S. Indian policy—as well as judicial interpretation of indigenous property entitlements—with the size of an ever greater number of the areas set aside (reserved) for Native use and occupancy demonstrating no relationship at all to the extent of aboriginal holdings or to more recent treaty guarantees of territoriality. Rather, federal policymakers, judges, and bureaucrats alike increasingly took to multiplying the number of Indians believed to belong to any given people by the number of acres it was thought each individual might use "productively." The aggregate figure arrived at would then be assigned as that people's reserved land base.[74] By the latter part of the nineteenth century, the process in Canada was much the same.[75]

In the United States, the trend culminated in passage of the 1887 General Allotment Act, a measure by which the government authorized itself to impose such terms upon every indigenous nation encompassed within the country's claimed boundaries.[76] At the stroke of the congressional pen, traditional Native modes of collective landholding were unilaterally abolished in favor of the self-anointedly more "advanced" or "civilized" Euro-American system of individual ownership.[77] The methods by which the act was implemented began with the compilation of official rolls of the members of each tribe in accordance with criteria sanctioned by the federal Bureau of Indian Affairs (BIA).[78] When this task was completed, each individual listed on a roll was allotted a parcel of land, according to the following formula:

1. To each head of a family, one-quarter section [160 acres].
2. To each single person over eighteen years of age, one-eighth section.
3. To each orphan child under eighteen years of age, one-eighth section.
4. To each other single person under eighteen years of age living, or who may be born prior to the date of the order . . . directing allotment of the lands, one-sixteenth section.[79]

Once each Native person had received his or her allotment, the balance of each reserved territory was declared surplus and made available to non-Indian settlers, parceled out to railroads and other corporations, and/or converted into federal parks, forests, and military compounds.[80] In this manner, the indigenous land base, which had still amounted to an aggregate of 150 million acres at the time the act went into effect, was reduced by approximately two-thirds before it was finally repealed in 1934.[81] Additionally, under provision of the 1906 Burke Act, which vested authority in the secretary of the interior to administer all remaining Native property in trust, a further "27,000,000 acres or two-thirds of the land allotted to individual Indians was also lost to sale" by the latter year.[82] What little territory was left to indigenous Nations at that point was thus radically insufficient to afford economic sustenance, much less to accommodate future population growth.[83]

Needless to say, Native people agreed to none of this. On the contrary, we have continuously resisted it through a variety of means, including efforts to secure some just resolution through U.S. courts. Our refusal to participate in allotment and similar processes has often resulted in our being left effectively landless, defined as non-Indians, and worse.[84] The response of the Supreme Court to our due-process initiatives has been to declare, in the 1903 case *Lone Wolf v. Hitchcock*, that the United States enjoys a permanent "trustee relationship" to its Native "wards," affording it a "plenary power" over our affairs which frees it to "change the form of" our property—from land, say, to cash or other "benefits"—at its own discretion. As a concomitant, the Court argued that the United States holds a unilateral right, based in no discernible legal doctrine at all, to abrogate such terms and provisions of its treaties with indigenous Nations as it may come to find inconvenient while still binding us to the remainder.[85]

By 1955, things had reached such a pass that Native peoples were required for the first time to demonstrate that they had acquired title to their lands from a European or Euro-American power rather than the other way around.[86] Even in cases where such recognition of title was clear and apparent—the *Rainbow Bridge* and *GO Road* cases of the 1980s, to name two prime examples—U.S. courts have consistently ruled that the "broader interests" of North America's settler society outweighs the right of indigenous owners to make use of their property in a manner consistent with their own values, customs, and traditions.[87] In other instances, such as *U.S. v. Dann*, treaty land has been declared vacant even though Native people were obviously living on it.[88]

Canadian courts, although not necessarily citing specific U.S. precedents, has followed much the same trajectory. This has been perhaps most notable in the 1984 *Bear Island* case, in which it was concluded that, Crown law to the contrary notwithstanding, federal law allowed provincial extinguishment of aboriginal title claims to "unoccupied" territories.[89] Relatedly, opinions have been rendered in several other instances— the 1973 *Calder* case, for example, and the *Cardinal* case a year later—holding that federal Canadian law functions independently of any historical guarantees extended to Native people by Great Britain, a position essentially duplicating the effect of *Lone wolf*.[90] Indeed, Canada has recently gone so far as to claim the kind of permanent trust authority over indigenous Nations within its ostensible boundaries earlier asserted by the United States[91] The rights of Native people in Canada have of course suffered accordingly.[92]

Whatever merit may once have attended such legalistic maneuvering by the United States and Canada—and it was always dubious in the extreme—it has long since evaporated. The Charter of the United Nations has effectively outlawed the assertion of perpetual and nonconsensual trust relationships between nations since 1945, a circumstance reaffirmed and amplified by the 1960 Declaration on the Granting of Independence to Colonial Countries and Peoples.[93] The *Lone Wolf* court's grotesque interpretation of U.S. prerogatives to exercise a "line item veto" over its treaties with indigenous Nations has been thoroughly repudiated by the 1967 Vienna Convention on the Law Treaties.[94] And, since the World Court's 1977 advisory opinion in the *Western Sahara* case, claims to primacy based in the notion of *Territorium res Nullius* have been legally nullified.[95]

RIGHTS OF CONQUEST

It has become rather fashionable in many quarters of North America's settler societies to refer to indigenous peoples as having been "conquered."[96] The basic idea has perhaps been expressed best and most forcefully by the U.S. Supreme Court in its 1955 *Tee-Hit-Ton* opinion.

> Every American schoolboy knows that the savage tribes of this continent were deprived of their ancestral ranges by force and that, even when the Indians ceded millions of acres by treaty in return for blankets, food and trinkets, it was not a sale but the conquerors' will that deprived them of their land.[97]

"After the conquest," the court went on, Indians "were permitted to occupy portions of the territory over which they had previously exercised 'sovereignty,' as we use the term. This is not a property right but amounts to a right of occupancy which the sovereign grants and protects against intrusion by third parties but which right of occupancy may be terminated and such lands fully disposed of by the sovereign itself without any legally enforceable obligation to compensate the Indians."[98] This curiously bellicose pontification, advanced a scant few years after U.S. jurists had presided over the conviction at Nuremberg of several German officials—including judges—in no small part for having vomited up an almost identical rhetoric,[99] is all the more peculiar in that it appears to bear virtually no connection to the case supposedly at hand.

> The Alaska natives [who had pressed a land claim in Tee-Hit-Ton] had never fought a skirmish with Russia [which claimed their territories before the United States] or the United States. . . . To say that the Alaska natives were subjugated by conquest stretches the imagination too far. The only sovereign act that can be said to have conquered the Alaska natives was the *Tee-Hit-Ton* opinion itself.[100]

If it may be taken as a rudiment that any conquest entails the waging of war by the conqueror against the conquered, then the sweeping universalism evident in the high court's pronouncement goes from the realm of the oddly erroneous to that of the truly bizarre. While the United States officially acknowledges the existence of well over four hundred indigenous nations within its borders, it admits to having fought fewer than fifty "Indian Wars" in the entirety of its history.[101] Assuming that it was victorious in all of these—in actuality, it lost at least one[102]—and could on this basis argue that it had conquered each of its opponents, the United States would still have to account for the nature of its contemporary relationship to several hundred *unconquered* indigenous nations by some other means.

Lumping the Native peoples of Canada into the bargain, as the language of *Tee-Hit-Ton* plainly suggests was its intent, renders the court's reading of history even more blatantly absurd. North of the border, with the exception of two campaigns mounted to quell Louis Riel's rebellious Métis during the mid-nineteenth century, nothing that might rightly be termed an Indian war was fought after 1763.[103] On the contrary, it was explicit and successfully enforced Crown policy from that point onward to avoid military conflicts with North America's indigenous Nations by every available means.[104] Of all imaginable descriptions of what might constitute a basis for Britain's assertion of rights in Canada, then, "conquest" is without doubt among the most wildly inaccurate.[105]

Benighted as was the *Tee-Hit-Ton* court's knowledge of historical fact, its ignorance of relevant law appears to have been even worse. The difficulties begin with the court's interpretation of the ancient notion of the "rights of conquest," which it erroneously construed as asserting that any nation possessed of the power to seize the assets of another holds a "natural" right to do so ("might makes right," in other words).[106] In reality, if the doctrine had ever embodied such a principle—and no evidence has ever been produced to show that it did—it had not done so for some nine hundred years.[107] By the sixteenth century, Vitoria, Matías de Pas, and others had codified conquest rights as an adjunct or subset of the discovery doctrine, constraining them within very tight limits.[108]

Such rights might be invoked by a discovering power, they wrote, only on occasions where circumstances necessitated the waging of a just war. With respect to the New World, the bases for the latter were delineated as falling into three categories: first, instances in which, without provocation, a Native people physically attacked representatives of the discovering Crown; second, instances in which the Natives arbitrarily refused to engage in trade with Crown representatives; and, third, instances in which Native people refused to admit Christian missionaries among them. Should any or all of these circumstances be present, the jurists agreed, discoverers held the right to use whatever force was necessary to compel compliance with international law.[109] Having done so, they were then entitled to compensate themselves from the property of the vanquished for the costs of having waged the war.[110] In all other instances, however, legitimate acquisition of property could occur only by consent of its indigenous owners.[111]

The problem is that in the entire history of Indian-white relations in North America, there is not a single instance in which any of the three criteria can be documented.[112] Hence, contra the *Tee-Hit-Ton* court's all-encompassing declaration that Euro-American title to the continent derives from conquest, such a result does not obtain, legally at least, even with regard to the relatively few instances in which wars were actually fought.[113] It follows that the only valid land title presently held by either the United States or Canada is that accruing from bilateral and mutually consensual treaties through which certain Native lands were ceded to those countries or predecessor powers like England and France.[114]

Earlier U.S. jurists and legislators understood the law, even if the *Tee-Hit-Ton* court did not. One consequence was the 1787 Northwest Ordinance, in which the Congress foreswore all wars of conquest against Native peoples and pledged the country to conducting its relations on the basis of treaties negotiated in "utmost good faith."[115] As has been mentioned, John Marshall classified contentions that North America's indigenous nations had been conquered as "extravagant and absurd."[116] Elsewhere, he observed that "law which regulates, and ought to regulate in general, the relations between the conqueror and conquered, [is] incapable of application" to American Indians.[117] Even the *Martin* court, hostile to Native interests by any estimation, was at pains to state that "English [and, by extension, U.S.] rights in America were *not* claimed by right of conquest (emphasis added)."[118] Probably the most definitive assessment was that offered by Indian Commissioner Thomas Jefferson Morgan in 1890, after the Indian Wars had run their course.

> From the execution of the first treaty made between the United States and the Indian tribes residing within its limits . . . the United States has pursued a uniform course of extinguishing Indian title only with the consent of those tribes which were recognized as having claim to the soil by reason of occupancy, such consent being expressed by treaties.[119]

In light of all this, it is fair to say that there is not a scintilla of validity attending the *Tee-Hit-Ton* opinion, either legally or in any other way. The same holds true for the dominant society's academic and popular discourse of conquest, perhaps best represented by the two-thousand-odd "Cowboys and Indians" movies produced by Hollywood over the past seventy-five years.[120] To pretend otherwise, as the *Tee-Hit-Ton* court did, does nothing to legitimate Euro-American claims of primacy over Native territories. Rather, it is to enter a tacit admission that, in the United States at least, much land has been acquired in the most illegitimate fashion of all—the waging of aggressive war—and that a considerable part of the continent constitutes what one analyst has termed "occupied America."[121]

EXTINCTION

Although both the United States and Canada officially maintain that genocide has never been perpetrated against the indigenous peoples within their borders,[122] both have been equally prone to claim validation of their title to Native lands on the basis that "group extinction" has run its course in a number of cases. Where there are no survivors or descendants of preinvasion populations, the argument goes, there can be no question of continuing aboriginal title. Thus, in such instances, the land—vacated by the literal die-off of its owners—must surely have become open to legitimate claims by the settler states under even the most rigid constructions of *territorium res nullius*.[123]

While the reasoning underpinning this position is essentially sound, and in conformity with accepted legal principles, the factual basis upon which it is asserted is not. With the exception of the Beothuks of Newfoundland, whose total extermination was complete at some point in the 1820s, it has never been demonstrated that any of the peoples Native to North America, circa 1500, have ever been completely eradicated.[124] Take the Pequots as a case in point. In 1637, they were so decimated by a war of extermination waged against them by English colonists that they were believed to have gone out of existence altogether. Even their name was abolished under colonial law.[125] For three centuries, Pequots were officially designated as being extinct. Yet today the federal government has been forced, grudgingly, to admit that several hundred people in Connecticut are directly descended from this "extirpated" nation.[126]

Similar examples abound. The Wampanoags of Massachusetts were declared extinct in the aftermath of the 1675 King Philip's War, but managed to force recognition of their continuing existence during the 1970s.[127] More or less the same principle applies to a number of other peoples of the Northeast:[128] the Piscataways, Yamasees, Catawbas, and others of the Southeast, all of whom were reportedly extinct by 1800;[129] the Yuki, Yahi, and others of Northern California, largely annihilated through the "cruelties of the original settlers" prior to 1900;[130] and so on around the country. James Fenimore Cooper's "Last of the Mohicans" wasn't, nor was Alfred Kroeber's Ishi really the "last of his tribe."[131] In sum, the fabled "Vanishing Red Man," alternately bemoaned and celebrated with a great deal of glee in turn-of-the-century literature, didn't.[132]

By and large, extinction is and has always been more a classification bestowed for the administrative convenience of the settler states than a description of physical or even cultural reality. The classic example occurred when, during the decade following the adoption of House Resolution 108 in 1953, the United States Congress systematically terminated its recognition of more than one hundred indigenous peoples.[133] Some, like the Menominees of Wisconsin, were eventually able to obtain formal "reinstatement."[134] The majority, however, like the Klamaths of Oregon and an array of smaller peoples in Southern California, have been unsuccessful in such efforts. They remain officially dissolved, whatever remained of their reserved territories absorbed by the surrounding settler state.[135]

In other instances, the United States has simply refused ever to admit the existence of indigenous peoples. Notably, this pertains to the Abnakis of Vermont, who, having never signed a treaty of cession, actually hold title to very nearly the entire state.[136] Other examples include the Lumbees of North Carolina, perhaps the most populous indigenous people in all of North America, and a number of fragmentary groups like the Miamis of Ohio scattered across the Midwestern states.[137] While not following precisely the same pattern,

Canada has also used policies of declining to acknowledge Native status and/or refusing to recognize the existence of entire groups as a means of manipulating or denying altogether indigenous rights to land and sovereign standing.[138]

While neither such official subterfuges nor the popular misconceptions attending them have the least effect in terms of diminishing the actual rights of the peoples in question, they do place the settler states in positions of patent illegality. Among other things, it is readily arguable that official declarations that still-viable human groups have gone out of existence, coupled to policies designed and intended to bring this about, constitute the crime of genocide, not only within the definition of the term as originally advanced by Raphaël Lemkin during the Second World War, but as it is now codified in international law.[139]

MERGER WITH SETTLER SOCIETY

A final line of argument extended by the United States and Canada to justify their denials of indigenous rights to self-determination is that most Native peoples have long since commingled with the settler societies of both countries to the point, in many if not most cases, of rendering our sovereignty self-nullifying.[140] Although it is true that international law recognizes the "voluntary merger" of one nation into another as the sole sure and acceptable means by which national identity and concomitant national rights can be extinguished, it is dubious whether the description actually applies to any but a handful of North America's indigenous nations (if at all).[141]

> In many instances there is simply no evidence of a voluntary merger by treaty agreements or in any manner. One will search the treaties of the Six Nations Confederacy and no doubt many other Indian nations in vain for such evidence. . . .Very few treaties, perhaps none, include provisions even remotely suggesting voluntary merger or voluntary surrender of sovereignty [although a] few treaties contain provisions subjecting the Indian parties to United States law. . . . Many Indian nations such as the Hopi have never made a treaty or agreement with the United States and [therefore] cannot be said to have assented to a merger.[142]

The state contended in *Worcester* v. *Georgia* that since, under Article III of the Treaty of Hopewell, the Cherokee Nation had voluntarily placed itself under the military protection of the United States, it had effectively relinquished its national sovereignty, merging with "the stronger power."[143] Chief Justice Marshall rejected this argument unequivocally and in terms which encompass all indigenous Nations finding themselves in a comparable situation:

> [T]he settled doctrine of the law of nations is that a weaker power does not surrender its independence—its right of self-government—by associating with a stronger, and taking its protection. A weak state, in order to provide for its safety, may place itself under the protection of one more

powerful, without stripping itself of the right of government, and ceasing to be a state.[144]

That Marshall's 1832 opinion yields a continuing validity is amply borne out in the status accorded such tiny protectorates as Liechtenstein and Monaco in Europe itself, examples which—along with Luxembourg, Grenada, the Marshall Islands, and a number of other small nations around the world whose right to sovereignty is not open to serious challenge—also preempt questions of scale.[145] As Onondaga leader Oren Lyons has aptly put it, "Nations are not according to size. Nations are according to culture. If there are twenty people left who are representing their nation ... they are a nation. Who are we to say less?"[146]

Other mainstays of the merger argument are the facts that Native peoples both north and south of the border have become increasingly assimilated into settler culture, accepted citizenship in both the United States and Canada, adopted forms of governance explicitly subordinated to those of the settler states, and are now thoroughly encompassed by the statutory codes of the latter.[147] Even the most cursory examination of the record reveals, however, that none of this has occurred in anything resembling a "voluntary" manner on the part of the indigenous Nations involved. Indeed, Native resistance to all four aspects of the process has been, and in many cases continues to be, substantial.

For starters, the kind and degree of cultural assimilation among Native people evident today in both countries results not from any choice made by Indians to "fit in," whether collectively or individually, but from extraordinarily draconian conditions imposed upon us by the settler-state governments. From at least as early as the last quarter of the nineteenth century, the United States and Canada alike implemented policies of compulsory assimilation involving direct intervention in the domestic affairs of all indigenous nations within their respective spheres.[148] Among the techniques employed was the systematic subversion of traditional Native governments through the creation, underwriting, and other support for oppositional factions, and routine disruption of customary social and spiritual practices.[149] Most especially in the United States, but also to a considerable extent in Canada, the early phases of such initiatives were coupled to the previously discussed program of land allotment and manipulation of "tribal" membership.[150] Meanwhile, the traditional economies of an ever increasing number of Native peoples throughout North America were undermined and in many cases obliterated altogether.[151]

While all of this was obviously devastating to the ability of indigenous nations to maintain their cohesion and cultural integrity, the real linchpin of assimilation policy on both sides of the border was the imposition of universal compulsory "education" upon Native children.[152] Between 1880 and 1930, up to 80 percent of all American Indian youngsters were sent, almost always coercively, often forcibly, to remote boarding schools, far from family, friends, community, nation, and culture. Thus isolated, shorn of their hair, compelled to dress in Euro-American attire, forbidden to speak their Native languages or follow their spiritual beliefs, subjected to severe corporal punishment and/or confinement for the slightest breach of "discipline," the students were typically held for years, systematically indoctrinated all the while to accept Christianity, speak "proper" English, and generally adopt Western values and perspectives.[153]

The express objective of the boarding school system was, according to U.S. Superintendent of Indian Schools Richard H. Pratt, to "kill the Indian" in each pupil, converting them into psychological and intellectual replications of non-Indians.[154] The broader goal, articulated repeatedly by the administrators of U.S. assimilation policy as a whole, was to bring about the functional disappearance of indigenous societies as such by some point in the mid-1930s.[155] The intent in Canada was no different, albeit geared to a somewhat slower pace.[156] While such a process of sociocultural "merger" can by no conceivable definition be described as voluntary, it is glaringly genocidal under even the strictest legal definition of the term.[157]

Citizenship fares little better as a justification for statist presumption. Indians, as a rule, sought to become citizens of neither the United States nor Canada. On the contrary, the record demonstrates conclusively that in the latter country we began to be treated as subjects at a time when we were strongly and all but unanimously asserting the exact opposite. Consider, for example, the following observation, drawn from the opinion of a twentieth-century Canadian court:

> It is well-known that claims have been made from the time of Joseph Brant [Thayendanegea, a Mohawk who led a faction of his people to fight on the British side during the U.S. War of Independence, and afterwards into Canada] that the Indians were not really subjects of the King but an independent people—allies of His Majesty—and in a measure at least exempt from the civil laws governing the true subject. "Treaties" had been made in which they were called "faithful allies" and the like. . . . As to the so-called treaties, John Beverly Robinson, Attorney-General for Upper Canada, in an official letter to Robert Wilmot Horton, Under Secretary of State for War and Colonies, March 14, 1824, said: "To talk of treaties with the Mohawk Indians, residing in the heart of one of the most populous districts of Upper Canada . . . is much the same, in my humble opinion, as to talk of making a treaty of alliance with the Jews of Duke Street. . . ."[158]

More formally, in the sense of enfranchisement and the like, citizenship was not extended to indigenous people until An Act to Encourage the Gradual Civilization of the Indian Tribes was effected by the Province of Canada in 1857.[159] Since the law made acceptance voluntary—Indians had to apply, and were declared legally "white" upon acceptance—there were relatively few takers.[160] Hence, pursuant to the 1867 British North American Act (Constitution Act), Native citizenship in Canada was simply made declarative, irrespective of objections raised by its alleged beneficiaries.[161] As Prime Minister Sir John A. MacDonald put it in 1887, "the great aim of [such] legislation has been to do away with the tribal system and assimilate the Indian people in all respects with the other inhabitants of the dominion, as speedily as they are fit for the change."[162]

In the United States, citizenship was first imposed upon Native people in a large-scale fashion during the 1880s, as a *quid pro quo* in the release of individually allotted land parcels from trust status.[163] In 1924, an act was passed unilaterally conferring citizenship upon all Indians who had been overlooked in earlier processes, or who had proven resistant to accepting it.[164] As in Canada, "The grant of citizenship was not sought by the Indian population, and many Indian nations have consistently and vigorously denied United States citizenship. The Six Nations Confederacy, to use a now familiar example, has repeatedly gone on public record to reject United States citizenship and deny the federal government's power to make them citizens."[165]

> It has never been held by any court, national or international, that the unilateral conferral of citizenship upon a population deprives them of their separate nationhood. The ultimate question is, after all, whether Congress [or the Canadian parliament] has the right or the legal power under international law to legislate over Indian nations without their consent.[166]

As to the fact that indigenous governments are presently considered as parts of the settler-state governmental hierarchies themselves, Native people no more chose this status than they did U.S. or Canadian citizenship or any other aspect of assimilation.[167] Traditional forms of governance throughout the United States were systematically supplanted, nation by nation, under the 1934 Indian Reorganization Act (IRA) with a constitutional structure designed by the BIA.[168] In the great majority of cases, the resulting "tribal councils" were patterned more after corporate boards than actual governing bodies, while all of them derived their authority from and were underwritten by the United States rather than their own ostensible constituents.[169]

Although superficially democratic in its implementation—referenda were conducted on each reservation prior to its being reorganized—the record is replete with instances in which federal officials misrepresented what was happening in order to convince Native voters to cast affirmative ballots.[170] In certain instances—among the Lakota, for example, where a sufficient number of dead persons to swing the outcome were later shown to have "voted"—outright electoral fraud prevailed.[171] Hopi provides another useful illustration.

> [Indian Commissioner John] Collier reported to the Secretary of Interior in 1936 that [in 1935] the Hopis had accepted the IRA by a vote of 519 to 299, the total votes cast representing 45 percent of the eligible voters, [yet he] came up with a figure of 50 percent for the percentage of voters coming to the polls a year later, in 1936, to vote on the constitution in, in his annual report for 1937. [But] according to the statistics contained in the ratified and Interior-approved constitution itself, only 755 people voted in the constitutional referendum. This is 63 fewer people than voted in the 1935 referendum on the Indian Reorganization Act. How can 818 voters constitute 45 percent of the eligible voters in 1935 and, a year later, 755

voters constitute 50 percent? . . . Clearly, Collier made up his own statistics, and perpetrated a good deal of deception in order to make it seem the
Hopis [embraced the IRA], when they did not.[172]

Moreover, a "number of Hopis assert today that voters were told they were
voting for retention of their land, not for reorganization; that registration papers
were falsified; and that votes were fabricated."[173] In reality, voter turnout was
less than 30 percent.[174] Even this does not tell the whole story, since, as was
made clear to BIA representatives at the time, the bulk of eligible voters did not
abstain. Instead, they opted to exercise their traditional right of signifying "no"
by actively boycotting the proceeding.[175] Tabulated in this fashion, the best contemporary estimate is that fewer than 15 percent of all eligible Hopi actually
voted for reorganization, while more than 85 percent voted against it.[176]
Nonetheless, it remains the official position of the United States that the IRA
council is the "legitimate" government of the Hopi people.

In Canada, meanwhile, provision was first made in the 1876 Indian Act to
establish a system of "band governments" under federal rather than Native
authority.[177] In 1880, the law was amended to deprive traditional chiefs (i.e.,
leaders) of their authority as rapidly as elected officials became available.[178] In
1884, the Indian Advancement Act was passed for, among other things, the specific purpose of preparing federally created and funded band councils to assume
functions roughly analogous to municipal governments.[179] In 1920, an amendment to the prevailing Indian Act of 1906 empowered the councils, by simple
majority vote, to make Canadian citizens of their constituency as a whole.[180]
And so it has gone, right up through the 1982 rewriting of the Canadian Constitution, a document which explicitly delineates the location and prerogatives
of Native governments *within* the settler-state corpus.[181]

Under the circumstances already described in this section, suggestions that
other unilaterally imposed "accommodations of" Native people within U.S. and
Canadian statutory codes might somehow imply the legitimate merger of
indigenous Nations with the settler states are too ludicrous to warrant serious
response.[182] On balance, both the arrangement and the duplicitous nature of
the arguments used to rationalize and defend such ideas are entirely comparable to those employed by France with respect to Algeria during the early
1950s.[183] As such, they are frankly colonialist and therefore in violation of black
letter international law.[184]

No mere adjustments to the status quo—the enactment of another statute
here, a constitutional amendment there—can rectify a situation which is so fundamentally at odds with legality. The only possible course by which either
Canada or the United States can redeem its posture as an outlaw state is to recall
and act upon the 1832 observation of John Marshall that

> Indian nations [have] always been considered as distinct, independent
> political communities, retaining their original natural rights. . . . The very
> term "nation," so generally applied to them, means "a people distinct from
> others." . . . The words "treaty" and "nation" are words of our own lan-

guage, selected in our diplomatic and legislative proceedings, by ourselves, having a definite and well-understood meaning. We have applied them to other nations of the earth. They are applied to all in the same sense.[185]

THE MARSHALL INNOVATION

It will undoubtedly be argued that there is yet another way out of the box of illegality in which the settler states would otherwise appear to be trapped, and that Marshall himself supplied it a year before he made the above-quoted statement. This is found in a formulation extended by the chief justice in an 1831 opinion, *Cherokee v. Georgia*, as he struggled with the impossible task of reconciling the legal realities of indigenous sovereignty to the insistence of his own country upon asserting its dominion over them.[186] After conceding that argumentation "intended to prove the character of the Cherokees as a state, as a distinct political society, separated from others, capable of governing itself, has . . . been completely successful,"[187] he went on to observe:

> [Y]et it may well be doubted whether those tribes which reside within the acknowledged boundaries of the United States can, with strict accuracy, be denominated foreign nations. They may, more correctly, perhaps be denominated domestic dependent nations.[188]

There were several bases upon which Marshall rested this idea, probably most importantly the element of discovery doctrine vesting sole rights of territorial acquisition in discovering Crowns he had previously explored in his *McIntosh* opinion.[189] While, as has been mentioned, the intent of this proviso was to regulate affairs among the European powers, not Indians, Marshall reconfigured it as a kind of restraint of trade measure imposed upon the indigenous Nations themselves. From there, he was able to extrapolate that, insofar as discovering powers enjoyed a legitimate right to constrain Native peoples in the alienation of their property, to that extent at least the sovereignty of the discoverer stood at a level higher than that of the discovered. Ultimately, from a juridical perspective, this was the logical loophole employed to recast the relations between the United States and indigenous Nations not as an association of peers, but in terms of supremacy and subordination.[190]

Although Marshall's interpretation stood the accepted meaning of international law squarely on its head—and there is ample indication he was fully aware of this[191]—it served the purpose of rationalizing U.S. expansionism quite admirably.[192] From the foundation laid in *Cherokee*, it was possible for American jurists and policymakers alike to argue that indigenous Nations were always sovereign enough to validate U.S. territorial ambitions through treaties of cession, never sovereign enough to decline them (indeed, after 1831, Native refusals to comply with U.S. demands were often enough construed as "acts of aggression" requiring military response).[193] Here, too, lay the groundwork for the eventual assertion of perpetual trust discussed above in relation to *Lone wolf*, allotment, reorganization, and all the rest.[194]

So useful has the doctrine emanating from Marshall's quartet of Indian cases—*Peck, McIntosh, Cherokee,* and *Worcester*—proven in enabling the U.S. judiciary to justify, or at least to obfuscate, its Indian policy that Canadian courts have openly and increasingly embraced it. This began at least as early as 1867, when a Quebec court quoted an entire passage from *Worcester* in the landmark case, *Connolly* v. *Woolrich*.[195] In its 1973 *Calder* opinion, the Supreme Court of Canada lavished praise on the *McIntosh* opinion as "the *locus classicus* of the principles governing aboriginal title."[196] By 1989, in determining the outcome of the *Bear Island* case, a Canadian appellate court simply abandoned its country's legal code altogether, adopting as precedents what it deemed to be the "relevant" aspects of U.S. common law. Most especially, these included the "domestic dependent nation" formulation advanced by Marshall in *Cherokee*.[197] Canadian policymakers have, of course, trotted dutifully down the same path.[198]

Whatever its utility for settler states, however, the Marshall doctrine does not add up to internationally valid law. On the contrary, the *Cherokee* opinion in particular cannot be honestly said to stand muster even in terms of its adherence to U.S. constitutional requirements. This is because, irrespective of the nomenclature he applied, when the chief justice held that indigenous Nations occupy both a position within the federal dominion and a level of sovereignty below that of the central government, he was effectively placing us on the same legal footing as the individual states of the Union.[199] This he could not do, by virtue of the previously-mentioned constitutional prohibition against treaty making by and with such subordinate sovereignties, while simultaneously arguing that we should be treated as fully independent Nations for purposes of conveying land title through treaties.[200]

The matter cannot be had both ways. Either we were and are sovereign for purposes of treating, or we were and are not. In the first instance, we could not have been and thus are not now legally subordinated to any other entity. In the second, we could not have been considered eligible to enter into treaties with the federal government in the first place, a matter which would serve to void all pretense that the United States holds legitimate title to any but a tiny fraction of its claimed territoriality outside the original thirteen Atlantic Coast states.[201]

By insisting upon playing both ends against the middle as he did, Marshall affected no reconciliation of conflicting legal principles whatsoever. Rather, he enshrined an utterly irreconcilable contradiction as the very core of federal Indian law and policy. In the process, he conjured up the fiction of "quasi-sovereign nations"—aptly described by one indigenous leader as "the judicial equivalent of the biological impossibility that a female can be partly pregnant"—a concept which has been firmly repudiated in international law.[202] As a consequence, so long as the United States continues to rely upon the Marshall doctrine in defining its relationship to Native peoples, it will remain in a legally untenable posture. No less does this hold true for Canada.

SUBVERSION OF INTERNATIONAL LAW

The second half of the 1960s saw the growth of a strong and steadily more effective movement toward national liberation among the Native peoples of North America. Initially concentrated in the United States, such initiatives had become notoriously more evident in Canada as well by the mid-1970s.[203] Meanwhile, south of the border, traditional Elders joined forces with younger militants to engage in an extended series of confrontations, some of them armed, with federal authorities.[204] These were highlighted by a protracted fishing rights campaign in Washington state (1964–69), the thirteen-month occupation of government facilities on Alcatraz Island (1969–70), the seizure of BIA headquarters in Washington, D.C. (1972), and the 71-day siege of the Wounded Knee hamlet, on the Pine Ridge Reservation (1973).[205]

By the latter year, an organization calling itself the American Indian Movement (AIM) had emerged as the galvanizing force within the liberation struggle and had become the target of severe physical repression by the federal government.[206] It was in this context, with world attention drawn to U.S.-Indian relations by the extraordinary pattern of events, that Lakota Elders convened a meeting on the Standing Rock Reservation for purposes of establishing an organization to carry the question of indigenous treaty rights before the United Nations. Charged with responsibility for carrying out this task was AIM leader Russell Means, who in turn named Cherokee activist Jimmie Durham to direct the day-to-day operations of what was dubbed the International Indian Treaty Council (IITC).[207]

Within months, Durham had established the presence of "AIM's international diplomatic arm" at both the U.N. headquarters in New York and the Palace of Nations in Geneva, Switzerland and had begun lobbying for hearings on settler state denial of self-determination to indigenous Nations and other abuses. This agenda dovetailed neatly with investigations already underway in several U.N. agencies and led to an unprecedented conference on discrimination against Native peoples in Geneva during the summer of 1977, attended by representatives of some ninety-eight indigenous Nations of the Western Hemisphere.[208] In some ways prefiguring a special session of the Russell Tribunal convened in Rotterdam to consider the same matters two years later,[209] the 1977 "Indian Summer in Geneva" sparked serious discussion within the United Nations concerning the need for a more regularized body to consider indigenous issues.[210]

Meanwhile, undoubtedly in part to preempt just such developments, the U.S. Congress came forth in 1975 with a statute bearing the supremely unlikely title of "American Indian Self-Determination and Educational Assistance Act."[211] While the act did nothing at all to meet the requirements of international legal definition—quite the opposite, it offered little more than a hiring preference to Native people in programs attending policies implemented "in their behalf" by the federal government[212]—U.S. representatives at the U.N. were quick to use it in asserting that questions of indigenous self-determination in the United States were "superfluous" since it was the only country in the world to specifically guarantee such rights within its own statutory code.[213]

This in itself was insufficient to halt the international process, given that a U.S. domestic law, no matter how it was presented, could hardly be argued as bearing upon the circumstances of Native peoples elsewhere. Thus, after much maneuvering, the United Nations Working Group on Indigenous Populations, a subpart of the Economic and Social Council (ECOSOC), was established in 1981.[214] Its mission was to conduct biannual sessions at the Palace of Nations during which Native delegations would present information and to submit regular reports to ECOSOC's Commission on Human Rights, with the preliminary goal of completing a then ongoing global study of the conditions imposed upon Native peoples.[215] After 1984, although Durham and others had hoped to see a direct application of existing law to Native circumstance, the working group was also mandated to produce a whole new draft declaration of indigenous rights for endorsement by the U.N. General Assembly.[216]

There followed a lengthy period of procrastination and outright obstruction on the part of various nation-state delegations. Those of Canada and the United States, to take notable examples, tied things up for several *years* while arguing that the draft document, like the name of the working group itself, should be couched in terms of populations rather than peoples.[217] This was because the former term, used interchangeably with minorities, is employed with reference to demographic subsets of given polities, a classification automatically placing them within the parameters of their respective countries' "internal" affairs.[218] Peoples, on the other hand, are construed as distinct polities on their own, and, as such, are universally guaranteed the unfettered right of self-determination under international law.[219]

It was not until 1989 that the two North American settler states abandoned their terminological objections, and then only with the caveat that they were doing so with the specific understanding that use of the word peoples would not be construed as conveying legal connotations.[220] By then, their joint bottleneck had stalled the formulating procedure to the point that draft declaration, originally intended for consideration by the General Assembly during the U.N.'s 1992 Year of Indigenous Peoples, could not be completed on that schedule.[221] Another year was required before the document was reviewed and tentatively approved by Native delegations, a further eighteen months before it had been signed off by the working group and its immediate parent, ECOSOC's Sub-Commission on Prevention of Discrimination and Protection of Minorities.[222]

Matters finally came to a head in October 1996, when, prior to its submission to ECOSOC's main body, and thence the General Assembly, a subgroup of the Commission on Human Rights convened in Geneva to review the draft. When the panel, composed exclusively of nation-state representatives, set out to "revise" the document in a manner intended quite literally to gut it, a unified body of indigenous delegates demanded that it be sent forward unchanged. U.S. representatives, who had for the most part remained a bit more circumspect in their approach over the preceding twenty years, then at last openly announced that the function of the proposed declaration was, in their view, to confirm rather than challenge the convoluted doctrines through which their country purportedly legitimates settler hegemony.[223] The United States, they made clear, would reject anything else, a position quickly seconded by Canada's representatives. This affront precipitated a mass walkout by Native delegates, thereby bringing the entire process to a temporary halt.[224]

PROSPECTS AND POTENTIALS

The events in Geneva represent something of a crossroads in the struggle for Native sovereignty and self-determination, not only in North America, but globally. The sheer audacity with which the United States and Canada have moved to convert a supposedly universal declaration of indigenous rights into little more than an extrapolation of their own mutual foreclosure upon the most meaningful of these clearly describes one direction in which things are moving. If the North American settler states are successful in pushing through their agenda, indigenous rights the world over will be formally defined in much the same truncated and subordinative fashion as is presently the case here. Native peoples everywhere will then be permanently consigned to suffer the same lack of recourse before the ICJ and other international adjudicating bodies that they have long experienced in U.S. and Canadian courts.[225]

In the alternative, if the all but unanimous indigenous refusal to agree to substantive alteration of the draft document they themselves endorsed proves inadequate to compel its eventual acceptance by the General Assembly, other options must be found. The most promising of these would appear to reside in a generalized Native repudiation of any statist version of the proposed declaration of indigenous rights combined with a return to the strategy advocated by Durham and others during the late 1970s.[226] This, quite simply, devolves upon the devising of ways to force acknowledgment of indigenous rights under existing law rather than the creation of a new instrument.[227]

There are numerous routes to this end, beginning with the seeking of ICJ advisory opinions on the broader applicability of its interpretations in the *Island of Palmas* and *Western Sahara* cases.[228] Perhaps more important are a range of possibilities by which the ICJ and/or appropriate U. N. organs might be compelled to advance concrete interpretations of the meaning inherent to assorted declarations, covenants, and conventions—the 1966 International Covenant on Economic, Social and Cultural Rights, for example, and the 1966 International Covenant on Civil and Political Rights—vis-à-vis indigenous peoples.[229] Probably salient in this regard is the 1960 Declaration on the Granting of Independence to Colonial Countries and Peoples (General Assembly Resolution 1514 (XV)), the fifth point of which stipulates that:

> Immediate steps shall be taken, in Trust and Non-Self-Governing Territories or all other territories which have not yet attained independence, to

transfer all powers to the peoples of those territories, without conditions or reservations, in accordance with their freely-expressed will or desire, without any distinction as to race, creed or colour, to enable them to enjoy complete independence and freedom.[230]

The nature of the "immediate steps" to be taken are neither mysterious nor left to the interpretive discretion of colonizing states. Rather, they are spelled out clearly in Articles 73–91 of the United Nations Charter.[231] In essence, all such territories/peoples must be inscribed by the colonizer on a list maintained by the U.N. Trusteeship Council, which then must approve a plan, including a timetable, by which complete decolonization will occur at the earliest feasible date.[232] The colonizer is then required to submit regular reports to the council on progress made in fulfillment of the plan.[233] The process culminates in a referendum or comparable procedure, monitored by the United Nations and sometimes conducted under its direct supervision, by which the colonized people determine for themselves exactly what they wish their political status to be, and what, if any, relationship they wish to maintain with their former colonizers.[234]

One significant hurdle which must be cleared in the course of bringing such elements of black letter law to bear on the question of Native rights are the provisions contained in Article 1 (4) of the United Nations Charter and Point 7 of General Assembly Resolution 1514 (XV) guaranteeing the territorial integrity of all states.[235] By and large, the meaning of these clauses has been interpreted in accordance with the so-called "Blue Water Principle" of the 1960s, a doctrine holding that in order to be eligible for decolonization, a territory must be physically separated from its colonizer by at least thirty miles of open ocean.[236] By this standard, most indigenous peoples are obviously not and will never be entitled to exercise genuine self-determining rights.

There are, however, substantial problems attending the Blue Water formulation, not just for indigenous peoples but for everyone. It would not, for instance, admit to the fact that Germany colonized contiguous Poland during World War II, or that the Poles possessed a legitimate right to decolonization. Plainly, then, a basic reformulation is in order, starting perhaps from the basic premise that "integrity" is not so much a matter of geography as it is a question of whether a given territory can be shown to have been legitimately acquired in the first place. Thus, the definitional obstacle at hand readily lends itself to being rendered far less "insurmountable" than it might now appear.[237]

Ultimately, such issues can be resolved only on the basis of a logically consistent determination of whether indigenous peoples actually constitute "peoples" in a legal sense. While the deliberately obfuscatory arguments entered on the matter by the United States, Canada, and several other settler states during the 1980s have by this point thoroughly muddied the situation with respect to a host of untreatied peoples throughout the world, the same cannot be said with respect to the treatied peoples of North America. As has been discussed in this essay, we have long since been formally recognized by our colonizers not only as peoples, but as Nations, and are thereby entitled in existing law to exercise the rights of such *regardless* of our geographic disposition.[238]

The path leading to an alternative destiny for indigenous peoples is thus just as clear as that the settler states would prescribe for us. By relentless and undeviating assertion of the basic rights of treatied peoples—at all levels, through every available venue and excluding no conceivable means of doing so—we can begin to (re)secure them, restoring to ourselves and our posterity our/their rightful status as sovereign and coequal members of the community of nations, free of such pretense as IRA-style "self-governance" and subterfuges like the "Self-Determination" Act. In achieving success in this endeavor, we will eventually position ourselves to assist our relatives in other parts of the world, untreatied and thus unrecognized as being imbued with the same self-determining rights as we, to overcome the juridical/diplomatic quandary in which this circumstance places them.

Notes

1. See generally, Douglas Sanders, "The Re–Emergence of Indigenous Questions in International Law," *Canadian Human Rights Yearbook* 3 (1983); S. James Anaya, "The Rights of Indigenous Peoples and International Law in Historical and Contemporary Perspective," in Robert N. Clinton, Nell Jessup Newton, and Monroe E. Price, eds., *American Indian Law: Cases and Materials* (Charlottesville, VA: Michie Co., 1991).

2. It is of course true that Mexico is geographically part of the North American continent. Since its colonial legal tradition is Iberian rather than Anglo-American, however, it is excluded from the present analysis (which is thus restricted to the area north of the Río Grande). Those interested in the circumstances pertaining to Ibero-America would do well to reference Greg Urban and Joel Sherzer, eds., *Nation-States and Indians in Latin America* (Austin: University of Texas Press, 1991). Of additional interest is Roxanne Dunbar Ortiz, *Indians of the Americas: Human Rights and Self-Determination* (London: Zed Press, 1984).

3. Perhaps the most coherent articulation of the thinking embodied in this claim will be found in Charles F. Wilkinson's *Indians, Time and Law* (New Haven, CT: Yale University Press, 1987). For more analyses specific to Canada, see Russel Barsh and James Youngblood Henderson, "Aboriginal Rights, Treaty Rights, and Human Rights: Indian Tribes and Constitutional Renewal," *Journal of Canadian Studies* 17:2 (1982); Paul Williams, "Canada's Laws About Aboriginal Peoples: A Brief Overview," *Law & Anthropology* 1 (1986); Shorn H. Venne, "Treaty and Constitution in Canada," in Ward Churchill, ed., *Critical Issues in Native North America*, Doc. 62 (Copenhagen: IWGIA, 1989).

4. See, e.g., the statements quoted by Jimmie Durham in his *Columbus Day* (Minneapolis: West End Press, 1983). For detailed analysis of the actualities involved, see Carol J. Minugh, Glenn T. Morris, and Rudolph C. Ryser, eds., *Indian Self–Governance: Perspectives on the Political Status of Indian Nations in the United States of America* (Kenmore, WA: World Center for Indigenous Studies, 1989).

5. For further details, see Ward Churchill, "Subterfuge and Self–Determination:

Suppression of Indigenous Sovereignty in the 20th Century United States," in *Z Magazine* (May 1997).

6. See, e.g., Robert M. Carmack, ed., *Harvest of Violence: The Maya Indians and the Guatemala Crisis* (Norman: University of Oklahoma Press, 1988); John G. Taylor, *Indonesia's Forgotten War: The Hidden History of East Timor* (London: Zed Books, 1991). On the historical treatment of Native peoples both north of the Río Grande and south, see David E. Stannard, *American Holocaust: Columbus and the Conquest of the New World* (New York: Oxford University Press, 1992). For particular emphasis on the U.S. portion of North America, including current data on health, life expectancy, and so forth, see Ward Churchill, *A Little Matter of Genocide: Holocaust and Denial in the Americas* (San Francisco: City Lights Books, 1997).

7. Most notably, this applies to the counterinsurgency campaign waged during the 1970s against the American Indian Movement by U.S. civil authorities, backed up by the military, and, to a lesser extent, actions undertaken against the Mohawk Warriors Society by Canadian military and police units twenty years later; see Bruce Johansen and Roberto Maestas, *Wasi'chu: The Continuing Indian Wars* (New York: *Monthly Review*, 1978); Ward Churchill and Jim Vander Wall, *Agents of Repression: The FBI's Secret Wars Against the Black Panther Party and the American Indian Movement* (Boston: South End Press, 1988); Geoffrey York and Loreen Pindera, *People of the Pines: The Warriors and the Legacy of Oka* (Boston: Little, Brown, 1991).

8. On England, see Michael Hecter, *Internal Colonialism: The Celtic Fringe in British National Development, 1536–1966* (Berkeley: University of California Press, 1975); Peter Berresford Ellis, *The Celtic Revolution: A Study in Anti-Imperialism* (Talybont, UK: Y Lolfa Cyf., 1985). On Spain, see Robert P. Clark, *Negotiating with ETA: Obstacles to Peace in the Basque Country, 1975–1988* (Reno: University of Nevada Press, 1990); Cyrus Ernesto Zirakzadeh, *A Rebellious People: Basques, Protests, and Politics* (Reno: University of Nevada Press, 1991).

9. There is much theoretical precedent for such an outcome with respect to enunciating principles of self-determination, not least within such ostensibly liberatory perspectives as Marxism-Leninism; see Walker Connor, *The National Question in Marxist-Leninist Theory and Strategy* (Princeton, NJ: Princeton University Press, 1984). For a concrete example of the United States, and Canada secondarily, manipulating the codification of international law in such fashion as to protect their own prerogatives to engage in certain of the practices ostensibly proscribed, see Lawrence J. LeBlanc, *The United States and the Genocide Convention* (Durham, NC: Duke University Press, 1991).

10. It might be useful for some readers at this point to offer a reference addressing the meaning of the term self–determination in not only its theoretical but also its legal and practical applications; see generally, Michla Pomerance, *Self-Determination in Law and Practice* (The Hague: Marinus Nijhoff, 1982).

11. The first indication that this is so may be found in the 1867 Quebec case *Connolly v. Woolrich* (11 LCJ 197) in which a Canadian court considering the validity of a marriage effected under Native tradition for purposes of determining inheritance rights repeated verbatim a lengthy passage from Chief Justice of the U.S. Supreme Court John Marshall's opinion in *Worcester v. Georgia*, 6 Peters 515 (1832). For a comprehensive overview of this phenomenon, see Bruce Clark, *Indian Land Title in Canada* (Toronto: Carswell, 1987).

12. See, e.g., J. V. Stalin, *Marxism and the National and Colonial Questions* (New York: International, 1935); V. I. Lenin, *The Right of Nations to Self–Determination: Selected Writings* (New York: International, 1951); Louis L. Snyder, *The Meaning of Nationalism* (New

Brunswick, NJ: Rutgers University Press, 1954); Ernst Gellner, *Nations and Nationalism* (Ithaca, NY: Cornell University Press, 1983).

13. For a variety of viewpoints, all arriving at more or less the same conclusion, see Ernst Cassirer, *The Myth of the State* (New Haven: Yale University Press, 1946); Perry Anderson, *Lineages of the Absolute State* (London: New Left Books, 1974); L. Tivey, ed., *The Nation-State* (New York: St. Martin's Press, 1981); J. Frank Harrison, *The Modern State: An Anarchist Analysis* (Montreal: Black Rose Books, 1984)

14. For further clarification, see Hugh Seton–Watson, *Nations and States: An Inquiry into the Origins of Nations and the Politics of Nationalism* (Boulder, CO: Westview Press, 1977); Anthony D. Smith, *State and Nation in the Third World* (Brighton, UK: Harvester Press, 1983).

15. As American Indian Movement leader Russell Means quipped during a talk delivered in Denver on October 9, 1996, "to be accurate, the United Nations should really have been called the United States. But the name was already taken" (UN, tape on file).

16. Sovereignty is a theological concept originally associated with the transcendent power of the deity. It was secularized during the sixteenth century when the French theorist Jean Bodin used it to describe the authority of the Crown, beyond which no world was seen to exist (monarchs, ruling by "divine right," were in his view accountable only to natural and supernatural law). Eventually, during the era of the American and French revolutions, the idea was reworked so that sovereignty might be understood as something vested in the people themselves, or, most recently, in the states supposedly embodying their "will"; L. Oppenheim, *International Law*, (London: Longman's, Green, 1955), 120–22; Carl Schmidt, *Political Theology: Four Chapters on the Concept of Sovereignty* (Cambridge: MIT Press, 1985).

17. This is not to say that the actions themselves bear an intrinsic illegitimacy, simply that they do not represent a negation of sovereignty. Even in the most extreme instances—the unconditional surrenders and subsequent occupations of Germany and Japan at the end of World War II, for example—it is understood that such outcomes are of a temporary nature, that the sovereignty of the defeated nations remains intact, and that their self–determining existence will resume at the earliest possible date. For elaboration of the legal and other principles involved, see Michael Walzer, *Just and Unjust Wars: A Moral Argument with Illustrations* (New York: Basic Books, 1977).

18. For an interesting array of perspectives on, and especially sensitive handling of, this matter, see R.B.J. Walker and Saul H. Mendlovitz, eds., *Contending Sovereignties: Redefining Political Community* (Boulder, CO: Lynne Rienner, 1990).

19. For a good summary, see Jack Weatherford, *Indian Givers: How the Indians of the Americas Transformed the World* (New York: Fawcett Columbine, 1988).

20. Felix S. Cohen, "Original Indian Title," *Minnesota Law Review* 32 (1947): 44, n. 34. Vitoria's *De Indis et de Ivre Belli Reflectiones* (Washington, DC: Carnegie Institution, 1917 reprint of 1557 original), a compilation of meditations begun in 1532, was more or less definitive and endorsed as legal doctrine by both the Iberian monarch and the pope. Among other things, Vitoria—and, by extension, the Vatican and the Spanish Crown—acknowledged indigenous peoples' ownership of their lands and other property, their right to govern themselves within these territories, and their right to convey citizenship; Felix S. Cohen, "The Spanish Origin of Indian Rights in the United States," *Georgetown Law Journal* 31:1 (1942); Lewis Hanke, *The Spanish Struggle for Justice in the Conquest of America* (Philadelphia: University of Pennsylvania Press, 1947); Etienne Grisel, "The Beginnings of International Law and General Public Law Doctrine: Francisco de Vitoria's *De Indis prior*," in Fredi Chiapelli, ed., *First Images of America*, 2 vols. (Berke-

ley: University of California Press, 1976). More broadly, see Robert A. Williams, Jr., *The American Indian in Western Legal Thought: The Discourses of Conquest* (New York: Oxford University Press, 1990).

21. See Howard Peckham and Charles Gibson, eds., *Attitudes of the Colonial Powers Toward the American Indian* (Salt Lake City: University of Utah Press, 1969).

22. Quoted in Francis Paul Prucha, *American Indian Policy in the Formative Years: The Trade and Intercourse Acts, 1790–1834* (Lincoln: University of Nebraska Press, 1970), 141.

23. Quoted in George Dewey Harmon, *Sixty Years of Indian Affairs: Political, Economic, and Diplomatic, 1789–1850* (Chapel Hill: University of North Carolina Press, 1941), 16.

24. *Worcester v. Georgia*, at 559. For further amplification, see Howard Berman, "The Concept of Aboriginal Rights in the Early History of the United States," *Buffalo Law Review* 27 (Fall 1978).

25. Edwin de Witt Dickenson, *The Equality of States in International Law* (Cambridge, MA: Harvard University Press, 1920). The principle at issue was consistently recognized by the U.S. judiciary with respect to American Indians as late as the 1883 case *Ex Parte Crow Dog* (109 U.S. 556), in which the court held that the United States lacked a jurisdictional standing to prosecute criminal offenses committed in Indian Country. Congress responded by passing the 1885 Major Crimes Act (ch. 120, 16 Stat. 544, 566, now codified at 25 U.S.C. 71), unilaterally extending the reach of U.S. courts into reserved territories with regard to seven felonious offenses. Hence, it was not until *United States v. Kagama* (118 U.S. 375 [1886]) that the Supreme Court began to speak of the federal government possessing an "incontrovertible right" to exercise jurisdiction over Native lands; see Sidney L. Harring, *Crow Dog's Case: American Indian Sovereignty, Tribal Law, and United States Law in the Nineteenth Century* (Cambridge, UK: Cambridge University Press, 1994). Usurpation of Native jurisdiction in Canada began earlier, with the 1803 Act for Extending Jurisdiction of the Courts of Justice in the Provinces of Upper and Lower Canada, to the Trial and Punishment of Persons Guilty of Crimes and Offenses within Certain Parts of North America Adjoining to Said Provinces (43 Geo. III, c. 138), amplified and extended into the civil domain by the 1821 Act for Regulating the Fur Trade and Establishing a Criminal and Civil Jurisdiction within Certain Parts of North America (1 & 2 Geo. IV, c. 66); Bruce Clark, *Native Liberty, Crown Sovereignty: The Existing Aboriginal Right of Self–Government in Canada* (Montreal: McGill–Queens University Press, 1990), 124–27. For a strongly articulated Native repudiation of the U.S. performance, see the testimony of Vine Deloria, Jr., during the 1974 "Sioux Sovereignty Hearing" conducted before a federal court in Lincoln, Nebraska; Roxanne Dunbar Ortiz, ed., *The Great Sioux Nation: Sitting in Judgment on America* (New York/San Francisco: International Indian Treaty Council/Moon Books, 1977), 141–46. On Canada, see the positions advanced by Ontario Region Chief Gordon Peters, John Amagolik, Doris Ronnenberg, and others in Frank Cassidy, ed., *Aboriginal Self–Determination: Proceedings of a Conference Held September 30–October 3, 1990* (Lantzville, BC: Oolichan Books, 1991), 33–60.

26. This prescription for the interaction of nations was worked out very well by the time of Dutch jurist Hugo Grotius' *De Jure Belli ac Pacis Libri Tres: In quibus ius naturae & Gentium, item iuris publicipraecipua explicantur* (Paris: Buon, 1625). For interpretation, see, Hidemi Suganami, "Grotius and International Equality," in Hedley Bull, Benedict Kingsbury, and Adam Roberts, eds., *Hugo Grotius and International Law* (Oxford, UK: Clarendon Press, 1990).

27. A particularly astute rendering of this principle will be found in John Howard Clinebell and Jim Thompson, "Sovereignty and Self–Determination: The Rights of

Native Americans Under International Law," *Buffalo Law Review* 27 (Fall 1978).

28. Suganami, "Grotius and International Equity," *op. cit.* Also see Hedley Bull, "The Grotian Conception of International Relations," in Herbert Butterfield and Martin Wright, eds., *Diplomatic Investigations: Essays in the Theory of International Politics* (London: Allen & Unwin, 1966); Cornelius J. Murphy, "Grotius and the Peaceful Settlement of Disputes," Grotiana 4 (1983). For translation of Grotian thought into the relatively more concrete terms of contemporary legal/diplomatic practice, see Martin Lachs, "The Grotian Heritage, the International Community and Changing Dimensions of International Law," in *International Law and the Grotian Heritage* (The Hague: T.M.C. Asser Instituut, 1985).

29. See generally, Vitoria, "On the Law of War," in *De Indis et De Jure Belli Relaciones, op. cit.* More particularly, see Walzer, *op. cit.,* 51–53; and *Report of the Special Committee on the Question of Defining Aggression,* Gen. Ass. Off. Rec. No. A/9619, 29 sess. 19 (1974), 10–13. On the military dimension of U.S.–Indian relations, see, e.g., Alan Axelrod, *Chronicle of the Indian Wars from Colonial Times to Wounded Knee* (New York: Prentice Hall, 1993).

30. As the point is delineated in the United Nations Resolution on the Definition of Aggression, U.N.G.A. Res. 3314 (XXIX), 29 U.N. GAOR, Supp. No. 31, 142, U.N. Doc. A/9631 (1975), "No territorial acquisition or special advantage resulting from aggression is or shall be recognized as lawful." This is an element of what has come to be known as the Nuremberg Doctrine; see, e.g., Quincy Wright, "The Law of the Nuremberg Trials," *American Journal of International Law* 41 (Jan. 1947). For the text of the instrument by which the international community accepted this doctrine, see "Agreement for the Prosecution and Punishment of the Major War Criminals of the European Axis Powers and Charter of the International Military Tribunal" ("London Agreement," Aug. 8, 1945) in Burns H. Weston, Richard A. Falk, and Anthony D'Amato, *Basic Documents in International Law and World Order,* (St. Paul, MN: West Publishing, 1990), 138–39. On the role of the United States in articulation of the Nuremberg principles and its endorsement of them, see Bradley F. Smith, *The Road to Nuremberg* (New York: Basic Books, 1981); *The American Road to Nuremberg: The Documentary Record, 1944–1945* (Stanford, CA: Hoover Institution Press, 1982). With respect to the crimes for which the German leadership was tried in this connection, see Office of United States Chief Council for Prosecution of Axis Criminality, *Nazi Conspiracy and Aggression* (Washington, DC: U.S. Government Printing Office, 1946).

31. The point is exceedingly well established; see, *Pomerance, Self–Determination in Law and Practice, op. cit.*; W. Ofuatey–Kodjoe, *The Principle of Self–Determination in International Law* (Hamden, CT: Archon Books, 1972); A. Rigo Sureda, *The Evolution of the Right to Self–Determination: A Study of United Nations Practice* (Leyden, Netherlands: A.W. Sijhoff, 1973); Lee C. Buchheit, *Secession: The Legitimacy of Self–Determination* (New Haven: Yale University Press, 1978); Ved Nanda, "Self–Determination Under International Law: Validity of Claims to Secede," *Case Western Journal of International Law* 13 (1981).

32. This principle was enunciated by Supreme Court Justice Robert H. Jackson, at the time serving as lead prosecutor for the United States, in his opening statement to the court at Nuremberg on November 21, 1945; International Military Tribunal, *Trial of the Major War Criminals before the International Military Tribunal,* 42 vols. (Nuremberg: Allied Control Authority, 1949) Vol. 2, 98–155. Also see Jackson's *The Nürnberg Case* (New York: Alfred A. Knopf, 1947).

33. On the contrary, instruments such as the Universal Declaration of the Rights of

Peoples ("Algiers Declaration," July 4, 1976), go in precisely the opposite direction; for text, see Richard Falk, *Human Rights and State Sovereignty* (New York: Holmes & Meier, 1981), 225–28.

34. This has been so since at least as early as publication of Grotius' 1625 *De Jure Belli, op. cit.*, and was reconfirmed quite forcefully by the renowned jurist Emmerich de Vattel in his massive three–volume *The Laws of Nations* (Philadelphia: T. & J.W. Joseph, 1883 reprint of 1758 original; Washington, DC: Carnegie Institution, 1925 reprint). Most definitively, the Vienna Convention on the Law of Treaties (U.N. Doc. A/CONF.39/27 at 289 [1969], 1155 U.N.T.S. 331, reprinted in 8 I.L.M. 679 [1969]) is explicit in positing that a "'treaty' means an agreement concluded *between States* in a written form and governed by international law (emphasis added)." It was agreed by those who met to formulate the convention that its contents are "merely expressive of rules which existed under customary international law"; *United Nations Conference on the Law of Treaties, Official Records, Second Session* (A Conf.39/11 Add.1 [1969]). See generally, Shabati Rosenne, *The Law of Treaties: A Guide to the Legislative History of the Vienna Convention* (Leyden: A. W. Sijhoff, 1970); Sir Ian Sinclair, *The Vienna Convention on the Law of Treaties* (Manchester, UK: Manchester University Press, 1984). With particular reference to the fact that the Vienna Convention merely codified existing custom rather than creating new law, see Samuel Benjamin Crandell, *Treaties: Their Making and Enforcement*, (New York: Columbia University Press, [2d ed.]1916).

35. Oppenheim, International Law, *op. cit.*, 146, 148; H. Chen, *International Law of Recognition* (Leyden, Netherlands: A.W. Sijhoff, 1951), 194. It is crucial to emphasize that one nation does not "create" another by entering into a treaty with it. Sovereignty is not *imparted* through treaty recognition. Rather, a treaty represents the acknowledgment by each party of the other's *preexisting* standing as a sovereign nation. In effect, then, the hundreds of European and Euro–American treaties with North America's indigenous peoples are all reiterations of the involved states' formal recognition that the Natives were and had always been inherently sovereign. For a good sampling of instruments deriving from the colonial era, see Alden T. Vaughan, *Early American Indian Documents: Treaties and Laws, 1607–1789* (Washington, DC: University Publications of America, 1979).

36. Art. I, § 10 of the U.S. Constitution precludes any private concern or level of government below that of the federal authority itself from entering into a treaty. The courts have interpreted this in terms of a "rule of reciprocity": Since lesser entities are prohibited from treating, the federal government is equally prohibited from treating with them. It follows that any entity with which the government treats must be, by definition, another sovereign national entity. This being true, Article VI, Cl. 2—the so–called "Supremacy Clause"—stipulates that ratified treaties "are superior to any conflicting state laws or constitutional provisions"; Rennard Strickland, et al., eds., *Felix S. Cohen's Handbook on Federal Indian Law* (Charlottesville, VA: Michie Co., 1982), 62–63.

37. A notable example is to be found in George III's Royal Proclamation of 1763 (RSC 1970, App. II, No. 1, at 127) and subsequent legislation; Jack Stagg, *Anglo–Indian Relations in North America to 1763 and an Analysis of the Royal Proclamation of 7 October 1763* (Ottawa: Carlton University Press, 1981). A useful summary and assessment of implications will be found in Clark, Native Liberty, *Crown Sovereignty, op. cit.*, esp. 134–46. Also see the opening chapter of Dorothy V. Jones, *License for Empire: Colonialism by Treaty in Early America* (Chicago: University of Chicago Press, 1982).

38. Under Art. II, Cl. 2 of the U.S. Constitution, treaties are negotiated by the president or his delegate(s), but do not become law until confirmed by two–thirds vote of the

Senate. The standard count on ratified treaties has until recently been 371, the complete texts of which are collected in Charles J. Kappler, ed., *Indian Treaties, 1778–1885* (New York: Interland, 1973). Lakota scholar Vine Deloria, Jr., has, however, collected a further two dozen such instruments overlooked by Kappler (these are to be included in an as yet unpublished study). As concerns unratified treaties, it should be noted that U.S. courts have in numerous instances opted to view them as binding upon Indians while exempting the United States from even a pretense of compliance with terms delineating reciprocal obligations. An especially egregious example concerns the more than forty unratified treaties with California's Native peoples used by the federal judiciary to impose the so–called "Pit River Land Settlement" during the late 1960s; see generally, Florence Connolly Shipeck, *Pushed into the Rocks: Southern California Indian Land Tenure, 1769–1986* (Lincoln: University of Nebraska Press, 1988).

39. *Canada: Indian Treaties and Surrenders from 1680 to 1890* (Ottawa: Queen's Printer, 1891; reprinted by Coles [Toronto], 1971; reprinted by Fifth House [Saskatoon], 1992). A useful interpretation will be found in John Leonard Taylor's "Canada's North–West Indian Policy in the 1870s: Traditional Premises and Necessary Innovations," in J. R. Miller, *Sweet Promises: A Reader on Indian–White Relations in Canada* (Toronto: University of Toronto Press, 1991).

40. *Opinions of the Attorney General* (Washington, DC: U.S. Government Printing Office, 1828), 613–8, 623–33. The validity of Wirt's equating the legal standing of indigenous nations to that of "any other nation" has been repeatedly conceded by the Supreme Court: e.g., *Holden v. Joy*, 84 U.S. 17, Wall. 211 (1872); *United States v. 43 Gallons of Whiskey*, 93 U.S. 188 (1876); *Washington v. Fishing Vessel Association*, 443 U.S. 675 (1979).

41. Wilcomb E. Washburn, *Red Man's Land, White Man's Law: The Past and Present Status of the American Indian*, (Norman: University of Oklahoma Press, [2d. ed.]1995), 57. It is worth noting, to reinforce the point, that under provision of the1796 Trade and Intercourse Act (Ch. 30, 1 Stat. 469) all U.S. nationals intending to travel into Indian Country were required to obtain a passport.

42. Robert T. Coulter, "Contemporary Indian Sovereignty," in National Lawyers Guild, Committee on Native American Struggles, *Rethinking Indian Law* (New Haven, CT: Advocate Press, 1982), 117. He cites M. Whitman, *Digest of International Law* §1 at 2 (1963) on this point.

43. This is all but axiomatic; see, e.g., Wilfred C. Jencks, *Law in the World Community* (New York: Oxford University Press, 1967), 31, 83–87.

44. *Opinions of the Attorney General* (Washington, DC: U.S. Government Printing Office, 1821), 345.

45. For a prime example of such argumentation, see Wilcomb E. Washburn, *The Indian in America* (New York: Harper & Row, 1975).

46. For good surveys of such contentions, see Reginald Horsman, *Expansion and American Policy, 1783–1812* (Lansing: Michigan State University Press, 1967); Richard Drinnon, *Facing West: The Metaphysics of Indian Hating and Empire Building* (Minneapolis: University of Minnesota Press, 1980). Also see Richard E. Buel, Jr., *Securing the Revolution: Ideology in American Politics, 1789–1815* (Ithaca, NY: Cornell University Press, 1972).

47. To be fair about it, the U.S. founders and their heirs are by no means the only parties to advance this sort of spurious argument. The English themselves, for example, claimed to have inherited discovery rights to Mikmakik (Nova Scotia) from France under the 1713 Treaty of Utrecht, despite a firm French denial that they held title to

what was in fact acknowledged Mi'kmaq territory. To further complicate matters, Canadian courts now contend that their country has inherited title from Great Britain, although they, no more than anyone else, can say exactly when or how Mi'kmaq title was ever extinguished; W.E. Daugherty, *The Maritime Indian Treaties in Perspective* (Ottawa: Indian and Northern Affairs Canada, 1981), 45–47; Peter A. Cumming and Neil H. Mickenberg, *Native Rights in Canada* (Toronto: General Publishing/Indian–Eskimo Association of Canada, 1972), 95.

48. The complete text of the Treaty of Paris (Sept. 3, 1783) is included in Ruhl J. Bartlett, ed., *The Record of American Diplomacy: Documents and Readings in the History of U.S. Foreign Relations*, (New York: Alfred A. Knopf, [4th ed.]1964), 39–42. Under both British common law and relevant international law, to quit a claim of interest in a property or territory means that unclouded title reverts to the original owners. In this case, other than in those relatively small areas to which the Crown had acquired an outright title through purchase or other agreement, this would be the indigenous nations whose lands were (and are) at issue.

49. Most important was Innocent III's bull *Quod super his*, promulgated in1210 to legitimate the Crusades. Relying on the intervening theoretical work of Thomas Aquinas and others, Innocent IV subjected his predecessor's bull to the question of whether it was "licit to invade a land which infidels possess, or which belongs to them?" He ultimately answered in the affirmative, but only under specific circumstances and in recognition of the "natural rights" of those invaded to their property; James Muldoon, *The Expansion of Europe: The First Phase* (Philadelphia: University of Pennsylvania Press, 1977), 191–92. Also see Brian Tierney, *The Crisis of Church and State, 1050–1300* (Engelwood Cliffs, NJ: Prentice–Hall, 1964), 155–6. On development of the Innocentian position by Vitoria, et al., see Hanke, *Spanish Struggle for Justice, op. cit.*; Williams, *American Indian in Western Legal Thought, op. cit.*; John Taylor, *Spanish Law Concerning Discoveries, Pacifications, and Settlements Among the Indians* (Salt Lake City: University of Utah Press, 1980); L.C. Green and Olive P. Dickason, *The Law of Nations in the New World* (Edmonton: University of Alberta Press, 1989).

50. See generally, Mark Frank Lindsey, *The Acquisition and Government of Backward Country in International Law: A Treatise on the Law and Practice Relating to Colonial Expansion* (London: Longman's, Green, 1926); W. J. Mommsen and J. A. de Moor, *European Expansion and the Law: The Encounter of European and Indigenous Law in 19th and 20th Century Africa and Asia* (Oxford: Berg, 1992).

51. *Bull Sublimis Duis*, promulgated by Pope Paul III in 1537; quoted in Frank Mac-Nutt, *Bartholomew de Las Casas* (Cleveland: Arthur H. Clark, 1909), 429. It is worth noting that understanding of the principle involved was still demonstrated by U.S. courts well into the twentieth century. In *Deere v. St. Lawrence River Power Company*, 32 F.2d 550 (2d Cir. 1929), for example, it was admitted that, "The source of [Native] title is no letters patent or other form of grant by the federal government. . . . Indians claim immemorial rights, arising prior to white occupation, and recognized and protected by treaties between Great Britain and the United States and the United States and the Indians [under which] the right of occupation of [their] lands . . . was not granted, but recognized and affirmed."

52. This amounted to a universalization of the principle expounded by Pope Alexander VI in his *bull Inter Caetera* of May 4, 1493, dividing interests in the Southern Hemisphere of the New World between Spain and Portugal; Paul Gottschalk, *The Earliest Diplomatic Documents of America* (Berlin: P. Gottschalk, 1927), 21.

53. *Worcester v. Georgia* at 544.

54. *Johnson & Graham's Lessee* v. *McIntosh*, 21 U.S. (8 Wheat.) 543 (1823) at 572.

55. Quoted in Washburn, *Red Man's Land, op. cit.*, 56. Precisely the same understanding continued to be demonstrated by the federal judiciary, however occasionally, throughout the nineteenth century. In *Jones* v. *Meehan*, 175 U.S. 1 (1899), for instance, the court admitted that the "United States had [by a 1785 Treaty with the Wyandots, Delawares, Chippewas, and Ottawas] relinquished and quitclaimed to said nations respectively all the lands lying within certain limits, to live and hunt upon, and otherwise occupy as they saw fit; but the said nations, or either of them, were not at liberty to dispose of those lands, except to the United States."

56. Washburn, *Red Man's Land, op. cit.*, 56. For an almost identical statement, this one made in a legal opinion rendered on May 3, 1790, see Andrew A. Lipscomb and Albert Ellery Bergh, eds., *The Writings of Thomas Jefferson*, 20 vols. (Washington, DC: Thomas Jefferson Memorial Association, 1903–1904), Vol. VII, 467–69. Further comments will be found in Merrill D. Peterson's *Thomas Jefferson and the New Nation* (New York: Oxford University Press, 1970), 771, 820–21.

57. *Worcester* v. *Georgia* at 545.

58. See generally, David M. Pelcher, *The Diplomacy of Annexation: Texas, Oregon and the Mexican War* (Columbia: University of Missouri Press, 1973).

59. Cohen, "Original Indian Title," *op. cit.*, 35; for the text of the Treaty Between the United States and France for the Cession of Louisiana (Apr. 30, 1803), see Bartlett, *Record of American Diplomacy, op. cit.*, 116–17. Also see Alexander de Conde, *This Affair of Louisiana* (New York: Charles Scribner's Sons, 1976).

60. Treaty of Peace, Friendship, Limits, and Settlement Between the United States and Mexico, Feb. 2, 1848; for text, see Bartlett, *Record of American Diplomacy, op. cit.*, 214–16. On the causes of the conflict preceding the treaty, see Gene M. Brack, *Mexico Views Manifest Destiny: An Essay on the Origins of the Mexican War* (Albuquerque: University of New Mexico Press, 1975).

61. The Hawaiian Archipelago was annexed by the United States in 1898, following an 1893 coup d'etat carried out by American nationals—supported by U.S. troops—against its indigenous government, a constitutional monarchy. In 1959, following a referendum conducted in a manner violating the most basic requirements of the United Nations Charter (the settler population as well as the much smaller Native population was allowed to vote), it was incorporated into the United States as its fiftieth state; Michael Kioni Dudley and Keoni Kealoha Agard, *A Call for Hawaiian Sovereignty* (Honolulu: Na Kane O Ka Malo Press, 1990); Haunani Kay Trask, *From a Native Daughter: Colonialism and Sovereignty in Hawai'i* (Monroe, ME: Common Courage Press, 1993).

62. *American Journal of International Law* 22 (1928): 1928; reporting the *Island of Palmas* case (*U.S.* v. *Netherlands*, Perm. Ct. Arb., Hague, 1928).

63. 41 U.S. (6 Pet.) 367 (1842) at 409.

64. U.S. ambitions in North America were hardly confined to the forty–eight contiguous states and Alaska. There was, for example, serious consideration given during the late 1860s to the idea of seizing all of what is now Canada west of Ontario. The idea of gobbling up what remained of Mexico after 1848 was also a perennial favorite. For varying perspectives, see Albert K. Weinberg, *Manifest Destiny: A Study of National Expansionism in American History* (Baltimore: Johns Hopkins University Press, 1935); Frederick Merk, *Manifest Destiny and Mission in American History: A Reinterpretation* (New York: Alfred A. Knopf, 1963); Sidney Lens, *The Forging of the American Empire* (New York: Thomas Y. Crowell, 1971); Reginald Horsman, *Race and Manifest Destiny: The Origins of American Racial Anglo–Saxonism* (Cambridge, MA: Harvard University Press, 1981).

65. A point worth making is that, given the realities of global demography, the whole idea of *territorium res nullius* has always lacked applicability anywhere outside Antarctica and a few remote sandspits scattered across the Seven Seas. There were an estimated billion people on the planet when the Supreme Court penned its *Martin* opinion in 1842—upwards of three–quarters that number in 1492—less than 20 percent of them of European derivation; see, e.g., Kenneth C. Davis, *Don't Know Much About Geography: Everything You Ever Wanted to Know About the World but Never Learned* (New York: William Morrow, 1992), 300.

66. The idea found form in 1066, when Pope Alexander recognized the conquest of Saxon England, vesting underlying fee title to English land in the Norman invaders. Thereafter, as a part of their policy of abolishing the preexisting system of collective land tenure, the Normans established an evolving structure of rules to individuate Saxon property titles on the basis of certain forms of utilization or "development"; Carl Erdmann, *The Origin of the Idea of the Crusade* (Princeton, NJ: Princeton University Press, 1977), 150–60. More broadly, see Otto Freidrich von Gierke, *Political Theories of the Middle Ages* (Boston: Beacon Press, 1958). By the time of the American War of Independence, philosopher John Locke had discovered what he believed to be a liberatory usage of the Norman system, arguing that individual developmental usage of given tracts of land bestowed upon those who engaged in it a "natural right" to ownership which transcended all state prerogatives to preempt title; Crawford Brough Macpherson, *The Political Theory of Possessive Individualism: Hobbes to Locke* (Oxford, UK: Clarendon Press, 1962). For application of all this specifically to North America, see Williams, *American Indian in Western Legal Thought, op. cit.*, esp. 233–80.

67. This is the premise underlying the 1862 Homestead Act (*U.S. Statutes* at Large, Vol. XII, 392) by which any U.S. citizen could claim a quarter–section (160 acres) of "undeveloped" land in exchange merely by paying an extremely nominal "patent fee" to offset the expense of registering it. He or she then had a specified period of time, usually five years, to fell trees, build a house, plow fields, etc. If these requirements were met within the time allowed, the homesteader was issued a deed to the property. For background, see Robert A. Williams, Jr., "Jefferson, the Norman Yoke, and American Indian Lands," *Arizona Law Review* 29 (1987).

68. For analysis, see Alden T, Vaughan, *The New England Frontier* (Boston: Little, Brown, 1965), 113–21; Francis Jennings, "Virgin Land and Savage People," *American Quarterly* 23 (1971).

69. Letter from the Massachusetts Bay Company to Governor John Endicott, Apr. 17, 1629; N. Shurtleff, ed., *Records of the Governor and the Company of the Massachusetts Bay in New England* (Boston: William White, 1853). At 100 of Vattel's *Laws of Nations, Book I* (*op. cit.*), the Puritans are praised for their "moderation" in adopting this posture, as are William Penn's Quakers in Pennsylvania.

70. *Cohen's Handbook, op. cit.*, 55.

71. The U.S. invocation of *territorium res nullius* has proceeded along a number of tracks, not all judicial. An especially glaring illustration has been the deliberate and systematic falsification of indigenous historical demography to make it appear that the preinvasion population of North America was not more than a million when, in fact, the best available evidence suggests that it was at least 12.5 million and perhaps as large as 18.5 million. The methods used by major Euro–American historians and anthropologists in undercounting Native people are covered very well by Francis Jennings in the chapter entitled "The Widowed Land" in his *The Invasion of America: Indians, Colonialism and the Cant of Conquest* (New York: W.W. Norton, 1975). More credible estimates of the

indigenous population, circa 1500, will be found in Henry F. Dobyns, *Their Number Become Thinned: Native American Population Dynamics in Eastern North America* (Knoxville: University of Tennessee Press, 1983). In any event, the aggregate Native population has been reliably estimated as having been reduced to something less than a million by 1800. The settler population, meanwhile, had burgeoned to approximately fifteen million. For regional breakouts, see Russell Thornton, *American Indian Holocaust and Survival: A Population History Since 1492* (Norman: University of Oklahoma Press, 1987).

72. Vattel, *The Laws of Nations, op. cit.*, Book I, 99. This was not one of Vattel's more tenable positions. If settlement and cultivation were actually employed to determine the quantity of land nations "have occasion for," the territoriality of Canada, Australia, Brazil, Russia, and several other countries would be immediately diminished by more than half. Nothing in the formulation admits to the legitimacy of speculative acquisition such as the United States engaged in during the nineteenth century, or of current policies "banking" land against anticipated future needs. By the same token, no nation would be able to maintain commons areas such as national wilderness areas, wildlife preserves, military training areas, and so forth, on pain of losing the right to possess them. Nor does Vattel's overall system of legal equity allow for the application of one set of standards to indigenous nations, another to settler states.

73. *Fletcher v. Peck*, 10 U.S. (6 Cranch.) 87 (1810). By all indications, this aspect of Marshall's opinion was an expediency designed to facilitate redemption of scrip issued to troops during the American decolonization struggle in lieu of cash. These vouchers were to be exchanged for land parcels in Indian Country once victory had been achieved (Marshall and his father received instruments entitling them to 10,000 acres apiece in what is now Kentucky, part of the more than 200,000 acres they jointly amassed there). The question was how to validate title to such parcels, a matter belatedly addressed by Peck. Having thus solved his and his country's immediate problem, all indications are that the chief justice promptly dropped Vattel's dubious premise—see note 72, above—in favor of a more subtle approach in his efforts to validate U.S. title to Native lands. For details on the Marshalls' Kentucky land transactions, see Jean Edward Smith, *John Marshall: Definer of a Nation* (New York: Henry Holt, 1996), 74–75. On the case itself, see C. Peter McGrath, *Yazoo: The Case of Fletcher v. Peck* (New York: W.W. Norton, 1966).

74. Although there were obvious antecedents in New York state and elsewhere, the clearest early formal indication of this policy came in the 1854 Treaty with the Omahas, Article 6 of which specifies that the Indians will accept a survey of their land and assignment of individual allotments at some future date; Vine Deloria, Jr., and Clifford M. Lytle, *American Indians, American Justice* (Austin: University of Texas Press, 1983), 8. On the New York precedents, see Franklin B. Hough, ed., *Proceedings of the Commission of Indian Affairs, Appointed by Law for Extinguishment of Indian Title in the State of New York* (Albany, NY: John Munsell, 1861); Helen M. Upton, *The Everett Report in Historical Perspective: The Indians of New York* (Albany, NY: New York State Bicentennial Commission, 1980).

75. For an overview of Canadian practice, see, e.g., the description offered in George F. G. Stanley's *The Birth of Western Canada* (Toronto: University of Toronto Press, 1975); George Brown and Ron McGuire, *Indian Treaties in Historical Perspective* (Ottawa: Indian and Northern Affairs Canada, 1979). Perhaps the main distinction to be drawn between Canada and the United States in terms of setting aside reserved areas was that, in the latter, priority was given to concentrating all of a given people—sometimes several peoples—in one locality. This had the effect of creating vast expanses of "Native–free"

territory, but often left indigenous nations with relatively large blocks of land on which we were able to hold ourselves together, socially and politically, at least for a while. Canada opted to reverse this emphasis, preferring a strategy of divide and rule which has resulted in an amazing proliferation of tiny "band" reserves scattered across the map; see generally, Boyce Richardson, *People of Terra Nullius: Betrayal and Rebirth of Aboriginal Canada* (Vancouver; Seattle: Douglas & McIntyre; University of Washington Press, 1993).

76. 25 U.S.C.A. § 331, also known as the Dawes Act in recognition of its primary congressional sponsor, Massachusetts Senator Henry Dawes; see generally, D.S. Otis, *The Dawes Act and the Allotment of American Indian Land* (Norman: University of Oklahoma Press, 1973).

77. The purpose of the act was sometimes framed in superficially noble–sounding terms, as when in 1881 President Chester A. Arthur described an early draft as a means to "introduce among the Indians the customs and pursuits of civilized life"; quoted in Deloria and Lytle, *American Indians, American Justice, op. cit.*, 8. At other times, it has been officially referenced with far more accuracy, as when Indian Commissioner Francis Leupp called it "a great pulverizing engine to grind down the tribal mass"; Francis A. Leupp, *The Indian and His Problem* (New York: Scribner's, 1910), 93.

78. This in itself constituted a gross violation of Native sovereignty insofar as it was a direct intervention by the United States in the internal affairs of each indigenous nation for purposes of defining its citizenry. Insofar as the means employed to determine Native identity was explicitly racial—the use of a blood quantum system—this U.S. aggression was doubly sinister, representing as it did a prefiguration of apartheid; for analysis, see George M. Frederickson, *White Supremacy: A Comparative Study in American and South African History* (New York: Oxford University Press, 1981). Canada effected similar interventions, albeit without the U.S. larding of scientific racism, creating categories of "status" and "non-status" Indians; see, e.g., Bill Wilson, "Aboriginal Rights: A Non- Status Indian View," in Menno Boldt and J. Anthony Long, *The Quest for Justice: Aboriginal People and Aboriginal Rights* (Toronto: University of Toronto Press, 1985). On the problematic nature of the term tribe—as opposed to nation or people—see the essay, "Naming Our Destiny: Toward a Language of American Indian Liberation," in Ward Churchill, *Indians Are Us? Culture and Genocide in Native North America* (Monroe, ME: Common Courage Press, 1994). Of related interest, see Robert A. Williams, Jr., "Documents of Barbarism: The Contemporary Legacy of European Racism and Colonialism in the Narrative Traditions of Federal Indian Law," *Arizona Law Review* 31:2 (1989).

79. Deloria and Lytle, *American Indians, American Justice, op. cit.*, 9.

80. See generally, Janet A. McDonnell, *The Dispossession of the American Indian, 1887–1934* (Bloomington: University Press of Indiana, 1991). On railroads, etc., see, e.g., H. Craig Miner, *The Corporation and the Indian: Tribal Sovereignty and Industrial Civilization in Indian Territory, 1865–1907* (Columbia: University of Missouri Press, 1976).

81. Kirk Kicking Bird and Karen Ducheneaux, *One Hundred Million Acres* (New York: Macmillan, 1973); Otis, *Dawes Act and Allotment, op. cit.*; McDonnell, *Dispossession of the American Indian, op. cit.*

82. 34 Stat. 182. All told, only about eleven million acres actually remained reserved for Native usage by 1973; Washburn, *Red Man's Land, op. cit.*, 145, 150.

83. Leaving aside property alienated as a result of the Burke Act, land was allotted in correspondence to the number of Indians surviving, circa 1890, the nadir point of indigenous population decline in North America; Thornton, *American Indian Holocaust and Survival, op. cit.*, 159–85. The Native population has by now "rebounded" to at least

ten times its turn–of–the–century size. For implications, see Ward Shepard, "Land Problems of an Expanding Indian Population," in Oliver La Farge, ed., *The Changing Indian* (Norman: University of Oklahoma Press, 1943); Ethel J. Williams, "Too Little Land, Too Many Heirs: The Indian Heirship Land Problem," *Washington Law Review* 46 (1971).

84. A good example is that of the traditionalist Cherokees who refused even to enroll as such with the Dawes Commission during the early twentieth century. Not only were they accorded no land rights whatsoever, they were ultimately disenfranchised as Cherokees; Emmett Starr, *A History of the Cherokee Indians* (Oklahoma City: Warden, 1922).

85. *187 U.S. 553.* For analysis, see Ann Laque Estin, *"Lone wolf v. Hitchcock: The Long Shadow,"* in Sandra L. Cadwalader and Vine Deloria, Jr., eds., *The Aggressions of Civilization: Federal Indian Policy Since the 1880s* (Philadelphia: Temple University Press, 1984).

86. *Tee-Hit-Ton v. United States*, 348 U.S. 272.

87. Most especially see *Badoni v. Higginson*, 638 F.2d, 10th Cir. (1980), *cert. denied*, 452 U.S. 954 (1981), otherwise known as the "Rainbow Bridge Case"; *Lyng v. Northwest Indian Cemetery Protective Association*, 485 U.S. 439 (1988), otherwise known as the "G–O Road Case." Related opinions will be found in *Montana v. United States, 450 U.S. 544* (1981); *Brendale v. Confederated Tribes and Bands of the Yakima Nation*, 109 S.Ct. 2994 (1989).

88. See, e.g., *United States v. Dann*, 470 U.S. 39 (1985).

89. *Attorney General of Ontario v. Bear Island Foundation*, 49 OR 353 (HC), affirmed (1989) 68 OR 394 (CA).

90. *Calder v. Attorney General for British Columbia*, SCR 313, 333, 344 (1973); *Cardinal v. Attorney General Alta*, 2 SCR 695 (1974). In substance, Canada wishes to have it both ways, claiming simultaneously that the legitimacy of its land title accrues from cessions made by Native peoples in their treaties with the Crown and that since the Canadian government itself never negotiated or ratified the instruments, it is not obligated to honor the range of reciprocal commitments the Crown made to Native people. A good overview of such thinking is provided in Peter Hogg, *The Liability of the Crown* (Toronto: Carswell, 1989).

91. For a fairly exhaustive overview of the official position, see *Canada, Lands, Revenues and Trust Review* (Ottawa: Supplies and Services, 1988–1990).

92. See, e.g., *Isaac v. Davey*, 5 OR (92d) 610 (1974); *Sandy v. Sandy*, 27 OR (2d) 248 (1979); *Four B. Manufacturing v. United Garment Workers of America*, 1 S.C.R. 1031 (1980). For interpretation and analysis, see Bruce Clark, *Indian Title in Canada* (Toronto: Carswell, 1987); Richardson, *People of Terra Nullius, op. cit.*

93. 59 Stat. 1031, T.S. No. 933, 3 Bevans 1153m 1976 Y.B.U.N. 1043 (June 26, 1945); U.N.G.A. Res. 1514 (XV), 15 U.N. GAOR, Supp. (No. 16) 66, U.N. Doc. A/4684 (1961). For texts, see Weston, et al., *Documents in International Law, op. cit.*, 16–32, 343–34.

94. It is important to reiterate that the Vienna Convention merely codified existing, customary treaty law. In other words, the Supreme Court's opinion in *Lone wolf* was legally invalid at the time it was rendered; Rosenne, *Law of Treaties, op. cit.*; Sinclair, *Vienna Convention on the Law of Treaties, op. cit.*

95. International Court of Justice, *Advisory Opinion on Western Sahara* (The Hague: International Court of Justice, 1975), 46. For analysis, see Robert Vance, "Questions Concerning Western Sahara: Advisory Opinion of the International Court of Justice, October 16, 1975," *International Lawyer* 10 (1976); "Sovereignty Over Unoccupied Territories: The Western Sahara Decision," *Case Western Reserve Journal of International Law* 9 (1977).

96. Aside from the several books already cited, see, as examples of academic usage, William H. Leckie's *The Military Conquest of the Southern Plains* (Norman: University of Oklahoma Press, 1963); Dan Thrapp's *The Conquest of Apacheria* (Norman: University of Oklahoma Press, 1967); Harry A. Stroud's *The Conquest of the Prairies* (Waco, TX: Texian Press, 1968); Patricia Nelson Limerick's more recent and much–touted *The Legacy of Conquest: The Unbroken Past of the American West* (New York: W.W. Norton, 1987).

97. *Tee-Hit-Ton v. U.S.* at 291.

98. Ibid. at 289–90.

99. There were two primary levels to this. The first was the "Trial of the Major Nazi War Criminals," in which both Supreme Court Justice Robert H. Jackson and former Attorney General Francis Biddle assumed leading roles—Jackson as lead U.S. prosecutor, Biddle as a member of the tribunal itself—in which diplomats Joachim von Ribbentrop and Constantin von Neurath were convicted of conspiring to wage aggressive war, largely on the basis of having pursued policies framed in terms precisely like those articulated in *Tee–Hit–Ton*. Ribbentrop was executed as a result, while Neurath was sentenced to fifteen years imprisonment, serving eight; Eugene Davidson, *The Trial of the Germans, 1945–1946* (New York: Macmillan, 1966), 147–76. The second was the so-called "Justice Case" of 1947, in which former Ohio Supreme Court Justice Carrington T. Marshall served as a tribunal member. In this case, fourteen high-ranking members of the German judiciary were tried and convicted of having committed crimes against humanity, mainly because of the various legalistic rationalizations they had advanced in justification of nazism's pattern of aggression; John Alan Appleman, *Military Tribunals and International Crimes* (Westport, CT: Greenwood Press, 1971 reprint of 1954 original), 157–62.

100. Nell Jessup Newton, "At the Whim of the Sovereign: Aboriginal Title Reconsidered," *Hastings Law Journal* 31 (1980): 1215, 1244. The Pacific coast of North America, as far south as California, was claimed by Russia during the early 1740s; William Cortez Abbott, *The Expansion of Europe: A History of the Foundations of the Modern World*, 2 vols. (London: G. Bell & Sons, 1919) Vol.1, 193–94. As has been mentioned, the United States purchased Russia's rights in what are now the states of Oregon, Washington, and Idaho in 1846. In 1867, with passage of the British North American Act making Canada a dominion of the Commonwealth, Russian claims to present-day British Columbia were also extinguished by purchase. The United States followed up the same year, buying out Russia's rights in Alaska; Samuel Eliot Morrison, *The Oxford History of the American People* (New York: Oxford University Press, 1965), 706, 765, 806.

101. "The Indian wars under the United States government have been more than 40"; U.S. Bureau of the Census, *Report on Indians Taxed and Not Taxed (1890)* (Washington, DC: U.S. Government Printing Office, 1894), 638. It should be noted that the term used is entirely inappropriate. Given that all the conflicts in question were precipitated by invasions of Indian Country rather than Indian invasions of someone else's domain, they should be referred to as "White Man's Wars," "Settlers' Wars" or, most accurately, "U.S. Wars of Aggression against Indians."

102. This was "Red Cloud's War" in present-day Wyoming, 1866–68; see the relevant chapter in Dee Brown's *Bury My Heart at Wounded Knee: An Indian History of the American West* (New York: Holt, Rinehart & Winston, 1970). On U.S. failure to comply with the terms and provisions of the treaty by which peace was temporarily restored, see Edward Lazarus, *Black Hills, White Justice: The Sioux Nation versus the United States, 1775 to the Present* (New York: HarperCollins, 1991).

103. On the "Riel Rebellions" of 1868 and 1885, see D. Bruce Sealey and Antoine S.

Lussier, *The Métis: Canada's Forgotten People* (Winnipeg: Manitoba Métis Association Press, 1975).

104. As an example, when Governor Frederick Seymor of British Columbia observed in a December 1864 letter to the Colonial Office in London that he "might find [himself] compelled to follow in the footsteps of the Governor of Colorado ... and invite every white man to shoot each Indian he may meet," he was firmly rebuked by Secretary of State Edward Cardwell and reminded that the "imperial government's policy was to quite the opposite effect"; quoted in Clark, *Native Liberty, Crown Sovereignty, op. cit.*, 61. Seymor's reference was to Colorado Territorial Governor John Evans, who had not only issued the statements indicated, but who had been complicit in the wholesale massacre of noncombatant Cheyennes and Arapahos at Sand Creek a month before Seymor's missive was written; David Svaldi, *Sand Creek and the Rhetoric of Extermination: A Case-Study in Indian White Relations* (Washington, DC: University Press of America, 1989).

105. Indeed, Canadian courts have themselves been exceedingly careful to avoid constructions based on notions of conquest. This has been so since at least as early as the 1773 case, *Mohegan Indians v. Connecticut*, in which the Privy Council opined that "the medieval concept" of conquest was simply "inadequate" to meet Crown needs in much of the New World. The "realities of colonial administration" in North America dictated, the Council affirmed, a more "prudent" course of recognizing the status of indigenous nations and guaranteeing our rights; J. H. Smith, *Appeals to the Privy Council from the American Plantations* (New York: Columbia University Press, 1950), 417. With this said, however, it is important to note that such policy by no means prevailed throughout the British Empire; see, e.g., Byron Farwell, *Queen Victoria's Little Wars* (New York: W. W. Norton, 1972).

106. This, again, is very close to—indeed, interchangeable with—the Hitlerian conception of the rights of the stronger over the weaker; see, e.g., the explanations of *Lebensraumpolitik* ("politics of living space") offered in *Mein Kampf* (Boston: Houghton-Mifflin, 1962 reprint of 1925 original); *Hitler's Secret Book* (New York: Grove Press, 1961); *Hitler's Secret Conversations* (New York: Signet, 1961).

107. The Greek and Roman imperial systems, for example, manifested no conception of conquest rights remotely comparable to that voiced in *Tee-Hit-Ton*; see, e.g., William Scott Ferguson, *Greek Imperialism* (New York: Houghton-Mifflin, 1913); Earl of Cromer, *Ancient and Modern Imperialism* (New York: Longman's, Green, 1910). By the time of the Norman Conquest of 1066, it was articulated canon law that such seizures were valid only when occurring under the divine authority of the Church: See Erdmann, *Origin of the Idea of the Crusade, op. cit.*, 150–60; Walter Ullmann, *Medieval Papalism: The Political Theories of the Medieval Canonists* (London: Methuen, 1949); James Muldoon, "The Contributions of the Medieval Canon Lawyers to the Foundations of International Law," *Traditio* 28 (1972). Accepted notions of natural law also run directly counter to that argued by the Supreme Court in *Tee-Hit-Ton*; see, e.g., Otto Frederick von Gierke, *Natural Law and the Theory of Society, 1500–1800* (Cambridge, UK: Cambridge University Press, 1934); Lloyd Weinreb, *Natural Law and Justice* (Cambridge, MA: Harvard University Press, 1987).

108. These ideas were tentatively codified in the1512 Laws of Burgos; see generally, Hanke, *Spanish Struggle, op. cit.*; James Muldoon, *Popes, Lawyers and Infidels: The Church and the Non-Christian World, 1250–1550* (Philadelphia: University of Pennsylvania Press, 1979).

109. Vitoria, "On the Law of War," *op. cit.*; Jorge Díaz, "Los Doctrinas de Palacios Rubios y Matías de Paz ante la Conquista America," in *Memoria de El Colegio Nacional*

(Burgos: Colegio Nacional, 1950). Overall, see Williams, *American Indian in Western Legal Thought, op. cit.*, 85–108.

110. "[W]hatever is done in the right of war receives the construction most favorable to the claims of those engaged in a just war"; Vitoria, "On the Law of War," *op. cit.*, 180.

111. Cohen, "Spanish Origins," *op. cit.*, 44; Robert A. Williams, Jr., "The Medieval and Renaissance Origins of the Status of American Indians in Western Legal Thought," *Southern California Law Review* 57:1 (1983).

112. Nothing in international law precluded indigenous peoples from defending themselves when attacked or invaded. Nor did it prevent them from expelling or otherwise punishing missionaries who violated Native law while residing in Indian Country, or from breaking off trade relations with entities which could be shown to have cheated them. In every instance, without exception, in which bona fide Indian-white warfare is known to have occurred the requisite provocation to legitimate Native resort to arms is abundantly evident. *Ipso facto*, European and Euro-American claims to having engaged in just wars against the indigenous peoples of North America are invalidated. For a succinct overview of the presumptive right of any nation to defend its territorial integrity and political sovereignty against violation by other nations, see Walzer, *Just and Unjust Wars, op. cit.*, 53–55.

113. This goes back to the point made in note 30, above, and accompanying text.

114. This is essentially the conclusion drawn by the U.S. government's Indian Claims Commission, which, despite thirty years of exhaustive study, concluded in its final report that it had been unable to find any sort of title by which to validate the country's claims to approximately 35 percent of its purported territoriality; Indian Claims Commission, *Final Report* (Washington, DC: U.S. Government Printing Office, 1978). For analysis, see Russel Barsh, "Indian Land Claims Policy in the United States," *North Dakota Law Review* 58 (1982); "Behind Land Claims: Rationalizing Dispossession in Anglo–American Law," *Law & Anthropology* 1 (1986).

115. 1 Stat. 50. The British/Canadian counterpart—or, more accurately, precursor—is the Royal Proclamation of 1763 which specifies, among other things, that North America's indigenous peoples should remain "unmolested and undisturbed" by the Crown and its subjects; Stagg, *Anglo-American Relations, op. cit.*

116. See note 57, above.

117. *Johnson* v. *McIntosh* at 591.

118. See note 63, above.

119. U.S. Department of Interior, *Report of the Commissioner of Indian Affairs for 1890* (Washington, DC: U.S. Government Printing Office, 1891), xxix.

120. For academic articulations of the theme, see note 96, above. On the films, see Ralph and Natasha Friar, *The Only Good Indian . . . The Hollywood Gospel* (New York: Drama Book Specialists, 1972); William Raymond Stedman, *Shadows of the Indian: Stereotypes in American Culture* (Norman: University of Oklahoma Press, 1982). On cinematic counterparts north of the border, see Daniel Francis, *The Imaginary Indian: The Image of the Indian in Canadian Culture* (Vancouver: Arsenal Pulp Press, 1992). On the capacity of such a disinformational onslaught to indoctrinate the general populace to accept sheer falsity as truth, see Jacques Ellul, *Propaganda: The Formation of Men's Attitudes* (New York: Alfred A. Knopf, 1965).

121. This brings the principle delineated in note 30 into play. More broadly, see C. A. Pompe, *Aggressive War: An International Crime* (The Hague: Martinus Nijhoff, 1953). For use of the referenced term, see Rudolfo Acuña, *Occupied America: The Chicano's Struggle for Liberation* (San Francisco: Canfield Press, 1972).

122. For excellent samples of rhetoric, see LeBlanc, *United States and the Genocide Convention, op. cit.*; Robert Davis and Mark Zannis, *The Genocide Machine in Canada: The Pacification of the North* (Montreal: Black Rose Books, 1973); Terrance Nelson, et al., *Genocide in Canada* (Ginew, Manitoba: Roseau River First Nation, 1997).

123. Questions as to when extinction occurred are largely academic since whenever the final die–out transpired—even if only in the past fifteen minutes—it remains presumptive that there are no heirs to contest title or receive compensation.

124. L. F. S. Lupton, "The Extermination of the Beothuks of Newfoundland," *Canadian Historical Review* 58:2 (1977).

125. The colonists sought "'to cut off the Remembrance of them from the Earth.' After the war, the General Assembly of Connecticut declared the name extinct. No survivors should be called Pequots. The Pequot River became the Thames, and the village known as Pequot became New London"; Drinnon, *Facing West, op. cit.*, 55.

126. Mashantucket Pequot Indian Claims Settlement Act (S.1499; signed Oct. 18, 1983). At least one analyst has seized upon this fact to "prove" that what was done to Pequots was never really genocide in the first place; Steven T. Katz, "The Pequot War Reconsidered," *New England Quarterly* 64 (1991).

127. See generally, Paul Brodeur, *Restitution: The Land Claims of the Mashpee, Passamaquoddy, and Pennobscot Indians of New England* (Boston: Northeastern University Press, 1985).

128. Road Island Indian Claims Settlement Act of 1978 (94 Stat. 3498). More broadly, see Harry B. Wallace, "Indian Sovereignty and the Eastern Indian Land Claims," *New York University Law School Review* 27 (1982).

129. See, e.g., Charles M. Hudson, "The Catawba Indians of South Carolina: A Question of Ethnic Survival," in Walter L. William, ed., *Southeastern Indians Since the Removal Era* (Athens: University of Georgia Press, 1979).

130. More broadly, see Lynwood Carranco and Estle Beard, *Genocide and Vendetta: The Round Valley Wars of Northern California* (Norman: University of Oklahoma Press, 1981).

131. James Fenimore Cooper, *The Last of the Mohicans* (New York: Barnes and Noble, 1992 reprint of 1826 original); Ishi, *Last of His Tribe* (Berkeley, California: Parnassus Press, 1964). For the record, the Mohicans were administratively amalgamated with the fragments of several other peoples under the heading "Stockbridge-Munsee" during the nineteenth century.

132. See, e.g., B. O. Flower, "An Interesting Representative of a Vanishing Race," *Arena* (July 1896); Simon Pokagon, "The Future of the Red Man," *Forum* (Aug. 1897); William R. Draper, "The Last of the Red Race," *Cosmopolitan* (Jan. 1902); Charles M. Harvey, "The Last Race Rally of Indians," *World's Work* (May 1904); E. S. Curtis, "Vanishing Indian Types: The Tribes of the Northwest Plains," *Scribner's* (June 1906); James Mooney, "The Passing of the Indian," *Proceedings of the Second Pan American Scientific Congress, Sec. 1: Anthropology* (Washington, DC: Smithsonian Institution, 1909–1910); Joseph K. Dixon, *The Vanishing Race: The Last Great Indian Council* (Garden City, NY: Doubleday, 1913); Stanton Elliot, "The End of the Trail," *Overland Monthly* (July 1915); Ella Higginson, "The Vanishing Race," *Red Man* (Feb. 1916); Ales Hrdlicka, "The Vanishing Indian," *Science* 46 (1917); J.L. Hill, *The Passing of the Indian and the Buffalo* (Long Beach, CA: n.p., 1917); John Collier, "The Vanishing American," *Nation* (Jan. 11, 1928). For implications of this literary barrage, see Ellul, *Propaganda, op. cit.*

133. Larry W. Burt, *Tribalism in Crisis: Federal Indian Policy, 1953–1961* (Albuquerque: University of New Mexico Press, 1982); Donald L. Fixico, *Termination and Relocation: Federal Indian Policy, 1945–1960* (Albuquerque: University of New Mexico Press, 1986).

It is worth mentioning that termination of recognition flies directly in the face of the international legal principle delineated in note 42 and accompanying text.

134. Nicholis Peroff, *Menominee DRUMS; Tribal Termination and Restoration, 1954–1974* (Norman: University of Oklahoma Press, 1982).

135. See, e.g., Theodore Stern, *The Klamath Tribe: The People and Their Reservation* (Seattle: University of Washington Press, 1965); Shipeck, *Pushed Into the Rocks, op. cit.*

136. The U.S. position is that any surviving Abnakis fled to Canada after they were subjected to wholesale massacre by George Rogers Clark's Ranger Company in 1759; see Collin G. Calloway, *The Western Abenaki of Vermont, 1600–1800: War, Migration, and the Survival of an Indian People* (Norman: University of Oklahoma Press, 1991).

137. See generally, L. Weatherhead, "What Is an Indian Tribe? The Question of Tribal Existence," *American Indian Law Review* 8 (1980); David Rotenberg, "American Indian Tribal Death: A Centennial Remembrance," *University of Miami Law Review* 41 (1986).

138. Wilson, "Aboriginal Rights," *op. cit.*; B. Morris and R. Groves, "Canada's Forgotten Peoples: The Aboriginal Rights of Metis and Non–Status Peoples," *Law & Anthropology* 2 (1987). A prime example of Canadian–style non–recognition concerns the Lubicon Lake Cree, a group overlooked in the process of negotiating Treaty 6. When the Ottawa government realized its error, it attempted to lump the Lubicons in with an entirely different, albeit related, group, and has yet to acknowledge the full extent of Lubicon rights; John Goddard, *Last Stand of the Lubicon Cree* (Vancouver: Douglas & McIntire, 1991).

139. For the original definition, see Raphaël Lemkin, *Axis Rule in Occupied Europe* (Washington, DC: Carnegie Institution, 1944), 79. With respect to black letter law, Article II of the 1948 Convention on the Prevention and Punishment of the Crime of Genocide makes it illegal to cause "serious bodily or mental harm . . . with intent to destroy, in whole or in part, a national, ethnical, racial or religious group, as such (emphasis added)" or deliberately inflict "conditions of life calculated to bring about its physical destruction in whole or in part." Article III makes it a crime not only to commit such acts, but to conspire to commit them, to attempt to commit them, to incite others to do so, or to be in any way complicit in their perpetration; Weston, et al., *Documents in International Law, op. cit.*, 297. For further analysis, see Rennard Strickland, "Genocide at Law: An Historic and Contemporary View of the American Indian Experience," *University of Kansas Law Review* 34 (1986).

140. On the U.S., see, e.g., American Indian Policy Review Commission, "Separate and Dissenting Views," *Final Report* (Washington, DC: U.S. Government Printing Office, 1976), 574. For analysis, see F. Martone, "American Indian Tribal Government in the Federal System: Inherent Right or Congressional License?" *Notre Dame Law Review* 51 (1976). On Canada, see, e.g., *Report of the Special Committee of the House of Commons on Indian Self–Government* (Ottawa: Supplies and Services, 1983); *Response of the Government to the Report of the Special Committee on Indian Self–Government* (Ottawa: Indian Affairs and Supplies and Services, 1984).

141. Oppenheim, *International Law, op. cit.*, 120.

142. Coulter, "Contemporary Indian Sovereignty," *op. cit.*, 118.

143. 7 Stat. 18, 19 (1785).

144. *Worcester v. Georgia* at 560–61.

145. Such comparisons are made by Vine Deloria, Jr., in his *Behind the Trail of Broken Treaties: An Indian Declaration of Independence*, (Austin: University of Texas Press, [2d. ed.]1984), 161–86.

146. Oren Lyons, "Introduction: When You Talk About Client Relationships, You Are

Talking About the Future of Nations," in *Rethinking Indian Law, op. cit.*, iv. Lyons is correct. There is nothing in international law establishing a minimum population level, below which a group loses its nationhood. Grenada, it should be remembered, has a total population of only 120,000, and, although it has recently suffered gross violation at the hands of the United States, is recognized as enjoying the same sovereign rights as any other nation.

147. Policy Review Commission, *Final Report, op. cit.*; *Response of the Government, op. cit.*

148. See generally, Henry E. Fritz, *The Movement for Indian Assimilation, 1860–1890* (Philadelphia: University of Pennsylvania Press, 1963); Fred Hoxie, *A Final Promise: The Campaign to Assimilate the Indians, 1880–1920* (Lincoln: University of Nebraska Press, 1984).

149. See, e.g., William Hagan, *Indian Police and Judges: Experiments in Acculturation and Control* (New Haven, CT: Yale University Press, 1966); Curtis E. Jackson and Marcia J. Galli, *A History of the Bureau of Indian Affairs and Its Activities Among the Indians* (San Francisco: R&E Associates, 1977); Douglas Cole and Ira Chaikan, *An Iron Hand Upon the People: The Law Against the Potlatch on the Northwest Coast* (Vancouver, BC: Douglas & McIntire, 1990); Katherine Pettitpas, *Severing the Ties That Bind: Government Repression of Indigenous Religious Ceremonies on the Prairies* (Winnipeg: University of Manitoba Press, 1994).

150. Otis, Dawes Act, *op. cit.*; McDonnell, *Dispossession of the American Indian, op. cit.* Good readings with respect to Canada will be found in Brian Slattery's *Ancestral Lands, Alien Laws: Judicial Perspectives on Aboriginal Title* (Saskatoon: University of Saskatchewan Native Law Center, 1983), and the early chapters of Michael Asch's *Home and Native Land: Aboriginal Rights and the Canadian Constitution* (Toronto: Methuen, 1984).

151. Perhaps the most striking example was when in 1873 General Phil Sheridan called for the deliberate extermination of an entire species of large mammals, the North American bison (buffalo), in order to "destroy the commissary" of the Plains Indians; General Philip Sheridan to Commanding General William Tecumseh Sherman, May 2, 1873; quoted in Paul Andrew Hutton, *Phil Sheridan and His Army* (Lincoln: University of Nebraska Press, 1985), 246. At one point in the mid-1870s, Congress considered legislation to preserve what was left of the dwindling herds. Sheridan vociferously opposed it, suggesting that the legislators instead "strike a medal, with a dead buffalo pictured on one side and a discouraged Indian on the other," and present it to the buffalo hunters; John R. Cook, *The Border and the Buffalo: An Untold Story of the Southwest Plains* (New York: Citadel Press, 1976), 163–5. Also see William T. Hornaday, *Exterminating the American Bison* (Washington, DC: Smithsonian Institution, 1899); Tom McHugh and Victoria Hobson, *The Time of the Buffalo* (New York: Alfred A. Knopf, 1972).

152. For a contemporaneous and quite glowing affirmation of the centrality of "instruction" to the entire Canadian assimilation process, see Thompson Ferrier, *Our Indians and Their Training for Citizenship* (Toronto: Methods Mission Rooms, 1991). For a bit longer view on its role in the United States, see Evelyn C. Adams, *American Indian Education: Government Schools and Economic Progress* (New York: King's Crown Press, 1946). Appropriate contextualization will be found in Martin Carnoy's *Education as Cultural Imperialism* (New York: David McKay, 1974).

153. The time period indicated represents only the most intensive phase of the process. It actually began earlier and lasted much longer in both countries. On the United States, see *Michael C. Coleman, American Indian Children at School, 1850–1930* (Jackson: University Press of Mississippi, 1993); David Wallace Adams, *Education for Extinction: Ameri-*

can Indians and the Boarding School Experience, 1875–1928 (Lawrence: University Press of Kansas, 1995). On Canada, see Celia Haig-Brown, *Resistance and Renewal: Surviving the Indian Residential School* (Vancouver: Tillacum Library, 1988); J.R. Miller, *Shingwauk's Vision: A History of Native Residential Schools* (Toronto: University of Toronto Press, 1996).

154. Col. Richard H. Pratt, *Battlefield and Classroom: Four Decades with the American Indian, 1867–1904* (New Haven, CT: Yale University Press, 1993 reprint of 1906 original), 293.

155. See, e.g., Leupp, *Indian and His Problem, op. cit.*

156. See generally, Jean Barman with Yves Hébert and D. McCaskill, eds., *Indian Education in Canada: The Legacy* (Vancouver: Nakoda Institute and University of British Columbia Press, 1986); Noel Dyck, *What Is the Indian "Problem"? Tutelage and Resistance in Canadian Indian Administration* (St. John's: Institute of Social and Economic Research, Memorial University of Newfoundland, 1991).

157. Not only do the criteria of the Genocide Convention delineated in note 139 apply here, but also the provision under Article II making it a crime of genocide to transfer children from targeted racial, ethnical, national, or religious groups systematically, with intent to bring about destruction of the group as such.

158. *Sero* v. *Gault*, 50 OLR 27 (1921). Robinson's position, adopted by the Sero court, totally ignores the fact that the treaties in question already existed and that the Crown had long maintained a formal diplomatic mission to the Mohawks and others of the Six Nations; James Thomas Flexner, *Lord of the Mohawks: A Biography of Sir William Johnson* (Boston: little, Brown, 1979). On the service rendered to the Crown by Brant and the Mohawks, see Barbara Greymount, *The Iroquois in the American Revolution* (Syracuse, NY: Syracuse University Press, 1975).

159. S Prov. c 1857, c. 26. For analysis, see J. Tobias, "Protection, Civilization, Assimilation: An Outline of Canada's Indian Policy," *Western Canadian Journal of Anthropology* 4:2 (1976).

160. The racially idiosyncratic aspects of the law are hardly unparalleled; see, e.g., Noel Ignatiev, *How the Irish Became White* (New York: Routledge, 1995). More broadly, see Theodore W. Allen, *The Invention of the White Race: Racial Oppression and Social Control* (London: Verso, 1994).

161. In statutory terms, Canada's national policy was first given form by An Act for the Gradual Enfranchisement of the Indians, the Better Management of Indian Affairs, and the extend Provisions of the Act (31 Vict. c. 42, SC 1869, c. 6) and An Act to Amend and Consolidate the Laws Respecting Indians (SC 1880, c. 28). Despite Canada's supplanting of its original 1871 Constitution Act with another in 1982, evolution of its policy on Native citizenship has been consistent from start to finish: see, e.g., The Indian Advancement Act (1884, SC 1884, c. 28), the Indian Act (RSC 1886, c. 43), the second Indian Act (RSC 1906, c. 81), An Act to Amend the Indian Act (SC 1919–1920, c. 50), the third Indian Act (RSC 1927, c. 98), An Act to Amend the Indian Act (SC 1932–33, c. 42), the fourth and fifth generations of Indian Acts (SC 1951, c. 29; RSC 1952, c. 149; RSC 1970, c. 1–16), as well as 1988 amendments to the 1970 Indian Act; Indian and Northern Affairs Canada, *Indian Acts and Amendments, 1868–1850* (Ottawa: Treaties and Historical Research Center, 1981). For interpretation, see J. Leighton, *The Development of Federal Indian Policy in Canada, 1840–1890* (London, Ont.: University of Western Ontario, 1975); Bernard Schwartz, *First Principles: Constitutional Reform with Respect to the Aboriginal Peoples of Canada, 1982–1984* (Kingston, Ont.: Institute of Intergovernmental Relations, Queen's University, 1986).

162. Quoted in M. Montgomery, "The Six Nations and the MacDonald Franchise,"

Ontario History 57:1 (1965): 37. Although it was not until 1933 that a supplemental amendment to the Indian Act formally authorized the government to naturalize even non-applying Natives at its own discretion, this had been de facto policy for more than fifty years; Clark, *Native Liberty, Crown Sovereignty, op. cit.*, 156–57.

163. Deloria and Lytle, *American Indian, American Justice, op. cit.*, 9–10.

164. Indian Citizenship Act, ch. 233, 43 Stat. 253 (1924), now codified at 8 U.S.C. § 1401 (a) (2).

165. Coulter, "Contemporary Indian Sovereignty," *op. cit.*, 118. Also see Deloria, *Trail of Broken Treaties, op. cit.*, 18.

166. Coulter, "Contemporary Indian Sovereignty," *op. cit.*, 118.

167. Indigenous governments are now officially described as being a "third level of governance" in the U.S., below that of the federal and state governments, but generally above those of counties and municipalities; U.S. Senate, Select Committee on Indian Affairs, *Final Report and Legislative Recommendations: A Report of the Special Committee on Investigations* (Washington, DC: 101st Cong., 2d Sess., U.S. Government Printing Office, Nov. 20, 1989). In Canada, on the other hand, it is official policy to view "federal and provincial governments as at a higher level than aboriginal governments"; Clark, *Native Liberty, Crown Sovereignty, op. cit.*, 154; J. Anthony Long and Menno J. Boldt, eds., *Governments in Conflict? Provinces and Indian Nations in Canada* (Toronto: University of Toronto Press, 1988).

168. Ch. 576, 48 Stat. 948; now codified at 25 U.S.C. 461–279; also referred to as the Wheeler-Howard Act, in recognition of its congressional sponsors. For an overly sympathetic overview, see Vine Deloria, Jr., and Clifford M. Lytle, *The Nations Within: The Past and Future of American Indian Sovereignty* (New York: Pantheon, 1984).

169. The constitutions were boilerplate documents hammered out by technicians at BIA headquarters in Washington, DC: see generally, Graham D. Taylor, *The New Deal and American Indian Tribalism: Administration of the Indian Reorganization Act, 1934–1935* (Lincoln: University of Nebraska Press, 1980).

170. See, e.g., the accounts of Rupert Costo and others in Ken Philp, ed., *Indian Self-Rule: First-Hand Accounts of Indian/White Relations from Roosevelt to Reagan* (Salt Lake City: Howe Bros., 1986).

171. On this and other sorts of fraud perpetrated in the "Sioux Complex" of reservations, see Thomas Biolosi, *Organizing the Lakota: The Political Economy of the New Deal on the Pine Ridge and Rosebud Reservations* (Tucson: University of Arizona Press, 1992).

172. Richard O. Clemmer, *Continuities of Hopi Culture Change* (Albuquerque: Acoma Books, 1978), 60–61. Also see Charles Lummis, *Bullying the Hopi* (Prescott, AZ: Prescott College Press, 1968).

173. Clemmer, *Continuities, op. cit.*, 61.

174. Steven M. Tullberg, "The Creation and Decline of the Hopi Tribal Council," in *Rethinking Indian Law, op. cit.*, 37.

175. The BIA official assigned responsibility for reorganizing Hopi was Oliver LaFarge. He compiled what he called a "running narrative" of the process which confirms all points raised herein, communicating his concerns to Indian Commissioner Collier as he went along. In the manuscript, which unfortunately remains unpublished (it is lodged in the LaFarge collection at the University of Texas, Austin), he remarks at page 8: "[I]t is alien to [the Hopis] to settle matters out of hand by majority vote. Such a vote leaves a dissatisfied minority, which makes them very uneasy. Their natural way of doing is to discuss among themselves at great length and group by group until public opinion as a whole has settled overwhelmingly in one direction. . . . Opposition is expressed by

abstention. Those who are against something stay away from meetings at which it is discussed and generally refuse to vote on it (emphasis added)."

176. Frank Waters, *Book of the Hopi* (New York: Ballantine, 1969), 386.

177. David C. Hawkes, *Aboriginal Self–Government: What Does It Mean?* (Kingston: Ont.: Institute for Intergovernmental Relations, Queen's University, 1983), 9.

178. This was subjected to legal challenge in the 1977 case of *Davey* v. *Isaac* (77 DLR (3d) 481 (SSC)). Predictably, the courts confirmed the "right" of the federal government to effect such interventions in the internal affairs of indigenous nations.

179. *Special Report on Indian Self-Government, op. cit.*; *Response of the Government, op. cit.*

180. Noel Lyon, *Aboriginal Self-Government: Rights of Citizenship and Access to Government Services* (Kingston, Ont.: Institute for Intergovernmental Relations, Queen's University, 1986), 15.

181. For analysis, see Asch, *Home and Native Land, op. cit.*; Schwartz, *First Principles, op. cit.*; E. Robinson and H. Quinney, *The Infested Blanket: Canada's Constitution: Genocide of Indian Nations* (Winnipeg: Queenston House, 1985).

182. One example of what is at issue here is Public Law 280 (ch. 505, 67 Stat. 588 (1953); now codified at 18 U.S.C. § 1162, 25 U.S.C. §§ 1321–1326, 28 U.S.C. §§ 1360, 1360 note), placing American Indian reservations in a dozen U.S. states under state rather than federal criminal jurisdiction. While the Indians involved ostensibly "consented" to this diminishment of their standing to essentially the level of counties, their alternative was outright termination. In California, the process has gone further, with the placement of many reservations under county jurisdiction as well; Carole Goldberg, "Public Law 280: The Limits of State Jurisdiction Over Reservation Indians," *UCLA Law Review* 22 (1975); "The Extension of County Jurisdiction Over Indian Reservations in California: Public Law 280 and the Ninth Circuit," *Hastings Law Journal* 25 (1974). More recently, under the 1988 Indian Gaming Act (Public Law 100–497), a number of peoples have been coerced into placing themselves under state regulatory authority for purposes of engaging in gambling operations. In the alternative, they faced continuing destitution; see generally, William R. Eadington, ed., *Indian Gaming and the Law* (Reno: Institute for the Study of Gaming and Commercial Gambling, University of Nevada, 1990). Suffice it to say that such impositions do not conform to international legal definitions of "voluntary merger."

183. The French sought to circumvent the U.N. Charter requirement that they decolonize all "non-self-governing territories" under their control by declaring Algeria to be an integral part of the "Home Department" (i.e., France itself) pursuant to its 1834 annexation of the entire Maghrib region. Such sophistry was rejected by the international community; see, e.g., J.L. Miège, "Legal Developments in the Maghrib, 1830–1930," in *European Expansion and the Law, op. cit.*; Joseph Kraft, *The Battle for Algeria* (Garden City, NY: Doubleday, 1961).

184. See note 93, above, and accompanying text.

185. *Worcester* v. *Georgia* at 559–60.

186. 30 U.S. (5 Pet.) 1. For background, see Starr, *History of the Cherokee Indians, op. cit.*; Thurman Wilkins, *Cherokee Tragedy: The Ridge Family and the Destruction of a People* (New York: Macmillan, 1970). On the case itself, see J. Burke, "The Cherokee Cases: A Study in Law, Politics, and Morality," *Stanford Law Review* 21 (1969).

187. *Cherokee* v. *Georgia* at 16.

188. Ibid. at 17.

189. A good overview of the flow and interrelationship of Marshall's "Indian cases," as well as their implications for both Native and Euro–American societies, will be found in

G. Edward White, *The Marshall Court and Cultural Change, 1815–1835* (New York: Macmillan, 1988), esp. chap. 10. Also see Robert A. Williams, Jr., "The Algebra of Federal Indian Law: The Hard Trail of Decolonizing the White Man's Jurisprudence," *Wisconsin Law Review* 31 (1986).

190. For a fuller exposition, see Williams, *American Indian in Western Legal Thought, op. cit.*, 312–17, 321–23.

191. A year later, in *Worcester* (at 559), Marshall again remarked upon how the doctrine "excluded [Native peoples] from intercourse with any other European potentate than the first discoverer of the coast of the particular region claimed" as being the "single exception" to the fullness of our sovereignty under international law. This time he framed the matter more correctly, however, by going on to observe that "this was a restriction which those European potentates imposed upon themselves, as well as upon the Indians." In other words, all parties being equal, there was no implication of supremacy or subordination involved. Even at that, Marshall overstated the case. Under the law, absent a treaty or agreement to the contrary, indigenous nations were free to trade with anyone they wished. It was the European powers themselves which were constrained from trading with Natives in one another's discovery domains; aside from the citations contained in note 52, above, see generally, Gordon Bennett, *Aboriginal Rights in International Law* (London: Royal Anthropological Association, 1978).

192. While Marshall was ostensibly writing about the specific circumstances of the Cherokee Nation, he couched his opinion in terms of all Native peoples within claimed U.S. boundaries. At the time, this already included the vast Louisiana Territory, to which the Jefferson administration had purchased French acquisition rights but in which there was virtually no U.S. settlement. Hence, while Marshall's characterization of the "domestic dependency" of indigenous nations might have borne a certain resemblance to the situation of the Cherokee, encapsulated as it was within the already settled corpus of the United States, the same can hardly be said of more westerly peoples like the Cheyenne, Comanche, Navajo, and Lakota. In this sense, the views expressed in *Cherokee* were not so much an attempt to apprehend extant reality as they were an effort to forge a sort of judicial license for future U.S. aggression. There is thus considerable merit to the observation of Glenn T. Morris, offered during a 1987 lecture at the University of Colorado, that, far from constituting an affirmation of indigenous rights, as is commonly argued (e.g., Wilkinson, Indians, *Time and Law, op. cit.*), the Marshall doctrine is "fundamentally a sophisticated juridical blueprint for colonization."

193. A good illustration is that of the U.S. military campaign against the Lakota and allied peoples in 1876–77. During the late fall of 1875, the administration of President Ulysses S. Grant issued instructions that all Lakota residing within their own territories, recognized by treaty in both 1851 and 1868, should assemble at specific locations therein by a given date in January 1876. When the Indians failed to comply, Grant termed their refusal of his presumption an "act of war" and sent in the army to "restore order"; for details, see John E. Gray, *Centennial Campaign: The Sioux War of 1876* (Norman: University of Oklahoma Press, 1988).

194. For elaboration, see Ward Churchill, "Perversions of Justice: Examining the Doctrine of U.S. Rights to Occupancy in North America," in David S. Caudill and Steven Jay Gould, eds., *Radical Philosophy of Law: Contemporary Challenges to Mainstream Legal Theory and Practice* (Atlantic Highlands, NJ: Humanities Press, 1995).

195. On the nature of the Canadian case, see note 11, above.

196. SCR 313 at 380. Contextually, see John Hurley, "Aboriginal Rights, the Constitution and the Marshall Court," *Revue Juridique Themis* 17 (1983).

197. In concluding that the federal government of Canada enjoys a unilateral prerogative to extinguish indigenous rights, the court noted that it had been "unable to find a Canadian case dealing with precisely the same subject" and that it would therefore rely on a U.S. judicial interpretation found in *State of Idaho v. Coffee* (56 P 2d 1185 [1976]); 68 OR (2d) 353 (HC), 438 at 412–13.

198. In general, see Slattery, *Ancestral Lands, Alien Laws, op. cit.*; and "Understanding Aboriginal Rights," *Canadian Bar Review* 91 (1987).

199. At the point at which Great Britain abandoned its struggle to retain the thirteen insurgent American colonies, each became an independent state in its own right. Their subsequent relinquishment of sovereignty and consensual subordination to federal authority was exactly comparable to that imposed by the United States as a result of the Cherokee opinion upon indigenous nations; see generally, Peter S. Onuf, *The Origins of the Federal Republic: Jurisdictional Controversies in the United States, 1775–1787* (Philadelphia: University of Pennsylvania Press, 1983).

200. See note 36 and accompanying text. Incidentally, the explanation offered by Bruce Clark of the difference between U.S. and Canadian approaches to Indian relations—that the Native right to sovereignty is protected in the Canadian Constitution but not in that of the U.S.—is erroneous; *Native Liberty, Crown Sovereignty, op. cit.*, 56–57. Indigenous sovereignty is protected under Article I of the U.S. Constitution for reasons indicated herein. That the southern settler-state government ignores this fact as a matter of policy hardly negates its existence.

201. For a sustained but unsuccessful effort by several scholars to get around this problem, see Imre Sutton, ed., *Irredeemable America: The Indians' Estate and Land Tenure* (Albuquerque: University of New Mexico Press, 1986).

202. The description comes from Russell Means, in a lecture delivered at the University of Colorado, July 1986. With respect to formal repudiation, see note 93 and accompanying text.

203. It is important to note that resort to armed struggle by bona fide national liberation movements is entirely legitimate. United Nations Resolution 3103 (XXVII; Dec. 12, 1972) declares that "the struggle of people under colonial and alien domination and racist régimes for the implementation of their rights to self–determination and independence is legitimate and in full accordance with the principles of international law." Accordingly, Section I, Clause 4 of Protocol I Additional to the Geneva Conventions of August 12, 1949, and Relating to the Protection of Victims of International Armed Conflicts, done at Geneva on June 10, 1977, expressly includes "armed conflicts in which peoples are fighting against colonial domination or alien occupation and against racist régimes in the exercise of their right to self-determination, as enshrined in the Charter of the United Nations...." Resolution 3103 goes on to state that "any attempt to suppress the struggle against colonial and alien domination and racist régimes is incompatible with the Charter of the United Nations . . . and constitutes a threat to international peace and security"; Weston, et al., *Documents in International Law, op. cit.*, 230–46. In effect, resort to arms in order to restore inherent sovereignty is lawful, while use of armed force to suppress or deny it is not.

204. On the fishing rights struggle, see *American Friends Service Committee, Uncommon Controversy: Fishing Rights of the Muckleshoot, Puyallup, and Nisqually Indians* (Seattle: University of Washington Press, 1970). On Alcatraz, see Troy R. Johnson, *The Occupation of Alcatraz Island: Indian Self–Determination and the Rise of Indian Activism* (Urbana: University of Illinois Press, 1996). On the BIA building takeover, see Deloria, *Behind the Trail of Broken Treaties, op. cit.* On Wounded Knee, see Robert Burnette and John Koster, *The Road to Wounded Knee* (New York: Bantam, 1974).

205. On the early phases, see, e.g., Stan Steiner, *The New Indians* (New York: Harper & Row, 1968); Alvin M. Josephy, Jr., *Red Power: The American Indians' Fight for Freedom* (New York: McGraw–Hill, 1971). On the Anishinaabe Park occupation in northwestern Ontario and other subsequent events in Canada, see the various issues of *Akwesasne Notes*, 1970–75, inclusive.

206. On the growth of AIM, see Paul Chaat Smith and Robert Allen Warrior, *Like a Hurricane: The American Indian Movement from Alcatraz to Wounded Knee* (New York: New Press, 1996). On the repression, see Johansen and Maestas, *Wasi'chu, op. cit.*; Churchill and Vander Wall, *Agents of Repression, op. cit.*; Peter Matthiessen, *In the Spirit of Crazy Horse*, (New York: Viking, [2d. ed.]1991).

207. Deloria, *Behind the Trail of Broken Treaties, op. cit.*

208. On the famous "Indian Summer in Geneva," see "The United Nations Conference on Indians" in Jimmie Durham, *A Certain Lack of Coherence: Writings on Art and Cultural Politics* (London: Kala Press, 1993).

209. Russell Tribunal, *The Rights of the Indians of the Americas* (Rotterdam: Fourth Russell Tribunal, 1980).

210. Sanders, "Re–Emergence of Indigenous Questions," *op. cit.* Also see Gordon Bennett, "The Developing Law of Aboriginal Rights," *The Review* 22 (1979).

211. 88 Stat. 2203; now codified at 25 U.S.C. 450a and elsewhere in Titles 25, 42 and 50, U.S.C.A. It is worth noting that in 1984 Canada made an abortive attempt to come up with its own version of this handy statute. Entitled "An Act Relating to Self-Government for Indian Nations" (Federal Bill c–52), the measure dissolved in the mists of transition from liberal to conservative government; Clark, *Native Liberty, Crown Sovereignty, op. cit.*, 169. As it stands, Canada relies upon the Section 35 (1) of the 1982 Constitution Act, a component of the so-called Charter of Rights and Freedoms specifically enumerating the "Rights of the Aboriginal Peoples of Canada." The provisions found therein seem clear enough—among other things, it states unequivocally that the "existing aboriginal and treaty rights of the aboriginal peoples of Canada are hereby recognized and confirmed"—to assure indigenous self-determination in a genuine sense; L. C. Green, "Aboriginal Peoples, International Law, and the Canadian Charter of Rights and Freedoms," *Canadian Bar Review* 61 (1983); K. McNeil, "The Constitution Act, 1982, Sections 25 and 35," *Canadian Native Law Reporter* 1 (1988). It should be noted, however, that in practice the courts of Canada have quietly voided these apparent guarantees by subjecting them to "reasonability tests" during a pair of 1989 cases. In *R. v. Dick* (1 CNLR 132 [BC Prov. Ct.]), the Provincial Court of British Columbia found the exercise of aboriginal rights to be unreasonable insofar as it conflicted with provincial statutes. In R. v. Agawa (65 OR 92d) 505 [CA]), the Ontario Court of Appeal reached the same conclusion with respect to treaty rights; see generally, Venne, "Treaty and Constitution in Canada," *op. cit.*; Thomas Berger, "Native Rights and Self-Determination," *The Canadian Journal of Native Studies* 3:2 (1983).

212. Michael D. Gross, "Indian Self-Determination and Tribal Sovereignty: An Analysis of Recent Federal Policy," *Texas Law Review* 56 (1978). For background, see Jack D. Forbes, *Native Americans and Nixon: Presidential Politics and Minority Self-Determination* (Los Angeles: UCLA American Indian Studies Center, 1981).

213. Samples of the rhetoric indulged in at the U.N. by U.S. representatives is laced throughout Jimmie Durham's Columbus Day (Minneapolis: West End Press, 1983). For responses, see Alexander Ewen, ed., *Voices of Indigenous Peoples: Native People Address the United Nations* (Santa Fe, NM: Clear Light, 1994).

214. Douglas Sanders, "The U.N. Working Group on Indigenous Peoples," *Human*

Rights Quarterly 11 (1989); Jimmie Durham, "American Indians and Carter's Human Rights Sermons," in *A Certain Lack of Coherence, op. cit.*

215. José R. Martinez Cobo, *Study of the Problem of Discrimination of Indigenous Populations* (U.N. Doc. /CN.4/Sub.2/1983/21/Ass.83, Sept. 1983). For context and amplification, see *Independent Commission on Humanitarian Issues, Indigenous Peoples: A Global Quest for Justice* (London: Zed Books, 1987).

216. On the decision to draft a new instrument, see S. James Anaya, "The Rights of Indigenous Peoples and International Law in Contemporary and Historical Perspective," in Robert N. Clinton, Nell Jessup Newton, and Monroe E. Price, eds., *American Indian Law: Cases and Materials* (Charlottesville, VA: Michie Co., 1991). For further background, see Dunbar Ortiz, *Indians of the Americas, op. cit.*; Sanders, "Re-Emergence of Indigenous Questions," *op. cit.*

217. Sanders, "U.N. Working Group," *op. cit.*

218. Article 1 (7) of the United Nations Charter specifically excludes intervention "in matters which are essentially within the jurisdiction of any state" and exempts member states from having "to submit such matters to settlement" by the community of nations; Weston, et al., *Documents in International Law, op. cit.*, 17. For analysis, see generally, Joseph B. Kelly, "National Minorities in International Law," *Denver Journal of International Law and Politics* 3 (1973); L. Mandell, "Indians Nations: Not Minorities," *Les Cahiers de Droit* 27 (1983).

219. Article 1 (2) of the United Nations Charter has required since 1945 that all member states "respect . . . the principle of equal rights and self-determination of peoples." Since then, it has become almost pro forma to incorporate the following sentence into international legal instruments: "All peoples have the right to self-determination; by virtue of that right they freely determine their political status and freely pursue their economic, social and cultural development"; see, e.g., Article 1 (1) of the 1967 International Covenant on Economic, Social and Cultural Rights (U.N.G.A. Res 2200 (XXI), 21 U.N. GAOR, Supp. (No. 16) 49, A/6316 (1967), reprinted in 6 I.L.M. 360 (1967); Article 1 (1) of the 1967 International Declaration on Civil and Political Rights (U.N.G.A. Res. 2200 (XXI), 21 U.N. GAOR, Supp. (No. 16) 52, U.N. Doc. A/6316 (1967), reprinted in 6 I.L.M. 368 (1967); and the Preamble to the 1986 Declaration on the Right to Development (U.N.G.A. Res. 41/128, 41 U.N. GAOR, Supp. (No. 53) U.N. Doc. A/41/925 (1986). The 1960 Declaration on the Granting of Independence to Colonial Countries and Peoples (*op. cit.*) not only includes the same language as point 2, but obviously incorporates the concept into its very title. Moreover, as in point 1, it states that the "subjection of peoples to alien subjugation, domination and exploitation constitutes a denial of fundamental human rights, is contrary to the Charter of the United Nations and is an impediment to world peace and cooperation"; Weston, et al., *Documents in International Law, op. cit.*, 17, 371, 376, 485, 343–44. See generally, Pomerance, *Self-Determination in Law and Practice, op. cit.*; Ofuatey-Kodjoe, *Principles of Self-Determination, op. cit.*; Rigo-Sureta, *Evolution of the Right to Self-Determination, op. cit.*

220. See, e.g., Article 1 (3) of the International Labor Organization Convention (No. 169) Concerning Indigenous and Tribal Peoples in Independent Countries; International Labor Conference, The Indigenous and Tribal Peoples Convention (76th Sess., Prov. Rec. 25, 1989).

221. The timing, corresponding with the quincentenary of the Columbian landfall in America, was selected as optimal for obtaining speedy passage of the proposed declaration by the General Assembly.

222. See generally, Isabelle Schulte-Tenckhoff, "The Irresistible Ascension of the UN Draft Declaration on the Rights of Indigenous Peoples: Stopped Dead in Its Tracks?" *European Review of Native American Studies* 9:2 (1995).

223. It should be noted that the United States has conducted itself in a similar fashion throughout the history of the United Nations, beginning with the 1946 deliberations over the content of a draft convention on prevention and punishment of genocide. In that instance, U.S. representatives acted decisively to delete an entire article on cultural genocide, which they correctly interpreted as describing much of their own country's Indian policy. Even then, the United States refused to ratify the law for forty years, until it felt it could exempt itself from aspects it found inconvenient; LeBlanc, *United States and the Genocide Convention, op. cit.* The same pattern of obstructing and subverting the formation of international law has continuously marked U.S. performance over the years, most recently with respect to its refusal to accept a universal prohibition against the use of antipersonnel mines unless it—alone among nations—could be formally exempted from full compliance.

224. The substance of this paragraph has been confirmed by several of the indigenous delegates in attendance, notably Sharon H. Venne, Moana Jackson, Glenn T. Morris, Josh Dillabaugh, Mona Roy, Troy Lynn Yellow Wood, Phyllis Young, and Russell Means.

225. Aside from the many references already made which bear on this point, see Robert T. Coulter, "The Denial of Legal Remedies to Indian Nations Under U.S. Law," in *Rethinking Indian Law, op. cit.*

226. It is unlikely that, absent at least some pretense of genuine Native endorsement, any form of declaration will be passed by the General Assembly at all. From an indigenous perspective, this would be an entirely acceptable outcome since, at least in this instance, something is definitely not better than nothing. From the settler-state perspective, of course, the precise opposite pertains. Hence, the United States in particular has set out to co-opt key indigenous organizations into accepting some compromise formulation. Ironically, it appears that the once militantly principled IITC—which has by now drifted very far from its roots, having long since incorporated itself (shedding control by the elders, original trustees, and grassroots supporters in the process)—has proven one of the more receptive in this regard; Churchill, "Subterfuge and Self–Determination," *op. cit.* The seeds for this ugly development were noted by some observers as far back as 1979; Jimmie Durham, "An Open Letter to the Movement," in *A Certain Lack of Coherence, op. cit.*

227. This is the route implicitly suggested in A. Kienetz, "Decolonization in the North: Canada and the United States," Canadian Review of Studies in Nationalism 8:1 (1986). Also see S. Powderface, "Self–Government Means Biting the Hand that Feeds Us," in Leroy Little Bear, Menno Boldt, and Jonathan Long, eds., *Pathways to Self-Determination: Canadian Indians and the Canadian State* (Toronto: University of Toronto Press, 1984).

228. See notes 62 and 95, above, and accompanying text.

229. See 219, above.

230. Weston, et al., *Documents in International Law, op. cit.*, 344. Both the United States and Canada will undoubtedly argue that Native territories within their borders are already self-governing—as the U.S. at least has already argued, they are self-determining under its laws—but neither can argue that indigenous nations presently enjoy complete independence, or that they have ever been afforded an opportunity to do so.

231. Ibid., 27–30.

232. As is stated at Point 6 of Resolution 1514, "Inadequacy of political, economic,

social or educational preparedness should never be used as a pretext for delaying independence"; ibid., 344.

233. In cases where the colonizer is found to have falsified reporting data in ways which allowed it to rig outcomes, the colony is reinscribed on the list of non-self-governing territories and the entire process starts over under direct U.N. supervision (rather than monitoring). Witness the recent case of New Caledonia; G.A. Res. 41/41A UN GAOR Supp. (No. 53), UN Doc. A/41/53 (1986) at 49. Also see "Report of the Special Committee on the Situation with Regard to the Implementation of the Declaration on the Granting of Independence to Colonial Countries and Peoples," 41 UN GAOR (No. 23), UN Doc A/41/23 (1986). For further background, see Stephen Bates, *The South Pacific Island Countries and France: A Study of Inter-State Relations* (Canberra: Australian National University, 1990), 77. Both Hawai'i and Puerto Rico are presently subject to this same procedure. On Hawai'i, see note 61, above, and accompanying text, as well as Ramon Lopez-Reyes, "Reinscription: The Right of Hawai'i to be Restored to the United Nations List of Non-Self-Governing Territories," in Ward Churchill and Sharon H. Venne, eds., *Islands in Captivity: Findings of the International Tribunal on the Rights of Indigenous Hawaiians* (Boston: South End Press, forthcoming). On Puerto Rico, see, e.g., Ronald Fernandez, *Prisoners of Colonialism: The Struggle for Justice in Puerto Rico* (Monroe, ME: Common Courage Press, 1994).

234. A colonized people is not legally required to opt for complete independence in order to exercise its complete independence and separation from its colonizer in exercising its right to self–determination. Instead, it may elect to limit its own sovereignty to some extent, as in the case of Greenland; Gudmunder Alfredsson, "Greenland and the Law of Political Decolonization," *German Yearbook of International Law* 25 (1982); Nannum Hurst, *Autonomy, Sovereignty and Self–Determination* (Philadelphia: University of Pennsylvania Press, 1990). Colonizing states, however, are legally required to acknowledge without qualification the right of colonial subjects to complete independence and separation and to do nothing at all to orchestrate any other outcome to the process of decolonization. Independence is thus legally presumed to be the outcome of any decolonizing process unless the colonized themselves demonstrate unequivocally that they desire a different result; Nanda, "Self-Determination Under International Law," *op. cit.*; Buchheit, Secession, *op. cit.*

235. Weston, et al., *Documents in International Law*, *op. cit.*, 17, 344.

236. The principle was adopted in response to the "Belgian Thesis," a proposition put forth by that country as it was being forced to relinquish the Congo, that each of the Native peoples within the colony would be at least as entitled to exercise self-determining rights as would the decolonized Congolese state (which Belgium, after all, had itself created); *The Sacred Mission of Civilization: To Which Peoples Should the Benefit be Extended?* (New York: Belgium Government Information Center, 1953). While the Belgian position, that each indigenous nation possessed a right equal to or greater than the state, was essentially correct, it was advanced for transparently neocolonialist purposes and was therefore rebuffed; Roxanne Dunbar Ortiz, "Protection of American Indian Territories in the United States: Applicability of International Law," in *Irredeemable America*, *op. cit.*, esp. 260–61.

237. For discussion, see, e.g., Russel Barsh, "Indigenous North America and International Law," *Oregon Law Review* 62 (1983).

238. For elaboration of this argument, see Catherine J. Jorns, "Indigenous People and Self-Determination: Challenging State Sovereignty," *Case Western Reserve Journal of*

International Law 24 (1992). Potentially applicable precedents will be found in Jencks, *Law in the World Community*, *op. cit.*

2

The Past as Legacy and Project: Postcolonial Criticism in the Perspective of Indigenous Historicism

Arif Dirlik

Men [and women] make their own history, but they do not make it just as they please; they do not make it under circumstances chosen by themselves, but under circumstances directly encountered, given and transmitted from the past. The tradition of all the dead generations weighs like a nightmare on the brain of the living.

—Karl Marx

AFTER NEARLY A CENTURY-AND-A-HALF, Marx's statement[1] still provides a most cogent affirmation of historicity against both a libertarian obliviousness to the burden of the past and a determinist denial of the possibility of human agency. But I begin with this statement for still another reason. While Marx's own work lies at the origins of so much of present-day theorizing about society and history, against our theory-crazed times, when once again the logic of abstraction seems to take precedence over the evidence of the world, the statement is comfortingly common sensical.

Issues of historicity and common sense are both pertinent to the problem I take up in this discussion. The problem derives from a paradox in contemporary cultural criticism and politics. In academic circles engrossed with postmodernity/postcoloniality as conditions of the present, it is almost a matter of faith these days that nations are "imagined," traditions are "invented," subjectivities are slippery (if they exist at all), and cultural identities are myths. Claims to the contrary are labeled "essentialisms" and are dismissed as perpetuations of

Arif Dirlik teaches at Duke University, where he specializes in modern Chinese history. He is the author of *The Postcolonial Aura: Third World Criticism in the Age of Global Capitalism* (Boulder, CO: Westview Press, 1997) and editor of *What Is in a Rim? Critical Perspectives on the Pacific Region Idea* (Lanham, MD: Rowman and Littlefield, 1998). This paper was presented originally as a public lecture and keynote address at the Annual Graduate Student Conference at the Humanities Institute at Stony Brook, New York, 3 November 1995.

hegemonic constructions of the world. The denial of authenticity to cultural claims beyond localized constructions is accompanied by the denial to the past of any authority to authenticate the present. In the words of one "postcolonial critic," criticism, if it is to be thoroughly antihegemonic, needs to learn from the experiences of "those who have suffered the sentence of history-subjugation, domination, diaspora, displacement." Recognition of these experiences:

> forces us . . . to engage with culture as an uneven, incomplete production of meaning and value, often composed of incommensurable demands and practices, produced in the act of social survival. . . . It becomes crucial to distinguish between the semblance and similitude of the symbols across diverse cultural experiences . . . and the social specificity of each of these productions of meaning as they circulate as signs within specific contextual locations and social systems of value. The transnational dimension of cultural transformation—migration, diaspora, displacement, relocation—makes the process of cultural translation a complex form of signification. The natural(ized), unifying discourse of "nation," "peoples" or authentic "folk" tradition, those embedded myths of culture's particularity, cannot be readily referenced. The great, though unsettling, advantage of this position is that it makes you increasingly aware of the construction of culture and the invention of tradition.[2]

As if by some devilish design to mock the postcolonial argument, cultural politics in our day exhibits an abundance of such claims to cultural authenticity which, rather than disappear, would seem to be proliferating in proportion to the globalization of postmodernity—with deadly consequences for millions. Cultural nationalism, ethnicism, indigenism have emerged as markers of cultural politics globally; over the last decade ethnicity has moved to the center of politics, overshadowing earlier concerns with class and gender. Claims to cultural authenticity, moreover, have been accompanied by efforts to discover or restore authentic pasts as foundations for contemporary identity, most urgently among those who have suffered "the sentence of history."

The most basic problem presented by this paradoxical situation is the disjuncture between cultural criticism and cultural politics. Even as cultural criticism renders the past into a plaything at the hands of the present, the burden of the past haunts contemporary politics in a reassertion of cultural identities. Postmodern/postcolonial criticism would seem to have little to say on this situation, except to insist even more uncompromisingly on its own validity. Where the postmodern/postcolonial intellectuals themselves are concerned, the repudiation of essentialized identities and authentic pasts seems to culminate in a libertarianism that asserts the possibility of constructing identities and histories almost at will in those "in-between" spaces that are immune to the burden of the past (and the present, in its repudiation of "foundational" structures). Ironically, however, postmodern/postcolonial critics are unwilling to accord a similar liberty to those who seek to invoke the past in the assertion of cultural identities. They label all such attempts as misguided (or ideological) essentialisms that ignore the constructedness of the past. That groups that have "suffered the sentence of history" are internally divided and differentiated is not a particularly novel insight; what seems to be new about the current historical situation is the erasure in the name of difference of differences among such groups in their efforts to cope with "the sentence of history," especially those efforts that contradict the new ideology of postmodernism/postcolonialism. "In-betweenness," universalized as a human condition and extended over the past, is thus naturalized in the process and becomes a new kind of determinism from which there is no escape. At the same time, the label of *essentialism,* extended across the board without regard to its sources and goals, obviates the need to distinguish different modes of cultural identity formation that is subversive not only of critical but also of any meaningful political judgment. Below I address some questions raised by these different modes of cultural identity formation. To assert that cultural identity is ambiguous and the historical materials out of which it is constructed are invented is in some ways to state the obvious. The questions are, what do different modes of identity construction imply intellectually and politically, and how do we construe the relationships they presuppose between the present and the past? The discussion is organized around three questions that I take to be critical to distinguishing among these identity formations: (a) What is their relationship to power? (b) Are the pasts out of which they are formed reified pasts or pasts recognized in their historicity? and (c) What relationship do they establish between the past as legacy and the past as project? My critique of the discourses on these questions, both in legitimations of power and in postmodern/postcolonial responses to it, is informed strongly by a perspective afforded by indigenism, the ideological articulation of the aspirations to liberation of those Native peoples—designated the Fourth World in recent years—that I take to be the terminally marginalized of all the oppressed and marginalized peoples around the world. The discussion draws most directly on articulations of indigenism in North America and, to a lesser extent, among the peoples of the Pacific.

CULTURAL IDENTITY AND POWER

Leslie Marmon Silko prefaces her novel *Ceremony* with a song-poem (also entitled "Ceremony") that tells the reader that the story she is to tell is more than just a story. There may be a postmodern ring to the idea that stories create reality—the idea that drives Silko's narrative—but the intention is anything but postmodern. *Ceremony* is about the recovery of identity destroyed by war and cultural incoherence through a reliving of ancient stories; as a story itself, *Cere-*

mony seeks to create a reality for Native peoples different from the one that is in the process of destroying them. The theme of restoring an indigenous identity by salvaging the Native past from its distortions in Euro-American historiography is a common one among indigenous peoples from Native Americans to the Australian aborigines, from Hawai'ians to the Indians of Chiapas. As Haunani-Kay Trask, leader of the Hawai'ian sovereignty movement, puts it,

> Burdened by a linear, progressive conception of history and by an assumption that Euro-American culture flourishes at the upper end of that progression, Westerners have told the history of Hawai'i as an inevitable if occasionally bittersweet triumph of Western ways over "primitive" Hawai'ian ways. . . . To know my history, I had to put away my books and return to the land. I had to plant *taro* in the earth before I could understand the inseparable bond between people and 'aina [land]. I had to feel again the spirits of nature and take gifts of plants and fish to the ancient altars. I had to begin to speak my language with our elders and leave long silences for wisdom to grow. But before anything else, I needed to learn the language like a lover so that I could rock with her and lie at night in her dreaming arms.[4]

"Indigenous peoples," according to Cree author George Manuel, who is also the founding president of the World Council of Indigenous Peoples, are peoples "descended from a country's aboriginal population and who today are completely or partly deprived of their own territory and its riches."[5] They have been described also as "the fourth world: the world on the margin, on the periphery."[6] Annette Jaimes describes the various aspects of indigenism as follows:

> "In terms of economics, the Native peoples tend to have communal property, subsistence production, barter systems, low impact technologies and collective production. . . . In terms of political relations, Native people have consensual processes, direct "participatory" democracy, and laws embedded in oral traditions. . . . In respect to their social relations, they differ [from modern society], generally, in terms of matrilineality versus patriarchy, extended versus nuclear families, and low versus high population density. . . . Finally, regarding differences in world view, the Native peoples are polytheistic, derive an understanding of the world from the natural order's rhythms and cycles of life, and include animals and plants as well as other natural features in their conceptions of spirituality.[7]

The goal of indigenism, then, is to restore these features of Native life, which have been associated in Euro-American historiography with "primitivism." Fundamental to indigenism is the recovery of land and, with it, the special relationship to nature that is the hallmark of indigenous identity.

"Indigenous ideology," as its proponents present it, defies all the protocols associated with postmodern/postcolonial criticism—to the point where it could be said fairly that it replicates the colonizers' views of indigenous peoples. Not only does it affirm the possibility of "real" Native identity, but it asserts as the basis for such identity a Native subjectivity that has survived, depending on location, as many as five centuries of colonialism and cultural disorientation. Not only does it believe in the possibility of recapturing the essence of precolonial indigenous culture, but it bases this belief on a spirituality that exists outside of historical time. The very notions of *Indian* or *Hawai'ian* that are utilized to describe collective identities take for granted categories invented by colonizers and imposed upon the colonized in remapping and redefining diverse peoples in a Euro-American reconstruction of space in the process of colonization. An articulate spokesman for indigenous ideology such as Ward Churchill not only utilizes this terminology but also insists that the collectivities thus depicted are "referents" (to recall Bhabha's term in the quotation above) for Indian nationhood, or peoplehood.[8] In all these different ways, indigenous ideology would seem to provide a textbook case of "self-Orientalization" that replays the features ascribed to the Others of Eurocentric modernizationism, which have been analyzed by Fabian in his *Time and the Other*.[9] What Nicholas Thomas says of "New Age primitivism" in Australia could describe equally well the self-essentialization that is a feature of indigenous ideology in general:

> Constructing them as culturally stable since the beginning of humanity does imply an ahistorical existence, an inability to change and an incapacity to survive modernity; this essentialism also entails stipulations about what is and what is not appropriately and truly Aboriginal, which marginalizes not only urban Aboriginal cultures, but any forms not closely associated with traditional bush gathering.[10]

Not surprisingly, indigenous ideology has come under criticism from postcolonial positions, or positions that share certain basic premises with postmodern/postcolonial criticism. Gareth Griffiths, a prominent Australian proponent of postcolonial criticism, wonders, of the protests against oppression of "subaltern people," that "even when the subaltern appears to 'speak' there is a real concern as to whether what we are listening to is really a subaltern voice, or whether the subaltern is being spoken by the subject position they occupy within the larger discursive economy." Griffiths goes on to state that his goal is not to question whether the claim of Aboriginal peoples in Australia and elsewhere to restitution of their traditional lands and sacred places, or to the voices and practices of their traditional cultures, is legitimate. Nor do I question the importance of locality and specificity in resisting the generalizing tendencies and incorporative strategies of white society. . . . [I]t is not my business to comment on this. What I am concerned with is the impact of the representation of that claim when it is mediated through a discourse of the authentic adopted and promulgated by the dominant discourse which "speaks" the indigene within a construction whose legitimacy is grounded not in *their* practice but in *our* desire.[11]

Similarly, but obviously with fewer qualms about offending indigenous sensibilities, a Canadian postcolonial critic writes,

While post-colonial theorists embrace hybridity and heterogeneity as the characteristic post-colonial mode, some native writers in Canada resist what they see as a violating appropriation to insist on their ownership of their stories and their exclusive claim to an authenticity that should not be ventriloquized or parodied. When directed against the Western canon, post-modernist techniques of intertextuality, parody, and literary borrowing may appear radical and even potentially revolutionary. When directed against native myths and stories, these same techniques would seem to repeat the imperialist history of plunder and theft. . . . Although I can sympathize with such arguments as tactical strategies in insisting on self-definition and resisting appropriation, even tactically they prove self-defeating because they depend on a view of cultural authenticity that condemns them to a continued marginality and an eventual death. . . . Ironically, such tactics encourage native peoples to isolate themselves from contemporary life and full citizenhood.[12]

Nicholas Thomas has observed that cultural studies in the United States have been largely silent on the question of Native Americans: "In U.S. journals that address race, more reference is made to racism and colonial conflicts elsewhere—in South Africa or Britain—than to native American struggles."[13] One noteworthy exception that is pertinent to the discussion here may be the questions raised by anthropologist Jocelyn S. Linnekin about the claims to cultural authenticity of the Hawai'ian independence movement. In an article published in 1983, "Defining Tradition: Variations on the Hawaiian Identity," Linnekin argued not only that Hawai'ian society was internally differentiated (and hence not to be homogenized), but that the "traditions" that served as symbols of Hawai'ian nationalism—such as Hawai'ian seafaring capabilities or the "love of the land"—were invented traditions. Especially damaging were the questions she raised about the traditional sanctity of the island of Kahoolawe, used by the U.S. Navy for bombing practices. Her questions were to be used by the navy as legal evidence to justify continued use of the island as a target against Hawai'ian claims to the island's sanctity.[14]

Whether these critiques are based on sufficient readings of indigenous ideology is a question I will take up below. It is necessary here to examine more closely the relationship of indigenous self-assertion to its context in a colonial structure of power. Griffiths's concern that the dominant discourse "speaks" the indigene raises the important question that the reification of indigenous identity not only replicates the assumptions of the dominant discourse, but also opens the way to the "consumption" of indigenism by the dominant society; after all, people who are outside of history are more easily placed in museums and theme parks than those who are part of a living present, and exoticized cultures provide a ready-made fund for the production of cultural commodities.[15] What Griffiths overlooks, however, is that it is the power context rather than the reification that may be the more important problem. As the case of Linnekin shows, the denial of reified pasts is equally open to exploitation by power. Disney these days justifies its constructions of the past or of the Other on the grounds that, since all pasts are invented or constructed, their constructions are as valid as anyone else's. It is arguable that postmodern/postcolonial denials of historical or cultural truths render the past or other cultures more readily available for commodification and exploitation by abolishing the possibility of distinguishing one invention from another. The premise that all truths are "contingent" truths, without reference to the structures of power that inform them, opens the way to silencing "the subalterns" who cannot even claim authentic custody of their own identities against their "construction" by academic, commercial, or political institutions of power.

The importance of accounting for power relations in judgments on identity formation may be illustrated further by placing indigenous ideology within the context of the current proliferation of cultural nationalisms with which it shares much in common in terms of intellectual procedures. There has been a resurgence in recent years of fundamentalistic nationalisms or culturalisms against Euro-American ideological domination of the world, ranging from Islamic fundamentalism to Pan-Asianism, from assertions in Japan of an ideology of "Japaneseness" to the Confucian revival in Chinese societies. These revivals, while antihegemonic in some respects, are also fueled by newfound power in formerly Third World societies that have achieved success in capitalist development and all of a sudden find themselves in a position to challenge Euro-American models of development. They are also motivated, however, by efforts to contain the disintegrative consequences of such development. The assertion of homogenized cultural identities on the one hand celebrates success in the world economy but also, on the other hand, seeks to contain the disintegrative threat of Western commodity culture, the social incoherence brought about by capitalist development, and the cultural confusion brought about by diasporic populations that have called into question the identification of national culture with the space of the nation-state. Thus the Confucian revival among Chinese populations points to Chinese success in capitalist development to argue that the Confucian ethic is equal, if not superior to, the "Protestant ethic" which Max Weber credited with causative power in the emergence of capitalism in Europe; a "Weberized" Confucianism in turn appears as a marker of Chineseness regardless of time or place.

In the idea of a "cultural China" that has been promoted by proponents of a Confucian revival, cultural essence replaces political identity in the definition of Chineseness. At the same time, the idea is one in the promotion of which Chinese states, capital, and academic intellectuals (mostly in First World institutions) have played a crucial part. No less important is the fact that non-Chinese academics in the United States closely connected with academic and commercial institutions of power have participated in this revival, and have even played an important part in legitimizing it; Confucianism, reduced to a few ethical principles conducive to social and economic order, has been rendered in the process into an ideology of capitalist development, superior to the individualistic ideology of Euro-American capitalism in its emphasis on harmony and social cohesiveness. The latter aspect prompted the government of the People's Republic of China, in 1994, to declare a "Confucian renaissance" on the grounds that, with socialism having lost its ethical power to counter undesirable social tendencies, Confucianism might serve as a suitable native substitute.[16] Naturalized as a marker of Chineseness, Confucianism also serves to erase memories of a revolutionary past.

The tendencies toward the proliferation of fundamentalisms and culturalist nationalisms were no doubt on the mind of Samuel Huntington when he wrote in his celebrated 1993 essay,

> World politics is entering a new phase. . . . [T]he fundamental source of conflict in this new world will not be primarily ideological or primarily economic. The great divisions among humankind and the dominating source of conflict will be cultural. Nation states will remain the most powerful actors in world affairs, but the principal conflicts of global politics will occur between nations and groups of different civilizations. The clash of civilizations will dominate world politics. . . . With the end of the Cold War, international politics moves out of its Western phase, and its centerpiece becomes the interaction between the West and non-Western civilizations and among non-Western civilizations. . . . Civilization identity will be increasingly important in the future, and the world will be shaped in large measure by the interactions among seven or eight major civilizations. These include Western, Confucian, Japanese, Islamic, Hindu, Slavic-Orthodox, Latin American and possibly African civilization.[17]

A critique of cultural "essentialism" that offers no articulated means to distinguish between the essentialism of indigenous ideology and the essentialism of a Confucian revival or Huntington's vision of war among civilizations, may be methodologically justifiable; but it is, to say the least, morally irresponsible and politically obscene. Indigenous claims to identity are very much tied in with a desperate concern for survival; not in a "metaphorical" but in a very material sense. Indian lands in the United States., or what is left of them, are not just reminders of a bygone colonial past, but are still the objects of state and corporate destruction in what Churchill describes as "radioactive colonization."[18] In accordance with racist policies in effect since the nineteenth century, according to Annette Jaimes, Indian identity in the United States is determined either by the recognition of tribal governments or by what has been described as "the blood quantum," the degree of "Indian blood" in any one individual as certified by the Bureau of Indian Affairs (the minimum for qualification set at "quarter blood").[19] Churchill, who describes the implications of the "blood quantum" as "arithmetical genocide," writes,

> The thinking is simple. As the historian Patricia Nelson Limerick frames it: "Set the blood quantum at one-quarter, hold to it as a rigid definition of Indians, let intermarriage proceed as it has for centuries, and eventually Indians will be defined out of existence." Bearing out the validity of Jaimes' and Limerick's observations is the fact that, in 1900, about half of all Indians in this country were "full-bloods." By 1990, the population had shrunk to about twenty percent. . . . A third of all Indians are at the quarter-blood cut-off point. Cherokee demographer Russell Thornton estimates that, given continued imposition of purely racial definitions, Native America as a whole will have disappeared by the year 2080.[20]

Cultural identity, under such circumstances, is not a matter of "identity politics" but a condition of survival, and its implications may be grasped only by reference to structures of power. There is a world of difference between a "Confucian identity" promoted by states and capital and intended to carve out a place in a global structure of political and economic power, and an indigenous identity that may be essential to survival as a social and cultural identity against the depredations of power. Postmodern/postcolonial criticism, especially in the United States, has not only been insensitive to such differences in its unqualified affirmation of "hybridity and heterogeneity" but, as the quotation from Brydon above suggests, quite intolerant of any efforts to "construct" the past differently from what is allowable to "postcolonial critics"; in fact, it is difficult to see how Brydon's "join up or shut up attitude" differs in any significant sense from that of colonialist attitudes toward indigenous peoples.[21]

What renders indigenous ideology significant, however, is not what it has to reveal about postmodern/postcolonial criticism. Its intellectual and political significance rests elsewhere: in its claims to a different historicity that challenges not just postcolonial denials of collective identity but the structure of power that contains it. To criticize indigenous ideology for its reification of culture is to give it at best an incomplete reading. It also disguises the complexity of what indigenous authors have to say about the relationship between culture and history, which is considerably more radical ideologically than is suggested by its apparent culturalism.

CULTURAL IDENTITY/HISTORICAL TRAJECTORY

One of the celebrated conflicts in U.S. letters in recent years is that between the

Chinese-American writers Frank Chin and Maxine Hong Kingston. Following the publication of Kingston's *The Woman Warrior* in 1976, Chin launched an attack on the book for its misrepresentation of Chineseness. The attacks continue to this day but have been broadened now to include other prominent Chinese-American writers such as Amy Tan and David Hwang. Chin has accused all of these authors of stereotyping Chinese culture and distorting its realities by adopting what he takes to be a "missionary" view of Chinese society.[22]

Chin's attacks on these authors have been ascribed to his misogynistic attitudes and his envy at their success. Regardless of whether there is any merit to such charges, his own refusal to bring any kind of subtlety to his criticisms has not helped his cause. His insistence that his is the only viable and authentically "Chinese" position has further isolated him and, unfortunately, obviated the need for elaborating on his critique which, I believe, has much to say about the problem of history in a minority group's construction of its ethnicity.[23]

At the heart of this particular controversy is Kingston's (mis)use of Chinese legends and the liberties she took with the interpretation of Chinese characters (namely, the association of the character for woman with the character for slave) in *The Woman Warrior*. Kingston has conceded the liberties she took but has explained them in terms of literary license. Chin has refused to accept this excuse. Legends, to him, represent cultural truths that are not to be tampered with; Kingston's distortions of Chinese legends were all the more serious because, at the insistence of the publisher, she consented to having *The Woman Warrior* classified as autobiography rather than fiction, as originally intended, which further endowed her distortions with the status of truth. She thus played into the hands of the dominant society's stereotypes of Chineseness.

Kingston herself has expressed regrets that *The Woman Warrior* was indeed received as a description of Chinese society, contributing to the image of an exotic China. This may have something to tell us about the plight of minority literature, but it will not do to ascribe it just to the parochialism of the dominant society, as Frederick Buell has suggested recently.[24] The problem with Kingston's representation of Chineseness may lie not in the distortions of Chinese legends or characters (although these are certainly problems), but in the manner in which the relationship to the past is represented in *The Woman Warrior*. A comparison with Chin's representation of this relationship may lend us a clue. Chin's own work engages in a stereotyping of Chineseness by associating it with certain primordial characteristics; indeed it is arguable that Chin's notion of the cultural endowment of Chinese in his formal statements is one-dimensional in contrast to that of Kingston, who perceives in Chinese culture the location both for oppression and the struggle against it, as personified in the woman warrior.[25] Nevertheless, in his fiction, Chin presents a relationship to the past that resists appropriation into the image of an exotic China. Why one representation should lend itself to appropriation while the other should resist it is an important question that has been sidestepped in the whole controversy.

The part history plays in mediating the Chinese-American relationship to the Chinese past is crucial, I think, to understanding the difference. While complex, Kingston's representation of the past relegates it to a Chinese space, which then haunts the Chinese-American as burden or promise, but in either case as a legacy from a different time and place (*haunts* in an almost literal sense, as she uses the metaphor of *ghosts* to depict the presence of the past in the present). Chin in his fiction is relatively unconcerned with Chinese culture—except in relationship to the Chinese-American; it may be suggested even that he substitutes the culture of the Chinese-American as he understands it for Chinese culture. The relationship of Chinese-American to Chinese culture in his representation is a relationship both of sameness and difference, mediated by a history that is grounded in a U.S., not a Chinese, temporality. The difference between the two representations is the difference between Chinese culture as a past legacy that continues to haunt the American Chinese, versus Chinese culture as a source of struggle to define a Chinese-American identity that defies "death by assimilation" while reaffirming its irreducible Americanness. In this latter case, the past serves not merely as legacy to be left behind as the ghosts of China themselves eventually recede to invisibility; rather, it is a fundamental moment in the creation of a Chinese-American history even as that history is distanced from its sources in China. What makes Chin's version resistant to exoticism, as well as to assimilation, I think, is its claim to a Chinese-American historicity that derives its trajectory from the reworking of past legacy within an American topography, that makes it as American as any other history but at the same time proclaims a historicity that is different from, and challenges, American history as represented in dominant historiography—one that has written the Chinese-American out of history and has denied the Americanness of the Chinese-American in doing so. Also, in this representation, we might note, there is a shift of emphasis (in spite of Chin's own longings) from cultural legacy that resists history to a historical legacy that rephrases the question of cultural identity in terms of its historicity.[26]

Thus, despite his insistence on his being the only "real" Chinese around, it is arguable that Chin is the most "American" of all the Chinese-American writers, and it is his alternative vision of being American, rather than his insistence on his Chineseness, that endows his work with a radicalism that resists appropriation. The complexity of Chin's notion of Chineseness may be gleaned from the following passage in his novel *Donald Duk*:

> A hundred years ago, all the Chinatowns in America were Cantonese. They spoke Cantonese. The only Chinese Donald has any ears for is Cantonese. Donald does not like the history teacher, Mr. Meanwright. Mr. Meanwright likes to prove he knows more about Chinese than Donald Duk. Donald doesn't care. He knows nothing about China. He does not speak Mandarin. He does not care a lot about Chinatown either, but when Mr. Meanwright talks about Chinatown, Donald Duk's muscles all tighten up, and he wants Mr. Meanwright to shut up.[27]

It is Chinatown culture that is Chinese-American culture, and while Chin has taken liberties with representing this culture as a metonym for Chinese culture as a whole, it is Chinese-American culture that has been his major preoccupation. Early in his career, he acknowledged not only that Chinese-Americans were not recognized as "real" Chinese by those from China, but he complained about the confusion of Chinese-American with Chinese culture.[28] Interestingly from our present vantage point, the happy "in-betweenland" of postcolonialism appeared at the time as "no-man's land." He and Jeffrey Chan wrote of the concept of "dual personality" (the unblendable "blending of east and west") that pervaded studies of Chinese-Americans at the time:

> The concept of the dual personality successfully deprives the Chinese-American of all authority over language and thus a means of codifying, communicating, and legitimizing his experience. Because he is a foreigner, English is not his native tongue. Because he was born in the U.S., Chinese is not his native tongue. Chinese from China, "real Chinese," make the Chinese-American aware of his lack of authority over Chinese, and the white American doesn't recognize the Chinese-American's brand of English as a language, even a minority language, but as faulty English, an "accent." The notion of an organic, whole identity, a personality not explicable in either the terms of China or white America . . . has been precluded by the concept of the dual personality . . . the denial of language is the denial of culture.[29]

The realization of just such a personality, which is not a hybrid of two cultures but a product of historical experience, emerges then as the goal (this may be the reason that Chin consistently uses the derogatory term *Chinaman* to describe his characters, turning the tables on racist usage). The grounds of the experience are very much American, but to resist assimilation the experience must draw upon the Chinese past, the authenticity of which then becomes crucial to the plausibility of a Chinese-American identity. An underlying theme of a novel such as *Donald Duk* (as well as Chin's other writings) is the erasure of Chinese from American history (literally absent from the photograph at Promontory Summit, Utah, where the Union Pacific met the Central Pacific, after Chinese workers had done so much to build the railroad from Sacramento). The goal is to restore that history, but as Chinese, not as shadows of white society:

> "I think Donald Duk may be the very last American-born Chinese-American boy to believe you have to give up being Chinese to be an American," Dad says. "These new immigrants prove that. They were originally Cantonese, and did not want to be Chinese. When China conquered the south, these people went further south, into Vietnam, Laos, Cambodia, Thailand. They learned French. Now they're learning English. They still speak their Cantonese, their Chinese, their Viet or Lao or Cambodian, and French. Instead of giving anything up, they add on. They're includ-

ing America in everything else they know. And that makes them stronger than any of the American-born, like me, who had folks who worked hard to know absolutely nothing about China, who believed that if all they knew was 100 percent American-made in the USA Yankee know howdy doodle dandy, people would not mistake them for Chinese.[30]

In *Donald Duk*, legendary Chinese heroes appear as railroad foremen, and the 108 outlaws of the Chinese novel *Water Margin* offer their aid in the semblance of "the ghost riders in the sky."

The historicity of identity does not make it any the less whole, nor does the constructedness of the past make it any the less significant in shaping history. Each generation may rewrite history, but it does so under conditions where it receives as its historical endowment previous generations' constructions of the past. For the marginalized and oppressed in particular, whose histories have been erased by power, it becomes all the more important to recapture or remake the past in their efforts to render themselves visible historically, as the very struggle to become visible presupposes a historical identity. In the face of a "historiographic colonialism" that denies them their historicity, capturing the truth of history, of oppression and the resistance to it, is a fundamental task that for its accomplishment requires constant reference to the precolonial past.[31] But it is also the case that those who are engaged in a struggle for identity can least afford to dehistoricize or reify the past, for the struggle is always the struggle for the present and must address not just the legacy of the past but also problems of the present. Cultural identity itself, then, is a terrain of the very struggles that it inspires. Whether it is reified, hybridized, or historicized, the meaning to be attached to alternative constructions of cultural identity is inseparable from the totality of the struggle that provides its context. The Confucian revival, Kingston's feminist construction of China, and Chin's use of popular religious and literary traditions all construct Chineseness differently, but also with different implications for the relationship between culture and history. They also imply different relationships to social and political power.

Chin's use of the past provides a cogent illustration that cultural construction is not a "zero-sum" process (either Chinese or American) or a matter of hybridity or in-betweenness (neither Chinese nor American), but a historical process of production in which the dialectical interaction between past legacy and present circumstances produces cultural identities that are no less integrated for being historical, that derive their trajectories of change from the accretion of experiences that may be shaped by the legacies of the past but also transform the meaning of the latter, and in which local experience interacts with structural context to produce, at once, forces of difference and unity. Cultural essentialism does not consist merely of defining cultural essences, but requires the isolation of culture from history, so that those essences come to serve as abstract markers that have little to do with the realities of cultural identity. Notions of cultural purity and hybridity alike, ironically, presuppose a cultural essentialism; from a perspective that recognizes the historicity of culture, the question of essentialism becomes quite irrelevant. In this sense, assertions of hybridity or in-betweenness as well as claims to cultural purity are equally culturalist, the one because it rejects the spatiality and temporality of culture, the other because it renders into spatial differences what are but the temporal complexities of the relationship between the past and the present. The historicization of culture against such culturalism is also quite radical in its consequences, in that it opens the way to an insistence on different histories which, unlike the insistence on different cultural spaces or spaces in-between, are not to be contained within a cultural pluralism let alone assumptions of cultural unity; hence the resistance to appropriation of a historicized insistence on culture.

Historicizing Chinese culture, Chin's account seeks also to indigenize it in the topography of a new location for history, where it challenges the claims of the dominant culture. But its own claims are those of one group of settlers against other settlers; an assertion that the one group of settlers has the same claims on history as another. What, if any, alternative vision of the future is embedded in this alternative history remains unclear.

This is where the radicalism of indigenous ideology comes in. If Chin indigenizes Chineseness in a new historical location, indigenous ideology historicizes indigenism in the face of a new historical situation but without conceding its topographical claims and an alternative way of life embedded in that topography. Not only does it insist on a different history, in other words, but it does so through a repudiation of the very idea of history promoted by the settlers; as it refuses to distinguish temporality from spatiality. I suggested above that readings of indigenous ideology that ascribe to it a simple cultural essentialism may not be sufficient. Contrary to critics wedded to ideas of "heterogeneity and hybridity," who see in every affirmation of cultural identity an ahistorical cultural essentialism, indigenous voices are quite open to change; what they insist on is not cultural purity or persistence, but the preservation of a particular historical trajectory of their own. In this case, however, the trajectory is one that is grounded in the topography much more intimately. And it is one that is at odds with the notions of temporality that guide the histories of the settlers.[32]

Silko might be echoing Chin when she writes,

> The people nowadays have an idea about the ceremonies. They think the ceremonies must be performed exactly as they have always been done. . . . But long ago when the people were given these ceremonies, the changing began . . . if only in the different voices from generation to generation, singing the chants. You see, in many ways, the ceremonies have always been changing. . . . At one time, the ceremonies as they had been performed were enough for the way the world was then. But after the white people came, elements in this world began to shift; and it became necessary to create new ceremonies. . . . [T]hings which don't shift and grow are dead things. They are things the witchery people want. That's what the witchery is counting on: that we will cling to the ceremonies the way they were, and then their power will triumph, and the people will be no more.[33]

Change is necessary, but it is to be contained within the history of the ceremonies. And, in this case, the ceremonies are inseparable from the land. Silko's narrative is a confirmation of the coexistence of the timeless and the temporal—a sensibility of timeless validity and the changes that are necessary to sustain that sensibility. The Indian is responsible for both. It was Indian witchcraft that "invented" the whites, who threaten the eternally valid. While the Indian "invention" of the whites points to the Indians' responsibility for their own fate (rather than blaming the whites for it), it also reverses the historiographical relationship by making whites into creatures of a quintessentially Indian history.[34] Only by overcoming witchcraft can the Indian once again restore the sensibility that is necessary to the sustenance of life.

Indigenism thus conceived is both a legacy and a project (as is ethnicity, when viewed in this perspective). Arguing against the "determinism" of culturalism, Jean-Paul Sartre wrote in his *Search for a Method,*

> The project, as the subjective surpassing of objectivity toward objectivity, and stretched between the objective conditions of the environment and the objective structures of the field of possibles, represents *in itself* the moving unity of subjectivity and objectivity, those cardinal determinants of activity. The subjective appears then as a necessary moment in the objective process. . . . Only the project, as a mediation between two moments of objectivity, can account for history; that is, for human creativity.[35]

The project, Sartre noted, contains a "double simultaneous relationship. In relation to the given, the *praxis* is negativity; but what is always involved is the negation of a negation. In relation to the object aimed at, *praxis* is positivity, but this positivity opens unto the 'nonexistent,' to what *has not yet* been."[36]

To an indigenist such as Ward Churchill, indigenism is a "negation of the negation," which also affirms "that which is most alive and promising for the future of the Indian people."[37] By indigenism, Churchill writes,

> I mean that I am one who not only takes the rights of indigenous peoples as the highest priority of my political life, but who draws upon the traditions—the bodies of knowledge and corresponding codes of values—evolved over many thousands of years by native peoples the world over. This is the basis upon which I not only advance critiques of, but conceptualize alternatives to the present social, political, economic and philosophical status quo. In turn, this gives shape not only to the sorts of goals and objectives I pursue, but the kinds of strategy and tactics I advocate, the variety of struggles I tend to support, the nature of alliances I'm inclined to enter into, and so on.[38]

The point of departure for this indigenism is the present, and its goal is not to restore a bygone past, but to draw upon the past to create a new future (which also explains why Churchill uses the term *Indian,* fully aware of its colonial origins, as does Frank Chin with *Chinaman* and Trask with *Hawai'ian).* In working out the scope of indigenism, moreover, Churchill also strives to account for challenges that are very contemporary, such as problems of class, sexism, and homophobia.[39]

Likewise, Annette Jaimes describes indigenism as a "reworking of . . . concepts which are basic to an American Indian identity on the threshold of the Twenty-first century," and Trask, like most indigenous writers, links the struggles for Hawai'ian independence to the struggles of oppressed people around the world.[40] The same is true of writers of the Pacific, such as Albert Wendt and Epeli Hau'ofa, who have affirmed that the effort to recapture a Native identity and history may proceed only through struggles against colonialism that nevertheless recognize the historical transformations wrought by colonialism.[41] The effort to overcome Eurocentrism and colonialism does not require denial of an immediate past of which Euro-American colonialism was an integral part but presupposes an identity through a history of which Euro-American domination was very much a reality.[42]

What is of fundamental significance here (and distinguishes these arguments from postcolonialism), however, is a recognition that the common history that united the colonizer and the colonized was also a history of division. What the colonizer may have experienced as unification, the colonized experienced as an oppressive denial of Native identity. The insistence on a separate historicity is driven by this sense of division: To liberate Native history from "historiographic colonialism," it is necessary not just to revive memories of a precolonial past, but to write the ways in which the precolonial past was suppressed, as well as the ways in which it informed past struggles against colonialism. As the Australian aboriginal writer Mudrooroo Narogin puts it,

> It is no use declaring, as some Aborigines do declare, that the past is over and should be forgotten, when that past is only of two hundred years duration. It is far too early for the Aboriginal people to put aside that past and the effects of that past. Aboriginal people must come to realise that many of their problems are based on a past which still lives within them. If this is not acknowledged, then the self-destructive and community-destructive acts which continue to occur will be seen as only resulting from unemployment, bad housing, or ill-health, and once these are removed everything will be fine.[43]

Narogin's comments show that the struggle over history is no longer just a struggle between colonizer and colonized but among the colonized themselves; between those who would forget the immediate past and those who insist on remembering.[44] Indigenism's insistence on remembering the immediate past distinguishes it from reifications of precolonial cultural markers and renders it fundamentally threatening to the status quo, even when that status quo is redefined in terms of cultural diversity and difference. As Gillian Cowlishaw writes, "Forty thousand years of history and spiritual links with the land gain a more sympathetic hearing than accusations of past injustices and displaying of old wounds received in the struggle for equality."[45] The reasons are not very complex: The reification of the precolonial past may be accommodated within a cultural pluralism much more easily than the insistence on the construction of alternative futures that draw not only on primordial traditions but also on the struggles of the immediate past. The difference is the difference between a multiculturalism that enables assimilation without challenge to the social, political, and economic status quo, and a multihistoricalism that questions the totality of existing relations and the future of the history that legitimizes them.

The indigenous historical challenge, moreover, is not "metaphorical" but deeply material. The insistence on a special relationship to the land as the basis for indigenous identity is not merely spiritual, an affirmation of an ecological sensibility, but also calls for a transformation of the spatial arrangements of colonialism or postcolonialism. Indigenism, in other words, challenges not just relations between different ethnicities but the system of economic relations that provides the ultimate context for social and political relationships: capitalist or state socialist. In this challenge also lies the possibilities for opening up indigenism to other radical advocacies of social change. Instead of a multiculturalism that presupposes coexistence of multiple ethnicities identified by ahistorical cultural markers, which elevates ethnicity to a determining principle of social life without saying much about the political and economic system as a whole, the historicity of the indigenous argument permits the design of open-ended projects that promise a return to a genuinely common history once the legacy of the colonial past has been erased—not just ideologically but materially as well.

CONCLUDING REMARKS

In his critique of Jocelyn Linnekin's criticisms of the Hawai'ian independence movement, Jeffrey Tobin has called for greater attention to context in evaluating political movements and their constructions of Native identity. "It is important," he writes, "to distinguish between discourses that naturalize oppression and discourses that naturalize resistance."[46] Similarly, responding to critiques of "essentialism" by James Clifford and Edward Said, Nicholas Thomas writes that

> what . . . these critiques pass over is the extent to which humanism and essentialism have different meanings and effects in different contexts. Clifford writes as though the problem were merely intellectual: difference and hybridity are more appropriate analytically to the contemporary scene of global cultural transposition than claims about human sameness or bounded types. I would agree, but this does not bear upon the uses that essentialist discourses may have for people whose projects involve mobilization rather than analysis. Said might be able to argue that

nativism as a political programme or government ideology has been largely pernicious, but nativist consciousness cannot be deemed undesirable merely because it is ahistorical and uncritically reproduces colonial stereotypes. The main problem is not that this imposes academic (and arguably ethnocentric) standards on non-academic and non-Western representations, but that it paradoxically essentializes nativism by taking its politics to be uniform.[47]

Thomas also recognizes that "nativist-primitivist idealizations can only be productive . . . if they are completely complemented by here-and-now concerns, and articulated with histories that do not merely recapitulate the 'imperialist nostalgia' of the fatal-impact narrative."[48]

Ironically, the insistence of the postcolonial argument on history conceals a deeply ahistorical reluctance to distinguish anything but the local, imbedded in an ideology of "heterogeneity and hybridity." It is also an argument that undercuts the ability to resist oppression except on the level of "identity politics." It is ironic that the insistence on the inventedness and the constructedness of the past should not be accompanied by a more acute self-awareness of the inventions of postcolonialism itself, but instead should be disguised, as in the case of Linnekin, by claims to a disinterested search for truth. Viewed from these perspectives, postcolonialism itself appears as a project among competing projects, that reifies into the eternal condition of humanity the endowments of a limited group.[49] In this case, however, the project is one without a future, condemning everyone without distinction to existence in ethnic margins—including those in the margins whose efforts to overcome their marginality are subject to immediate condemnation.

The call for greater attention to political context in evaluations of identity construction is common sensical to the point of being trivial. Common sense, unfortunately, is never transparent but is loaded with ideological assumptions. The postmodern/postcolonial questioning of identity is itself quite common sensical; it is when it is generalized and universalized to the point where it will brook no deviation from its own assumptions that it becomes intellectually counterproductive and is driven into a political dead end that extinguishes the possibility of political alternatives. Sharpened awareness of the constructedness of identity or of history may have rendered political and moral choice more complex and difficult; it has not eliminated the necessity of choice. Postmodernism may be an ideology of defeat, as Terry Eagleton suggests, or a "matter of class," as Aijaz Ahmad puts it; in either case, it reifies into a general analytical or political principle what may be but a condition of our times.[50]

In a recent essay, I suggested that indigenism may be of paradigmatic significance in contemporary politics globally.[51] This is not to suggest that indigenism provides a ready-made utopia, as in New Age constructions of indigenism. Indigenous proponents of indigenism are quite aware of the problems of Native societies: that they have been disorganized by centuries of colonialism and reorganized in accordance with the political and cultural prerogatives of colonialism, which has led to a social and political disintegration, as well as a nearly total incoherence of Native identity, that will take enormous effort to overcome; that their cultures continue to be cannibalized by tourist industries and New Age cultural consumerism, often with the complicity of the Native peoples themselves; and that the dream of recovering the land, crucial both to material and spiritual existence, may be just that, a dream.[52] It may be out of this deep sense of the historical destruction of their societies that indigenous writers insist on recovering the process of history "as it really was"— for them. Because indigenous people were written out of history for being "unhistorical," it becomes all the more necessary to document meticulously the process whereby they were erased from history in order to recover historicity.[53]

The insistence on a separate history is itself not without problems, especially these days when tendencies to the ethnicization or even the biologization of knowledge threatens not only a common understanding of the world, but the possibility of common political projects as well. Although the cannibalization of indigenous cultures (by tourist or anthropologist) is very real, the fact remains that its very reality divides indigenous from nonindigenous projects—especially when issues of identity are framed around spiritualities that are accessible only to those on the inside.

Nevertheless, it is arguable that indigenism is as much a utopian aspiration that seeks to contain and overcome these problems as it is an expression of Native sensibilities. The same utopianism—history as project—also offers possibilities of common struggles and aspirations. Indigenous ideology, while insistent on a separate history, also finds common ground with other histories in the problems it addresses. What makes it particularly pertinent in our day are the questions it raises about the whole project of development, capitalist or socialist; although some indigenous writers have pointed to common features between socialism and indigenism, this is a socialism that is far removed from the state socialisms as we have known them, grounded in the reassertion of community.[54] The indigenous reaffirmation of a special relationship to the land as the basis of a new ecological sensibility obviously resonates with growing ecological consciousness worldwide. The indigenous reassertion of ties to authentic pasts is not as divisive as it may seem, but may contain a lesson that is broadly relevant. If the past is constructed, it is constructed at all times, and ties to the past require an ongoing dialogue between present and past constructions, except in linear conceptions of history where the past, once past, is irrelevant except as abstract moral or political lesson. The repudiation of linear temporality in indigenous ideology suggests that the past is never really past, but offers "stories" that may be required to resolve problems of the present, even as they are changed to answer present needs.[55] The notion of dialogue between past and present also suggests the possibility of dialogue across present-day spaces, among indigenous peoples and with the nonindigenous as well, in which lies the possibility of common understanding as well as common historical projects.

If indigenous ideology claims as its basis an indigenous sensibility, it also opens up to others through problems that cut across any ethnically defined identity, those of class and gender oppression in particular. Just as local political movements in our day have had to reconsider such problems as class, gender, and ethnicity in light of ecological and community needs, indigenous ideology has had to reconsider the meaning of indigenism in light of those problems. Surely such movements may learn from, and cross-fertilize, one another while respecting their different identities. If indigenism does have paradigmatic significance, it is because it shares with other political movements in our day both common problems, and the necessity of common action to resolve those problems.

I cannot think of a better way of concluding this discussion, and illustrating what I have just said, than to quote the eloquent words of a leader of a contemporary movement for indigenous self-assertion that has caught the attention of many in these bleak political times:

> Not everyone listens to the voices of hopelessness and resignation. Not everyone has jumped onto the bandwagon of despair. Most people continue on; they cannot hear the voice of the powerful and the fainthearted as they are deafened by the cry and the blood that death and misery shout in their ears. But in moments of rest, they hear another voice, not the one that comes from above, but rather the one that comes with the wind from below, and is born in the heart of the indigenous people of the mountains, a voice that speaks of justice and liberty, a voice that speaks of socialism, a voice that speaks of hope . . . the only hope in this earthly world. And the very oldest among the people in the villages tell of a man named Zapata who rose up for his own people and in a voice more like a song than a shout, said, **"Land and Liberty!"** And these old folks say that Zapata is not dead, that he is going to return. And the oldest of the old also say that the wind and the rain and the sun tell the campesinos when they should prepare the soil, when they should plant, and when they should harvest. They say that hope also must be planted and harvested. And the old people say that now the wind, the rain, and the sun are talking to the earth in a new way, and that the poor should not continue to harvest death, now it is time to harvest rebellion. So say the old people. The powerful don't listen, the words don't reach them, as they are made deaf by the witchery that the imperialists shout in their ears. "Zapata," repeat the youth of the poor, "Zapata" insists the wind, the wind from below, our wind. . . .[56]

The choices may be complex, but they are ours to make.

Acknowledgments

I would like to thank the Humanities Institute at Stony Brook, New York, for the invitation to the Annual Graduate Student Conference and the participants in the lecture for their enthusiastic and stimulating input. I also would like to thank Ward Churchill and Rob Wilson, as well as two anonymous readers for *AIRCJ*, for their support and comments.

Notes

1. Karl Marx, *The 18th Brumaire of Louis Bonaparte* (New York: International Publishers, 1967), 15.

2. Homi Bhabha, "The Postcolonial and the Postmodern: The Question of Agency," in *The Location of Culture* (London: Routledge, 1994), 171–97, 172.

3. Leslie Marmon Silko, *Ceremony* (New York: Penguin Books, 1977), 2.

4. Haunani-Kay Trask, "From a Native Daughter," in *From a Native Daughter: Colonialism and Sovereignty in Hawai'i* (Monroe, ME: Common Courage Press, 1993), 147–59, 149–54. Roger Moody, ed., *The Indigenous Voice: Visions and Realities* (Utrecht, Netherlands: International Books, 1993), offers the most comprehensive selection I am aware of, of indigenous problems and perspectives. See also Ward Churchill, "A Little Matter of Genocide: Sam Gill's *Mother Earth*, Colonialism and the Expropriation of Indigenous Spiritual Tradition in Academia, " in *Fantasies of the Master Race: Literature, Cinema and the Colonization of American Indians*, ed. M. Annette Jaimes (Monroe, ME: Common Courage Press, 1992), 187–213; Albert Wendt, "Novelists, Historians and the Art of Remembering," in *Class and Culture in the South Pacific*, ed. Antony Hooper et al. (Auckland, NZ and Suva, Fiji: Centre for Pacific Studies of the University of Auckland in collaboration with the Institute of Pacific Studies, The University of the South Pacific, 1987), 78–91; Epeli Hau'ofa, "Our Sea of Islands," in *A New Oceania: Rediscovering Our Sea of Islands* (Suva, Fiji: School of Social and Economic Development, The University of the South Pacific, 1993), 2–16; and Alan Duff, *Once Were Warriors* (Honolulu: University of Hawai'i Press, 1990).

5. Quoted in Ward Churchill, "I Am Indigenist: Notes on the Ideology of the Fourth World," in *Struggle for the Land: Indigenous Resistance to Genocide, Ecocide and Expropriation in Contemporary North America* (Monroe, ME: Common Courage Press, 1993), 403–51, 410.

6. Quoted in ibid., 411.

7. M. Annette Jaimes, "Native American Identity and Survival: Indigenism and Environmental Ethics," in *Issues in Native American Identity*, ed. Michael K. Green (New York: Lang, 1994).

8. Ward Churchill, "Naming Our Destiny," in *Indians Are Us? Culture and Genocide in Native North America* (Monroe, ME: Common Courage Press, 1994), 291–357, 300.

9. Johannes Fabian, *Time and the Other: How Anthropology Makes Its Object* (New York: Columbia University Press, 1983).

10. Nicholas Thomas, *Colonialism's Culture: Anthropology, Travel and Government* (Princeton, NJ: Princeton University Press, 1994), 176.

11. Gareth Griffiths, "The Myth of Authenticity," in *De-Scribing Empire: Post-colonialism and Textuality*, ed. Chris Tiffin and Alan Lawson (London: Routledge, 1994), 70–85, 75, 83. The title suggests, in spite of Griffiths's disclaimer, that what he says in this passage would apply to aboriginal claims as well and not just to the dominant discourse. An earlier work leaves no doubt that, under postcolonial conditions, "the demand for a new or wholly recovered pre-colonial reality," while "perfectly comprehensible . . . cannot be achieved," because "post-colonial culture is inevitably a hybridized phenomenon involving a dialectical relationship between the 'grafted' European cultural systems and an indigenous ontology, with its impulse to create or recreate an independent local identity." In Bill Ashcroft, Gareth Griffiths, and Helen Tiffin, eds., *The Empire Writes Back: Theory and Practice in Post-colonial Literatures* (London: Routledge, 1989), 195.

12. Diana Brydon, "The White Inuit Speaks: Contamination as Literary Strategy," in

The Post-Colonial Studies Reader, ed. Ashcroft, Griffiths, and Tiffin (London: Routledge, 1995), 136–42, 140–41; originally published in Ian Adam and Helen Tiffin, eds., *Past the Last Post: Theorizing Post-Colonialism and Post-Modernism* (New York: Harvester Wheatsheaf, 1991). Brydon's arguments are largely directed at Linda Hutcheon, who is much more sympathetic toward indigenous claims against the "settlers." See her "Circling the Downspout of Empire," in *The Post-Colonial Studies Reader,* 130–35. What Brydon has to say reveals more cogently than Griffiths that what postcolonial critics have to say on the subject of indigenism could be said easily without the aid of a "postcolonial consciousness." Thus, a former Smithsonian historian writes, "Those who decry the intrusion of the white presence in Indian history are often simply unwilling to recognize that Indian history is, for good or ill, shaped by the white presence, whether physically, in terms of European immigrants, or intellectually, in terms of Western historical or anthropological theories." Wilcomb E. Washburn, "Distinguishing History from Moral Philosophy and Public Advocacy," in *The American Indian and the Problem of History,* ed. Calvin Martin (New York: Oxford University Press, 1987), 91–97, 92.

13. Thomas, *Colonialism's Culture,* 172. This is not to say that such discussions do not exist. Thomas has in mind progressive cultural critics. As noted in the previous note, there is no shortage of criticisms of indigenous ideology, albeit without the marker of "postcoloniality." For a more sympathetic criticism that points out the origin, in Euro-American power and the Euro-American mapping of the world, of the concept of "Indianness" itself, see Robert F. Berkhofer, "Cultural Pluralism versus Ethnocentrism in the New Indian History," in *The American Indian and the Problem of History,* pp. 35–45.

14. Linnekin, "Defining Tradition: Variations on the Hawaiian Identity," *American Ethnologist* 10 (1983): 241–52. For a discussion of the case and the controversy it provoked between Linnekin and Haunani-Kay Trask, see Jeffrey Tobin, "Cultural Construction and Native Nationalism: Report from the Hawaiian Front," in Rob Wilson and Arif Dirlik, eds., *Asia/Pacific as Space of Cultural Construction,* special issue of *Boundary 2* 21:1 (Spring 1994): 111–33.

15. See, also, Thomas, *Colonialism's Culture,* chapter 1, for a discussion of this problem. In the United States, the New Age craze drew extensively on "tribal cultures" for its lore.

16. For further discussion, see Arif Dirlik, "Confucius in the Borderlands: Global Capitalism and the Reinvention of Confucianism," *Boundary 2* 22:3 (November 1995): 229–73. For the role of the state in this revival, see Allen Chun, "An Oriental Orientalism: The Paradox of Tradition and Modernity in Nationalist Taiwan," *History and Anthropology* 9:1 (1994): 1–29.

17. Samuel P. Huntington, "The Clash of Civilizations?" *Foreign Affairs* 72:3 (1993): 22–49.

18. Ward Churchill, "Radioactive Colonization: Hidden Holocaust in Native North America," in *Struggle for the Land,* 261–328. Where Indians refuse the use of reservations as dumping grounds, the state uses its power "to disestablish" the reservations, as is the case most recently with the Yankton Reservation in South Dakota. See *Indian Country Today* (3 August 1995). "Radioactive colonization" is also an ongoing threat in the South Pacific.

19. M. Annette Jaimes, "Some Kind of Indian: On Race, Eugenics, and Mixed Bloods," in *American Mixed Race: The Culture of Microdiversity,* ed. Naomi Zack (Boston: Rowman and Little, 1993), 133–53, 137.

20. Ward Churchill, "Nobody's Pet Poodle," in *Indians Are Us?,* 89–113. See pages 92–93 for the quotation.

21. If this seems like an exceptional case, we may take note here of the special issue

of *Public Culture* devoted to the critique of Aijaz Ahmad's *In Theory,* which also came under severe attack for its "transgressions" against postmodern/postcolonial criticism. Rather than address the issues raised by *In Theory,* most contributors to this special issue engaged in ad hominem attacks on Ahmad. Especially noteworthy are the red-baiting comments by Peter van der Veer and the religious bigotry displayed by Marjorie Levinson. *Public Culture* 6:1(1993).

22. Frank Chin, "Come All Ye Asian American Writers of the Real and the Fake," introduction to Jeffrey Paul Chan, Frank Chin, Lawson Fusao Inada, and Shawn Wong, eds., *The Big AIIIEEEEE! An Anthology of Chinese American and Japanese American Literature* (New York: Meridian, 1991), 1–92. All of the above-named authors were excluded from this collection.

23. For a discussion of these various issues, see Edward Iwata, "Word Warriors," *The Los Angeles Times* (24 June 1990).

24. Frederick Buell, *National Culture and the New Global System* (Baltimore: Johns Hopkins University Press, 1994), 180–81.

25. Chin, "Come All Ye Asian American Writers," passim.

26. I do not wish to overlook here the different experiences of oppression that inform the works of the two authors. Chin is concerned almost exclusively with the oppression of Chinese in general, and the "feminization," in the process, of Chinese men in particular. Kingston is concerned with the "double" oppression of Chinese women, as Chinese and women, the latter including oppression sanctified by Chinese cultural tradition. Although Chin is right to point out that Kingston's portrayal of Chinese tradition as relentlessly oppressive of women plays into the hands of Euro-American stereotypes of China, he nevertheless goes overboard in presenting his own portrayal of idyllic gender relations in Chinese history. All I would like to say on this issue here is that gender relations, too, must be rescued from cultural stereotyping and placed within historical context, as has been argued by writers on Third World gender relations since the publication of *The Woman Warrior.*

27. Frank Chin, *Donald Duk* (Minneapolis, MN: Coffee House Press, 1991), 34.

28. See the interview in Victor G. and Brett deBary Nee, *Longtime Californ': A Documentary Study of an American Chinatown* (New York: Pantheon, 1973), 359, for the interview. For the confusion of Chinese-Americans with Chinese, which ignores "the obvious cultural differences," see Frank Chin and Jeffery Paul Chan, "Racist Love," in *Seeing Through Shuck,* ed. Richard Kostelanetz (New York: Ballantine Books, 1972), 65–79, 77. This article, incidentally, should put to rest the notion that Chin's recent criticisms of Chinese-American writers are motivated by envy, because he and Chan raise here all the questions that have been brought up again in recent years. At the time, Chin was the only well-known Chinese-American writer.

29. Chin and Chan, "Racist Love," 76.

30. Chin, *Donald Duk,* 41.

31. Calvin Martin, "The Metaphysics of Writing Indian-White History," in *The American Indian and the Problem of History*, 27–34, 33.

32. The very notion of "first nations," which is especially common in Canada and Australia, in this sense, represents a compromise, since it makes it possible to speak of a second, third, etc., disguising within an ordinal succession of arrivals fundamentally irreconcilable ways of life and a history of colonization and repression. Against this compromise, however, we might note a historicization, as in the case of Annette Jaimes, who proclaims that Indian tribes have been open all along to outsiders, as shown in marriage practices, etc., which skirts around the issue of "openness" while making the quite valid

point that racial differences were not the most important criteria of difference.

33. Silko, *Ceremony,* 126.

34. Ibid., 135. This appropriation of whites for Indian history seems to have an interesting parallel among Australian aborigines, who have appropriated white social scientists for their own "traditions." Says one, "I am thrilled at the knowledge that has come through archeologists and scientists about the Aborigines. To me, it is as though the ancients are trying to relay a message not only to the Aboriginal race, but to the human race." Quoted in Robert Ariss, "Writing Black: The Construction of an Aboriginal Discourse," in *Past and Present: The Construction of Aboriginality,* ed. Jeremy R. Beckett (Canberra: Aboriginal Studies Press, 1994), 131–46, 136.

35. Jean-Paul Sartre, *Search for a Method,* tr. Hazel E. Barnes (New York: Vintage, 1968), 99, 101.

36. Ibid., 92.

37. Churchill, "Nobody's Pet Poodle," 107.

38. Churchill, "I Am Indigenist," 403.

39. Ibid., 418–20.

40. Jaimes, "Native American Identity and Survival," 276, and Trask, "Hawai'i: Colonization and Decolonization," in *Class and Culture in the South Pacific,* 154–74, 169–70.

41. Epeli Hau'ofa, "The Future of Our Past," in *The Pacific Islands in the Year 2000,* ed. Robert C. Kiste and Richard A. Herr (Honolulu: Pacific Islands Studies Program Working Paper Series, 1974), 151–70; and Wendt, "Towards a New Oceania," in *Writers in the East-West Encounter: New Cultural Beginnings,* ed. Guy Amirthanayagam (London: MacMillan Press, 1982), 202–15.

42. I am paraphrasing here Geoffrey M. White, *Identity Through History: Living Stories in a Solomon Islands Society* (Cambridge: Cambridge University Press, 1991).

43. Mudrooroo Narogin (Colin Johnson), *Writing from the Fringe: A Study of Modern Aboriginal Writing* (Melbourne: Hyland House, 1990), 25.

44. Klaus Neumann writes that "these days, Papua New Guineans . . . do not appear overtly interested in being told about the horrors of colonialism, as such accounts potentially belittle today's descendants of yesterday's victims." "'In Order to Win Their Friendship': Renegotiating First Contact," *The Contemporary Pacific* 6:1 (1994): 11–145, 122. Likewise, Deirdre Jordan notes the complaints of adult aboriginal students in Australia about emphasis on white oppression, "which seems designed to call forth in them responses of hostility and racism and which, they believe, causes a crisis of identity." "Aboriginal Identity: Uses of the Past, Problems for the Future?" in *Past and Present,* 109–30, 119. There are others, needless to say, who would suppress the past for reasons of self-interest.

45. "The Materials for Identity Construction," in *Past and Present,* 87–107, 87–88.

46. Tobin, "Cultural Construction and Native Nationalism," 131.

47. Thomas, *Colonialism's Culture,* 187–88.

48. Ibid., 189.

49. Frederick Buell, *National Culture and the Global System*, provides an example of the fetishism of hybridity. Buell is intolerant of any argument that suggests the possibility of integrated identity, and the main targets of his argument are those who would foreground divisions between oppressor and oppressed.

50. Terry Eagleton, "Where Do Postmodernists Come From?" *Monthly Review* 47:3 (1995): 59–70, 66; and Aijaz Ahmad, "The Politics of Literary Postcoloniality," *Race and Class* 36:3 (1995): 1–20, 16.

51. Dirlik, "Three Worlds or One, or Many? The Reconfiguration of Global Relations

under Contemporary Capitalism," *Nature, Society and Thought* 7:1 (1995): 19–42.

52. Churchill writes of the "go it alone" approach that he advocates: "I must admit that part of my own insistence upon it often has more to do with forcing concession of the right from those who seek to deny it than it does with putting it into practice." "I Am Indigenist," 432.

53. See, for example, Ward Churchill, "Bringing the Law Back Home: Application of the Genocide Convention in the United States," in *Indians Are Us?*, 11–63. The necessity of documentation is closely related to legal efforts to recover or protect treaty rights. It is also interesting that in a volume such as *The American Indian and the Problem of History*, while most of the nonindigenous contributors speak of different temporalities and conceptions of history, the distinguished indigenous scholar Vine Deloria, Jr., stands out for his advocacy of old-fashioned historical documentation.

54. Churchill, "I Am Indigenist," 409.

55. The rewriting of history implied here is not merely a matter of writing indigenous sensibilities into existing history, but rewriting history in accordance with indigenous sensibility. Lenore Coltheart offers a challenging discussion of the distinction between "history about Aborigines" and "Aboriginal history," in "The Moment of Aboriginal History," in *Past and Present*, 179–89.

56. Subcommandante Marcos, quoted in Alexander Cockburn, "Jerry Garcia and El Sup," *The Nation* (28 August/4 September 1995), 192.

PART II

INTERNATIONAL INDIGENOUS RIGHTS

Native American tribes' earliest attempt to seek legal redress outside of the established American system of jurisprudence occurred in the1831 court case Cherokee Nation v. Georgia. Here the Cherokee Nation attempted to affirm its status as a foreign nation to restrain the state of Georgia from annihilating the Cherokee as a political entity. Chief Justice John Marshall averted the creation of a new level of legal relationship between Indian tribes and the United States by stating that the term "foreign nation" was not applicable to the Cherokee and that its relationship with the United State could best be considered as a denominated domestic dependent nation. The proper forum for tribal pursuit of legal remedies was through the Supreme Court as a subordinate power, not on an equal footing with the United States as a nation.

Despite being relegated to a "government ward," Indian Nations have sought higher courts for remedies not available through the U. S. court system. The Hopi Nation asserted its rights as a sovereign nation and sent a delegation for recognition to the United Nation in 1959. In 1977, the Lakota Nation presented its treaty case for the return of the sacred Black Hills before a United Nations Nongovernmental Organization Conference on Discrimination Against Indigenous Populations in Geneva, Switzerland, charging that they could not receive a fair hearing in the United States court system and that the United States had unilaterally violated treaties made with Indian Nations throughout its history. Again in 1980, Lakota Elders were heard by the United Nations Commission on Human Rights and the

Commission on Prevention of Discrimination and Protection of Minorities. Despite the above, the United Nations has not generally been viewed as a forum to which Indian Nations may take their concerns.

A second, but equally pressing issue in establishing and protecting indigenous rights is the form in which testimony and historical memory is acceptable in the Western legal system. Traditionally, Indian histories were oral histories. This included their sacred truths of creation, the lives and movement of the people, as well as the important events in the history of the individual tribes. Written histories did exist, however, in the form of petroglyphs, wood and tusk carvings, and winter-counts recorded on animal skin. These records of history were ignored or considered unreliable by Euro-American courts for establishing land ownership, sovereignty, and issues of jurisdiction and self-regulation.

Authors Quesenberry and Korsmo move the discussion in the previous chapter on nationalism and sovereignty in a different direction in presenting the unprecedented opportunities available at the international level. They explore the seeking of long-term protection of indigenous rights and Native people through new United Nations initiatives and through Canadian court recognition of the validity of oral histories, family lineages, songs, and description of cultural and historical events. The opportunities suggested here through the United Nations and its subsidiary bodies and the recognition of the validity of oral history, herald a new stage and script for the documentation and protection of indigenous sovereignty, culture, and respect.

In his contribution to this book, Stephen V. Quesenberry, a lawyer and the director of litigation of California Indian Legal Services, provides us with an examination of the recent United Nations initiatives on the rights of indigenous people and their relevance to Native American tribes. Importantly, Quesenberry considers not only the text of the treaties; but the complex process of their development, implementation, and ratification. Additionally, he offers strategies for broader and more active tribal participation in international standard-setting processes, reviews major U. N. treaties on indigenous and human rights, and assesses their relevance to, and possible strategic use by, Native American politicians. Quesenberry provides seven specific strategies for increasing the participation in activities relating to the rights of indigenous peoples with special attention to the International Decade of Indigenous People. In his conclusion, the author relates that there is still much work to be done and that the momentum must be sustained by broad, active participation from indigenous peoples and Native organizations. He states that Indian tribes and national Indian organizations can and should participate actively in international activities such as the drafting of laws and policies by the United Nations Commission on Human Rights.

Fae Korsmo's article "Claiming Memory in British Columbia: Aboriginal Rights and the State," addresses a critical issue facing indigenous people. While the author concentrates on aboriginal peoples from British Columbia, the question raised is germane to all indigenous populations: Is oral history to be regarded on the same level with written history? More importantly, the answer to this question is the critical issue in determining historical coherence and continuity in sorting out aboriginal title to traditional homelands.

Korsmo provides an excellent discussion of the issues of sovereignty, jurisdiction, and self-regulation in validating the Gitksan and Wet'suwet'en claim to their traditional lands. The author states that the tribes were asking for nothing less than aboriginal sovereignty, a status that had been denied them by both the British and Canadian governments. The claims by the Gitksan and Wet'suwet'en forced the courts to take a stand on aboriginal title and raised fundamental questions of rights of ownership, use, conservation, and the management of land and natural resources. In this legal battle, the primary question, as expressed by the Gitksan and Wet'suwet'en people, is what is recognized as legitimate history. "Whose memories become history?" As Chief Justice Antonio Lamer stated, "the ruling requires the courts to come to terms with the oral histories of aboriginal societies, which for many aboriginal nations, are the only record of their past."

3

Recent United Nations Initiatives Concerning the Rights of Indigenous Peoples

Stephen V. Quesenberry

 RECENT DEVELOPMENTS[1] WITHIN THE UNITED NATIONS (U.N.) and its subsidiary bodies present opportunities for an unprecedented dialogue on the relationship between States[2] and indigenous peoples and the rights of these peoples under international law. These opportunities may not be pressed to fullest advantage in the United States, however, because knowledge of the United Nations' work on indigenous rights is not widespread among Native American communities, nor is the United Nations generally viewed as a forum to which they may bring their concerns.[3] Indeed, it would be rare for Native American tribes, whose attention is increasingly focused on congressional actions that threaten their political and economic survival, to divert limited resources from domestic issues to the international dialogue on the rights of indigenous peoples. Nevertheless, it is at the international level and within the United Nations that the best hope for long-term protection of indigenous peoples may lie.

The first section examines the recent U.N. initiatives on the rights of indigenous peoples and their relevance to the situation of Native American tribes. The second section offers strategies for broader and more active tribal participation in these international standard-setting processes. A basic premise of the following discussion is that efforts to achieve progressive change in United States Indian law and policy can be strengthened and promoted by the increased participation of Native American tribes and organizations at the United Nations.

UNITED NATIONS INITIATIVES CONCERNING INDIGENOUS PEOPLES

By resolution 48/163 of December 21, 1993, the General Assembly of the

Stephen V. Quesenberry is a lawyer and the director of litigation of California Indian Legal Services, a statewide nonprofit corporation organized to provide legal representation to low income individuals regarding issues of federal Indian law. Quesenberry also has been active in advocacy efforts for the international protection of human rights, especially the rights of indigenous peoples.

United Nations proclaimed the International Decade of the World's Indigenous People (International Decade), commencing December 10, 1994.[4] The International Decade has both symbolic and practical aspects: symbolic in the sense that it represents a heightened awareness, within the international community, of the rights of indigenous peoples as proper subjects of international law, and practical in the sense that it includes a program of action for achieving specific objectives keyed to an ongoing process of international action on indigenous issues. Indeed, the General Assembly resolution was largely a response to a number of actions taken by U.N. bodies, specialized agencies, nongovernmental organizations (NGOs), and individual indigenous representatives and organizations over the past few years.

During the International Decade, indigenous groups will be targeting specific goals. Foremost among these are General Assembly adoption of an international declaration on the rights of indigenous peoples, the creation of a permanent forum within the United Nations for indigenous peoples, and the convening of a world summit on indigenous peoples. A permanent forum for indigenous peoples is essential to bridge the gap between mere aspirations and the full realization of indigenous rights as concrete, enforceable obligations acknowledged and respected by the international community. The forum must have full participator and representative rights within the United Nations and be invested with sufficient powers to carry out its assigned functions such as overseeing the implementation, in concert with concerned U.N. bodies, of the draft declaration and other international instruments relevant to the lives, rights and affairs of indigenous peoples.

Much of the effort during the International Decade will focus on forging partnerships between indigenous peoples and State governments to achieve the goals and objectives of a comprehensive U.N. program of action for the International Decade.[5] These partnerships, coupled with a sharply defined program of action for the International Decade, are essential to achieving constructive movement on indigenous issues within the International Decade. Thus far, two technical meetings on the planning of the International Decade have been convened in Geneva, the first in July 1994, and the second, July 20–21, 1995, attended by representatives of States and indigenous and nongovernmental organizations. Subsequent to the first technical meeting in 1994, the secretary-general submitted to the General Assembly a preliminary report on a comprehensive program of action for the International Decade.[6] The General Assembly adopted the short-term program for 1995 in its Resolution 49/214 of December 23, 1994. The short-term program, which appears in an annex to the secretary's report, encourages State governments to support the International Decade by contributing to the U.N. Trust Fund for the International Decade, and, in consultation with indigenous people: (1) preparing relevant programs, plans, and reports in relation to the International Decade, (2) seeking means of giving indigenous people greater responsibility for their own affairs and an effective voice in decisions on matters which affect them, and (3) establishing national committees or other mechanisms to ensure that the objectives and activities of the International Decade are planned and implemented on the basis of a full partnership with indigenous people.[7]

Following the July 1995 technical meeting, the General Assembly adopted the comprehensive program of activities for the International Decade in its Resolution 50/157 of December 21, 1995.[8]

The ILO Convention on
Tribal and Indigenous Peoples

In 1989, the International Labor Organization (ILO) adopted the Convention Concerning Indigenous and Tribal Peoples in Independent Countries, Convention No. 169.[9] It updated an earlier ILO convention, No. 107, on the same subject.[10] These conventions are the only international treaties on the recognition and protection of the rights of indigenous peoples. Convention No. 169 has been ratified by ten countries.[11] Neither the United States nor Canada has ratified it.

Convention No. 169 has been heavily criticized by many indigenous groups, their criticism primarily directed at the caveat in Article 1(3) that "[t]he use of the term 'peoples' in this Convention shall not be construed as having any implications as regards the rights which may attach to the term under international law." This language precludes the critical linkage in international law between the term "peoples" and the right of self-determination, a linkage that is essential to full recognition of the legal status of indigenous peoples under international law and the realization of the dual goals of stability and certainty in the evolving relationships between these peoples and State governments. The qualification of the term peoples is thus viewed by these indigenous groups as undermining the major goals of the convention.

While Convention No. 169 is by no means a perfect statement of the aspirations of indigenous peoples, it does mark a major shift from the earlier assimilationist orientation of Convention No. 107 to a recognition of "the aspirations of these peoples to exercise control over their own institutions, ways of life and economic development and to maintain and develop their identities, languages and religions, within the framework of the States in which they live. . . ."[12] Rather than dwell too long on the limitations of the convention, it seems more prudent for indigenous representatives to build upon its positive elements, such as the principle of self-identification,[13] in their advocacy for an international declaration on the rights of indigenous peoples and for a U.N. convention on the same subject.

The Draft Declaration on the
Rights of Indigenous Peoples

Within the U.N. human rights bodies, the Working Group on Indigenous Populations (WGIP), created by the Sub-Commission on the Prevention of Discrimination and the Protection of Minorities, has been the main forum for participation at the international level by indigenous peoples. The WGIP is open to all representatives of indigenous peoples and their communities and organizations.

The openness of its sessions, which includes the participation of representatives of governments, NGOs, and U.N. agencies, has strengthened its position as a focal point of international action on indigenous issues. The WGIP is today one of the largest U.N. forums in the field of human rights. One of the most significant accomplishments of the WGIP is its completion, after years of intensive discussion, of a draft declaration on the rights of indigenous peoples.

As part of an international standard-setting process, the draft declaration is, literally, law in the making. Review of the draft declaration has been guided by General Assembly Resolution 41/120 (December 4, 1986) entitled, "Setting international standards in the field of human rights," which set guidelines for the development of international legal instruments dealing with human rights.[14] Among these is the requirement that the instrument "[b]e consistent with the existing body of international human rights law." In addition, the draft declaration "identifies new rights in response to the particular situations of indigenous peoples."[15] Thus, the draft declaration reflects both existing and evolving standards of international human rights law in the specific context of indigenous peoples. And, as has been the case with other U.N. declarations, it will provide the legal basis and political momentum for the eventual adoption of a U.N. convention on indigenous peoples.

The draft declaration is divided into eight parts: I—general principles; II—life, integrity, and security; III—cultural, religious, and linguistic identity; IV—education and public information; V—economic and social rights; VI—land and resources; VII—indigenous institutions; and VIII—implementation. It is a comprehensive document that builds on the existing body of international law and also identifies new rights in response to the particular situations of indigenous peoples. For these reasons, the document should be of particular interest to tribal and indigenous peoples in countries where laws provide limited or no protection for indigenous rights, including rights to land, culture, language, and self-determination. Even in countries where some protections are provided, for example in the United States, there is widespread dissatisfaction with the pace and quality of implementation of these rights by government agencies and officials.

One of the issues that is likely to remain a major part of the agenda of the new intersessional working group created by the Commission on Human Rights to review the draft declaration is whether a definition of *indigenous peoples* should be included in the draft.[16] Leaving the term undefined has raised a number of State concerns, among them the political implications of the linkage in international law between the term *peoples* and the principle of self-determination.[17] If the determination of indigenous status is solely a matter of self-identification, some States argue that any stateless group, including ethnic and national minorities, would be in a position to claim such status and with it, the right to self-determination.[18] Indigenous representatives, on the other hand, argue that the definition is a concern of the indigenous themselves and should not be subject to a State's concept of which groups or persons are included in the term. Indeed, Article 8 of the draft declaration confirms "the right [of indigenous peoples] to identify themselves as indigenous and to be recognized as such."[19]

In a seminal 1971 United Nations study of discrimination against indigenous populations conducted by Jose Martinez Cobo, the right of self-identification was tied to specific criteria.[20] Cobo's definition, while useful, is not entirely satisfactory. Then again, there is no need to rush to definition where "no simple formula will be completely adequate to capture all the manifestations of complex phenomena, particularly in dynamic, changing contexts."[21] But definitions determine rights, and to that extent it is not unreasonable for States to insist that agreement be reached on at least some basic criteria of "indigenousness." However difficult that task may be, it cannot be ignored and will undoubtedly be an issue when the intersessional working group convenes in Geneva this November.

The draft declaration prepared by the WGIP was adopted by the sub-commission on August 26, 1994, by Resolution 1994/45[22] and forwarded to the full commission for review.

Creation of the Intersessional Working Group on the Draft Declaration

Instead of adopting the draft declaration on the rights of indigenous peoples as recommended by the sub-commission, the Commission on Human Rights decided to establish its own intersessional working group to prepare another draft, taking into consideration the WGIP draft.[23] While the adoption of a draft U.N. declaration on the rights of indigenous peoples remains on the commission's human rights agenda, indigenous organizations are understandably concerned that their draft of the declaration, which was the subject of years of intense discussion and clarification, may be rewritten or revised by the intersessional working group in ways that would substantially reduce its intended scope and protections.

Over the years, the sessions of the WGIP have been the most informal and open sessions within the U.N. system. Participation by indigenous organizations regardless of official NGO status under Economic and Social Council (ECOSOC) Resolution No. 1296 (XLIV) was encouraged and welcomed. This policy ensured that interested indigenous individuals and organizations would have a direct voice in the discussions and drafting of the declaration. Because of this unprecedented participation, there is a sense of ownership of the draft declaration among these organizations. It is a product of their efforts, achieved with input from, but not directed by, State governments.

Indigenous groups initially feared that the new intersessional working group, whose procedures for participation[24] are more formal and potentially restrictive than those of the WGIP, might diminish the influence and control that indigenous peoples have thus far exercised over the development of the draft declaration. To address these concerns, the commission invited applications to participate in the intersessional working group by national indigenous organizations "not in consultative status with the ECOSOC." The ECOSOC Committee on Non-Governmental Organizations (NGO Committee) reviews the applications and any other relevant information, "including any views received from the States concerned." There was some concern that this opportunity for State review and comment might ultimately limit the participation by grassroots national indigenous organizations, especially those that have been most aggressive in their advocacy and criticism of State indigenous law and policy. These fears have not been borne out.

At the 1995 session of the intersessional working group, ninety-nine organizations of indigenous people applied for accreditation. Of these, seventy-eight organizations were approved and representatives of thirty-four actually attended the session.[25] During the 1996 session, forty-seven indigenous organizations accredited in accordance with Commission Resolution 1995/32 attended the intersessional working group.[26] While it appears that the accreditation process has not posed a significant obstacle to broad participation by indigenous groups, some have voiced concerns that the process needs to be further expedited to ensure that all applications are considered and acted upon by the time the session for which accreditation is sought commences.

The Study of Treaties, Agreements, and Other Constructive Arrangements between States and Indigenous Populations

In 1988, on the recommendation of the Commission on Human Rights, ECOSOC appointed Miguel Alfonso Martinez, an independent expert from Cuba and member of the United Nations Sub-Commission on the Prevention of Discrimination and the Protection of Minorities, special rapporteur to the sub-commission,[27] with the mandate[28] to prepare a study of treaties, agreements, and other constructive arrangements between States and indigenous populations.[29] The purposes of the study are set forth in the Commission on Human Rights Resolution 1988/56 of March 9, 1988, and, as explained by the Special Rapporteur, its "ultimate purpose" is:

> . . . to offer elements concerning the achievement, on a practical level, of the maximum promotion and protection possible, both in domestic and international law, of the rights of indigenous populations and especially of their human rights and fundamental freedoms.[30]

The study will provide a valuable source of information on treaties and other legal instruments used by States and indigenous peoples in the historical course of their dealings.

Divided generally into three parts, the study will (1) analyze "the origins of the practice of concluding treaties, agreements, and other constructive arrangements between indigenous populations and States"; (2) evaluate "the contemporary significance of those legal instruments"; and (3) consider "the potential value of [the instruments] as elements for the regulation of the future relationships between indigenous populations and States."[31] It will also provide an important analysis of State compliance with and implementation of these agreements. Ultimately, in addition to its relevance to the international standard-setting process, the study should provide the basis for States, in consultation with indigenous peoples, to consider possible constitutional, legislative, and administrative measures to address indigenous concerns, especially self-determination issues, within the State-indigenous relationship; and to determine the relevance of early treaties and other instruments to contemporary indigenous issues.

Early in the study process, the special rapporteur prepared a comprehensive questionnaire for the study, which was widely circulated to States and indigenous groups and organizations during 1991 and 1992. The questionnaire contains separate sets of questions for State governments and indigenous groups and organizations. It seeks information on the current status of any treaties, agreements, or constructive arrangements between States and indigenous peoples, also focusing on their purposes, the circumstances of their negotiation, their substantive provisions, any administrative and judicial interpretations, and their implementation (or lack thereof). Importantly, the questionnaire solicits specific recommendations regarding the future role of these treaties and other instruments.

The number of responses to the questionnaire from both States and indigenous groups has been disappointing, though the special rapporteur has supplemented this information with research and site visits to some of the countries with substantial indigenous populations, including the United States. Oral and written testimony gathered through meetings, hearings, and personal interviews also have been incorporated into the preliminary reports.[32]

The special rapporteur has submitted three progress reports on the study to the sub-commission, the most recent at the August 1996 session of the group.[33] These reports have been generally well received by both State governments and indigenous groups; however budgetary constraints have imposed practical limitations on the study. Because there is no travel budget for the special rapporteur, he has had to rely on the financial support of indigenous NGOs for travel expenses to conduct field research and site visits.

It was originally anticipated that the study would be completed and a final report submitted to the sub-commission in 1995. However, health problems of the special rapporteur and the study's limited budget have delayed his work. The new completion date for the study is 1997.

STRATEGIES FOR INCREASED INVOLVEMENT BY INDIGENOUS GROUPS IN THE WORK OF THE UNITED NATIONS AND ITS BODIES

Before discussing strategies for supporting the initiatives discussed above, it is worth considering why Indian tribes in the United States should participate in the development of international standards for protection of the rights of indigenous peoples.[34] There are a number of compelling reasons.

First, with regard to the draft declaration, this is a document that will establish key international standards for the recognition[35] and protection of the rights of indigenous peoples. These international standards, even if not accepted by a particular State through adoption or ratification, exert considerable pressure on State policy, articulated through State legislative or executive actions and implemented by the State's courts. In addition, some standards are already part of international treaty law or are considered evolving standards of international common law.

Second, the more active and vocal the indigenous participation at the international level, the more likely it is that a State will acknowledge and respond to legitimate indigenous concerns. It can be politically embarrassing for a State to be brought to task in an international forum by indigenous groups alleging violations of human rights. This is as it should be. States should not be immune from criticism in international fora when human rights, including rights of indigenous peoples, are at stake.

Third, many tribal and indigenous groups in the United States and elsewhere have reached an impasse in their relationships with national governments, thus restricting significant movement on indigenous concerns at the domestic level. The recent congressional recommendations to cut back Bureau of Indian Affairs' and tribal priority funding, to tax selected Indian economic enterprises, and to waive the immunities of Indian tribes are evidence of this. In the face of such regressive domestic measures, which undermine the economic basis for tribal self-governance and self-determination, Indian tribes should consider whether, in addition to any domestic remedies, the human rights activities of the United Nations provide an alternative for addressing their concerns. Moreover, by pressing for international consensus on standards for the protection of indigenous rights as human rights, including the right to development, Indian tribes can elevate and broaden the discussion, removing it from the constraints of domestic law and policy. An international dialogue increases the base of participation, both as to States and indigenous groups, making it less likely that one powerful State or group of States will be able to dictate the agenda. Progress at the international level on indigenous issues and concerns, therefore, can create political momentum and pressure for similar progress at the domestic level.

Fourth, the draft declaration contains legal standards that extend beyond the protections afforded specific areas of indigenous concern under the laws of the United States and elsewhere. As the chairperson of the WGIP pointed out, the draft declaration includes new rights developed in response to the demands of particular situations.[36] Indigenous rights, like human rights in general, are not static, wooden things. They are evolving, vital, and influenced by many different political, social, economic, and judicial currents in the stream of human development.

Finally, the work of the United Nations on indigenous issues is especially important because its scope is global. We live in a shrinking world whose farthest reaches are brought into our personal and vicarious experiences through major technological advances. What happens in Chechnya reverberates on Indian reservations in South Dakota. The historical experiences of Native Americans, steeped in the blood of gross violations of human rights, have their modern-day counterparts in Colombia, El Salvador, Bosnia, Chechnya, Rwanda, South Africa, and other countries. The difference is that technology's global window has made it increasingly difficult for States to hide these violations or escape international condemnation. In this atmosphere of international scrutiny, as we view our not-so-distant neighbors through the "windows" of our global village, the possibility of consensus on human rights standards that could only be dreamed of in the past is now within reach. Yet this unprecedented potential will remain unfulfilled unless peoples throughout the world, especially indigenous peoples, demand that States adhere to basic standards for the protection of human rights as a matter of international law, the law of the global village. This is where the United Nations plays a critical role. It is the forum in which this process, this dialogue, can and should occur.

Strategies for Increasing the Extent and Effectiveness of Participation by Indian Tribes in the Development of International Standards for Protection of the Rights of Indigenous Peoples

Thus far, Native American participation at the United Nations, especially at the WGIP, has been primarily through a handful of United States-based indigenous NGOs. With the completion of the draft declaration and its acceptance by the subcommission, there is a need for broader-based support. This broader base means Indian tribes and indigenous organizations, including national Indian organizations such as the National Tribal Chairmen's Association, the National Congress of American Indians,[37] and the American Association on Indian Affairs. Their active involvement in the International Decade of Indigenous People, especially in the development of a United States plan for the Decade, is critical to achieving the overall goals of the decade.

The counterpart to indigenous participation in the International Decade, and to indigenous efforts seeking international consensus on standards governing the rights of indigenous peoples, is the participation of States. The U.N. comprehensive program for the Decade envisions this participation as a partnership between States and indigenous peoples and organizations for the purpose of planning and implementing the activities of the decade. For Indian tribes and national Indian organizations in the United States, this means a partnership with the United States government. Such a proactive role for the United States, however, seems problematic unless the tribes demand it and demonstrate that both domestic and international interests will be well served by an active United States role.[38] Certainly one of the strongest incentives for United States participation will be a strong showing of broad-based and active support for the decade by Indian tribes, national Indian organizations, and United States-based indigenous NGOs.

The following are suggested strategies for increasing the participation by indigenous groups and organizations in the United Nations activities relating to the rights of indigenous peoples, with special attention to the International Decade of Indigenous People:

> 1. Identify existing networks of those indigenous and nonindigenous groups involved in the U.N.–sponsored work on indigenous issues. Use these networks, or create new networks, as mechanisms for obtaining and exchanging information and for participating in the international standard-setting processes of the United Nations.

Indigenous NGOs based in the United States are a logical starting point, followed by nonindigenous NGOs that have demonstrated their support on indigenous issues. The network of indigenous organizations outside the United States is rapidly expanding, although only a handful of NGOs worldwide have ECOSOC consultative status.

> 2. Identify resources to support effective participation at relevant sessions of U.N. bodies in New York and Geneva. For example, using the NGO network mentioned above, identify: (a) lawyers, law professors, and students who are familiar with the United Nations and its work on indigenous issues and who would be willing to assist in a paid or volunteer capacity; and (b) funding for travel and projects related to the International Decade of Indigenous People. Two potential sources of funding are the United Nations Voluntary Fund for Indigenous Populations[40] and the Voluntary Fund for the International Decade.[41]

> 3. Request that the United States government take steps to implement the domestic components of the United Nations' comprehensive program of action for the International Decade.[42] Specific steps should include the formation and funding of a national commission composed of indigenous and United States–government representatives who would develop a United States–specific action plan for the decade. This plan would complement the international action plan and also provide a national forum for indigenous groups to raise issues relating to the development of international standards on indigenous peoples and how that process should influence United States Indian policy.

> 4. In conjunction with the formation of a national commission for the Decade, establish a clearinghouse on international indigenous issues that would be responsible for compiling and disseminating materials on the decade, especially documents relating to international and domestic standard setting on the rights of indigenous peoples. The clearinghouse could either become part of the activities of the national commission or could be housed within one of the United States-based indigenous NGOs or national Indian organizations. Since both options would require fund-

ing, the United States should be asked to provide all or part of the funds as a demonstration of its commitment to the goals of the decade.

5. Support the work and recommendations of the special rapporteur on the treaty study, whose final report is due this year. The study provides Indian tribes a unique opportunity to present, through an international study, an account of their historical dealings with the United States as confirmed in treaties and other legal instruments.[43]

6. Apply to the Office of the Coordinator for the International Decade, U.N. Centre for Human Rights, for certification to participate in the sessions of the Commission on Human Rights' intersessional working group on the elaboration of a draft declaration on the rights of indigenous peoples. The intersessional working group meets each year in Geneva. Its next session has been scheduled for October 27–November 7, 1997.[44]

Resolution 1995/32 of the Commission on Human Rights outlines the process for participation in the intersessional working group. In the resolution, the Commission speaks of the "participation of other relevant organizations of indigenous people, in addition to non-governmental organizations in consultative status with the Economic and Social Council." Because Indian tribes are vested with the inherent powers of a sovereign, there could be some question as to whether the phrase "organizations of indigenous people" is meant to include tribal governments. Presumably, an indigenous governmental *organization* would be eligible to apply. Indian tribes, however, are not mere governmental organizations. They are the government itself. This ambiguity in the accreditation appears to have been resolved by a liberal construction and application of the term *organization*. At least one North American Indian tribal government has been accredited under the procedures outlined in Resolution 1995/32.[45]

Applications should be sent to the Council Committee on Non-Governmental Organizations for review and consultation with the State concerned (the United States).[46]

CONCLUSION

International discussion of human rights issues has increasingly focused on the nature and content of the rights of indigenous peoples. In every part of the world there are peoples who identify themselves as tribal or indigenous and who seek the right to self-determination. Most of these movements and struggles for self-determination are centuries old, are rooted in past injustices, and find expression in terms, such as *cultural integrity* and *autonomy*. Ultimately, they reflect varying degrees of the indigenous peoples separation in status, in both a political and territorial sense, from that of the State. The struggles of these peoples, expressed in contemporary terms through the human rights mechanisms of the United Nations and other international bodies have, at long last, resulted in their aspirations being moved to the forefront of the international human rights agenda.

This increased international dialogue on indigenous issues, however, has not been free of conflict. Some States have expressed the fear that nascent indigenous nationalism threatens the integrity of States and have raised questions concerning the definition and rights of indigenous peoples, especially the right to self-determination. Others contend that the relationship between States and indigenous peoples within their territories is a matter of domestic, rather than international, concern. Still, in spite of this resistance, the number of States participating in the international dialogue is increasing, and the potential for progressive changes in the relationship of States and indigenous peoples seems greater than ever. But there is still much work to be done, and the momentum created by the recent completion of a draft declaration on the rights of indigenous peoples must be sustained by broad, active participation from indigenous peoples and organizations in the continuing review of the draft by the United Nations Commission on Human Rights.

Indian tribes and national Indian organizations in the United States can and should participate actively in these international activities. Their participation is especially important in the review of the draft declaration, the completion of the U.N. Treaty Study, and the development of a United States plan to implement the U.N. program of action for the International Decade of the Worlds Indigenous People. It is only through such participation that the aspirations of the tribal and indigenous peoples of the United States and elsewhere may eventually be translated into the concrete reality of international legal standards for the protection of their rights. United States–based indigenous NGOs and representatives have played a key historical role in pressing for and achieving major changes in the way that the United Nations and its constituent State members deal with indigenous peoples. It is now time for Indian tribes and national Indian organizations to participate more directly and actively, both in the international dialogue on indigenous rights and in the domestic dialogue with the United States government regarding the content of these rights and their implementation within the United States political and legal systems.

Notes

1. This article was originally written in October 1995. In the intervening two years, the work of the United Nations and indigenous peoples has progressed on a number of fronts, though more slowly than hoped for, especially with respect to efforts to reach accord on the basic text of the Draft Declaration on the Rights of Indigenous Peoples. Where practical, the author has attempted to update the original text to include more

recent developments.

2. The term *States*, as used in this paper, means the sovereign nations that are members of the United Nations, not their constituent units. The term does not refer to states such as California, Arizona, or Nevada, of which United States of America is composed.

3. This is not to say that Indian organizations in the United States are unaware of the United Nations' activities with respect to tribal and indigenous peoples. In December 1993, the National Congress of American Indians (NCAI) adopted Resolution NV-93-11, a Resolution to Support and Promote the Adoption of the Draft U.N. Declaration on the Rights of Indigenous Peoples.

4. G.A. Res. 163, U.N. GAOR, 48th Sess., Supp. No. 49, A/48/49 (Vol. I), at 281 (1994).

5. In Resolution 49/214 (December 23, 1994), the General Assembly established the operational focus of the decade as "Indigenous people: partnership in action." G.A. Res. 214, U.N. GAOR, 49th Sess., Supp. No. 49, A/49/49 (Vol. I), at 237 (1995).

6. U.N.Doc. A/49/444 (September 28, 1994).

7. Ibid., note 5, at 239,19.

8. G.A. Res. 157, U.N. GAOR, 50th Sess., Supp. No. 49, at 219, U.N. Doc. A/50/49 (1996).

9. ILO, *Official Bulletin*, vol. LXXII, 1989, Ser. A., no. 2, p. 63; entry into force: September 5, 1991.

10. Convention No. 107 (1957), Convention Concerning the Protection and Integration of Indigenous and Other Tribal and Semi-Tribal Populations in Independent Countries. This convention remains in force for those States that have ratified it but have not ratified the revising convention, Convention No. 169.

11. Bolivia, Colombia, Costa Rica, Denmark, Guatemala, Honduras, Mexico, Norway, Paraguay, and Peru. The convention entered into force on 5 September 1991. (*Found at* URL=http://ilolex.ilo.ch:1567/public/50normes/ilolex/sqcgi/query, *visited on*19 August 1997.)

12. Preamble to Convention No. 169.

13. Article 1(2) of Convention 169 states that the principle of self-identification is "a fundamental criterion for determining the groups to which the provisions of this Convention apply. . . ."

14. G.A. Res. 120, U.N. GAOR, 41st Sess., Supp. 53, A/41/53, at 178 (1987).

15. Statement of Madame Erica-Irene A. Daes, Chairperson of the WGIP. Technical review of the United Nations draft declaration on the rights of indigenous peoples, U.N. Doc. E/CN.4/Sub.2/1994/2 (April 5, 1994).

16. This issue also has been raised in preliminary discussions on the establishment of a permanent forum on indigenous peoples within the United Nations. A workshop on this issue was held on 26–28 June 1995, in Copenhagen, Denmark, in which representatives from both State governments and indigenous groups participated. The report of the workshop reflects the concern of some participants that "in the absence of a universally applicable definition, discussions on a possible permanent forum would be impossible." U.N. Doc. E/CN.4/Sub.2/AC.4/1995/7, at 4, 10 (July 12, 1995). The Commission on Human Rights has requested that the High Commissioner, Center for Human Rights, convene a second workshop prior to the 1997 session of the WGIP, drawing upon the results of the Copenhagen workshop. See Resolution 1997/30, *found at* URL=http://193.135.156.15/html/menu4/chrres/1997.res/30.htm, *visited on* 19 August 1997.

17. Articles 1(2) and 55 of the U.N. Charter refer to "the principle of equal rights and

self-determination of peoples." Common Articles 1(1) of the 1966 International Covenants on Civil and Political Rights, and on Economic, Social and Cultural Rights include the statement: "indigenous peoples have the right of self-determination. By virtue of that right they freely determine their political status and freely pursue their economic, social and cultural development."

18. One article concludes that the content of the right to self-determination for indigenous peoples is equated "with . . . 'internal' self-determination in contradistinction to 'external' self-determination," which may only come into play if representative government fails. Brolman and Zieck, "Some Remarks on the Draft Declaration on the Rights of Indigenous Peoples," *Leiden Journal of Internatal Law* 8 (1995):103, 107–08. The authors criticize the draft because it does not completely renounce the possibility of external self-determination, which includes the right to secession under certain circumstances, and because the right of internal self-determination, as stated therein, implies a right to autonomy that sets up a competing nationalism within the boundaries of the State. Ibid., at 111.

19. This "absolutist concept" of the right to self-identification may "stretch the concept of 'indigenousness' beyond credulity, and increase the level of state resistance to the recognition of indigenous rights and status under international law." Corntassel and Hopkins Primeau, "Indigenous 'Sovereignty' and International Law: Revised Strategies for Pursuing 'Self-Determination'," *International Human Rights Quarterly* 17 (1995): 343, 365.

20. In his 1971 study, Cobo provided the following definition of *indigenous peoples*: "Indigenous communities, peoples and nations are those which, having a historical continuity with pre-invasion and pre-colonial societies that developed on their territories, consider themselves distinct from other sectors of the societies now prevailing in those territories. They form at present non-dominant sectors of society and are determined to preserve, develop and transmit to future generations their ancestral territories, and their ethnic identity, as the basis of their continued existence as peoples, in accordance with their own cultural patterns, social institutions and legal systems." See technical review of the United Nations draft declaration on the rights of indigenous peoples, U.N. Doc. E/CN.4/Sub.2/1994/2, at 3, 10 (5 April1994).

21. P. Thornberry, Keele University, "Indigenous Peoples: Reflections on Concept and Definition," a paper presented to the Working Group on Indigenous Populations at its 1995 session. Thornberry further reflects that if there is to be a definition, "[t]he identification of a cluster of relevant elements in the concept of indigenous has much to recommend it. It is important not to produce a narrow result and attempt to reduce indigenousness to only one 'supreme' factor." In other words, functionality and flexibility should be the key requirements.

22. U.N. Doc. E/CN.4/1995/2-E/CN.4/Sub.2/1994/56, at 103 (29 October 1994).

23. See Comm. on Human Rts. Res. 1995/32, U.N. ESCOR, 1995, Supp. No. 3, at 110, U.N. Doc. E/1995/23-E/CN.4/1995/176 (3 March1995).

24. Ibid., Annex to Resolution 1995/32 of the Commission on Human Rights.

25. Report of the Working Group established in accordance with Commission on Human Rights Resolution 1995/32 of 3 March 1995, U.N. Doc. E/CN.4/1996/84 (4 January1996).

26. U.N. Doc. E/CN.4/1997/102 (10 December 1996).

27. ECOSOC Resolution 1988/134 (27 May 1988), U.N. ESCOR, 1st Sess. 1988, Supp. No. 1, at 51, U.N. Doc. E/1988/88 (1989).

28. ECOSOC Resolution 1989/77 (24 May 1989), U.N. ESCOR, 1st Sess. 1989,

Supp. No. 1, at 62, U.N. Doc. E/1989/89 (1990).

29. The International Indian Treaty Council, a United States–based indigenous NGO with offices in San Francisco, California, first proposed a treaty study in 1977.

30. Report of the Working Group on Indigenous Populations, Annex III, Outline of the Study on Treaties, Agreements and Other Constructive Arrangements Between States and Indigenous Populations by Special Rapporteur, Miguel Alfonso Martinez. U.N. Doc. E/CN.4/Sub.2/1988/24/Add.1, at 3, 10 (24 August 1988).

31. Ibid., at 6, s 21-23.

32. In September 1994, California Indian Legal Services (CILS) submitted answers to the special rapporteur's questionnaire. In its responses, CILS focused on the eighteen unratified California Indian treaties, highlighting the disastrous effects of the U.S. Senate's refusal to ratify the treaties, including the widespread impoverishment and the near-extermination of California's indigenous peoples. CILS recommended comprehensive remedial measures in the form of legislation to redress the status and funding problems of California's tribes, especially the unacknowledged tribes.

33. U.N. Doc. E/CN.4/Sub.2/1996/23 (15 August 1996).

34. Some Indian tribes from the United States have used the various U.N. human rights fora, including the WGIP and the sub-commission, to raise issues concerning their rights as indigenous peoples. In the sub-commission, this has been done through indigenous NGOs, such as the International Indian Treaty Council, the Indigenous World Association, and the Indian Law Resource Center.

35. The term *recognition* is a misnomer in the sense that indigenous peoples claim they are already separate nations and, as such, always have had the right to self-determination.

36. See above, the text accompanying note 15.

37. At the historic Tribal Leaders Meeting with President Clinton on 29 April 1994, NCAI President Gaiashkibos stressed the need for the United States to embrace a policy of real self-determination for all indigenous peoples and urged the president and the nation to take the lead in ensuring passage of the draft U.N. declaration on the rights of indigenous peoples.

38. On 2 April 1992, the United States Senate ratified the International Covenant on Civil and Political Rights (ICCPR), eighteen years after it was signed by President Jimmy Carter. Subsequently, in 1995 the United States presented its initial report on compliance with the ICCPR to the U.N. Human Rights Committee, as required by Article 40 of the ICCPR. This periodic reporting requirement places United States' compliance within the provisions of the ICCPR, including the right of self-determination of peoples (Article 1), under public scrutiny. An active United States' role, in partnership with Indian tribes and Indian organizations, to implement a national plan for the International Decade would be consistent with, and would further implementation of, the United States' obligations under the ICCPR. This kind of partnership can only enhance the United States' international standing on human rights issues.

39. The following indigenous NGOs have ECOSOC consultative status: Aboriginal and Torres Strait Islander Commission (Australia), Grand Council of the Crees (Canada), Indian Council of South America (Peru), Indian Law Resource Center (United States), Indigenous World Association (United States), International Indian Treaty Council (United States), International Organization of Indigenous Resource Development (Canada), National Aboriginal and Islander Legal Service Secretariat (Australia), Sami Council (Finland), and World Council of Indigenous Peoples (Canada). See, List of Indigenous Organizations, U.N. Doc. E/CN.4/Sub.2/AC.4/1994/CRP.1 (1 June 1994),

for a list of over 200 indigenous peoples, nations, and organizations that have participated in some capacity at the United Nations.

40. With financial assistance from the Voluntary Fund on Indigenous Populations, fifty-two indigenous participants were able to attend the July 1995 session of the Working Group on Indigenous Populations in Geneva. Report of the Working Group on Indigenous Populations at its thirteenth session, U.N. Doc. E/CN.4/Sub.2/1995/24, at 11, 30 (10 August 1995).

41. In its Resolution 48/163 of 21 December 1993, the General Assembly authorized the secretary-general to establish a voluntary fund for the International Decade and accept contributions from State governments and other entities. The Voluntary Fund is intended to support projects in all the areas identified in the resolution and is also a "source of funding for consultancies, information activities, publications, meetings and other activities that promote the objective of the Decade." Preliminary report on a comprehensive programme of action for the International Decade of the World's Indigenous People, U.N. Doc. A/49/444, at 14, 56 (28 September 1994).

42. Ibid., at Annex I (Draft programme of activities for the International Decade), Item 6, page 21.

43. With reference to California's unacknowledged tribes, it is hoped that the treaty study will reflect information provided to the special rapporteur on the eighteen treaties negotiated during 1851 and 1852 between the United States and various tribes and bands of California Indians, but subsequently rejected and placed under seal by the United States Senate. Not only are the treaties historical evidence of the government's bad faith, they have particular relevance today. The treaties' unfulfilled promises are the source of continuing problems concerning tribal status, lack of adequate land and housing, and denial of basic health, education and welfare services to many California Indians.

44. Commission on Human Rights Resolution 1997/31, *found at* URL=http://193.135.156.15/html/menu4/chrres/1997.res/31.htm, *visited on* 19 August 1997.

45. The Lummi Indian Business Council is listed as an observer/participant in the inter-sessional working groups report on its 1995 session. U.N. Doc. E/CN.4/1996/84 (January 4, 1996).

46. The procedure for application and the required information to be provided are set forth in the Annex to Resolution 1995/32 of the Commission on Human Rights.

4

Claiming Memory in British Columbia: Aboriginal Rights and The State

Fae L. Korsmo

INTRODUCTION

 WHILE ATTENDING A MEETING of a Saami organization in northern Sweden, I introduced myself to an older fellow during a coffee break. "From America?" he asked and paused. "When do you go back?" I replied that I planned to return in a couple of months. He smiled. "You'll go back," he said, "and we will forget you were ever here." This remark from a Saami who was old enough to remember the era of segregation, the political mobilization of northern Europe's indigenous people, the lawsuits, the endless negotiations and promises of the Swedish government, juxtaposed the ephemeral nature of my visit and the extended encounter of a colonial endeavor. Whose memories would become history? Here I would like to explore the significance of memory in the assertion of Native claims. I turn to Canada, specifically British Columbia, where claims processes have been underway for a long time.

Proving the existence of aboriginal rights in common law requires a reconstruction of a people's past presented in a way that satisfies Western legal traditions. Evidence must be internally consistent, chronological, and documented. Crucial gaps in time or knowledge must be explained. Observers of the trial and readers of the decisions rendered in *Delgamuukw* v. *The Queen*[1] have criticized the process and outcome as expressions of colonialism and ethnocentrism.[2] This essay does not dismiss the criticisms, but analyzes the texts of the decisions issued by the British Columbia Supreme Court and the British Columbia Court of Appeal as representations of the state's concept of itself in opposition to societies claiming to be whole, original, and sovereign.

The European state, while extending its authority to new territories, lost its memory. Colonial officials had no need to justify the intrusions of settlers in terms of who they were or where they came from; they were busy creating facts for future claims. This is an essential feature of colonialism: looking forward to becoming established and creating a mythology binding newcomers to the territory.

Fae L. Korsmo is an associate professor of political science at the University of Alaska, Fairbanks.

The people already living in or near the area have no role in the new myths, except perhaps as enemies or a dying race. They represent a noble yet doomed past that must be prevented from becoming a present-day threat. Insofar as the colonial mythology has put the burden on the indigenous societies to justify their claims in terms of their origins and hardy continuity, the doctrine of aboriginal title is part of colonialism and therefore dooms the indigenous claimants to failure. But there is something else in contemporary aboriginal claims, a reminder to the colonial state of its own homelessness and fragmentation. By demanding a show of coherence and continuity from aboriginal claimants, the state exposes itself to scrutiny. As a result, the claims reveal not only the fissures and discontinuities in the aboriginal society's recollections but also the differences among government officials, settlers, and others whose accounts are taken as evidence. Allowing these differences to surface as contestable claims is part of the postcolonial experience. Yet, as seen in cases such as *Delgamuukw*, the transition from a myth-making colonial state to a postcolonial cacophony of diverse voices is hardly complete.

The legal doctrine of aboriginal title emerged from the contingencies of encounter in the New World. The explorer's and conqueror's calculation of the Native society's relative strength (and other factors such as usefulness and willingness to cooperate) helped to determine whether to leave them alone, establish alliances and joint ventures, or enslave them. The test for proving aboriginal title arose out of these political considerations. Did you resist us? Did you keep your culture intact? Did we recognize your power? Did we keep records of your whereabouts and your battles with neighboring tribes? In other words, did your forms of resistance resemble ours? Were you sufficiently like us to gain our recognition, yet different enough to be kept separate?

The elements of this test require a high degree of self-consciousness possessed by the indigenous society in order to act and respond to intrusions as a social unit, to reciprocate, in other words, the Europeans' recognition. Needless to say, this delicate balance of sameness and difference would be difficult to demonstrate. Indeed, the more statelike the aboriginal claim, involving elements of separate statelike institutions, the less likely the aboriginal claimants are to convince courts of their claim. The less familiar and more "primitive" the claim, such as nonexclusive hunting and fishing rights, the more likely its success.

The Gitksan and Wet'suwet'en claims considered in *Delgamuukw* involved comprehensive ownership and jurisdiction in addition to aboriginal rights, the latter taking a kind of fall-back position should the claims of ownership and jurisdiction fail.[3] While a few commentators see a necessary linkage between the three, it is more common to distinguish between (1) aboriginal title or aboriginal rights, (2) ownership or proprietary rights, and (3) jurisdiction or legal authority over a territory. Thus, *Delgamuukw* presents a single case from which to examine three levels of group autonomy, ranging from a tolerated yet easily extinguished use of resources to a sovereign ability to make and enforce rules regarding the use of resources. Not surprisingly, the trial judge and the majority of the Court of Appeal focused on the aboriginal rights claim and rejected the ownership and jurisdiction claims. An analysis of their opinions in conjunction with the dissents reveals correspondingly divergent images of the state as a rigid, solid frame versus a fluid, protective layer. The major part of this article will consider the three levels of group autonomy, beginning with sovereignty and jurisdiction. But first, let us turn to a brief background of *Delgamuukw*.

BRITISH COLUMBIA AND ABORIGINAL PEOPLES

The first recorded encounter between Europeans and the Native inhabitants of what is now British Columbia occurred in 1774, when a Spanish navigator met a group of Haida on the coast. Four years later, James Cook spent time refitting for his Pacific voyage and trading with the locals at Nootka Sound.[4] The years between this initial contact and the discovery of gold in the Fraser River in 1858 were characterized, according to Robin Fisher, by a fur trade that may have influenced the power relationships among the various aboriginal groups but did not disrupt their ways of life. In fact, the aboriginal groups often controlled the trading relationships with the Americans and Europeans rather than the other way around.[5] Not until 1849, three years after the Oregon Boundary Treaty established the southern border of British control in the western part of North America, did Britain establish a colony, the Colony of Vancouver Island, and put the Hudson's Bay Company in control of it.[6]

The gold rush brought hundreds of fortune seekers to British Columbia. In 1858, the British government responded to the influx of gold seekers by taking over the Hudson's Bay Company's jurisdiction and consolidating Vancouver Island with the mainland to establish the Colony of British Columbia. The governor of the new colony, James Douglas, who had also been the Hudson's Bay Company's chief factor on Vancouver Island, favored white settlement over a transient mining population, and settlement soon followed. Douglas, according to Paul Tennant, actually recognized aboriginal title and, during his tenure with the Hudson's Bay Company, treated with Native groups on Vancouver Island to purchase lands and establish reserves.[7] He arranged no treaties on Vancouver Island after 1854, however, and, on the mainland, he arranged none at all. Instead, he granted small reserves and allowed Native individuals to homestead (or "pre-empt") land in the same way as white settlers could. Tennant claims that Douglas did not continue treatymaking because he envisioned an assimilated aboriginal population who would maintain neither their collective identity nor their lands.[8]

Douglas's successors continued the assimilationist policy with even greater force. In 1866, the British Columbia legislature forbade aboriginal people from pre-empting land without executive permission.[9] In 1871, British Columbia joined the Confederation of Canada as a province. The federal government reserved for itself exclusive jurisdiction over aboriginal peoples. At the time of British Columbia's acceptance into confederation, the federal government of

Canada was busy signing treaties with aboriginal groups west of Ontario (the so-called prairie treaties) and, through the Indian Act, setting up an administration for aboriginal communities.[10] The provincial government of British Columbia resisted federal intrusion and, by and large, maintained that aboriginal title did not exist in the province. In the meantime, aboriginal groups resisted white settlement and brought their land claims to both capitals, Victoria and Ottawa.

Among those who claimed that miners and settlers were intruding upon their aboriginal lands were Gitksan chiefs. The 1984 claim brought by Gisday Wa and Delgam Uukw, on behalf of their houses and other Gitksan and Wet'-suwet'en houses and hereditary chiefs, was a renewal of a one-hundred-year-old effort, although clearcut logging had replaced mining and settlement as the major source of land encroachment. The chiefs brought the claim to court to force the province to recognize title and jurisdiction to territories encompassing about twenty-two thousand square miles on and around the Skeena, Bulkley, and Nechako river systems.[11] The court claim came only after repeated attempts to negotiate failed.

The Gitksan and Wet'suwet'en claim relied on the presentation of evidence that included oral histories, family lineages, songs, and descriptions of the potlatch or feast system of governance. In most Western courts of law, much of this evidence would constitute hearsay, but in the *Delgamuukw* case, it was used (although not entirely accepted, as the next sections will show) to demonstrate the vital and enduring relationship between people and land.

The Gitksan and Wet'suwet'en claimants also tried to demonstrate a continuous presence lasting thousands of years in what is now British Columbia. These two groups, among the thirty or more ethnolinguistic aboriginal groups in the area now covered by the province, had established complex trade relationships along the coast and inland long before their involvement in the Hudson's Bay Company fur trade. Their economy evolved from hunting, trapping, fishing, and gathering to a mixed economy that incorporated wage labor in the fishing, transportation, and lumber industries. Throughout the many economic changes, the people retained their social structures, including the clans, the houses within clans, crests, songs, and, of course, the feast, also known as the potlatch.[12]

A good deal of the evidence, in other words, consisted of collective memories, both recent and ancient, the pieces of which struck the trial judge, Chief Justice Allan McEachern, as confusing or questionable.[13] Some of the stories were not consistent with others. Some were incomplete or without reference to specific dates. Many did not establish specific land uses attaching to specific areas of land. Indeed, the words of the chief justice give the impression he is trying—not always successfully—to establish definite references in time and space. And this is not a comfortable position. When one is afloat, one is easily deceived. The fluid state has no center.

The following three sections treat the claims to sovereignty and jurisdiction, property, and aboriginal rights.

SOVEREIGNTY, JURISDICTION, AND SELF-REGULATION

Unlike other claimants of aboriginal title, the Gitksan and Wet'suwet'en chiefs who filed suit on behalf of their houses and members of their houses also asserted rights of authority over the territory, such as the right to prevent settlement and resource use by outsiders. The chiefs described a complex, multifaceted feast system as evidence of internal governance.[14] But Chief Justice McEachern was not satisfied that the feast was used as a "legislative institution" with regard to the administration and regulation of territory.[15] He found inconsistent practices respecting internal boundaries and remained unconvinced that the Gitksan and Wet'suet'en had a land law system consisting of legislative and enforcement mechanisms.[16] The rules and norms described by the plaintiffs as "law" seemed to McEachern "a most uncertain and highly flexible set of customs which are frequently not followed by the Indians themselves."[17]

The chief justice suspected the plaintiffs' attorney of trying to manufacture a system of governance out of the "undefined, unspecific forms of government which the chiefs are just beginning to think about."[18] As to the alleged self-governing rights of the Gitksan and Wet'suwet'en peoples that would prevail against the province if a conflict arose between aboriginal and provincial law, McEachern pronounced this a "new theory of government."[19]

In sum, the chief justice did not find that either the plaintiffs or their ancestors governed the territory according to their own legal system. In fact, prior to the assertion of British sovereignty in the nineteenth century, the chief justice concluded, the Gitksan and Wet'suwet'en people had little need for laws of general application. Individuals may have followed local customs at their convenience, but this could not be called obedience to the law.[20]

The Court of Appeal upheld Chief Justice McEachern's conclusion with regard to jurisdiction. Both McEachern and the Court of Appeal majority (Macfarlane, Taggart, Wallace) interpreted the jurisdiction claim as a broad claim to sovereignty that would, if recognized, establish a third order of government and limit provincial and federal jurisdiction. The doctrine of tribal sovereignty in the United States, it was emphasized, does not exist in Canada. Instead, Canada was established on the principle of Crown (or parliamentary) sovereignty and, with confederation, a division of powers between the federal and provincial levels.[21]

In Chief Justice McEachern's and the Court of Appeal's assessment, the Gitksan and Wet'suwet'en plaintiffs were asking for no less than aboriginal sovereignty: the authority to legislate and execute laws in their territories and to resist the enforcement of provincial law. Dissenting opinions by Court of Appeals judges Lambert and Hutcheon, however, did not consider the plaintiffs' claim to jurisdiction as a claim to sovereignty. Rather, they were seeking recognition of the right to exercise control over their community, land, and institutions, regulating internal relationships in accordance with their own customs and traditions. This right to "self-government" or "self-regulation" rested on flexible customs, traditions, and practices that may appear to contain inconsistencies to outsiders, but certainly the common law provides plenty of inconsistencies as well. In other words, the dissenting judges saw the jurisdiction claim as naturally connected with the aboriginal title claim, stemming from aboriginal customs, traditions, and practices, and giving the Native societies the requisite power to continue to develop their culture, society, and economy unhindered by logging, mining, or other ventures by nonaboriginal companies. As such, the right to self-regulation can be seen as an existing right protected by Section 35 of the Constitution Act, 1982.[22]

Aboriginal sovereignty carries with it the notion of absolute authority as well as the executive and legislative functions of the British and Canadian governments. By defining jurisdiction as absolute authority, the courts deny the legality of aboriginal self-government and leave any kind of concurrent powers to be decided through negotiations with the very governments whose standards the aboriginal institutions fail to meet. Aboriginal societies do not resemble the Western state as solidified in a constitutional frame and therefore cannot enjoy any separate authority. Yet there is no room for them within that frame.

Only in the dissent do we see a different kind of state, one that admits of failure and nonawareness, where the common law is "not well or universally understood."[23] Just as a multiethnic, dispersed population living across a vast territory requires laws of general application to maintain a social unit, the customs, traditions, and practices of a small aboriginal society may demand a high degree of flexibility to cope with diminished or threatened resources. If evidence of inconsistencies can be found, then this evidence itself could be taken as an indication of aboriginal law.[24] Rule creation is part of social formation, then; violations of the rules indicate the rules' existence rather than their absence.

But, one may argue, someone in the group must recognize the violations and be able to meet them with sanctions. Following the logic of the dissent, perhaps the violations were needed due to exigencies recognized within the culture, or perhaps a deeper, primary rule prevailed, such as individual autonomy.[25] In any case, the aboriginal conception of rules is not required to fit the state's prevailing definition, for the state itself is transformed and deepened by admitting alternate systems.

Much has been said about different forms of resistance among minorities and marginalized peoples.[26] But in *Delgamuukw*, it is the state that resists cooptation of its narrative by a minority group that wishes to erode the state's power to define itself. The claim of ownership and jurisdiction bears a disquieting resemblance to the feudal unity of sovereignty and property, a combination often claimed by a colonial state.[27]

PROPERTY, OWNERSHIP, EXCLUSIVITY

The ownership claim of the Gitksan and Wet'suwet'en plaintiffs invited the courts to take a stand on aboriginal title. Was it equivalent to a proprietary interest in land, or was it merely a personal right of use that depended for its origins and maintenance on the good will of the sovereign? Chief Justice McEachern accepted the authority of *St. Catherine's Milling & Lumber Co.* v. *The Queen*,[28] and found that aboriginal rights are nonproprietary rights of occupation for residence and aboriginal use and that they can be extinguished at the pleasure of the sovereign.[29] A proprietary interest, on the other hand, would confer on the owners a right to use the land as they see fit, even though the Crown might hold the underlying or radical title. The Supreme Court of Canada in *Guerin v. The Queen*, found a middle ground between personal usufruct and beneficial ownership as follows:

> Indians have a legal right to occupy and possess certain lands, the ultimate title to which is in the Crown. While their interest does not, strictly speaking, amount to beneficial ownership, neither is its nature completely exhausted by the concept of a personal right. It is true that the sui generis interest which the Indians have in the land is personal in the sense that it cannot be transferred to a grantee, but it is also true . . . that the interest gives rise upon surrender to a distinctive fiduciary obligation on the part of the Crown to deal with the land for the benefit of the surrendering Indians.[30]

In other words, aboriginal title differs from property rights by the inability to sell or transfer, yet because the Crown has the unique ability to alienate Native lands, it takes on a special duty to consider aboriginal interests.31 In addition, as will be discussed below, aboriginal title confers limited rights based on the historical patterns of use and occupation unique to the aboriginal culture.

The plaintiffs in *Delgamuukw* accordingly went beyond the strictures of aboriginal title and asked for a declaration that their rights of ownership included the right to use, harvest, manage, conserve, and transfer the lands and natural resources within the claimed territory. In response, Chief Justice McEachern differentiated between use (e.g., hunting and fishing) and settlement (permanent or semipermanent dwellings) and between exclusive and enforceable rights of possession and shared or noncontested use-rights.[32] For the Gitksan and Wet'-suwet'en to show proprietary interests, they had to demonstrate exclusive possession and continuous dwelling, both of which would be defended against outsiders. The chief justice found that, apart from the village sites, the plaintiffs or their ancestors did not possess other parts of the claimed territory. Since the British Columbia government included village sites within reserves and those reserves were regulated by statute, the court did not touch on the legal status of village sites. Instead, McEachern and the Court of Appeal focused on the claims for territory lying outside the village dwellings. Did plaintiffs occupy these areas to the exclusion of others? Did they establish and recognize boundaries?

According to McEachern and the Court of Appeal majority, the plaintiffs failed to establish exclusive possession and failed to provide agreement on the boundaries between the territories allegedly belonging to individual houses. There were two major reasons for the failure of the ownership claim. First, contradictory evidence did not persuade the courts of recognized boundaries between house territories. If the houses did not recognize one another's claims, how then could the state be expected to recognize the sum of their claims? Second, McEachern did not find evidence of *exclusive* use and occupation *prior* to the assertion of British sovereignty. He found that

> at the date of British sovereignty the plaintiffs' ancestors were living in their villages on the great rivers in a form of communal society, occupying or using fishing sites and adjacent lands as their ancestors had done for the purpose of hunting and gathering whatever they required for sustenance. They governed themselves in their villages and immediately surrounding areas to the extent necessary for communal living, but it cannot be said that they owned or governed such vast and almost inaccessible tracts of land in any sense that would be recognized by the law.[33]

To put it another way, wrote McEachern, other groups of people could have settled near the villages, and no Gitksan or Wet'suwet'en law would have challenged their settlement.[34] The occupation was nonexclusive, unenforceable, and unrecognized. It was incidental to the search for food, a product of survival rather than ritual. It could not be called ownership.

Dissenting judges Lambert and Hutcheon disagreed with the stark distinction between the aboriginal rights of use and property or ownership rights. Lambert treated the claim to ownership as encompassing a claim to aboriginal title; Hutcheon drew upon the writings of the first Hudson's Bay Company trader in the area, William Brown, to conclude that the Gitksan and Wet'-suwet'en people held possession of lands far from the villages and regarded themselves as owners.[35] In fact, Lambert concluded that the proper test was not the existence of explicit tribal laws against intruders, but rather whether the people regarded themselves as having the right of exclusive use.[36]

Lambert exposes the subjectivity of law regardless of its source. The only difference between the explicit laws sought by McEachern and the subjective version of one's own rights is that the former entails a recognition of another society that may need to see a law of general application and an enforcement mechanism before their members will stay away. The calculation necessary to make such explicit laws (explicit, that is, to the other) could not be expected to occur in the absence of threat. To require such an assertion of exclusivity (in terms understood by contemporary Canadian courts) prior to British sovereignty applies a theory of the modern state as an instrument of property protection to a nonstate society in precontact days. On the other hand, the subjective test brings up the possibility of an arbitrary and contingent history of state formation and acquisition of territory: We are here because we regard ourselves as having exclusive rights and will act accordingly (e.g., claiming underlying title to aboriginal lands). By treating the plaintiffs and their ancestors as subjects (not of the Crown but as autonomous actors capable of rational decision) equipped with a degree of self-knowledge, one can also see the state as subjectivity, this time inscribed as a highly contingent set of rewards and punishments for individual actions rather than a historical and legal necessity. To see aboriginal rights as equivalent to proprietary interests, the agents of the state are forced to destroy the framework from within.

ABORIGINAL RIGHTS

When Judge Mahoney enumerated the criteria for establishing aboriginal title in the 1979 decision, *Hamlet of Baker Lake* v. *Minister of Indian Affairs and Northern Development*,[37] he established a certainty that was seized upon by courts faced with considerable uncertainty. The *Baker Lake* criteria have become a standard to uphold or modify. To establish aboriginal title, according to this standard, plaintiffs must prove (1) that they and their ancestors were members of an organized society; (2) that the organized society occupied the specific territory over which plaintiffs assert aboriginal title; (3) that the occupation was to the exclusion of other organized societies; and (4) that the occupation was an established fact at the time Britain asserted sovereignty. Chief Justice McEachern used the *Baker Lake* criteria and added a requirement of his own: that plaintiffs establish indefinite, long use of aboriginal lands, stretching back in time before the possibility of European influence.[38] Justifying this time requirement using precedent such as the 1990 fishing rights case of *R.* v. *Sparrow*,[39] the majority of the Court of Appeal concluded that the aboriginal practices had to be integral to the unique culture of the original society to establish any kind of aboriginal rights to land, be it title or limited use-rights (e.g., nonexclusive hunting and fishing). The time requirement simply reflected the evolutionary nature of culture.[40]

Taking the criteria one by one, the trial judge did find evidence of a rudimentary form of social organization among the ancestors of the Gitksan and Wet'suwet'en plaintiffs in the precontact period. He also found evidence of occupation and doubted that other organized societies established themselves in the heart of Gitksan or Wet'suwet'en territory on a permanent basis. Finally, some Gitksan and Wet'suwet'en people had been present in their villages and surrounding lands for a long time before British sovereignty.[41]

For previous aboriginal practices to provide the basis of current aboriginal rights, they had to be integral to the distinctive culture of the aboriginal society and not brought about by European influence. Trapping animals for the fur trade, for example, would not establish occupancy; neither would mining under European employ.[42] Hunting over a vast territory prior to the European encounter might establish the basis for continued nonexclusive rights to hunt for sustenance. Subsistence activities of the past, however, set the limits for the continuance of such activities; they do not necessarily provide the basis for commercial activities of the future.

How is a court to know that, at the time of contact, aboriginal societies used specific territories in culturally distinct ways? There are, of course, the statements of the Elders and the anthropologists, but Chief Justice McEachern turned instead to the written observations of Europeans, finding that many of the oral histories and much anthropological evidence amounted to bias.[43] By emphasizing the Europeans' interpretation of aboriginal customs, the chief justice acknowledged another, implicit requirement for proof of aboriginal rights: recognition by the colonial state.

Judge Wallace, in a separate, concurring opinion for the B.C. Court of Appeal, also emphasized the necessity of recognition by the European society:

> Prior to the exercise of sovereignty and the introduction of the common law, the issue of aboriginal "rights" did not arise. For the aboriginal peoples to have the right, vis-à-vis European settlers, to engage in those traditional practices and uses of land which were integral to their aboriginal society there must be recognition of such a right by those outside the aboriginal community and some mechanism requiring them to respect such a "right." An enforceable right, as against European settlers, came only with the protection which was extended to aboriginal rights by the adjusted common law.[44]

In other words, if aboriginal practices were not recognized as "rights" by the Europeans and somehow incorporated into common law, they would not survive as aboriginal rights today.

Menno Boldt has pointed out that such limitations put on aboriginal rights make these claims quite senseless as a strategy to enhance the status of Native peoples.[45] The purity and distinction required of the aboriginal practice combined with the subjectivity of the European observers put in mind a visit to a museum. The use of such criteria freezes aboriginal rights in time, hearkening back to an origin we can only imagine.[46] Indeed, the trial judge found that the state had extinguished whatever aboriginal rights existed by encouraging settlement of British Columbia. The B.C. Court of Appeal disagreed with extinguishment but limited the unextinguished rights to nonexclusive use for aboriginal purposes.

Lambert's dissent rejected the "frozen title theory," asserting that aboriginal title depends not on time immemorial possession, but on established possession at the time England claimed sovereignty over the territory.[47] Furthermore, Lambert wrote, it is a mistake to draw a sharp distinction between ownership and aboriginal rights; the ownership claim encompasses aboriginal rights. Indeed, that is the idea behind aboriginal title.[48]

Aboriginal rights, then, according to Lambert, arose from past customs and traditions and continued to exist after the colonial state was established. The content of those rights should be determined by the aboriginal society's own description, not that of the European newcomers. The right may include modern means of land use, depending on how aboriginal practices evolved over time, but this is a matter for further litigation rather than negotiation.[49]

To put it another way, the task for the claimants is to connect their origins with the present and rename the contributions of the Euro-Canadians. This is a creative, invigorating enterprise, culminating in elaborate presentations of cultural knowledge before the courts. This can and does occur in Lambert's state, a state that has affirmed its commitment to diversity through the Constitution Act of 1982. The state exists only as it is reflected in the self-assertions of its citizens.

Such do-it-yourself projects meet with skepticism in McEachern's state. Under the guise of historical research, they reconstruct the past according to present aspirations. The claims cannot succeed, but they do make visible the lack of fit between aboriginal societies' conceptions of themselves and the state's constitutional categories of power.

The notion of aboriginal rights implies a truth of origins, if only we could discover it and translate it into modern terms. That the common law incorporates such a term indicates how we grasp at the sanctity of beginnings and cannot help but envy societies that have not lost their memories. If anything, the myth of the state relies on timelessness, a rational solution to tribalism, a structure always available to be discovered or carried to new lands.[50]

MABO AND NATIVE CLAIMS: A NEW MODEL FOR CANADA?

In *Mabo* v. *Queensland*,[51] the High Court of Australia overturned years of precedent that justified the extinguishment of aboriginal rights and in this decision affirmed the aboriginal title of the Meriam people to the lands of the Murray Islands. The majority opinion in *Mabo* resembles Lambert's dissent; indeed Lambert cited *Mabo* as an important authority. *Mabo* raised aboriginal title to the status of property rights, a right against the state, unless the state (Queensland), in a valid exercise of legislative or executive power, revealing clear and plain intention to do so, extinguished the title (and such extinguishment would bear the obligation to compensate). A year after the high court's decision in the *Mabo* case, Australia enacted a law for the recognition, protection, and extinguishment of Native title.[52] Does this represent the beginnings of an inclusive state or simply another crack in the structure—like common law—that allows aboriginal groups to gain a hearing but not to find a place? And if they do find a place, what happens to competing claims, not the least those claims disputed among different aboriginal groups? Does the inclusive state simply become the captive of different groups at any given moment?

Questions like these have come to the fore for federal and British Columbia officials in the negotiations leading to the Nisga'a Agreement-in-Principle of February 1996. The Nisga'a land claim, like that of the Gitksan and Wet'-suwet'en chiefs, goes back about a hundred years. The *Calder* decision of 1973 acknowledged the existence of aboriginal title, but the details were to be hammered out by negotiations.[53] The resulting agreement includes not only Nisga'a ownership of 1,930 square kilometers of land in the lower Nass Valley and former reserve lands, but also self-government, a separate Nisga'a court, and a percentage of the salmon harvest.[54] The agreement represents the first comprehensive land claims settlement in British Columbia, possibly a model for other claims processes in the province. Not surprisingly, opposition political parties and resource-based interest groups such as the nonaboriginal commercial fishery, are challenging the settlement.[55]

CONCLUSION

As more aboriginal claims are negotiated, it is helpful to compare the state's and the Native claimants' positions along the separate dimensions suggested by Tzvetan Todorov.[56] First, there is a value judgment: Is the other party good or bad, inferior or superior? Second, what kind of relationship is established: distance, submission, or identification? Third, what must be known of each other? There is a range of knowledge, from absolute ignorance to as much knowledge as an outsider could have of the other party.

The Native claims seem to seek distance, as emphasized in the Gitksan and Wet'suwet'en claims of ownership and jurisdiction, the ability to expel outsiders and maintain internal control. To achieve that distance, however, one must present a great deal of knowledge about one's own legal and social systems in terms that are as familiar as possible to the courts. Presumably once formal recognition of a separate, parallel system has taken place and mechanisms for compensation and future negotiations incorporate the recognition of equal parties, then little need will exist for extensive knowledge of the other party's history.

Recognition of the desired distance, however, cannot follow a history of countless interactions with the Europeans and colonial institutions. Chief Justice McEachern did not see enough evidence of resistance, nor did he see familiar aboriginal executive and legislative institutions he could identify as legitimate. Without physical barriers, aboriginal societies from the origin to the present have to strain to separate their histories from the observers, the traders, the police, the settlers. It is impossible to provide the requisite familiarity with Native institutions and demonstrate the requisite distance in the same claim. Indeed, the more aboriginal groups pursue their claims, the more terminology and conceptual categories they must adopt from dominant institutions, thus presenting their uniqueness in familiar terms.

Least troublesome for the state is the acknowledgment of nonexclusive aboriginal rights to take food for sustenance, an activity not only deemed primitive but also quite easy to regulate and subordinate to other resource use, reducible as it is to units, times, and places. This is the kind of knowledge the fish and game management agencies can incorporate into their plans.

But if we were to abandon the structural model of the state and accept the dissenting voices in *Delgamuukw*, would we have anything but the elevation of subjectivity to icons? Right now the state offers the forum to present one's stories and reserves the right to accept or reject, in total or in part, to call them hoaxes or wounds in need of balm. If the state becomes transformed in this process to the fluid protective layer some would like to see, there has to be identification rather than distance. Whether one calls it co-management, co-optation, or integration, leadership circles in Native and nonnative societies overlap and lead to even more vehement cries for distance and secrecy, more virulent claims of superiority.

Furthermore, we see quests for what appear to be the other's defining characteristics. "Indigenous knowledge," "indigenous ways of knowing" appeal to members of the postcolonial state who have forgotten how to communicate with the physical-spiritual world. Using the proceeds from subsurface resources to build schools appeals to indigenous leaders who have been isolated from the most important human-to-human communications regarding resource distribution.[57] Distance is fast disappearing as an option, as is absolute ignorance of the other.

If the state does cloak the masks of diverse subjects, the inquiry into origins becomes less a search for truth than yet another means to resist contemporary assimilative pressures. Claims processes encourage the dusting off of traditions and institutions, but do not guarantee them a viable future. Like the provisions of the Australian Native Title Act of 1993, claims processes require a certain amount of identification and sharing of knowledge between parties and try to avoid built-in assumptions of inferiority or superiority. They rarely settle anything once and for all.

Whose memories become history? In British Columbia, aboriginal groups urge the rethinking of centuries. They have only partly succeeded. Compared to the comprehensive settlements with the aboriginal peoples in Canada's North,[58] the British Columbia groups, with the exception of the Nisga'a, have not attained the three levels of autonomy claimed in *Delgamuukw*. Greater degrees of contact and resource exploitation will complicate the achievement of distance.

Notes

1. The trial decision was reached in 1991 by Chief Justice Allan McEachern of the Supreme Court of British Columbia. See 79 D.L.R. (4th) 185 [1991] 3 W.W.R. 97, 25 A.C.W.S. (3d) 1012. The published version available to the author is found in *Smithers Registry*, no. 0843 (B.C.S.C.), 1–394. The appeal was heard by the British Columbia Court of Appeal, 104 D.L.R. (4th) 470 [1993]. Throughout the rest of the article, the two *Delgamuukw* decisions will be cited, with page numbers, as *Smithers* (the trial decision by Chief Justice McEachern) and 104 D.L.R. (4th) 470 (the appeals decision).The Canadian Supreme Court is scheduled to review the case in June 1997.

2. For critical discussions of the trial decision by anthropologists, see Michael Asch, "Errors in *Delgamuukw*: An Anthropological Perspective," in *Aboriginal Title in British Columbia*, ed. Frank Cassidy (Montreal: Oolichan Books and The Institute for Research on Public Policy, 1992), 221–43; Michael Asch and Catherine Bell, "Definition and Interpretation of Fact in Canadian Aboriginal Title Litigation: An Analysis of *Delgamuukw*," *Queens Law Journal* 19:2 (1994): 503–50; and Robin Ridington, "Fieldwork in Courtroom 53: A Witness to *Delgamuukw*," in *Aboriginal Title in British Columbia*, 206–20.

3. The plaintiffs' counsel first indicated that they were seeking no less than recognition of aboriginal ownership and jurisdiction, but later during the trial altered the claim to include aboriginal rights. *Smithers*, 1991, part 6, section 1, 39.

4. Robin Fisher, *Contact and Conflict: Indian-European Relations in British Columbia, 1774–1890*, 2d ed. (Vancouver: UBC Press, 1992), 1–2.

5. Ibid., chs. 1–2.

6. Paul Tennant, *Aboriginal Peoples and Politics: The Indian Land Question in British*

Columbia, 1849–1989 (Vancouver: UBC Press, 1990), 17.

7. Ibid., ch. 2.

8. Ibid., 26–37. Hamar Foster suggests that resistance to treatymaking may have come from the aboriginal groups themselves. He also points out that although formal treatymaking ceased, informal land purchases continued into the 1860s. See Foster, "Letting Go the Bone: The Idea of Indian Title in British Colombia, 1849–1927," in *Essays in the History of Canadian Law,* vol. 6, ed. Hamar Foster and John McLaren (Toronto: University of Toronto Press, 1995), 43–46.

9. Foster, "Letting Go the Bone," 54.

10. Only one of these treaties, Treaty No. 8, was applied to British Columbia, and only to the northern interior groups of Beaver, Slave, and Sekani Indians. See Tennant, *Aboriginal Peoples,* 65–67, and Dennis F.K. Madill, "British Columbia Indian Treaties in Historical Perspective" (Unpublished monograph, Department of Indian and Northern Affairs, Research Branch, Corporate Policy, Ottawa, 1981), 43–63.

11. Gisday Wa and Delgam Uukw, *The Spirit in the Land: Statements of the Gitksan and Wet'suwet'en Hereditary Chiefs in the Supreme Court of British Columbia, 1987–1990* (Gabriola, BC: Reflections, 1992), 1–2.

12. This summary of the evidence is taken from Gisday Wa and Delgam Uukw, *The Spirit in the Land,* 25–46.

13. *Smithers,* 56–59.

14. Gisday Wa and Degam Uukw, *The Spirit in the Land,* 30–35.

15. *Smithers,* 215.

16. Ibid.

17. Ibid., 219.

18. Ibid., 218.

19. Ibid., 219.

20. Ibid., 221.

21. The question of whether aboriginal societies possess inherent powers of self-governance can be answered at several levels: the self-conception of the group, the constitutional arrangements of the state, and the international legal norms of self-determination and human rights. In U.S. constitutional jurisprudence, the doctrine of tribal sovereignty arose as a means to limit the jurisdiction of state governments over Indian tribes and to justify the inclusion of tribes under the umbrella of the federal government. Eroded during eras of assimilation and termination, the doctrine of tribal sovereignty was renewed in the 1970s. Generally, tribes have the powers to determine their membership criteria, regulate tribal property, tax, maintain law and order, manage hunting and fishing, and regulate health and safety. Although comprehensive claims agreements in Canada, such as the Nisga'a agreement mentioned below, do include some similar powers for Canadian aboriginal groups, the process of recognizing such powers seems to have emerged only in the last two decades, and on a case-by-case basis as a result of negotiations. As a constitutional entrenchment of aboriginal rights, the Canadian Charter of Rights and Freedoms includes a section (35) on aboriginal rights (see below, note 22). Some Canadian legal scholars conclude that the aboriginal rights mentioned in section 35 include an inherent right of self-government. For background on tribal powers and U.S. policy, see David H. Getches et al., *Cases and Materials on Federal Indian Law,* 3d ed. (St. Paul, MN: West Publishing Co., 1993), passim; Charles F. Wilkinson, *American Indians, Time and the Law* (New Haven, CT: Yale University Press, 1987). For Canadian sources on self-government, see John Borrows, "Constitutional Law from a First Nation Perspective," *University of British Columbia Law Review* 28:1 (1994): 1–47;

and Bob Freedman, "The Space for Aboriginal Self-Government in British Columbia," *University of British Columbia Law Review* 28:1 (1994): 49–90.

22. 104 D.L.R. (4th) 470 at 762. Section 35(1) of the Constitution Act of 1982 reads, "The existing aboriginal and treaty rights of the aboriginal peoples of Canada are hereby recognized and affirmed."

23. 104 D.L.R. (4th) 470 at 719.

24. 104 D.L.R. (4th) 470 at 718.

25. The idea of primary and secondary rules comes from H. L. A. Hart, *The Concept of Law* (New York: Oxford University Press, 1961), 92–114.

26. Sally Engle Merry, "Resistance and the Cultural Power of Law," *Law and Society Review* 29:1 (1995): 11–26.

27. Russel Lawrence Barsh and James Youngblood Henderson, *The Road: Indian Tribes and Political Liberty* (Berkeley: University of California Press, 1980), chs. 1–3; Gordon I. Bennett, "Aboriginal Title in the Common Law: A Stony Path through Feudal Doctrine," *Buffalo Law Review* 27 (1978): 617–35.

28. 14 App. Cas. 46 [1888].

29. *Smithers*, 194.

30. 13 D.L.R. (4th) 321 [1984] at 339.

31. Whether this amounts to a fiduciary obligation has been the topic of debate. See Michael J. Bryant, "Crown-Aboriginal Relationships in Canada: The Phantom of Fiduciary Law," *UBC Law Review* 27:1 (1993): 19–49.

32. *Smithers*, 222.

33. Ibid.

34. Ibid.

35. 104 D.L.R. (4th) 470 at 758–60.

36. 104 D.L.R. (4th) 470 at 710–12.

37. 107 D.L.R. (3d) 513 at 542.

38. *Smithers*, 98, 212.

39. 1 S.C.R. 1075.

40. *Delgamuukw*, 104 D.L.R. (4th) 470 at 492 and 515.

41. *Smithers*, 227.

42. *Delgamuukw*, 104 D.L.R. (4th) 470 at 494 and 514.

43. *Smithers*, 50–52.

44. 104 D.L.R. (4th) 470 at 570.

45. Menno Boldt, *Surviving as Indians: The Challenge of Self-Government* (Toronto: University of Toronto Press, 1993), 29–30.

46. Brian Slattery, "Understanding Aboriginal Rights," *Canadian Bar Review* 66 (1987): 727–83.

47. 104 D.L.R. (4th) 470 at 628.

48. 104 D.L.R. (4th) 470 at 703–11.

49. 104 D.L.R. (4th) 470 at 644–57 and 741.

50. The philosophical origins of liberalism center around the social contract, a decision entered into by rational human beings to establish a government. The notion of social contract is ahistorical, and the modern democratic state, founded on the ideology of liberalism, is also seen in modern contract theory as an arrangement existing independently of particular historical circumstances. The timelessness of the state can be used as a justification for boilerplate applications of state action in varied circumstances, but it also seems virtually empty of content and therefore wide open to definition. For a survey of liberal theory, see Ian Shapiro, *The Evolution of Rights in Liberal Theory*

(Cambridge, England: Cambridge University Press, 1986).

51. 107 A.L.R. 1 [1992].

52. "Native Title Act 1993," no. 110, *Commonwealth Statutes Annotations* (31 December 1993), 2121.

53. *Calder v. the Attorney-General of British Columbia (B.C.)*, [1973] S.C.R. 313.

54. "Nisga'a Treaty Negotiations: Agreement-in-Principle," issued jointly by the Government of Canada, the Province of British Columbia, and the Nisga'a Tribal Council, 15 February 1996.

55. Mark Hume, "Angry Fishers Denounce Deal," *The Vancouver Sun,* 16 February 1996; Stewart Bell and Justine Hunter, "Nisga'a Deal Initialled into History," *The Vancouver Sun,* 16 February 1996.

56. Tzvetan Todorov, *The Conquest of America,* trans. Richard Howard (New York: HarperCollins, 1984), 185.

57. Todorov observes in his study of the encounter between Europeans and Native Americans that the latter favored communication with the world, the former favored exchanges between men. *The Conquest of America,* 252.

58. For brief overviews of the northern claims negotiations, see Peter Jull, *Constitution-Making in Northern Territories* (Northern Territory, Australia: Central Land Council, 1996), 14–18, and Letha J. MacLachlan, "Comprehensive Aboriginal Claims in the N.W.T.," *Information North* 18:1 (March 1992): 1–7.

PART III

ECONOMIC DEVELOPMENT

*Economic development is not a late twentieth-century phenomenon that has sud-
denly captured the imagination of Native American people, nor did it start, nor will
it stop, with gaming. Economic development can be traced historically to the time of
first European contact. Christopher Columbus commented that the Native people of
the Caribbean were eager to trade. The later founders of the Roanoke and
Jamestown settlements recorded a smilar eagerness. The next major extension of
economic development came through the fur trade, first involving the French,
Huron, Ottawa and the other indigenous people of present-day Canada, then the
Dutch and English with the major power south of the Great Lakes, the
Haudeonosaunee, or Iroquois Confederacy. Native American people were astute
businessmen and women and, for a period of time, maintained a superior position in
the trade relationship, later a balanced position, and ultimately as a result of the
overwhelming numbers and the technology of the Europeans, a subordinate position
in the economic marketplace.*

*Fluctuating federal policies such as the concentration of most Indian people on
reservations has severely penalized and restricted Native economic development.
Some tribes have successfully attracted non-Indian economic ventures. The Turtle
Mountain and Devils Lake Chippewa as well as the Mississippi Choctaw have had
success at managing electronic assembly plants, building military equipment, and
manufacturing greeting cards. Other tribes have established businesses of their own.
The Passamaquoddy and Penobscot Indians in Maine have invested in a number of
commercial enterprises. The Oglala Sioux of South Dakota purchased a meat-*

packing plant which provides high-quality beef for sale to restaurants, and the Blackfeet tribe of Montana founded the Blackfeet Indian Writing Company which makes pens, pencils, and markers. Many non-Indian firms are reluctant to invest capital on Indian reservations, however, for fear that they may not be protected by United States law but will be subject to federal Indian law under which Indian tribes exercise exclusions granted them by their Indian sovereignty. Indian Nations strongly resist any further dimunitization of their sovereignty or of their control of non-Indian commercial development on their lands. As this book goes to press, some Indian leaders fear that unless Indian tribes agree to waive their protections against lawsuits by non-Indian businesses operating on reservations, economic development will suffer further atrophy.

Ronald Trosper, director of the Native American Forestry Program at Northern Arizona University, begins our discussion of economic development with an intro-spective look into the concept of traditional Indian economic policy and the term "traditional Indian." In this article, Trosper does several important things. First, the paper analyzes the connectedness between a major world view of economic develop-ment and the types of economic policies this world view requires. Trosper defines and generalizes "traditional" American Indian views with the purpose of arriving at some clear implications this view has on the making of economic policy. Trosper also examines several examples of policies in contemporary Indian communities as a way to assess the usefulness and applicability of traditional American Indian views. The final section of the paper addresses areas for future research.

Trosper quotes Joseph Epes Brown and states that "The recent literature on American Indian world views demonstrates that American Indian cultures share an attitude of respect toward the world around us." Building upon this, Trosper offers four basic components characterizing the American Indian definition of respect. These are, community, connectedness, seventh generation, and humility. Briefly stated, Native American people believe that men and women are members of a com-munity that includes all beings, that everything is connected, that past generations left a legacy that is to be protected as far as the seventh generation, and that the nat-ural world is powerful, thus humanity should be humble. These four components of respect govern the type of economic development undertaken and the methods of organizing for development.

Based on this understanding of traditional American Indian viewpoint, the author then applies the four components to explore implications for development activities. This includes a discussion of ecosystem health, nuclear and hazardous waste disposal, gaming, savings, and investment, and community population levels. Equally important, Trosper projects the use of traditional American Indian view-points to discuss the issues of private property, corporations, and alternative institu-tions of land control, such as common property ownership. Lastly, Trosper offers the Menominee Tribe and the Taos Pueblo as examples of Indian communities which have pursued policies consistent with the traditional Native American view of respect.

Gaming, or gambling, on Indian reservations is one of most controversial of contemporary Native American political issues. It is an enterprise that embodies the *complex issues of sovereignty, tradition, and world view that Trosper examines. Gary Anders provides a clear and informative article on this extremely important approach to economic development, clarifying many of the perceptions and misperceptions that surround the "return of the Buffalo," as it has been called by many people.*

Anders begins his discussion with a brief history of Indian gaming that "sprang from a single bingo hall on the Seminole reservation in Florida," and has grown into a multimillion dollar industry. Following the Seminole experiment, high-stakes gaming flourished and was challenged in the federal court in California v. Cabazon Band of Mission Indians in 1987. In this case, the Supreme Court upheld the right of tribes as sovereign nations to conduct gaming on land held in federal trust for Indian people and ruled that individual states did not have the authority to regulate gaming if gaming is permitted in the affected state for any other purposes. For most states, state lotteries opened the door to Native American gaming operations.

Professor Anders provides an overview of Public Law 100-497, the Indian Gaming Regulatory Act (IGRA) that sought to balance Native American rights with the interests of individual states. For the purpose of IGRA and gaming regulation, types of gambling were broken down into Class I, II, and III. The author provides a description of the types of gaming that falls under each of these categories as well as the IGRA regulatory framework and reporting requirements for oversight and taxation. Basically, tribes do not have to pay taxes on gaming revenues to the state (hence the efforts by states to control gaming), however, tribes are required to deduct and withhold state and federal income tax and FICA from all non-Indian and non-resident Indian tribal employees. Additionally, Indian tribes are required to report winnings to the IRS and to withhold federal income taxes on gaming winnings.

The author next looks into tribal uses of gaming revenue, the economic and social impact of gaming, the negative impact of Indian casinos, and the conflicts that have arisen over Native American sovereignty as Indian tribes have attempted to negotiate with individual states (particularly Public Law 280 states) and the federal government. Tribal leaders believe that because their operations are on federal trust land, individual states have no jurisdiction. States, on the other hand, have complained that IGRA exempts tribes from paying taxes and that tribes have exceeded the types of gaming authorized by introducing gaming machines comparable to Las Vegas–style casinos. As the author explains, however, IGRA provides for the development of state-tribal agreements to balance the state interest against tribal interests and sovereignty. Most states have recognized the importance of gaming for economic development and have entered into agreements. Some states such as California have refused to negotiate with tribes who already have established gaming facilities that the state feels exceeds the legal IGRA definitions.

In view of these recent conflicts and in view of a long and fluctuating history of U.S. government regulation of Indian activities, Anders advised tribes to anticipate changes in current law. Most importantly, because gaming may not last, Anders encourages tribes to use casino profits to diversify their economic bases. Thus our discussion comes full circle, as gaming must be seen within a larger context of the struggle for more equitable power relations that will strengthen tribal independence and future prospects for prosperity and sovereignty.

5

Traditional American Indian Economic Policy

Ronald L. Trosper

MANY HAVE OBSERVED that Indian and mainstream values differ, but few have spelled out the implications of these differences for economic development policy. This paper presents a characterization of Indian values, derives some implications for traditional Indian economic policy, and provides two examples of Indian communities that have adopted policies consistent with its analysis. As tribes continue to assert their sovereign powers to control their own communities, a consideration of the connections between traditional American Indian world views and economic development policy can assist tribes and others in examining and selecting among current development alternatives.

Those studying economic policy in Indian communities recognize that Indians have different goals from those of the dominant society.[1] What are these goals and do they help explain why economic policy has been different in Indian communities? This paper begins by listing a set of assumptions that many Indian communities share. It then proceeds to explore the implications of these assumptions for economic development activities and institutions. Not surprisingly, the implications describe rules profoundly different from what *economic development* usually means. For example, traditional Indian economic policy would place an upper limit on consumption. High grading of renewable resources would not be allowed. Pure private property institutions for land management would be rejected. If economic development means mere growth in the production of goods and services, one might say that traditional Indian economic policy is not economic development at all. Recently, *development* has acquired adjectives in many applications: community development, human development, sustainable development. Traditional American Indian economic policy is a type of *development,* if the term is allowed to cover a wide field. This paper analyzes the connections between a major world view and the types of economic policies this world view requires. Whether these policies constitute development depends on one's definition of development.

The label *traditional Indian* can attract criticism for being too general, because Indian tribes and cultures vary significantly in time and space. Detailed application

Ronald L. Trosper is a professor of forestry and director of the Native American Forestry Program, Northern Arizona University. An earlier version of this paper, "Indian-Centered Economic Development," was presented at the University of Tulsa Centennial celebration on 16 April 1994.

of the concepts described below will vary from community to community. People do use *traditional Indian* to describe a viewpoint—not necessarily held by all—represented in many Indian communities.

This paper defines and generalizes "traditional" American Indian views with the purpose of deriving some clear implications for policy. It begins with a characterization of traditional Indian views. It then derives policy prescriptions following from those views; the prescriptions are a matter of deductions from assumptions rather than from a description of actual policies. No claim is made that the policies described in the second section of the paper or the institutions described in the third actually drive all business and economic decisions on reservations today. Such decisions are motivated by a variety of viewpoints; in fact, because of the dependency of tribes on the federal government, fully independent economic policymaking is hard to find. The fourth and fifth sections of the paper examine several examples of policies in contemporary Indian communities as a way to assess the usefulness and applicability of the analysis. The final section addresses areas of future research required to extend the analysis to challenges created by current advanced capitalist markets.

RESPECT DEFINES THE TRADITIONAL INDIAN VIEWPOINT

In order to describe traditional Indian economic policy, we must define the term *traditional Indian*. The recent literature on American Indian world views demonstrates that American Indian cultures share an attitude of respect toward the world around us.[2] Since *respect* can have many interpretations, one needs to specify its meaning further. To summarize traditional world views, this paper offers the following four basic components as a way to characterize the American Indian definition of respect:

Community: Men and women are members of a community that includes all beings. Each has its proper role, and each has obligations to others. The sacred aspect of this assumption is that all beings have spirit. The political aspect of this assumption is that human-to-human relationships are similar to human-to-animal and human-to-plant relationships. The economic aspect is that reciprocity in exchange must exist.

Connectedness: Everything is connected. While the idea of community provides a source of obligation and a guide to proper behavior, the idea of connectedness is a description of how the world is.

Seventh Generation: Past human generations left us a legacy, and we have a duty to pass that legacy to our great-grandchildren and beyond, as far as to the seventh generation.

Humility: In taking action, humanity should be humble. The natural world is powerful and well able to cause trouble if not treated properly.

These four components are distinct; while other world views share parts of them, the traditional Indian view includes them all. The first provides a way to derive ethical statements (what ought to be) about what policies should be selected, with a focus on today. The second furnishes a way to generate descriptions or models of the world (what is) in order to describe the consequences of policies. The third states the time dimension; although it is also an ethical position, it has such enormous implications for policy that separation from the first category is useful. The fourth, humility, can be presented as an aspect of the connectedness assumption as well, but humility involves more than just assuming that everything is connected; it is a statement about humanity's ability to understand the connections. The following describes each of these four components in more detail.

Community

J. Baird Callicott, a philosophy professor who studies land ethics, summarizes the views of Ojibwa and other Algonquian sources as follows:

> Nonhuman natural entities are personal beings, socially organized into families, clans, and nations not unlike the traditional Algonquins themselves. Relations with these other-than-human persons are, accordingly, socially structured. They are courteous, cautious, muted, reciprocal, deferential, diplomatic—forms of conduct that must be maintained to sustain the interspecies social structure and, so to speak, international balance of power.[3]

Indian discussions of what ought to be begin with the whole natural world included in the analysis. This is useful, because theories about how humans should treat humans are extensive in the literature of anthropology, sociology, political science, and philosophy. Each of the human-focused approaches should have implications when animals and all of nature are included.[4] Since community social structure can vary, this assumption that other beings are part of the same community as humans does not say much about the structure of the community. Callicott notes that the Sioux idea of community is closest to that of an extended family, while the Algonquian view is broader in extending to nations.[5] The stories about animals that act as humans demonstrate the ubiquity of the community concept. Coyote, Beaver, Blue Jay, and Buffalo are a few of the characters who provide examples and advice.[6] Often the lessons in the stories illustrate the importance of fulfilling one's social obligations, as well as the importance of connectedness and humility.

Further exploration of the community concept requires examination of community ideas common among Indian tribes. Many tribes reach community decisions by developing consensus. Successful individuals share their wealth with others, often through give-aways. Reciprocation among individuals cements personal relationships. Since animals and plants are community members, their interests must be represented in all activities. Each entity, including men and women, has a proper role. American Indians believe men and women should live in harmony with nonhuman beings.

Connectedness

The idea of connectedness is related to but different from the idea of community. While community creates obligations, connectedness is a way to describe how the world works. Richard Nelson, who has lived extensively with the Koyukon Indians of Alaska, reports an opinion from a Koyukon Elder:

> "The country knows," an elder told me. "If you do wrong things to it, the whole country knows. It feels what's happening to it. I guess everything is connected together somehow, under the ground."[7]

Many have described the native world view as "holistic."[8] The idea of a whole, however, requires definition of the edge of an entity, which can be difficult to do. Connectedness is more flexible, while still emphasizing a danger in treating any one entity or phenomenon in isolation.[9]

Seventh Generation

Because other traditions share the concern for future generations, the Iroquois statement of concern for the seventh generation has been popular among many tribes. Oren Lyons, an Iroquois leader and college professor, provides a statement from the Iroquois culture that underlies long-term resource use:

> We are looking ahead, as is one of the first mandates given to us as chiefs, to make sure and to make every decision that we make relate to the welfare and well-being of the seventh generation to come, and that is the basis by which we make decisions in council. We consider: will this be to the benefit of the seventh generation?[10]

He goes on to criticize contemporary shopping mall culture of shortsightedness. Nelson reports that the Koyukon manage their world for sustained yield, which is an immediate consequence of concern for distant generations.[11]

Part of the concern for the seventh generation is an assumption that today's resources have limited capacity. There is a zero-sum aspect to ecosystem management, an assumption that seems to deny the reality of rapid technological change. This assumption of limited capacity will be used in what follows; the final section of the paper addresses the impact of technological change on economic policy from a traditional Indian viewpoint.

Humility

The fourth component of respect is an attitude of humility. Actions to modify the world must be undertaken with care. Nelson provides this example from the Koyukon:

> When the river ice breaks up each spring, people speak to it, respectfully and acknowledging its power. Elders make short prayers, both Christian and traditional Koyukon, asking the ice to drift downstream without jamming and causing floods. By contrast, some years ago, the U.S. Air Force bombed an ice jam on the Yukon River to prevent inundation of

communities. Far from approving some villagers blamed subsequent floods on this arrogant use of physical force. In the end, nature will assert the greater power. The proper role for humans is to move gently, humbly, pleading or coercing, but always avoiding belligerence.[12]

The reason for humility is recognition of nature's power. Acting with caution is a matter of prudence; since humanity does not understand how nature is put together, massive interventions are dangerous.

One basis for this attitude is the experience of large change in the natural world. Native oral tradition, stretching back over generations, conveys images of a world in great change. The creation stories of the Navajo, Hopi, and Zuni have people journeying from world to world.[13] The Koyukon and Algonquin traditions have humans turning into animals and animals into humans.[14] The character of Coyote, in particular, stirs up great trouble with his recklessness. These stories of transformation support the idea that nature's power is so great that cataclysmic change has been experienced—and hence is always a real possibility.

Must Respect Have This Shape?

The answer is no. If one starts simply with respect for nature as a philosophical position, one needs to add some further cultural assumptions in order to provide specific components. Two examples are ecologist Aldo Leopold's early analysis and a recent book by philosopher Paul Taylor.

Aldo Leopold's land ethic often is summarized with the following quotation: "Quit thinking about land-use as solely an economic problem. . . . A thing is right when it tends to preserve the integrity, stability, and beauty of the biotic community."[15] This standard arises, for Leopold, in the context of treating land (or nature) as a community. As Callicott has explored in several essays, Leopold's concept of community and Native American land ethics are related.[16] Both contain the idea that humans and their environment are part of a community; and the interrelatedness, or connectedness, of all things is part of that idea. Leopold does not stress humility; nor does he stress long-term considerations directly. Following Leopold, Callicott does not stress humility (it is not an entry in his book's index), but he does defend Leopold's views against charges that they are "presumptuous" or "condescending."[17] Leopold says, "A land ethic changes the role of *Homo sapiens* from conqueror of the land-community to plain member and citizen of it."[18] It implies respect for his fellow-members and also respect for the community as such.

In *Respect for Nature: A Theory of Environmental Ethics,* Paul Taylor emphasizes community and connectedness as part of respect, which he calls a "biocentric outlook on nature." He omits discussion of long-term considerations as required by concern for the seventh generation. Neither does he clearly advocate humility, although he does advocate the "belief that humans are not inherently superior to other living things."[19]

Both Leopold and Taylor promote an ethic that reduces man from superiority over nature to equality with nature. This is close to the Native American view that humility, not hubris, is the proper attitude. Neither Leopold nor Taylor emphasizes concern for the seventh generation, although neither advocates short-term analysis of ecosystem management. Their ideas about respect for nature are more narrow that the traditional American Indian view as defined in this paper. Because of this, implications for economic policy derived from American Indian views may well differ from the implications drawn from analysis such as theirs.

Omission of Sacred Dimensions

The above presentation of the four components of respect omits discussion of sacred or spiritual dimensions. In contrast to many expositions of Native views, this essay examines the analytical and ethical assumptions that accompany the sacred views. Of course, religious beliefs and definitions of the sacred provide meaning and force to a world view. Unfortunately, to emphasize the sacred aspects in the secular field of economic policy would reduce the plausibility of the underlying argument. To limit analysis to the secular assumptions may appear to remove the adjective *traditional,* but the nonspiritual parts of a traditional Indian world view often remain active in the opinions of Christian and other nontraditional Indians. Fundamental world view assumptions survive loss of language and religion, although they are stronger among people who retain the support of language and religion.

IMPLICATION OF RESPECT FOR DEVELOPMENT ACTIVITIES

The four components of respect provide implications for both the type of economic development undertaken—the activities—and the methods of organizing for development—the institutions. This part of the paper addresses activities, and the next section addresses institutions. At least six types of constraints on economic development activities are consistent with respect:

1. High grading is not allowed
2. Consumption has an upper bound.
3. Ecosystem health should be maintained.
4. Nuclear or other hazardous waste disposal should be avoided.
5. Although modern market niches such as gambling and reduced-tax sales can be used, savings from profits should be very high.
6. A community's population levels should remain within the carrying capacity of a community's resources.

Although there are other topics that could be addressed, these six provide good illustrations of the ways in which traditional Indian economic policy might be identified.

Do not high grade

To high grade is to take the best products first. In a forest, high grading means to harvest all the large old trees first, or to take all of the valuable species first. In resource extraction, high grading means taking the oil closest to the surface or taking the best grade ores. Both community and connectedness oppose high grading. Since high grading involves possible elimination of a species or an age class, it means removing one whole part of a community. Since every entity is part of the community, none should be fully eliminated. Because everything is connected, extraction measures such as elimination of one component could have unintended consequences. Concern for the seventh generation requires leaving some of the best for use by great-grandchildren and their grandchildren.

Consumption has an upper limit

Both the community obligations of people and the connectedness of humanity's activities to the rest of the world suggest that there are limits to human use of community resources. In a community that includes plants and animals, humanity has a place with boundaries that should not be crossed. Connectedness and humility imply that extreme actions will lead to extreme responses: People should be moderate in extracting resources. The seventh generation assumption of limits to the world's productiveness supports this reasoning. Since savings constitute the difference between production and consumption of useful goods and services, consuming less than is produced yields savings for use by later generations.

Ecosystem health should be maintained

Closely related to the existence of an upper bound on consumption is maintenance of ecosystem health. Since any economic development strategy uses a reservation's land, respect for the land requires supporting ecosystem health to some extent. Ecologist Robert Constanza's summary chapter of his *Ecosystem Health* provides the following ecological definition:

> To be healthy and sustainable, a system must maintain its metabolic activity level as well as its internal structure and organization (a diversity of processes effectively linked to one another) and must be resilient to outside stresses over a time and space frame relevant to that system.[20]

Constanza proposes that a health index be defined as the product of three separate indices: vigor, organization, and resilience. Vigor is measured by productivity, the output of food or other measure of biomass.[21] Organization is measured by the complexity of the structures—the connections between species and the abiotic environment—and by the diversity of the species present. Resilience is hard to measure, because it describes the response of a system to disturbance. When long-time frames are involved, as is the case with ecosystems, a simulation model is needed to predict results; such models are hard to construct. The failure of resilience, such as when an ecosystem declines badly in its function, can be observed only after the decline has occurred. But even in these cases—a lake that has atrophied, a stream bed and banks that have eroded away, or a forest that has suffered a catastrophic fire after a hundred years of fire suppression—some modeling as well as historical research is needed to estimate how much time would be required to reconstruct the damaged system, if the source of the damage were to cease.

This three-part definition of ecosystem health embodies the basic components of respect. The ecosystem idea of vigor describes a characteristic of community. If all members of a community are accorded respect for their right to a livelihood, then each member will perform his or her role in the production of useful products for others, thereby contributing to the community. Respect for community means respect for diversity, which is part of the ecosystem health concept of organization. Connectedness is also related to organization; while the term *connectedness* is vague about the type of connections, *organization* suggests a structure. A healthy ecosystem will have resilience, which will help it survive until the seventh generation. The difficulty in constructing adequate simulation models for measuring resilience is consistent with humanity's need for humility. If the residents of a reservation want to use their ecosystems in a manner consistent with respect, they will preserve or promote ecosystem health. In greatly disturbed ecosystems, however, identifying the proper policies may be difficult.

Nuclear or Other Hazardous Waste Disposal Should Be Avoided

All four components of respect argue against hazardous waste disposal. Community with all other entities dictates that nothing be done to harm them; hazardous waste, while ostensibly controlled in landfills, has great potential to affect other community members. The connectedness assumption, combined with humility, denies the assumption that hazardous waste will, in fact, remain contained in whatever structure is provided for it. The seventh generation perspective reinforces the doubts generated by humility; if containment of the hazardous waste should fail, its negative effects will be felt by the seventh generation.

Although Modern Market Niches Such as Gambling and Reduced-Tax Sales Can Be Used, Savings and Investment from Profits Should Be Very High

The prescription for high savings rates derives from the assumption of duty to the seventh generation. If there is a belief in ultimate limitations in any one source of income, the generation that receives an influx of financial capital resulting from the profits in gambling will not assume that those profits are going to continue forever. Humility would suggest caution in believing the gambling niche will last forever; contemporary political opposition to the niche reinforces this worry. Concern for future generations will lead to a high savings rate.[22] The two other principles, community and connectedness, seem less relevant to this example. A casino can be set up as a border enclave that has little impact on reservation lands, with the exception of waste products. The greater concern, generated by connectedness assumptions, may be about the character of the Indian community rather than transformation of its land directly by the casino.

A Community's Population Levels Should Remain within the Carrying Capacity of a Community's Resources

The need to control population growth follows from all four of the components of respect. Community ethics require that humanity's role may limit an individual's right to dominate the community by expanding his own participation at the expense of other members. Because of connectedness, there will be unintended consequences if human population increases out of proportion to its place in the system. In any one generation, increases in total numbers would mean that the average impact of each individual on the ecosystem would have to be less. Consideration of the rights of the seventh generation means that the current generation should restrain use of the ecosystem so that it retains the capacity to provide adequately for the seventh generation. Humility also requires that humanity not expand its own population to unusually high levels.

Summary of Development Activities

These examples of the implications, for economic development activities, of an attitude of respect suggest that traditional Indian economic policy should be very different from what historically has been called economic development, namely high rates of increase in per capita income, combined with population growth and structural transformation.[23] Rates of resource exploitation should be adequate for subsistence but should be limited, and consumption levels should rise to a limit. The depth of the differences may explain the deep divisions that have occurred in many communities over proper economic development strategies. To the extent that one accepts the premises of traditional Indian values, one may approve of "nondevelopment" of the sort some Indian communities have chosen. Not developing, in the sense of increases in levels of consumption of goods, may be development from the viewpoint of the policies described above. As recent publications by the United Nations suggest, the old notion of economic development has come to be questioned by other societies as well.[24]

IMPLICATIONS FOR DEVELOPMENT INSTITUTIONS

Many advocate the selection of appropriate institutions as a way to have the right development activities emerge from the decisions of people in the institutional framework.[25] Private property and corporate ownership are two institutions that have been advocated for Indians to manage land. An examination of their inconsistencies with the four components of respect shows why many Indian tribes have refused to accept private property or corporate ownership as land management institutions. In the past, Indian tribes have used institutions of generosity, usufruct property rights, and tribal territorial boundaries; these institutions are consistent with respect.

Private Property

The institution of private property in land assigns an owner to each parcel of land. A landowner has full rights to manage it, sell commodities on it, and dispose of the property, including bequest to the landowner's children. He or she can exclude other persons from the land and sue in cases of trespass. The owner also has the right to sue others who cause damage to the land. The role of government is to enforce these rights and enforce any contracts mutually agreed to by a landowner and other persons.[26] When resources such as water or migratory animals affect the productivity of land, the private property institution is extended to include these resources, to ensure that everything of importance has an owner.[27]

Considering the first component of respect, community and private property are not consistent. An owner is placed in a position of dominance over other beings; if a man or woman can own land and everything on it, reciprocal symmetry does not apply. For example, an animal cannot own people in the same way. In a community, with its families, clans, towns, and nations, each participant has obligations. These requirements are enforced by the community's imposition of constraints on individual behavior. For a property owner, there are no such constraints. Obligations to other community members, particularly the nonhuman ones, cannot be enforced by other human members. The idea that a man or woman has a set of reciprocal relationships, a place in the food web, is undermined by the institution of private property. By ignoring community between humans and nonhumans, private property removes ethical obligations to nonhumans and humans without property.

The drawing of clear boundaries denies connectedness. If the parts of an ecosystem are subdivided into private property parcels, the owners must relate to each other through market exchanges such as leases, contracts, sales, and purchases of goods. In this way, self-interest overrides connectedness while ecosystem function is not disturbed and individual parcel productivity will be maintained. As owners use their land for their own purposes, however, connections will be broken and productivity will fall. To maintain parcel productivity, each owner will have to import resources.

Lack of large-scale coordination increases the probability that owners will experience catastrophic loss. In ecosystems where fire is common, control of fire on a parcel basis, through a general increase in fuels, can generate periodic catastrophes. An example is fire in forests protected for a hundred years. In a watershed in which periodic floods contribute to repairing ecosystem function by setting succession back and renewing soil nutrients, control of water through diversions, dams, and levees can have unintended systemwide consequences.

In ecosystems where large migrating animals are significant, fences and other characteristics of private property can remove species whose contribution to system productivity may be important.[28]

If private property rights are fully defined and if all participants understand the connections within an ecosystem, then each owner will have an interest in purchasing the needed ecosystem inputs from other owners. But private property systems rarely assign ownership rights to everything. Rights are defined as particular goods become scarce; enforcing rights to nonvaluable components is not cost effective. In addition, owners of parcels learn about their own land exclusively; information also becomes private. Under a private property system, there is little incentive to share knowledge about connections. If one owner hurts the resources of another, recourse is to a court system.

Concern for the seventh generation emerges from a view that assumes a community of humans will persist into the far future. A full private property system assumes that owners can sell to outsiders as well as members of the community. An Indian private property system would, in consideration of the seventh generation, allow sales of land only between tribal members. Since the institution of private property allows sales to anyone, it is not consistent with concern for the seventh generation.

The attitude of humility suggests the following question: If people do not understand the connections in the natural world, can they know which resources should be placed in private ownership, and who the owner should be? Also, can they know that the pattern of ownership among people will lead to the right levels of knowledge and the right private agreements to share resources? Because the answer to both these questions is no, private property is not consistent with humility.

Corporations Owning Land

The private property system has many inconsistencies with the four components of respect. One institution used within the private property system is the ownership of land by a fictitious person, a corporation owned by shareholders. When the Indian Reorganization Act of 1934 authorized creation of tribal corporations, some tribes adopted corporate charters. A corporation was imposed on the Menominee in 1963, when termination created Menominee Tribal Enterprises. In 1971, the Alaskan Native Claims Settlement Act imposed corporate structures in Alaska. Both the Menominee and Alaska Natives have had problems with corporations.[29]

Since corporations are part of private property systems, all of the objections raised about private property also apply to corporations. Corporations raise three additional problems: First, they are governed by majority rule, through a vote of the board of directors. Community consensus is not a requirement, which would violate most Indian notions of community action. Second, the financial accounts of a corporation are maintained using generally accepted accounting rules. Only products with market values that can be observed today are entered into these accounts. This limits recognition of connections between things and beings with and without market value. Third, standards of corporate profitability conflict with concern for the seventh generation. In the United States, corporate profitability is judged against rates of return in capital markets, which emphasize earning as much as possible in the short term. To earn rapid rates of return, both renewable and nonrenewable resources are consumed quickly.[30] Given all this, one would expect that American Indian and Alaska Native communities using corporate management would have difficulty implementing traditional Indian policies.

Alternative Institutions

Historically, neither private property nor corporate ownership of land was popular with Indians. What institutions are consistent with the four principles of respect? One is direct control of land by a governing body that makes land use decisions through community consensus. Another is the granting of specific, limited use rights to individual members of the community, with the provision that rights can be removed if misused.

Common property ownership, when defined as community control rather than simply open access, provides examples. Economists finally have realized that common property institutions can be successfully implemented for sustained use.[31] In the presence of economies of scale in the management of migratory animals, Nugent and Sanchez have shown the advantages of tribal chiefs in coordinating the allocation of land between cultivation and grazing.[32]

To look for alternative institutions, we can examine the traditional institutions that were in place when Europeans arrived. Across North America, three institutions coexisted: generosity, usufruct tenure for individuals, and tribal or band territorial division.[33] The institution of generosity is a rule that all members of a community must share goods and property. In societies with hierarchy, such as in the Pacific Northwest, the rich conducted potlatches in which they gave away many goods. In more level societies, such as in New England, everyone shared their possessions. Usufruct tenure is the principle that one has exclusive rights to the products of land one is using, but that ultimate ownership will revert back to the community upon relinquishment of use. Territorial division of land among bands of Indians accompanies a migratory lifestyle; at different times of the year, a band resides in different parts of its territory; lines between band territories are recognized and subject to conflict.

Fundamental in this constellation of institutions is the requirement to be generous. If all individuals and families are required to share their bounty with others, then everyone in a community has an interest in the productivity of his neighbor. Generosity creates connectedness in consumption, which complements the reality of connectedness in production. Just as selfishness is an institution that accompanies private property in land, generosity is an institution that accompanies communal land ownership.

In New England, Cronon provides the following quotation from Le Clerc, an observer of the time:

The Micmac of Nova Scotia . . . were "so generous and liberal towards one another that they seem not to have any attachment to the little they possess, for they deprive themselves thereof very willingly and in very good spirit the very moment when they know that their friends have need of it."[34]

In the South, the Choctaw situation was as follows:

> Choctaw chiefs . . . were primarily redistributors. They maintained power not by hoarding goods but rather by giving them away. As it operated aboriginally, redistribution was coupled with another concept: reciprocity, or the obligation eventually to return certain gifts of goods, labor, service, and favors. Together, redistribution and reciprocity governed the exchange of goods in Choctaw society.[35]

Thus, the Choctaw chiefs were similar to leaders in the Northwest, who competed with one another through potlatches.[36] These three examples, spanning the continent, are a small taste of the extent to which generosity was fundamental in traditional Indian societies.

Property ownership also existed in these traditional societies, but it was not private property ownership. Cronon provides the following description for New England:

> Property rights . . . shifted with ecological use. . . . Hunting grounds are the most interesting case of this shifting, nonagricultural land tenure. The ecological habits of different animals were so various that their hunting required a wide range of techniques, and rights to land use had to differ accordingly.
> What the Indians owned—or, more precisely, what their villages gave them claim to—was not the land but the things that were on the land during the various seasons of the year.[37]

In this interpretation, the rights to use things on the land were allocated to individuals, as part of the private property institution is supposed to hold. But the right was one of use, not ownership in the sense of exclusive control, including buying and selling. Other uses may overlap in the same geographical area. Ultimate ownership remained with the village as a whole.

With ownership dependent on use, exclusivity is determined by the territorial extent of each community of Indians. In the Pacific Northwest,

> Indians were very much aware of the region's character as a great watershed. Anthropologist Marian Smith observes that Indians from southeastern Puget Sound derived their major concept of social unity from the geographical concept of the drainage system.
> Often the names of a village site and the area that fed its river were the same. For example, the Puyallup River above its fork with the Carbon River was called "ts'uwa," as was the village at that spot. The Indians living there called themselves "the people of ts'uwa": "ts'uwadiabc."[38]

Cohen summarizes the evidence that shows that Indians in Puget Sound had clear property concepts about which villages owned rights to fish at particular sites, and individuals or groups of individuals owned weirs, dams, and traps that they constructed.[39] Cronon and White report that villages had boundaries in New England and among the Choctaw in the South.[40]

Fundamental for understanding the ability of these institutions to ensure respect for the land is attention to generosity. Even if individual members of a community control particular resources, the rest of the community has an immediate interest in the management of this resource. The richer the owner, the more he has to share with everyone else. Thus, connectedness is addressed directly. That only use-rights can be owned means that the community retains a sanction over misuse. In addition, use-rights leave ownership of the land in the community, which can preserve it for the seventh generation. Because the community retains control, the limits on a person's use-rights provide ways for the members of a group of Indians to insist that an individual obey the principles of proper behavior toward nonhuman entities and that management be undertaken with a spirit of humility.

THE APPLICABILITY OF THE ANALYSIS

This essay has provided proposals for economic development policy guided by Indian values. Respect imposes constraints on the shape of economic policy by barring excessive high grading, placing an upper limit on consumption, and maintaining ecosystem health. Institutions that encourage violation of these constraints, such as private property and corporate land ownership, are not consistent with respect. Do we observe any contemporary Indian communities pursuing traditional Indian economic policy? The answer is yes, but rarely. Most Indian tribes are not truly in control of selecting their economic policy institutions or the resulting activities, and they must be in control in order for this analysis to be tested.

Control of Indian economies from outside takes several forms. The most direct form is the explicit authority of the federal government to coerce tribal governments to sell the products of Indian land.[41] All of this authority, ultimately, is based on the plenary (absolute) authority of Congress as recognized by the Supreme Court throughout this century.

In addition to the authority to coerce tribal governments, the historical legacy of treaties has created dependency that assists in the coercion. The general pattern was for Indian tribes to exchange land for promises of a continuing supply of commodities and tools. These promises have evolved into a system of federal support systems: the Bureau of Indian Affairs' (BIA) programs to manage timber and other renewable resources, education programs, the Indian Health Service, and so on. These programs are part of the federal trust responsibility, and they derive from the legitimate source of the treaties. Because Indians now receive services paid for by the federal government, the threat of withholding services is always available. Because interest was not paid in the Indian Claims Commission process for land taken in the nineteenth century, Indians can show that they still have not been paid fair value for the land cessions.[42] They also know that current Indian resources are often utilized by non-Indians at prices that are unfairly low.[43] Since they have not been fully compensated, Indians retain the sense that federal support is owed to them. The perpetuation of support keeps in place the potential threat to remove the support.

A third form of federal control is the imposition of governing structures. Examples are the promulgation of constitutions under the Indian Reorganization Act by bare majorities in elections with few Indians voting, the governing structures imposed under termination, and the corporate structures imposed by the Alaska Native Claims Settlement Act.

The three forms of federal control were neither universal in scope nor fully successful. Through their own insistence on self-government, combined with good luck, some tribes have been able to preserve traditional governing structures or to create new ones. To determine if Indian tribes select traditional Indian development strategies when they can, we must study the choices made by the few tribes that have been able to retain or obtain some independence. Two tribes that have done so are the Menominee and the Taos Indians.

The Menominee Tribe

The Menominee's independence today is the result of political struggle. Because of the tribe's efforts and the help of Senator Robert LaFollette in the first decade of this century, the Menominee were able to build tribal institutions during the allotment era, when most tribal governments were being ignored or dismantled.[44] In 1909, when the Menominee established a tribal lumber mill to use their forest resource, the federal government was dividing the commonly held resources of other tribes among their members. Although the BIA asserted its authority over timber management, the tribe, through a series of lawsuits, was able to force the bureau to adhere to the tribe's standards for sustained-yield management.

In the early 1950s, a combination of factors made the tribe temporarily vulnerable to extreme federal coercion under the termination policy. The Menominee had won a judgment against the federal government, giving leverage to an aggressively anti-Indian senator, Arthur Watkins of Utah. There was no senator or governor helping them, as was the case with the Salish and Kootenai tribes in Montana. In Montana, both the Republican governor and Senator Mansfield opposed termination. As a result of their weak position, the reservation status of the Menominee tribe was terminated. A county government and a corporation replaced the tribal government and the BIA.

The decisions of the corporation to create artificial lakes, sell land in a housing development, and change the cutting practices in the forest met great opposition, leading to a movement within the tribe to restore reservation status and change the governing structure. The short-term outlook and the sale of land to outsiders by Menominee Tribal Enterprises, contrary to the consensus of the tribal members, was a major factor leading to the restoration of the Menominee reservation.

The new tribal structure has two governing boards, which serve as a check on each other. Major land-use decisions, especially regarding the tribal forest, require approval by both bodies. With its current governing structure, the Menominee tribe manages its forest in a manner consistent with maintaining ecosystem health. They do not high-grade the old growth, and they maintain species and structural diversity in the forest.

To achieve these goals, the Menominee employ principles of forest management that illustrate respect. They have given their forest manager the following management guidelines: (1) Produce trees with both quality and quantity; (2) Don't put all the eggs in one basket; and (3) Remember that we are borrowing the forest from our grandchildren.[45]

The first two principles illustrate community and connectedness. Production of quality and quantity requires growing trees to large size for quality, which compromises quantity production. The large stock of older trees indicates that they are not high-graded, which cuts out all of the high-quality trees at once. All species are supported under the principle of keeping the eggs (forest productivity) in different baskets (species). The idea that the forest is borrowed from future generations expresses the seventh-generation principle. Although none of these three principles clearly states the idea of humility, keeping all of the species present in the forest is an example of cautious management consistent with humility.

Taos Pueblo

From 1906 to 1970, the leadership of the pueblo of Taos Indians fought to preserve the ecosystem health of the drainage of the Rio Pueblo de Taos. The land was taken from them in 1906 and placed under the management of the U.S. Forest Service as part of the Carson National Forest in northern New Mexico. As explained by Paul Bernal, one of the leaders in the struggle to regain control of the land,

> In all of its programs the Forest Service proclaims the supremacy of man over nature; we find this viewpoint contrary to the realities of the natural world and to the nature of conservation. Our tradition and our religion require our people to adapt their lives and activities to our natural surroundings so that men and nature mutually support the life common to both. The idea that man must subdue nature and bend its processes to his purposes is repugnant to our people.[46]

He went on to complain about forest service logging plans:

> These plans tell us that the Forest Service will always be seeking ways to interfere with the natural ecology of the Rio Pueblo watershed and that it will claim the legal right to do so despite Indian rights under the 1933 act. Our religion is based upon the unity of man with nature in the Rio

Pueblo watershed. Any outside interference with natural conditions of the watershed interferes with our religion.[47]

Pueblo governor John C. Reyna explained the religious importance as follows:

The lake is as blue as turquoise. It is surrounded by evergreens. In the summer there are millions of wild flowers. Springs are all around. We have no buildings there, no steeples. There is nothing the human hand has made. The lake is our church. The mountain is our tabernacle. The evergreen trees are our living saints. They are with us perpetually. We pray to the water, the sun, the clouds, the sky, the deer. Without them we could not exist. They give us food, drink, physical power, knowledge.[48]

Although the watershed is sacred, it is not unused. One major source of conflict was different harvesting rules for deer. The Taos Indians kill deer at times different from those allowed under federal and state wildlife policies.[49]

In their struggle to obtain title to Blue Lake and the Rio Pueblo de Taos watershed, the Taos Indians had to confirm their religious devotion to the area by accepting limitations on development. The law that returned their land restricts use of the watershed to wilderness. The Taos Indians accepted this restriction with little complaint.[50]

In convincing President Nixon, the House of Representatives and the Senate to transfer land title to them, the Taos Indians emphasized the religious significance of the land. To avoid the argument that returning the land to them would set a precedent, they and their supporters argued that the Taos Indians were unique: No other Indians had such strong religious ties to particular land areas.[51] Of course, the claim was false, although politically convenient at the time. Connectedness assumes all humans are tied to their roots, and the connectedness assumption is widespread among Indians.

Both the Menominee and the Taos Indians illustrate Indian-inspired economic policy. Although their forest management practices differ from each other, both manage forests that non-Indians regard as wilderness. The Menominee Forest is roaded, with stumps as well as very large trees. The large trees and species diversity suggest forests as they were before non-Indian settlement. The Taos forest is accessible only by foot, does not support a mill, and is closer to wilderness as currently defined by non-Indians. The principles of respect support a wide range of policies, while excluding others.

A POSSIBLE COUNTEREXAMPLE

The examples of the Taos Pueblo and the Menominee tribe show that some Indian communities pursue policies consistent with respect. There are apparent counterexamples, however; the case of the Navajo is examined below. Some other counterexamples can be dismissed as instances of imposed institutions leading to disrespectful policies; an example of this is the clearcutting of the cedar forests of the Quinault Reservation. The Quinault Indian Nation had no power to determine the harvest policy, because of the imposition of a private property system, combined with federal administration of forest policy.

The case of overgrazing on the Navajo Nation, however, is not so easily dismissed. The situation has been extensively analyzed and is a rather typical example of an open-access property rights system leading to overuse: the tragedy of the commons.[52] The situation was created by the federal government, by regulation of land-use policies. When the federal government attempted to reduce sheep herds in the 1930s, the undemocratic and harsh method used created political opposition to such policies. But in the years since, the Navajo Nation has attained sufficient self-governing powers to control grazing if the political will existed to do so. After all, the Menominee example shows that political will can overcome deleterious institutions. It appears that the political will does not exist in the Navajo Nation. Why is this so?

An answer is provided in John Farella's careful study of Navajo philosophy, entitled *The Main Stalk*.[53] Although Navajo belief stresses the importance of harmony with the external world, Navajo concepts of society and the community of humans does not include the assumption of resource limitation that underlies most Indian thought regarding the seventh generation. In fact, many Navajo resist planning for the future. Farella summarizes his presentation as follows:

> First Man set about creating Navajo society so that, if man behaved selfishly, it would, at worst, harm no one, and at best benefit everyone. Further, his own actions are the model. Remember what Grey Mustache said, "What he did brought all these things into being that benefit mankind, the reason he did these things was for himself, for his own benefit . . . ."
>
> The essential foundation block in this endeavor was to assure that the process would be non-zero sum. Or in terms of the Navajo gloss, "ever increasing, never decreasing." As we have already pointed out, the mechanism for that is gender, sexuality, and reproduction. The way the system was "designed" was to ensure that growth could occur and that anyone's gain would not be contingent on another's loss. In fact, First Man did even better. He arranged it so that anyone's gain would, within limits, be of social benefit. . . .
>
> There is a paradoxical imperative at the base of Navajo Society—"To be social, one must be selfish." The above discussion points to a second underlying maxim or basic premise, namely, "don't compete." Obviously, the two can co-exist only in the non-zero-sum or "increase with no decrease" context.[54]

Farella's analysis of Navajo philosophy shows the Navajo do not share all of the assumptions included in the traditional Indian definition of respect used in this paper. The missing component is the seventh generation assumption of resource limits. Proper behavior leads to increase without decrease, suggesting an unlimited future.

Navajo philosophy does not provide a basis for the political will to revise an open-access grazing system. Today's traditional Navajo will insist that the world will adjust and will provide what is needed to those whose behavior is correct. Although these attitudes may have been influenced by early contacts with non-Indian culture, the Navajo example suggests caution in asserting that the idea of the traditional Indian used in this paper is a universal concept among Native peoples in the Americas. Acceptance of the four components of respect is common among Indians; it is not universal.

FUTURE RESEARCH

This paper has examined values that were probably developed in relatively closed communities, prior to contact with Europeans. In the five hundred years since the two halves of the earth began communicating with each other, the system of capitalism, with its high rate of technological change, has taken over the planet. How might this analysis be extended in relation to challenges posed by the current market situation? How might traditional Indian thought incorporate the following into the economic policy decisions: the exchange of species in ecosystems, major engineering events such as hydroelectric dams, and technological change? Another paper is needed to provide complete analysis of these examples. This paper concludes by suggesting an agenda for further work.

As Indian tribes attain control over their reservations, they will be faced with decisions about the management of ecosystems that have already been manipulated according to the engineering and management principles espoused by the federal government. Forests will have been clearcut, and fire will have been excluded; hydroelectric and irrigation dams will be in place. A return to a previous ecosystem may not be feasible. Are the policies advocated above a good, useful guide to management of resources and ecosystems after major disturbance?

The view that ecosystem health should be maintained provides fairly clear implications, given the above definition of ecosystem health.[55] It is worth noting, however, that there is no clear indication that the four components of respect tell one to return to a previous ecosystem: Respect applies to entities in existence today, and in the future.

Respect for natural systems is not consistent with one of the fundamental justifications for economic development under capitalism: the prospect of infinite growth of humanity's per capita income based on technological progress. Such rapid change denies one of the assumptions about duties to the seventh generation and is inconsistent with humility. The stories of man emerging through several worlds as well as the transformations of animals into men and women in traditional Indian stories suggest that the reality of change is part of the traditional world view. But change that is continually an increase in man's share of natural productivity may not be part of such a world view.

Technical progress in the modern industrial economy makes additional consumption appear feasible based on current resources. This possibility raises some key issues regarding an upper limit on consumption. One should distinguish between renewable and nonrenewable resources. When discussing both, technical change in the industrial economy has to be treated. Technical change has many components: (1) the ability to make an existing ecosystem more productive by applying improved knowledge of how the system works; (2) the addition of energy and resource inputs into an ecosystem, also making it more productive; and (3) the introduction of new commodities or new species. Future essays will consider what the four components of respect require regarding the use of new technology in economic policy.

CONCLUSION

The fact that many non-Indians are becoming more interested in Native American world views may be a result of the fact that the consequences of modern economic growth have made several of the assumptions of traditional Indian people seem more relevant.[56] The ubiquity of problems generated by the disposal of waste products has made the assumption of connectedness seem important. The possibility of major catastrophe based on global warming has given the assumption of humility more appeal. Difficulties based on mistaken application of technology seem to have the potential to affect our lives in the near future. The basis of the fears, however, is still limited to the impact of unintended consequences on human livelihood and on this generation and the next.[57] Although concern for the seventh generation and for nonhuman entities has not been as great, the concept of sustainable development is gaining popularity.[58]

This essay provides examples of economic policies based on four components of respect that can be called part of a traditional Indian world view. Resource exploitation should be limited, consumption should have an upper bound, ecosystem health should be supported, and population growth rates should be held to a low level. The author hopes that others will join in spelling out the implications in more detail. Although many people agree that traditional Indian values are relevant, the study of the implications of these values for contemporary management issues has just started.

Acknowledgments

The author thanks the referees of this chapter for many helpful suggestions.

Notes

1. David Vinje, "Cultural Values and Economic Development on Reservations," in *American Indian Policy in the Twentieth Century*, ed. Vine Deloria (Norman: University of

Oklahoma Press, 1985), 155–75; Delores J. Huff, "The Tribal Ethic, the Protestant Ethic and American Indian Economic Development," in *American Indian Policy and Cultural Values: Conflict and Accommodation,* ed. Jennie R. Joe (Los Angeles: American Indian Studies Center, 1986), 75–89; Stephen Cornell and Joseph Kalt, "Reloading the Dice: Improving the Chances for Economic Development on American Indian Reservations," in *What Can Tribes Do? Strategies and Institutions in American Indian Economic Development,* ed. Stephen Cornell and Joseph Kalt (Los Angeles: American Indian Studies Center, 1992), 1–59; Ronald L. Trosper, "Mind Sets and Economic Development on Indian Reservations," in Cornell and Kalt, *What Can Tribes Do?* 301–28.

2. Joseph Epes Brown, "Becoming Part of It," in *I Become a Part of It: Sacred Dimensions in Native American Life,* ed. D. M. Dooling and Paul Jordan-Smith (New York: HarperCollins Publishers, 1989), 9–20; J. Baird Callicott, "American Indian Land Wisdom? Sorting out the Issues," and "Traditional American Indian and Western European Attitudes toward Nature: An Overview," in Callicott, *In Defense of the Land Ethic: Essays in Environmental Philosophy* (Albany, NY: State University of New York Press, 1989), 177–201, 203–19; Richard K. Nelson, *Make Prayers to the Raven: A Koyukon View of the Northern Forest* (Chicago: University of Chicago Press, 1983); idem, "Searching for the Lost Arrow: Physical and Spiritual Ecology in the Hunter's World," in *The Biophilia Hypothesis,* ed. Stephen R. Kellert and Edward O. Wilson (Washington, DC: Island Press, 1993), 201–28.

3. Callicott, "American Indian Land Wisdom?" 216.

4. The work of John Rawls on justice as fairness is an example of the way that an assumption of constitution building among humans leads to statements about what ought to be. His first book on the topic, *A Theory of Justice* (Cambridge, MA: Harvard University Press, 1971), reviews the types of analysis presented in Western European thought, especially pp. 22–53. His recent *Political Liberalism* (New York: Columbia University Press, 1993) clarifies his intent to focus on the structure of democratic societies. Because of this emphasis on democracy, his work is potentially very helpful in analyzing Indian assumptions about the proper order of society, which typically are very democratic. In *Political Liberalism,* pp. 21 and 244–46, Rawls recognizes that his theory has not been extended to the rest of nature and expresses some doubt that it can be, based on the assumption that a constitution is an agreement among humans. Most traditional Indian world views, it appears, would not make the same assumption. In spite of this difference, Rawls's reflections on the political aspect of justice raise issues similar to those Callicott sees in traditional Indian societies.

5. Callicott, "American Indian Land Wisdom?" 216. Rawls distinguishes between a well-ordered democratic society, his object of study, and a community or an association (*Political Liberalism,* 40–43). In describing inclusion of nonhuman beings within a human social system, we must be careful to distinguish between different ideas. Rawls's differentiation of society, community, and association is helpful in this regard. The word *community* is used broadly by Callicott, and in the text of this essay, to include all three as possibilities.

6. Dooling and Jordan-Smith, ed. *I Become a Part of It: Sacred Dimensions in Native American Life* (New York: HarperCollins Publishers, 1989); Barry Holstun Lopez, *Giving Birth to Thunder, Sleeping with His Daughter: Coyote Builds North America* (New York: Avon Books, 1977); Ella E. Clark, *Indian Legends from the Northern Rockies* (Norman: University of Oklahoma Press, 1966); Mourning Dove, *Coyote Stories* (Lincoln: University of Nebraska Press, 1990).

7. Nelson, "Searching for the Lost Arrow," 220.

8. Brown, "Becoming Part of It," 19–20; Trosper, "Mind Sets," 310.

9. Marguerite Swift quotes her recent interview with Lacondon Indian leader Chan K'in: "The roots of all living things are tied together." See Swift, "Parallels Between Traditional Native American Land Ethics, the Emerging Western/Anglo Land Ethics, and Multiresource Management" (Master's thesis, Northern Arizona University, 1994), 24.

10. Oren Lyons, "An Iroquois Perspective," in *American Indian Environments: Ecological Issues in Native American History,* ed. Christopher Vecsey and Robert W. Venables (Syracuse, NY: Syracuse University Press, 1980), 173.

11. Nelson, "Searching for the Lost Arrow," 220.

12. Ibid., 215.

13. Frank Waters, *Book of the Hopi* (New York: Penguin Books, 1977); Paul G. Zolbord, *Dine bahane': The Navajo Creation Story* (Albuquerque: University of New Mexico Press, 1984); Barbara Tedlock, *The Beautiful and the Dangerous* (New York: Viking, 1992).

14. Nelson, "Searching for the Lost Arrow," in *Clothed-In-Fur and Other Tales: An Introduction to an Ojibwa World View,* ed. Thomas W. Overholt and J. Baird Callicott (Lanham, MD: University Press of America, 1982).

15. Aldo Leopold, *A Sand County Almanac, with Essays on Conservation from Round River* (New York: Ballantine Books, 1970), 262.

16. Callicott, "American Indian Land Wisdom?" 197–98.

17. Ibid., 198.

18. Leopold, *A Sand County Almanac,* 280.

19. Paul W. Taylor, *Respect for Nature: A Theory of Environmental Ethics* (Princeton, NJ: Princeton University Press, 1986), 99–100.

20. Robert Costanza, "Toward an Operational Definition of Ecosystem Health," in *Ecosystem Health: New Goals for Environmental Management,* ed. Robert Costanza, Bryan G. Norton, and Benjamin D. Haskell (Washington, DC: Island Press, 1992), 248.

21. Economists measure productivity as output per unit of input; in a closed ecological system, the input is energy from the sun, a constant, unless humans are supplying additional inputs.

22. Tietenberg provides a survey of economic models of sustainable development that also require high savings rates, usually 100 percent of the returns to exhaustible resources (which gambling might be). See Tom Tietenberg, *Environmental and Natural Resource Economics*, 3d ed. (New York: HarperCollins, 1992), 604–05. The literature on justice as fairness has started to consider an issue of just savings among many generations. See Jane English, "Justice Between Generations," *Philosophical Studies* 31 (1977): 91–104; and Rawls, *Political Liberalism,* 274.

23. Simon Kuznets, *Modern Economic Growth* (New Haven, CT: Yale University Press, 1972).

24. See United Nations Development Programme, *Human Development Report 1994* (New York: Oxford University Press, 1994).

25. Cornell and Kalt, "Reloading the Dice," Terry L. Anderson and Donald R. Leal, *Free Market Environmentalism* (Boulder, CO: Westview Press, 1991).

26. Edella Schlagger and Elinor Ostrom, "Property-Rights Regimes and Natural Resources," *Land Economics* 68:3 (1992): 249–62.

27. Anderson and Leal, *Free Market Environmentalism,* 161–65. In recent years, advocates of private property institutions generally have backed off urging them for Indians; see Jennifer Roback, "Exchange, Sovereignty, and Indian-Anglo Relations," in *Property Rights and Indian Economies,* ed.Terry L. Anderson (Lanham, MD: Rowman & Littlefield Publishers, 1992), 5–26.

28. Timothy F. H. Allen and Thomas W. Hoekstra, *Toward a Unified Ecology*. (New York: Columbia University Press, 1992), 256–81.

29. Gary C. Anders, "Social and Economic Consequences of Federal Indian Policy: A Case Study of the Alaska Natives," *Economic Development and Cultural Change* 37:2 (1989): 285–303.

30. To illustrate: If the real rate of interest is 3 percent and a generation is twenty-five years long, then the value today of one dollar's worth of consumption by the seventh generation, 175 years from now, is less than one cent. With such low value assigned, the consequences of today's action on the seventh generation will be ignored when principles of corporate profitability are applied to management decisions. The principle of maximizing the present value of a flow of income over time places very low weights on income in the far future.

31. Schlagger and Ostrom, "Property-Rights Regimes and Natural Resources," 249–62; Elinor Ostrom, *Governing the Commons: The Evolution of Institutions for Collective Action* (Cambridge, England: Cambridge University Press, 1990); Terry L. Anderson and Randy T. Simmons. *The Political Economy of Customs and Culture: Informal Solutions to the Commons Problem* (Lanham, MD: Rowman and Littlefield, 1993).

32. Jeffrey B. Nugent and Nicolas Sanchez, "Tribes, Chiefs, and Transhumance: A Comparative Institutional Analysis," *Economic Development and Cultural Change* 42:1 (1993): 87–113.

33. Although the literature on traditional Indian systems is large, the text relies on three sources: William Cronon, *Changes in the Land: Indians, Colonists, and the Ecology of New England* (New York: Hill and Wang, 1983); Richard White, *The Roots of Dependency: Subsistence, Environment, and Social Change among the Choctaws, Pawnees, and Navajos* (Lincoln: University of Nebraska Press, 1983); and Fay G. Cohen, *Treaties on Trial: The Continuing Controversy over Northwest Indian Fishing Rights* (Seattle: University of Washington Press, 1986).

34. Cronon, *Changes in the Land*, 61–62.

35. White, *The Roots of Dependency*, 42.

36. Cohen, *Treaties on Trial*, 19.

37. Cronon, *Changes in the Land*, 62–64.

38. Cohen, *Treaties on Trial*, 21.

39. Ibid., 22.

40. Cronon, *Changes in the Land*, 59; White, *The Roots of Dependency*, 37–38.

41. Russel Lawrence Barsh, "Indian Resources and the National Economy: Business Cycles and Policy Cycles," in *Native Americans and Public Policy*, ed. Fremont J. Lyden and Lyman H. Legters (Pittsburgh: Pittsburgh University Press, 1992), 193–221.

42. Leonard A. Carlson, "What Was It Worth? Economic and Historical Aspects of Determining Awards in Indian Land Claims Cases," in *Irredeemable America*, ed. Imre Sutton (Albuquerque: University of New Mexico Press, 1985), 87–109.

43. Trosper, "Who Is Subsidizing Whom?" in *American Indian Policy: Self-Governance and Economic Development*, ed. Lyman H. Legters and Fremont J. Lyden (Westport, CT: Greenwood Press, 1994), 175–89.

44. Brian C. Hosmer, "Creating Indian Entrepreneurs: Menominees, Neopit Mills and Timber Exploitation, 1890–1915," *American Indian Culture and Research Journal* 15:1 (1991): 1–28.

45. Marshall Pecore, "Menominee Sustained Yield Management: A Successful Land Ethic in Practice." *Journal of Forestry* 90:7 (July 1992): 12–16.

46. R. C. Gordon-McCutchan, *The Taos Indians and the Battle for Blue Lake* (Santa Fe,

NM: Red Crane Books, 1991), 157.

47. Ibid.

48. Ibid., 93.

49. Ibid., 39.

50. Ibid., 155.

51. Ibid., 192–93.

52. Gary D. Libecap and Ronald N. Johnson, "Legislating Commons: The Navajo Tribal Council and the Navajo Tribe," *Economic Inquiry* 18:1 (January 1980): 69–85.

53. John R. Farella, *The Main Stalk: A Synthesis of Navajo Philosophy* (Tucson: University of Arizona Press, 1984).

54. Ibid., 192–93.

55. In fact, the maintenance of ecosystem health may be an easier rule than implementation of management systems based on the net present value of private and social costs and benefits, which is the usual environmental economist's prescription. Calculation of true social value requires surveys and other techniques to estimate the public's valuation of natural phenomena. See Ronald G. Cummings, et al., ed., *Valuing Environmental Goods* (Totowa, NJ: Rowmand & Allanheld, 1986).

56. David Suzuki and Peter Knudtson, *Wisdom of the Elders: Sacred Native Stories of Nature* (New York: Bantam Books, 1992).

57. In his influential 1967 article, "Conservation Reconsidered" (*American Economic Review* 57: 777–86), economist John Krutilla emphasizes the usefulness of genetic diversity and other characteristics of natural environments. Although he refers to the future in general terms, he relies on the bequest motive ("a desire to leave one's heirs an estate") for supporting his conclusions. The article is reprinted in V. Kerry Smith, *Environmental Resources and Applied Welfare Economics* (Washington, DC: Resources for the Future, 1988), 263–73.

58. The literature on sustainable development is large and growing. An early book was Herman Daly's *Steady-State Economics*, 2d ed. (Washington, DC: Island Press, 1991). Two critical overviews of the literature are provided by Michael Redclift, *Sustainable Development: Exploring the Contradictions* (London and New York: Routledge, 1987), and Tom Tietenberg, *Environmental and Natural Resource Economics,* 599–626. See also United Nations Development Programme, *Human Development Report 1994*. Four earlier reports, 1990–1993, also stress sustainable development.

6

Indian Gaming:
Financial and Regulatory Issues

Gary C. Anders

If after a long period the Indian problem remains a problem still, it is because we have no sufficient knowledge of the people we are striving to teach. The solution of the problem is not to be reached until the stronger race shall understand the weaker, and, in the light of that understanding, shall deal with it wisely and well.

—George Bird Grinnell[1]

A BRIEF HISTORY OF INDIAN GAMING

 Casinos and bingo parlors have become recent additions to Indian[2] reservation landscapes. An industry of more than 120 casinos and 220 high-stakes bingo games in 24 states sprang from a single bingo hall on the Seminole reservation in Florida.[3]

High-stakes gaming grew as other Florida and California Indian tribes began offering cash prizes greater than allowed under state law. When the states threatened to close the operations, the tribes sued in federal court. In *California v. Cabazon Band of Mission Indians* ,[4] the Supreme Court upheld the right of tribes as sovereign nations to conduct gaming on Indian lands. The Court ruled that states had no authority to regulate gaming on Indian lands, if gaming is permitted for any other purpose.[5]

In light of the favorable Supreme Court decision, Congress passed Public Law 100-497, the Indian Gaming Regulatory Act (IGRA), in 1988, recognizing Indian gaming rights. IGRA faced strong opposition from Las Vegas and Atlantic City. States, however, lobbied for the legislation in an effort to establish some control over tribal gaming. In passing IGRA, Congress sought to balance Native American legal rights with the interests of the states and the gambling industry.[6]

Table 1 presents three classes of gaming defined under IGRA. IGRA requires states to negotiate in "good faith" with tribes seeking Class III gaming compacts. A tribal-state compact is a legal agreement that establishes the kinds of games

Gary C. Anders is professor of economics at the School of Management at Arizona State University, West. He has been a faculty fellow at the U. S. General Accounting Office and a visiting fellow at the Institute of Developing Studies at Sussex and the East-West Center. He has written extensively on Native American economic development and the economic impact of Indian casinos.

offered, the size of the facility, betting limits, regulation, security, and so forth. Compacts ensure that tribal governments are the sole owners and primary beneficiaries of gaming.

In 1996, Indian gaming exceeded $5 billion, accounting for approximately 10 percent of total U.S. gambling revenue according to *International Gaming and Wagering Business*.[7] Currently, 124 of the 557 federally recognized[8] tribes operate gaming facilities (see table 2). Indian gaming is highly diverse.[9] Casinos range from the palatial Foxwoods casino in Connecticut to trailers in remote locations offering a few slot machines.

IGRA REGULATORY FRAMEWORK

IGRA created a framework for regulation and oversight of tribal gaming with four interdependent levels: tribal, state, federal (including the Department of Justice, the Federal Bureau of Investigation, the Internal Revenue Service, and the Bureau of Indian Affairs), and, finally, the National Indian Gaming Commission (NIGC). Class I gaming is regulated solely by tribes. Class II gaming is regulated solely by tribes if they meet conditions set forth in IGRA. Regulation of Class III gaming is governed by tribal-state compacts.

In general, tribes enforce frontline gaming regulations. They establish their own gaming commissions and operate tribal police forces and courts to combat crime. They adopt ordinances, set standards for internal controls, issue licenses for gaming

Table 1
IGRA Types of Gambling

Class	Description
Class I	Social games for prizes of minimal value and traditional forms of Indian gaming engaged in as part of tribal ceremonies or celebrations.
Class II	Bingo and similar games, pull tabs, tip jars, punch boards, lotto, instant bingo, and some card games such as black jack and baccarat and excluding certain nonbanking card games.
Class III	All other forms of gaming, including banking card games, slot machines, craps, pari-mutuel horse racing, dog racing, and lotteries.

Table 2
Tribal-State Gaming Compacts

State	Tribal Compacts*
Arizona	16
California	5
Colorado	2
Connecticut	2
Idaho	2
Iowa	3
Kansas	3
Louisiana	3
Michigan	7
Minnesota	11
Mississippi	1
Montana	4
Nebraska	1
Nevada	2
New Mexico	14
New York	2
North Carolina	1
North Dakota	5
Oklahoma	2
Oregon	8
Rhode Island	1
South Dakota	9
Washington	12
Wisconsin	11

Source: National Indian Gaming Commission, 1996.
* Some tribes may have more than one compact for different types of games.

operations, and provide security and surveillance measures. Tribes or management contractors also manage tribal gaming operations. States enforce the provisions of Class III gaming compacts, which include background checks of employees and management company personnel. Some states, like Arizona, for example, coordinate background checks and other security measures with tribes.

At the federal level, the Department of the Interior determines which lands can be placed into reservation trusts, approves tribal-state compacts, rules on tribal gaming revenue allocation plans, and conducts audits of gaming operations. The Department of Justice enforces criminal violation of gaming laws, conducts background checks of key gaming employees, and conducts investigative studies. The Federal Bureau of Investigation and the Bureau of Indian Affairs provide oversight regarding crimes committed on reservations. The NIGC approves tribal resolutions and gaming ordinances, and it reviews the terms of Indian casino management contracts. The NIGC has the authority to enforce civil penalties, impose fines, and close an establishment. The NIGC has seventeen field employees to oversee the more than two hundred tribal gaming operations.[10]

INFORMATION DISCLOSURE, OVERSIGHT, AND TAXATION

IGRA provides tribal gaming operations with an exemption from the Freedom of Information Act. Unless the tribe agrees, federal and state regulators cannot publicly release or disclose financial information. This protective measure makes it nearly impossible to ascertain individual casino revenues.

According to the General Accounting Office, the regulations and reporting requirements for tribal casinos differ from Bank Security Act requirements, thereby affecting the information reported to the Internal Revenue Service. (See table 3 for a comparison of casino reporting requirements.) "These differences may cause problems for law enforcement officers looking for a consistent paper trail of records with which to trace all gaming activity of customers engaged in large cash transactions, as well as to help identify potential money laundering activities."[11]

Tribes do not have to pay taxes on their gaming revenues to the state or federal government.[12] Tribes are, however, legally required to deduct and withhold state and federal income tax and FICA from all non-Indian and nonresident Indian[13] tribal employees, pay federal employment taxes and the employer's share of FICA, and report payments to independent contractors. Additionally, Indian tribes are obligated to report gaming winnings to the Internal Revenue Service, withhold federal income taxes of statutorily defined gaming winnings and payments to nonresident aliens, report per capita distributions of more than $600 to the Internal Revenue Service, and withhold federal income tax on distributions of $6,400 or more.

Table 3
Comparison of Casino Currency Transaction Reporting
Requirements and Prohibitions

Requirements and Prohibitions	BSA* Casinos	Non-BSA Tribal Casinos	Nevada Casinos
Reporting requirements			
All cash in over $10,000	X	X	X
All cash out over $10,000	X		
All cash out over $10,000 except verified winnings	X		
Aggregation of multiple transactions during a day (in same gaming area of the casino)	X	X	
Aggregation of multiple transactions during a day (in different gaming areas of the casino)	X		
Detailed currency transaction reporting and record-keeping system	X	X	
Prohibited transactions			
Exchanging cash for over $2,500	X		
Exchanging cash for a casino check over $2,500	X		
Exchanging cash for a wire transfer over $2,500	X		

Source: U.S. GAO (1996). *Bank Security Act regulations as amended on 3 August 1995 were applied to tribal gaming operations, requiring tribes to report incoming and outgoing cash transactions of more than $10,000 in a 24-hour period.

TRIBAL USES OF GAMING REVENUE

IGRA requires that all tribal gaming revenue be used exclusively for tribal government operations, the general welfare of the tribe and its members, support of economic development, charitable contributions, and local government agencies. Tribal governments determine how to allocate the proceeds. Some tribes are using gaming profits to build houses, schools, day-care centers, clinics, and hospitals; to support social service programs, drug and alcohol treatment programs, roads, and sewer and water systems; and to fund retirement programs for their tribal elders as well as college scholarships.[14] A tribe may petition the secretary of the interior for approval of a plan for a per capita distribution of revenues. Instead of per capita payments, other tribes use gaming profits to expand employment opportunities by diversifying the reservation's economic basis.[15]

Economic and social conditions on many reservations are deplorable. In 1990, more than half of all Native Americans and Alaska Natives (50.7 percent) had incomes below the poverty line.[16] Reservation Indians have a life expectancy of 47 years, a suicide rate more than twice that of all other nonwhites, and the highest high school dropout rate among all nonwhites.[17] Alcoholism and drug abuse are prevalent, along with other health and social problems.[18] Health care for Native Americans is the poorest in the country. Reservation unemployment rates average 45 percent and can be as high as 80 percent of the total labor force. Only 28 percent of Indians with jobs earned more than $7,000 a year.[19]

In spite of this situation, Congress continues to cut substantially programs for Native Americans. Tribal leaders argue that gaming is one of the few revenue sources available to help offset federal cuts. According to Rick Hill, chairman of the National Indian Gaming Association (NIGA):

> Tribal gaming is the one successful economic venture that has worked virtually every place a tribe has established a gaming operation. Tribes are in the gaming business like states are in the lottery business, to establish and increase revenue for governmental operations and infrastructures.[20]

ECONOMIC AND SOCIAL IMPACT OF GAMING

Gaming has both positive and negative effects for Indians struggling for economic and cultural survival. According to the NIGA, an Indian gaming lobby, gaming creates jobs, reduces dependence on welfare, stimulates business activity, and generates tax revenue for states. Drawn largely from consulting studies, the NIGA cites the following examples.

Michigan Indian tribes operate 8 Class III gaming operations, employing nearly 2,000 workers, with an annual payroll estimated at $13.5 million and state and federal tax payments of nearly $700,000.[21] Minnesota's 17 casinos generate $390 million in revenues and have created more than 12,000 new jobs. In 1992, casinos paid more than $37 million in state and federal payroll taxes and benefits. Approximately 37 percent of the tribal gaming employees received state or federal welfare assistance prior to their employment, and another 31 percent were drawing unemployment compensation. Welfare payments in counties with casinos dropped 14 percent between 1987 and 1991, saving the state an estimated $7 million.[22]

Wisconsin tribes operate 15 Class III<%0> gaming facilities, with a total payroll of about $68 million. Half of the 4,500 casino employees were previously unemployed, and 20 percent were receiving welfare. Welfare costs in 11 rural counties with Indian casinos dropped 26 percent over three years, saving taxpayers $470,000 per month. In 1992, casino employees paid more than $380,000 in state income tax and $2.1 million in federal income tax. Tribal gaming operations spend nearly $62 million each year, creating 470 indirect jobs in other businesses.[23]

Tribal gaming in Washington State is estimated to have created 1,200 jobs, with a total economic impact of more than $65 million in 1993. Unemployment on the Tulalips' reservation has dropped from 65 percent to less than 10 percent since the tribe opened its gaming operation in 1991. The Tulalips' casino injects $25.4 million into the local economy yearly in wages and direct purchases from local businesses.[24] The Mashentucket-Pequots Foxwoods casino in Connecticut employs more than 20,000 workers, with an annual payroll of nearly $480 million. Every Foxwoods job supports 0.74 new jobs in the rest of Connecticut.

Every new job trims 0.154-0.260 recipients from Aid to Families with Dependent Children, saving the state between $9.6 and $16.0 million per year.[25]

These examples make a strong case for gaming. Tribes, formerly dependent upon government programs, are developing new managerial and professional competencies through gaming. Thompson asserts that unlike public sector programs, gaming gives Native Americans a choice in the direction of their economic development.[26] Gaming represents economic clout that brings tribal members together and connects their individual interests to larger national issues. Gaming elevates the standing of tribes and helps them mobilize as an effective political force. Such political mobilization can provide a training ground for younger leaders to cultivate the skills to effectively interact with non-Indians.

NEGATIVE IMPACT OF INDIAN CASINOS

The negative effects of Indian casinos, while more difficult to quantify, can be specified. First, there are attendant externalities including compulsive addictions, increased drug and alcohol abuse, crime, neglect and abuse of children and spouses, and missed workdays. As to problem gamblers, the state must pay to prosecute them, incarcerate them, and provide restitution to their victims. Researchers have estimated the social costs at between $12,000 and $50,000 for each problem gambler.[27] Estimates of compulsive gamblers range as high as 4–5 percent of the general adult population.

Second, the General Accounting Office notes that due to the nature of the business—primarily on a cash basis without receipts or other written records—there are opportunities for theft, embezzlement, and criminal infiltration.[28] In a review of 37 management contracts (signed before 1993, when the NIGC began oversight operations), the Interior Department concluded that there were excessive fees amounting to $62.2 million in 18 of them. The Bureau of Indian Affairs admitted that in the past, some tribes "entered into unconscionable contracts and leases" that called for "exorbitant or excessive fees." [29]

Third, because of the enormous profit potential, gaming may undermine the cultural integrity of Indian communities. The Prior Lake Skakopee Mdewakanton Dakota reservation in Minnesota is a high-profile example. The tribe's casino, Mystic Lake, is one of the premier Indian operations. Since opening in 1992, it has turned 150 members of the tribe into millionaires. Leonard Prescott, head of a corporation that runs the casino, says that, because of this success, dozens of people with dubious claims are clamoring for tribal membership. This has led to disputes over who is entitled to control the tribe's gaming operation.[30] Citing other examples, Pasquaretta[31] argues that the presence of high-stakes gaming aggravates existing conflicts within Native American communities.

Fourth, there are instances where small tribes with highly profitable casinos make large per capita payments; for example, Mystic Lake has paid $40,000 to $50,000 per month to enrolled tribal members. In most instances such large payments are not the case. Still, gaming exacerbates inequalities between urban and rural tribes[32] and between large tribes such as the Navajo and Hopi and other tribes. The Navajo and Hopi suffer extremely limited economic conditions but have chosen not to open casinos.

Fifth, the majority of casino jobs are low-wage, high-turnover positions.[33] The fewer high-paying professional and technical jobs require a college education. Unless the tribe has a strong training program, these jobs generally go to outsiders.

Sixth, there is evidence that gaming draws money from established businesses. When local retail establishments experience a significant decrease in sales, the employment gains in gaming may not be net increases but only shifts between industries.[34] Goodman argues that increases in gaming profits come at the expense of other taxable sectors of the economy.[35] For example, since Indian casinos do not pay taxes, lost tax revenue may have stimulated some state legislatures to legalize riverboats that can be taxed.

CONFLICTS OVER INDIAN SOVEREIGNTY

Relations between Indian tribes, states, and the federal government are predicated on three centuries of law and treaties. Tribal leaders believe that since their operations are on federal trust land, the state should have no jurisdiction. States have complained that IGRA exempts tribes from paying taxes while reducing states' regulatory control.[36] IGRA attempted to balance the state interests against tribal sovereignty by stipulating that Class III gaming could be offered only in conformance with a tribal-state compact. Having compacts gave states the power to exercise control over Indian gaming. Congress might have bypassed the states, as it did for Class II gaming, had it not been for states' insistence on some control over gaming activities within their borders.[37]

IGRA set time limits to protect tribes so that states could not stall the compact process. The law provides that if states refuse to negotiate in good faith for more than 180 days, tribes can ask the federal court to appoint a mediator. If the mediator fails to bring both sides together within 60 days, the mediator chooses the last best offer of either the tribe or the state. To address the possibility that states might not negotiate in good faith, Congress made the state's obligation judicially enforceable. The U.S. district courts have jurisdiction over cases initiated by an Indian tribe arising from the failure of a state to enter into good-faith negotiations.

Several tribes have initiated court cases under IGRA. In 1991, Alabama became the first state to argue that Congress did not have the constitutional authority to subject unconsenting states to the jurisdiction of the federal courts. This defense, based on the Eleventh Amendment, concerns the judicial powers of the state and federal governments.[38] In 1991, Arizona became the first state to argue that, on the grounds of the Tenth Amendment, Congress did not have the constitutional authority to compel states to have compacts with tribes. Court cases regarding whether IGRA violates the Tenth and Eleventh Amendments are on the docket in other states.

A recent Supreme Court decision in *Seminole Tribe of Florida* v. *Florida* may significantly affect the future of Indian gaming.[39] In September 1991, the Seminole Tribe sued the state of Florida for refusing to enter into compact negotiations. Florida's motion to dismiss the Seminole suit as violating the state's sovereign immunity was denied by the federal district court. The Eleventh Circuit Court of Appeals reversed the district court and held that the Eleventh Amendment barred the Seminole suit against the state. The Supreme Court ruled in favor of the state's sovereign immunity and against the tribal right to force the state to have compacts.

IGRA made the secretary of the interior the ultimate authority when an agreement on a compact could not be reached after 180 days. In lieu of successful compact negotiations, the interior secretary has the power to establish conditions and procedures for tribes to offer Class III gaming.[40] If the secretary chooses, the state of Florida and all states may find that a refusal to negotiate or waive the state's immunity may lead to a set of procedures that bypasses the state. The *Seminole* decision raises a new series of questions related to a state's right to prohibit gaming that Congress will eventually have to resolve.[41]

CHANGES IN IGRA

In light of recent developments, Indian tribes should anticipate changes in the current law. Several amendments to IGRA have already been proposed, and more will follow. For example, proposed legislation drafted by the Senate Indian Affairs Committee seeks stricter federal guidelines, including licensing of games, background checks of key casino employees, and accounting with respect to revenues and profits. Another proposal would let states refuse to allow Indian gaming within their borders. Still another amendment could eliminate a governor's veto authority over Indian gaming and instead only allow him or her to advise the Interior Department. Another proposed amendment would change Section 511(a) of the Internal Revenue Code, which would treat tribes as charitable organizations and tax tribal gaming revenues.

Indian leaders realize that gaming may not last. They are using casino profits to diversify their economic base and build infrastructure, schools, hospitals, and houses. Even where tribal gaming is thriving, it cannot quickly reverse generations of paternalism and failure.[42] There is also concern that these economic improvements facilitate cultural assimilation. Amending IGRA to widen the distribution of benefits and minimize the negative social consequences will be difficult,[43] but a backlash eliminating Indian gaming could be devastating.

Notes

1. George Bird Grinnell, "The Wild Indian" *Atlantic Monthly* 83 (1899): 20-29, at http://etext.lib.virginia.edu/conditions.html.

2. The terms *Native American* and *American Indian* will be used interchangeably.

3. Brian M. Greene, "The Reservation Gambling Fury: Modern Indian Uprising or Unfair Restraint on Tribal Sovereignty" *BYU Journal of Public Law* 10:1 (1996):93–116.

4. *California* v. *Cabazon Band of Mission Indians* (480 U.S. 202 [1987]).

5. In two famous cases (*Seminole Tribe of Florida* v. *Butterworth* [658 F.2d 310 (5th Cir. 1981)] and *California* v. *Cabazon Band of Mission Indians* [480 U.S. 202 (1987)]), the courts determined that if a state civilly regulates a form of gambling including bingo or "Las Vegas night," then the tribes have the right to conduct gaming operations on their own land. See Greene, "The Reservation Gambling Fury."

6. W. R. Eadington, *Native American Gaming and the Law*, (Reno, NV: University of Nevada, Institute for the Study of Gambling and Commercial Gaming, 1990).

7. About 55 percent of gambling revenues come from casinos in Nevada and New Jersey; another 40 percent comes from state lotteries and riverboats. See various issues of *International Gamming and Wagering Business*, 1996.

8. Tribes can be recognized in only two ways: by an act of Congress or by the lengthy and complex process with the Department of the Interior. The final determination on tribal recognition is made by the assistant secretary for Indian Affairs. A directory of federally recognized Indian Nations is maintained by the Bureau of Indian Affairs. Currently, over 109 groups are seeking recognition from the Department of the Interior for the purposes of establishing a reservation.

9. G. Anders, "Native American Casino Gambling in Arizona: A Case Study of the Fort McDowell Reservation" *Journal of Gambling* Studies 12:3 (1996): 253–67.

10. James Popkin, "Organized Crime May Infiltrate Indian Casinos," in *Gambling*, ed. Charles P. Cozic and Paul A. Winters (San Deigo, CA: Greenheaven Press, 1995).

11. U.S. General Accounting Office (GAO), *Money Laundering: Rapid Growth of Casinos Makes Them Vulnerable*, letter report (1996), GAO/GGD-96-28.

12. Brian M. Greene, "The Reservation Gambling Fury."

13. All Native Americans pay federal income, FICA, and Social Security taxes; however, Indians who live and work on federally recognized reservations are exempt from paying state income and property taxes. Each tribe sets its own membership rules. In order to be eligible for federal benefits, most tribes require a person to have one-fourth quantum blood degree of his or her tribe's blood to be an enrolled member. Some tribes have additional qualifications for membership.

14. Jonathan Gardner, "For Indians, a Winning Gamble" *Modern Healthcare* 26:20 (1996): 40–45.

15. G. Anders, "Native American Casino Gambling in Arizona"; Mary H. Cooper, "Native Americans' Future" *CQ Researcher* 6:26 (1996): 603–23.

16. U.S. Department of Commerce, Bureau of the Census, *1990 Census of Population and Housing* (Washington, DC: Government Printing Office, 1991).

17. Neal Lawrence, "Gambling on a New Life" *Midwest Today* (Jan. 1995).

18. Mary H. Cooper, "Native Americans' Future," 608.

19. Michelle Rushlo, "State's Job Boom Stops at Reservations," *Arizona Republic*, 14 May 1997.

20. Rick Hill, "Consider This," *Casino Journal* 9:3 (1996): 24, 102.

21. National Indian Gaming Association (NIGA), Web page (1997), http://www2.dgsys.com/ niga/regulatn.html.

22. Don Cossetto, "The Economic and Social Implications of Indian Gaming: The Case of Minnesota," *American Indian Culture and Research Journal* (Winter 1995): 119-32; NIGA Web page.

23. James M. Murray, "The Economic Impact of American Indian Gaming on the Government of the State of Wisconsin," (Green Bay: University of Wisconsin, Extension Cooperative Division, 1993); NIGA Web page.

24. NIGA Web page.

25. Ibid.

26. W. Thompson, *Native American Issues* (Santa Barbara, CA: ABC-Clio, 1996).

27. W. Thompson, R. Gazel, and D. Rickman, "The Economic Impact of Native American Gaming in Wisconsin," *Wisconsin Policy Institute Research Report* 8:3 (1995): 1–48.

28. U.S. General Accounting Office (GAO), *Money Laundering: Rapid Growth of Casinos Makes Them Vulnerable*, Letter Report GAO/GGA 96-28 (Washington, DC: Government Printing Office, 1996); Brian M. Greene, "The Reservation Gambling Fury," 95.

29. Neal Lawrence, "Gambling on a New Life."

30. A judge is reviewing the qualifications of eleven people who voted to approve the 1995 amendment to the tribal ordinance that was used to justify the enrollment of 43 others. See David Melmer, "Shakopee Election Challenged" *Indian Country Today* (8 Feb. 1996).

31. Paul Pasquaretta, "On the Indianness of Bingo: Gambling and the Native American Community" *Critical Inquiry* 20:4 (1994): 694–714.

32. Anthony Layng, "Indian Casinos: Past Precedents and Future Prospects" *USA Today* (1 Mar. 1996).

33. R. Keith Schwer and Jeffrey Waddoups, "Job Satisfaction in Gaming and Nongaming Occupations," Paper presented at the Western Social Science Association Meetings, 14 Apr. 1996, Reno, NV.

34. A Minnesota study raises questions about the extent to which that state's Indian casinos have benefited economies in rural counties, where most of the Indian casinos are located. The report claimed that business volume has actually fallen by 20–50 percent at restaurants located within a thirty mile radius of casinos with food service. See Neal Lawrence, "Gambling on a New Life."

35. Robert Goodman, *The Luck Business* (New York: Free Press, 1995).

36. Richard L. Worsnop, "Does Indian-Run Gambling Enjoy an Unfair Advantage?" *CQ Researcher* 4:11 (1994): 246.

37. James Belliveau, "Casino Gambling Under the Indian Gaming Regulatory Act: Narrangansett Tribal Sovereignty Versus Rhode Island Gambling Laws," *Suffolk University Law Review* 27:2 (1993): 391–423.

38. Brian M. Greene, "The Reservation Gambling Fury," 105.

39. 116 S.Ct. 1114 (1996).

40. Brain M. Greene, "The Reservation Gambling Fury," 114.

41. Charles Irwin, *A Discussion of the Seminole Decision* (Washington, DC: Tribal Gaming Commission Administrators, June 1996).

42. Neal Lawrence, "Gambling on a New Life."

43. Elsewhere I have argued for four changes in IGRA: (1) public disclosure of relevant financial information should be provided; (2) the powers of the NIGC should be strengthened; (3) the built-in inequality should be reduced by providing a mechanism for the redistribution of revenues to all tribes; and (4) tribes should be required to nego-

tiate to pay a percentage of the gambling revenues to states to cover lost tax revenue and the increased demand for social services.

PART IV

LAW AND JUSTICE

Chief Justice John Marshall, in 1823 when delivering the opinion of the Court in the case Johnson v. McIntosh, stated that "On discovery of this immense continent, the great nations of Europe were eager to appropriate to themselves so much of it as they could respectively acquire. . . . The potentates of the old world found no difficulty in convincing themselves that they made ample compensation to the inhabitants of the new [land], by bestowing on them civilization and Christianity, in exchange for unlimited independence." In their eyes, justice had been extended to the first nations of the new world.

Johnson v. McIntosh is the first of the John Marshall trilogy of cases which also includes Cherokee Nation v. Georgia, 1831, and Worcester v. Georgia, 1832. This trilogy constituted the early canons of federal Indian law. These three court cases established that title to Indian lands could not be passed to individuals or states, only to the federal government; that Indian tribes did not enjoy the unique status of foreign nations but were rather domestic dependent nations; and lastly, that Indian Nations were distinct communities with boundaries accurately described, in which state laws and non-Indian citizens had no authority. In Worcester v. Georgia, Marshall reiterated the decision rendered in Johnson v. McIntosh that the relationship between the new government and Indian Nations was committed exclusively to the government of the union.

Over 160 years have passed since the decisions of the Marshall Court, and hundreds of cases involving Indian Nations have since worked their way through the *judicial system and up to the Supreme Court bench. The decisions rendered with such clarity by the Marshall Court have been reduced from established precedent to a concept of a "backdrop," against which Indian cases are now heard. The Court ruled in the 1903 Lone Wolf v. Hitchcock case that "Plenary authority over the tribal relations of the Indians has been exercised by Congress from the beginning and . . . . The power exists to abrogate the provisions of an Indian treaty. . . ."*

In this section, Carole Goldberg and Donald Green provide us with two very current topics which are rooted in the distant past but have critical impact for contemporary Native people and Native communities. Of primary importance is an examination of the contextual nature of what has been defined as "American Indian Criminality." Donald Green's "The Contextual Nature of American Indian Criminality," reviews selected studies and presents data from the Uniform Crime Reports (UCR) to show several important contextual factors placing the study of Native American criminology within the sociological framework of the historical experience and treatment of Indian people in the United States. In reviewing previous studies, Green finds that they lack a sociological context; for example, federal Indian policies that resulted in a breakdown of traditional mechanisms of social control among the Eastern Cherokee and, in another, the two-decade federal government relocation program that uprooted large numbers of American Indians to urban areas. Particularly interesting is the author's presentation of the changing American Indian identity and aggregate-level analyses of crime that is available from the FBI recording arrest date systematically by race.

Based on this accumulated data, Green provides a table for "arrest for 1970, 1980, and 1990 for Index and Total Crimes by Race." This table compares arrests for the three years broken down by Native Americans, blacks, and whites, the actual change in numbers of arrests for these groups, and the percent change in number of arrests. The percentage change indicates that, in the two decades since 1970, American Indians have experienced the largest increase in arrest for index crimes among all racial groups examined. In a second table, the author provides for the "Arrest Rates (per 100,000) by race for 1970, 1980, and 1990, total and index crimes." This analysis "reveals significant differences in aggregate measures of American Indian arrests when alternate indicators of the American Indian population are utilized. . . ."

A study conducted by Gary D. Sandefur and Trudy McKinnell show the importance of bringing the contextual and sociological framework together to explain these findings. "[T]heir findings suggest that Indians residing in traditionally Indian areas of the country do differ from Indians who live in the so-called non-Indian states. American Indians living in Indian states had higher rates of poverty and family social disorganization, as well as lower per capita household incomes, both of which represent factors that have been found by previous criminological research to be highly correlated with aggregate crime rates." In closing, Green states that "The diversity of the American Indian experience in the United States requires that those who conduct research on American Indian crime patterns not view it as a generic phenomenon" but "must also attempt to identify situational and contextual factors that can account for differences within the American Indian population."

Another area of concern has been a perceived state of "lawlessness" on Indian reservations. This lawlessness, if it exists in fact, is the product of another misguided federal government edict: Public Law 280. On August 15, 1953, Congress passed PL 280, which empowered the states of California, Wisconsin, Nebraska, Minnesota, Oregon, and, in 1959, Alaska, to manage criminal justice on Indian reservations. The law opened the possibility of state jurisdiction over reservation courts where previously federal law, Congress, and the U.S. Supreme Court had upheld the separation of state and Indian government relations explicitly provided for in the Commerce Clause of the U.S. Constitution and had been articulated by the Marshall Court in Worcester v. Georgia, 1831. Public Law 280 did not usurp all federal responsibility, however, and specifically excepted from state jurisdiction the regulation and taxation of trust property and the hunting and fishing rights of Native American people.

Carole Goldberg calls Public Law 280 "law gone awry" in her article and explains how the law was able to take hold, with its destructive impact, in California. Because California Indian tribes had no ratified treaties with the U.S. government, because years of population loss and dislocation had disrupted tribal social and political organization, and because the Indian Service undermined traditional or popularly elected leaders, tribal leaders and tribal institutions over hundreds of years were hampered in their capacity to respond to changing social and economic conditions wrought by local, state, and federal authorities. As a result, Goldberg correctly points out, non-Indians were prepared to view tribes as "lawless," in the nineteenth century. This early concept of lawlessness was crucial to the passage of Public Law 280. Federal authorities had failed to control lawlessness in California Indian Country, and so the state would be given the opportunity.

Goldberg provides a summary of the direct and indirect effects of Public Law in California Indian Country. The issues go beyond simple law enforcement and affects the general welfare of tribes and tribal members in areas such as education, welfare, and health care. Of critical concern for the control of crime, or "lawlessness" on Indian reservations has been the tribal law enforcement organizations and tribal courts. Prior to passage of PL 280, the federal Courts of Indian Offenses handled dispute resolution on many reservations. The federal government has withdrawn funding and refused to support tribal justice systems in California "on the grounds that Public Law 280 made tribal jurisdiction unnecessary and perhaps even eliminated such tribal authority." Noting the consequent jurisdictional vacuum, Goldberg concludes with the irony that "Public Law 280 has itself become the source of lawlessness on reservations."

7

The Contextual Nature of
American Indian Criminality

Donald E. Green

SEVERAL REVIEWS OF THE CONTEMPORARY LITERATURE on American Indian criminality and criminal justice outcomes during the last decade have lamented the lack of volume, theoretical clarity, and methodological rigor of research in this area of criminology.[1] The present analysis of that literature suggests a somewhat more optimistic view. When these works are placed within the sociological framework of the Native American experience in the United States, several important contextual factors emerge that advance our understanding of crime patterns in this uniquely American racial group. This paper will review selected studies and present additional crime data from the Uniform Crime Reports (UCR) that establish the significance of these contexts and discuss their implications for future research.[2]

THE CONTEXTUAL NATURE OF
CRIMINOLOGICAL RESEARCH ON AMERICAN INDIANS

Perhaps the most overlooked factors in the study of American Indian criminality are the sociological contexts of the studies themselves. Consider one of the earliest studies to appear in the contemporary literature, authored by Norman S. Hayner and published in a prominent sociological journal in 1942.[3] Although this research was conducted during a period in which significant numbers of American Indians still lived on reservation lands that were relatively isolated from large, white, urban populations, extensive efforts by the federal government to dismantle traditional Indian culture and assimilate Indians into mainstream American society had taken their toll on many Indian Nations.[4] Not surprisingly, then, in this primarily descriptive work, Hayner stressed the importance of tribal social disorganization as an explanation for crime among American Indians. He used initial arrest statistics generated by the Federal

Donald E. Green is an assistant professor of sociology at the University of Wisconsin, Milwaukee. An earlier version of this paper was presented at the annual meetings of the American Society of Criminology in Chicago, Illinois, November 1988.

Bureau of Investigation (FBI)[5] to support his argument that crime among American Indians in the Pacific Northwest, who were the focus of his study, varied according to levels of social isolation from white populations and periods of economic prosperity resulting from monetary payments for natural resources. That is, less isolated populations and those that experienced greater monetary payments had higher rates of crime. Hayner concluded that these factors adversely affected tribal organization in these groups and provided the best explanation for their crime patterns.

Although social disorganization explanations for American Indian criminality have continued to appear in the literature,[6] more recent studies have found support for refined conceptualizations of this approach. And while these reconceptualizations are internally consistent with the data presented in these studies, the literature has failed to address the exogenous relationships between the sociological contexts of these studies and the shifting theoretical relationships among social disorganization variables and American Indian crime patterns. For example, in their 1970s case study of violent behavior among the Eastern Cherokee, French and Hornbuckle also found support for social isolation explanations for crime among American Indians but placed their findings within a "cultural frustration/subcultural control" perspective.[7]

In addition, the direction of the social isolation and crime relationship that French and Hornbuckle found is contrary to Hayner's earlier study. They argue that, rather than protecting traditional culture, years of living in a restrictive reservation environment created by paternalistic federal Indian policies resulted in a breakdown of traditional mechanisms of social control among the Eastern Cherokee. The authors stress that the breakdown was particularly evident among "marginal Indians," whom they defined as the majority of Native Americans living on and off reservations, torn between Indian and white worlds and not being fully accepted by either group. French and Hornbuckle contend that, as the influence of the traditional cultural norms and values of the Eastern Cherokee has continued to decline, nontraditional norms and values more supportive of interpersonal violence have emerged in response to the frustrating and tension-filled reservation experience. They conclude that the pattern of criminal behavior observed among this group is similar to that identified in urban black ghetto communities by Wolfgang and Ferracuti.[8]

Others have questioned whether these findings can be generalized, because the studies by French and Hornbuckle, Hayner, and others have lacked the possibility of statistical control for alternative explanations for criminal behaviors.[9] Acknowledging this problem, Larry Williams and his colleagues assessed the relative impact of three different approaches to American Indian criminality: social background characteristics, personality, and cultural factors.[10] Using survey data from a randomly selected sample of Native Americans living in the Seattle area during 1972, their step-wise multivariate regression analysis indicated little support for cultural conflict explanations, while support was found for several indicators of social disorganization, although these were more contemporary conceptualizations not necessarily specific to American Indians.

Williams and his colleagues found that indicators of familial disorganization, such as problems with marital adjustment and relative marital happiness, were significant predictors of self-reported arrests among these Seattle respondents, even after controlling for a number of personal and cultural variables such as self-esteem, degree of alienation, and support for assimilation into white culture.

Again, however, the sociological context of this study emerges as a neglected explanatory variable that is central to the theoretical implications of its findings. This research was conducted following a two-decade effort by the federal government to relocate large numbers of American Indians to urban areas in the United States.[11] Therefore, these findings should be considered in light of the fact that many urban American Indians in the sample may have experienced some of the previously documented adjustment problems that occurred during these federal relocation programs.[12] And while these experiences may have been no less difficult to endure than the conditions experienced by those who remained in rural/reservation areas, the lack of support for alternative explanations for the respondents' self-reported arrests may be due to unaccounted-for differences between urban and nonurban Indian populations.

The contextual nature of research on American Indian criminality is further demonstrated by two studies on the social reaction to American Indian offenders. Hall and Symkus compared sentencing decisions for both whites and Indians in a western state during the late 1960s and early 1970s.[13] They controlled for the effects of a number of legal and extralegal variables that past research has found to be important predictors of criminal court sentencing patterns, such as prior adult offenses and juvenile dispositions, education levels, employment status, and other socioeconomic background variables. Hall's and Symkus's findings indicated that even when comparisons were statistically controlled for both sets of variables, Native Americans, more than non-Indians, were both more likely to receive sentences that included incarceration and less likely to receive deferred sentences.

A second study by Bynum also focused on criminal justice outcomes among American Indians during the 1970s.[14] His research examined the effect of prior record and major disciplinary infractions while in prison—as well as selected sociodemographic characteristics of the offenders—on a parole board's release decisions in an upper Plains state. Bynum's findings indicated that not only did American Indians receive incarceration for offenses that non-Indians did not; they also served significantly greater portions of their original sentences than did non-Indians. Although the authors of these two studies did not explicitly acknowledge the social context in which their data collection occurred, it is significant to note that the time frame used in both coincides with that of increased Native American political activity.[15] Given the widely held view among criminologists and criminal justice practitioners that race per se has no direct effect on criminal justice outcomes,[16] one could possibly interpret these findings to mean that the differential criminal justice outcomes reported in these studies were evidenced only within the context of a highly visible political movement among various American Indian groups in these states and other regions of the county.

Another frequently ignored contextual factor in research literature on American Indian criminality is the lack of comprehensive data. This limitation forces researchers to omit a number of variables previously identified as significant predictors of crime patterns among other population groups. As a result, studies of American Indian criminality often propose theoretical arguments that extend well beyond the data presented. A good example of this problem can be found in aggregate-level analyses of national arrest data.[17] Notwithstanding the numerous studies that have stressed the importance of alcohol abuse in explaining frequency of involvement in illegal behaviors,[18] aggregate-level research on American Indian arrest rates has consistently documented the disproportionate number of American Indians involved in alcohol-related crime.[19] A study by Peak and Spencer is representative of this series of studies conducted over the last three decades focusing solely on univariate arrest statistics.[20] Although it is important to acknowledge Peak and Spencer for their efforts to examine Indian arrest rates both on and off reservations, they also devote considerable attention to "the Indian propensity for arrests involving alcohol-related offenses."[21] With the inability of univariate analyses such as these to assess alternative theoretical explanations adequately, it is not surprising that conclusions drawn from these studies too often focus primarily on the role that alcohol plays in the etiology of crime among American Indians, rather than on variables that may be antecedent to both its abuse and relationship to illegal behavior.

In fact, despite these frequently cited physiological and/or psychological explanations, there are still other studies suggesting that at least within particular social contexts, structural and/or economic explanations often used to account for crime patterns among non-Indian populations might best account for American Indian criminality. For instance, sociodemographic population characteristics such as age and sex have consistently been linked to criminality in non-Indian populations.[22] Similarly, in the previously mentioned study by Williams and his colleagues, the variables of age and sex were the most important predictors of self-reported arrests among their sample of urban American Indians.[23] And in an earlier study of the Shoshone-Bannock tribe on the Fort Hall Reservation, Minnis assessed the relationship between various indicators of the social structure of that Indian community and official tribal records of adult and juvenile law violations.[24] Using households as the unit of analysis, she argued that overcrowded conditions, high percentages of individuals on public assistance, and low education levels were linked to high levels of crime.[25]

In the following sections, perhaps the most recent sociological context of the American Indian experience in the United States to influence research on American Indian criminality—changing conceptions of American Indian identity—is presented and discussed.

AMERICAN INDIAN IDENTITY
AND THE UNITED STATES CENSUS DATA

Over the past few decades, demographic research on the American Indian has frequently discussed the consequences of a series of historical factors that have effected this population.[26] While debate continues concerning the exact number of American Indians prior to European contact, those who have focused their research efforts in this area generally agree that disease, war, and federal government policies directed toward these indigenous groups since their initial contacts with European societies have had devastating effects on American Indian populations.[27] Nagel and Snipp, for example, have noted that even conservative estimates of the Native American population indicate a decline from approximately two million people at the time of Columbus's arrival in 1492 to as few as 237,000 people in 1900.[28]

Since this population nadir, census figures from 1900 to the present suggest that the Native American population in the United States has increased over the past century at a rate that is perhaps as dramatic as the population declines prior to the 1900s. Nagel and Snipp, for instance, report that American Indian census data between 1890 and 1980 indicate an increase of 555 percent during this period.[29] Moreover, these researchers note that the largest increase occurred between the years 1950 and 1980, when the American Indian population increased from 343,000 to 1,357,000.[30] Even the most recent census data reveal a continuation of this trend, reporting the 1990 American Indian population at 1,959,234, although the degree of increase is less than that which occurred over the last three decades.[31]

Some demographers, however, have questioned whether this more recent American Indian population trend has been a natural one (i. e., the result of high birth and low death rates), arguing instead that the increase can be attributed primarily to changes in the way the Census Bureau counts American Indians.[32] Since 1950, the bureau has increasingly relied on respondents' self-identification of race in the enumeration process. Subsequently, some have suggested that more recent census data include a significant number of individuals, previously identified with other races, who now identify themselves as American Indian, at least for census-recording purposes.[33] Although explanations for this dramatic increase have been of significant interest to those concerned with the study of American Indian demography, criminological research on official rates of American Indian criminality—which employ census data to derive rates of involvement in crime—has completely ignored this issue. In the following review and extension of the literature on American Indian arrest rates, some preliminary indications will be presented of the degree to which this demographic phenomenon affects criminological research involving American Indian populations.[34]

CHANGING AMERICAN INDIAN IDENTITY
AND AGGREGATE-LEVEL ANALYSES OF CRIME

As previously mentioned, some of the more widely cited research on American Indian criminality has been based on national-level arrest data.[35] Collectively, this research can provide us with a rough chronological account of the rate of Native American involvement in crime since the FBI has been recording arrest data systematically by race.[36] Native American arrest rates have consistently increased from a low of 1,699 per 100,000 in 1935[37] to a high of 15,123 in 1960.[38] Following this peak, American Indian arrest rates show a more gradual decrease, with the most recently published studies (based on 1985 data) indicating an American Indian arrest rate of between 7,859.2[39] and 8171.5,[40] depending on whether the census figures used to calculate the rate per 100,000 population included Alaska Natives.

These reported increases in arrests between 1935 and 1960 are consistent with similar trends in census data reported by demographic research on the Native American population, at least between the years of 1935 and 1960.[41] Given these historical patterns, however, it is somewhat surprising that more recently published studies of American Indian arrest rates indicate a decrease in crime among this racial group while census figures indicate that the American Indian population continues to increase, especially during the last three decades.[42] Perhaps more importantly for our efforts to understand American Indian criminality, these indicators of involvement in crime suggest that the total Native American crime rate has decreased during a time when the overall amount of crime in the United States in general, and among other racial groups in particular, has experienced dramatic increases.[43]

This differential pattern of racial involvement in illegal behavior has continued into the 1980s. Table 1 presents the actual number of arrests for American Indians, blacks, and whites for the years 1970, 1980, and 1990 for all crimes and index crimes only. Between 1970 and 1980, the total number of arrests for index crimes increased for all groups. On the other hand, while the total number of arrests for all crimes increased for blacks and whites during the years 1970 through 1980, American Indian arrests for all crimes decreased during this period. An examination of the percent change in number of arrests provides a cogent illustration of these differences. As the bottom panel of table 1 indicates, the total number of Native American arrests for index crimes increased by 54.6 percent between 1970 and 1980, an increase that exceeds comparable totals for both blacks (39.4 percent) and whites (48.6 percent). During the same decade, however, American Indian arrests for all crimes decreased by 16.4 percent, while arrests for all crimes for both blacks and whites increased by 28.9 and 38.8 percent, respectively. These figures indicate that, unlike the patterns observed for blacks and whites, Native American arrests have both increased and decreased between the years 1970 and 1980, depending which category of crimes is examined.

In contrast to the 1970–80 data, table 1 indicates that the arrest patterns

Table 1
Arrests for 1970, 1980, and 1990 for Index and Total Crimes by Race*

Arrests	Native Americans	Blacks	Whites
1970			
Index Crimes	9,167	436,581	739,306
Total Crimes	130,981	1,739,306	4,373,157
1980			
Index Crimes	20,194	720,739	1,438,098
Total Crimes	109,480	2,375,204	7,145,763
1990			
Index Crimes	22,198	794,725	1,469,241
Total Crimes	122,586	3,224,060	7,712,339
Actual Change in Number of Arrests:			
1970–80			
Index Crimes	+11,027	+284,158	+698,792
Total Crimes	−21,501	+686,815	+2,772,339
1980–90			
Index Crimes	+2,004	+73,986	+31,143
Total Crimes	+13,106	+843,856	+566,576
1970–90			
Index Crimes	+13,031	+358,144	+729,935
Total Crimes	−8,395	+1,484,754	+3,339,182
Percent Change in Number of Arrests:			
1970–80			
Index Crimes	+54.6	+39.4	+48.6
Total Crimes	−16.4	+28.9	+38.8
1980–90			
Index Crimes	+9.0	+9.3	+2.1
Total Crimes	+10.7	+26.3	+7.4
1970–90			
Index Crimes	+58.7	+45.1	+49.7
Total Crimes	−6.4	+46.1	+43.3

* The FBI classifies the following offenses as index crimes (or Part 1 offenses): murder, rape, robbery, aggravated assault, burglary, larceny theft, and arson. Index crimes are basically felonies that are considered of most concern to the general public. The arson category is omitted from the table because it has been included as an index crime only since 1979. The total crime category includes both Part I and Part II offenses (which include simple assault, forgery and counterfeiting, fraud, embezzlement, buying, receiving or possessing stolen property, vandalism, carrying or possessing deadly weapons, prostitution and commercialized vice, sex offenses, drug-abuse violations, gambling, offenses against the family or children, liquor laws, drunkenness, disorderly conduct, vagrancy, and all other offenses that are violations of state or local laws, except the above offenses and traffic violations). Source: U.S. Department of Justice, Uniform Crime Reports, 1970, p. 131; 1980, p. 204; 1990, p. 192.

among these racial groups are considerably more consistent for the years 1980 through 1990. Arrests for the index and total crimes categories increased for all groups during this decade. The percent change figures indicate that arrests for index crimes were up 9.0 percent for American Indians and 9.3 percent for blacks, while index crime arrests were up only 2.1 percent for whites. A similar pattern emerges for all crimes, with blacks having the largest increase in arrests (26.3 percent), while American Indian and white increases were considerably smaller (10.7 and 7.4 percent, respectively).

Finally, a comparison of 1970–90 arrest data for these groups reveals a pattern more similar to the years 1970–80 than 1980–90. As was the case in 1970, the number of arrests for index crimes only has increased for all groups between 1970 and 1990, while the number of arrests for total crimes has decreased for American Indians only. The percentage change figures in table 1 indicate that, in the two decades since 1970, American Indians have experienced the largest increase in arrests for index crimes among all racial groups examined (+58.7 percent), while blacks and whites have experienced increases of 45.1 and 49.7 percent, respectively. However, the percent change figures in the bottom row of the table indicate that, while arrests for all crimes have continued to increase between the years 1970 and 1990 for both blacks and whites (46.1 and 43.3 percent, respectively), total arrests among American Indians during this same period have actually decreased 6.4 percent.

The differential patterns of arrest revealed by these data, particularly for the years 1970–90, clearly indicate the need for more scholarly inquiries to determine what factors have contributed to the varied picture of racial involvement in crime presented here. Sociological theories of law suggest that these rates are merely a reflection of an underlying practice of differential enforcement of criminal laws against Native Americans, as well as other racial groups. For example, conflict theories of criminal law posit that the formation and implementation of the criminal law is directly influenced by those groups in society that control its power and resources.[44] Through this influence, these more powerful groups have the ability to avoid sanctions against those behaviors that are in their best interest, while ensuring that behaviors detrimental to their interest but frequently engaged in by those groups not in power or control over resources are more frequently and severely sanctioned. The so-called labeling perspective in criminology also suggests that social reactions against certain forms of behavior are racially linked. Proponents of this view of the criminal law argue that, although all members of society engage in behaviors that could be considered illegal, in reality only those individuals with selected social characteristics—for example, being in a racial minority—are the object of society's reactions to crime.[45]

Still another possible factor to consider is the sociological context of changing patterns of American Indian identity and the potential measurement error American Indian census data may create for research on aggregate arrest rates among American Indians. Table 2 presents two methods of calculating American Indian arrest rates and compares them with rates of arrests for both blacks and whites for the years 1970, 1980, and 1990, in order to assess the degree to which these changing patterns of American Indian identity may alter arrest rates for this group. That is, two Native American arrest rates are presented: one based on actual census data and a second based on estimates derived from natural increases (the difference between births and deaths). These estimates have been determined previously by demographers who have examined the extent to which increases in the American Indian population, as indicated by census figures, are the result of changes in self-identification rather than a natural increase in the Native American population.[46] These latter figures then represent what would be considered the natural increase in the American Indian population in the United States over the last two decades.[47]

As table 2 indicates, based on actual census figures, American Indian arrest rates (per 100,000) for index crimes only were 1,156 in 1970, 1,419 in 1980, and 1,133 in 1990. The corresponding percent change figures reported in the bottom panel of the table indicate that American Indian arrests for index crimes increased by 18.5 percent between 1970 and 1980 and decreased by 20.2 percent between 1980 and 1990. The table also reveals a decrease of 2.0 percent in arrests for index crimes among American Indians over the past three decades.

Using demographic estimates of the natural increase in the Native American population to calculate their arrest rates reveals a somewhat different picture of American Indian criminality over this period of time. This alternative population base produces a change in the American Indian arrest rate for index crimes between 1970 and 1980 of almost twice that based on actual census data (18.5 percent versus 32.5 percent), although the latter rate more closely approximates the rate of change in index arrests during the same period for blacks (+39.5) and whites (+48.7). Differences among these two indicators of arrests for index crimes involving American Indians are not as pronounced for the 1980–90 period (–20.2 versus –25.6). In general, they follow a similar decline in arrests for index crimes among blacks (–17.0) and whites (–9.0). Interestingly, the 2.0 percent change figures between 1970 and 1990 present completely opposite patterns of American Indian arrests for index crimes over these three decades. The actual census-based rate reveals a decrease of 2.0 percent in arrests for index crimes among American Indians, while the rates based on estimated natural increases indicates an increase of 9.3 percent. Again, however, the natural increase-based rates more closely follow the three-decade pattern of increased index arrests among both blacks (+27.1) and whites (+43.6).

The percent change figures for American Indian arrests for all crimes consistently reveal a decrease in rates regardless of the population base employed, although there are considerable differences in the degree of change indicated for each. For example, when the natural increase base is used, the percent change figures for the periods 1970–80 (–53.4 versus –43.8) and 1970–90 (–62.1 versus –57.4) are reduced, while those for 1980–90 (–19.9 versus –24.3) are increased. Perhaps the more compelling finding in regard to these figures is the fact that, with the exception of the 3.9 percent decrease for whites between 1980 and 1990, overall rates of arrest for all crimes have increased for both blacks and whites during these three decades, while rates of arrest for all crimes among American Indians have decreased dramatically.

Table 1
Arrest Rate (per 100,000) by Race for 1970, 1980, and 1990
Total and Index Crimes

Arrest Rates	American Indian*	Black	White
1970			
Index Crimes	1,156 (1,286)	1,932	415
Total Crimes	16,517 (18,370)	7,471	2,457
1980			
Index Crimes	1,419 (1,905)	3,192	809
Total Crimes	7,694 (10,329)	10,519	4,020
1990			
Index Crimes	1,133 (1,417)	2,650	736
Total Crimes	6,258 (7,823)	10,752	3,862
Percent Change in Rates of Arrest:			
1970–80			
Index Crimes	+18.5 (+32.5)	+39.5	+48.7
Total Crimes	−53.4 (−43.8)	+29.0	+38.9
1980–90			
Index Crimes	−20.2 (−25.6)	−17.0	−9.0
Total Crimes	−19.9 (−24.3)	+2.2	−3.9
1970–90			
Index Crimes	−2.0 (+9.3)	+27.1	+43.6
Total Crimes	−62.1 (−57.4)	+30.5	+36.4

* Numbers in parentheses represent Native American crime rates based on demographic estimates of natural increases, defined by demographers as the difference between the number of births and deaths per year. Source: U.S. Bureau of the Census, 1970, 1980, 1990; U.S. Department of Justice, Uniform Crime Reports, 1970, p. 131; 1980, p. 204; 1990, p. 192.

While this analysis reveals significant differences in aggregate measures of American Indian arrests when alternate indicators of the American Indian population are used, the implications of these differences for future research are less clear. In general, the "natural increase" population estimates produce higher rates of arrests across all crime categories and time periods. Although the differences between the two indicators of criminality show some convergence between the 1970s and 1980s, comparisons between the 1980 and 1990 figures reveal that these differences may have started to increase again. This finding suggests that longitudinal research should further assess the extent to which this lack of congruence continues between American Indian census data and population estimates derived from alternative sources on American Indian populations.

Nevertheless, with the exception of the arrest rates for the 1970–90 period, these differences seem to raise more questions concerning the magnitude rather than the overall direction of these indicators. Assuming that these population differences are constant across all American Indian populations, this measurement issue may uniformly affect aggregate analyses of national arrest data only through the strength of various relationships among variables in this area of criminological research, rather than their direction. On the other hand, if the differential population figures reflect that changing patterns of American Indian identity are not invariant across Indian populations at state, county, and other units of analysis, future research that fails to account for this contextual factor would seem to be of limited value.

In this regard, it is instructive to note that several recent studies of American Indian demography have used a comparative strategy to assess the extent to which this measurement issue affects demographic research involving American Indian census data.[48] For example, noting that the "overcount" previously identified by demographers is less problematic for nineteen "Indian states" (i. e., states that historically have had large numbers of American Indians and in which Indian identity has remained relatively consistent over the years 1960–80), Sandefur and his colleagues have assessed differences between these states and all others on a number of sociodemographic and social indicators of the population.[49] Based on 1980 census data, their findings suggest that Indians residing in traditionally Indian areas of the country do differ from Indians who live in the so-called non-Indian states. American Indians living in Indian states had higher rates of poverty and family social disorganization, as well as lower per capita household incomes, both of which represent factors that have been found by previous criminological research to be highly correlated with aggregate crime rates.[50] Given these findings, it seems crucial that future aggregate-level analyses of American Indian arrests also assess the extent to which crime rates in "Indian states" differ from those in non-Indian states.[51] For example, should findings indicate that arrest patterns differ significantly on these grounds, states might prove to be the preferred unit of analysis for future aggregate-level research American Indian arrest rates. Currently I am analyzing arrest data for all fifty states to determine the extent to which this measurement issue affects American Indian arrest rates.[52]

A FRAMEWORK FOR FUTURE RESEARCH ON AMERICAN INDIAN CRIMINALITY

As the previous discussion indicated, the contextual nature of research findings on American Indian criminality has been virtually ignored in the literature. However, a review of some of the more widely cited studies in this area of criminology suggests that the sociological context of the Native American experience in the United States is a crucial concept for our understanding of crime and criminal justice outcomes among this racial group. Indicators of the concept not only emerge as important exogenous variables capable of bridging the theoretical gap between often divergent findings of past criminological research on American Indians, but they also raise significant methodological issues for future quantitative research on American Indian arrest rates.

Several other contextual factors should also be considered in future research on American Indian criminality. As recently suggested by Biolosi, a problem with many studies that focus on the American Indian experience is the tendency to assume a monolithic conception of Indian culture.[53] Although the history of the American Indian reveals that, in general, Indians have shared similar experiences as the victims of cultural, social, and economic deprivations, the degree of deprivation clearly differs by tribal group, as well as by individual. Regardless of the level of analysis, research on Native American criminality should assess more thoroughly those factors that can account for differential rates of criminal behavior within Indian populations.

The assumption of a monolithic Indian culture also raises questions concerning those studies that continue to suggest that culture conflict is a primary explanation for American Indian criminality. There is little argument that traditional Indian cultures have conflicted directly with Anglo-American culture, but the importance of this variable for our contemporary understanding of American Indian crime patterns may be considerably reduced. American Indians today are a diverse, young, and increasingly urban population that participates to varying degrees in both the remnants of the traditional tribal culture and that of the dominant society.[54] To the extent that research on American Indian criminality fails to take into account the diversity of the Indian experience in the United States, our knowledge about Indian crime patterns will continue to be limited to overgeneralizations based on an unrealistic view of what it means to be an American Indian in contemporary society. In addition, many American Indians today have little knowledge of their traditional cultures precisely because of the continuous subjugation and exploitation of Indian people; therefore, the use of culture conflict variables to explain racial differences in patterns of crime could lead to a misspecified model of American Indian criminality.

In fact, it is plausible to argue that a decline in the degree of culture conflict among American Indians has paralleled the previously noted changing forms of Indian identity. Rather than culture conflict, American Indian identity may now be a more important variable to consider in future efforts to develop an etiology of crime among American Indians. As previously noted, scholars of the Native American experience in the United States have noted recently the emergence of new dimensions of American Indian identity.[55] Consequently, it seems crucial that future studies of American Indian crime patterns incorporate a method of conceptually defining and measuring this dimension of "Indianness" to account for variation in the degree of American Indian identity among those individuals who engage in illegal behavior.

Research on this dimension of American Indian criminality may find that Indian identity and criminality are inversely related. For example, individuals of Indian descent who have lost ties to their tribal cultures may be more likely to engage in crime than those who have not. As an explanation for crime and delinquency, social control theories in criminology emphasize the importance of an individual's social bond to society through attachments to significant others and involvement in conventional activities.[56] If this perspective is applied to American Indian criminality, involvement in illegal behavior among this racial group may well be explained by the lack of a social bond to contemporary Indian society. For example, findings from a recent study on American Indian delinquency suggest that illegal behavior among Indian youth is the result of a lack of attachment to and involvement in both Indian and non-Indian societies.[57] Future research on self-reported American Indian criminality should test the applicability of social control theories as explanations of American Indian criminality by including indicators of individual involvement in contemporary Indian society, such as participation in powwows, membership in tribal, pan-tribal, or pan-Indian organizations, and perhaps other, more traditional ceremonies.[58]

It is also instructive to consider the findings of Williams's and his colleagues' study based on a random sample of American Indians in Seattle.[59] They report that degree of Indianness, measured as a composite of their respondents' ancestry, religion, attendance at powwows, and perceptions of their ethnicity, was positively related to self-reported arrests. Based on this finding, they argue that active participation in Indian community affairs may raise the visibility of individual Indians to agents of social control. These findings, linked with the studies reporting differential treatment of American Indians in the criminal justice system during periods of increased political activity, support the argument that the Native American resurgence in the form of highly visible political activities may not bode well for the future experiences of politically active American Indians with the formal social control system in the United States.

The diversity of the American Indian experience in the United States requires that those who conduct research on American Indian crime patterns not view it as a generic phenomenon. In order to assess between racial group differences in general patterns of crime, future criminological research must include more comprehensive data on American Indians in current macrolevel and microlevel research efforts on the etiology of and social reaction to crime. Studies must also attempt to identify situational and contextual factors that can account for differences within the American Indian population by using comparative samples of Indian offenders across tribal groups. The agenda outlined here may seem to involve as long and difficult a task as the struggle of American Indians themselves to achieve racial and social equity; nevertheless, it is deserving of just such an effort.

Notes

1. Philip A. May, "Contemporary Crime and the American Indian: A Survey and Analysis of the Literature," *Plains Anthropologist* 27:97 (August 1982): 225–38; Donald E. Green, "American Indian Criminality: What Do We Really Know?" in *American Indians: Social Justice and Public Policy, Ethnicity and Public Policy Series,* vol. 9, ed. Donald E. Green and Thomas V. Tonnesen (Milwaukee, WI: University of Wisconsin System, Institute on Race and Ethnicity, 1991), 223–70.

2. Although a number of studies have examined crime among indigenous groups in North America, the focus of this discussion will be on United States studies that have examined crime and criminal justice outcomes among American Indians living in the contiguous forty-eight states, because they are more directly comparable to the contemporary criminological literature. For example, research on Canadian indigenous populations is hampered by a lack of race-based data to facilitate comparative studies with United States crime figures. Moreover, race-based statistics on criminality and criminal justice outcomes continue to be a source of controversy in Canada. "Taboo on Race-based Figures Debated," *Milwaukee Journal*, 2 August 1992.

3. Norman S. Hayner, "Variability in the Criminal Behavior of American Indians," *American Journal of Sociology* 47 (1942): 75–84.

4. Vine Deloria, Jr. and Clifford M. Lytle, *American Indians, American Justice* (Austin, TX: University of Texas Press, 1983); Stephen Cornell, *The Return of the Native: American Indian Political Resurgence* (New York: Oxford University Press, 1988).

5. For an excellent discussion of the origins as well as current issues involving this source of criminological data, see Albert D. Biderman and James P. Lynch, *Understanding Crime Incidence Statistics: Why the Uniform Crime Report (UCR) Diverges from the National Crime Survey (NCR)* (New York: Springer-Verlag, Inc., 1991).

6. Charles Reasons, "Crime and the American Indian," in *Native Americans Today: Sociological Perspectives*, ed. Howard M. Bahr, Bruce A. Chadwick, and Robert C. Day (New York: Harper & Row, 1972), 319–26; Sidney Harring, "Native American Crime in the United States," in *Indians and Criminal Justice,* ed. Laurence French (Totowa, NJ: Allanheld, Osumn & Co. Publishers, Inc., 1983), 93–108; Ronald B. Flowers, "Native American Crime," in *Minorities and Criminality* (New York: Greenwood Press, 1988), 105–118.

7. Laurence French and Jim Hornbuckle, "An Analysis of Indian Violence: The Cherokee Example," *American Indian Quarterly* 3 (1977): 335–56.

8. Marvin Wolfgang and Franco Ferracuti, *The Subculture of Violence* (London: Tavistock, 1967).

9. Green, "American Indian Criminality"; Larry E. Williams, Bruce A. Chadwick, and Howard M. Bahr, "Antecedents of Self-Reported Arrest for Indian Americans in Seattle," *Phylon* 40:3 (Fall 1979): 243–52.

10. Williams, Chadwick, and Bahr, "Antecedents of Self-Reported Arrest."

11. Alan L. Sorkin, *The Urban American Indian* (Lexington, MA: Heath, 1978); Cornell, *Return of the Native*.

12. Ibid.

13. Edwin L. Hall and Albert A. Symkus, "Inequality in the Types of Sentences Received by Native Americans and Whites," *Criminology* 13 (1975): 199–222.

14. Tim Bynum, "Parole Decision-Making and Native Americans," in *Race, Crime and Criminal Justice,* ed. R. L. McNeely and C. E. Pope (Newbury Park, CA: Sage, Inc., 1981), 75–87.

15. Cornell, *Return of the Native*.

16. Charles Welford, "Labeling Theory and Criminology: An Assessment," *Social Problems* 22 (February 1975): 332–45; William Wilbanks, *The Myth of a Racist Criminal Justice System* (Monterey, CA: Books/Cole, 1987).

17. Omer Stewart, "Questions Regarding American Indian Criminality," *Human Organization* 23 (1964): 61–66; Reasons, "Crime and the American Indian"; Flowers, "Native American Crime"; Ken Peak and Jack Spencer, "Crime in Indian Country: Another 'Trail of Tears,'" *Journal of Criminal Justice* 15 (1987): 485–94.

18. Jerrold E. Levy, Stephen J. Kunitz, and Michael Everett, "Navajo Criminal Homicide," *Southwestern Journal of Anthropology* 25 (1969): 124–52; Robert E. Kuttner and Albert B. Lorincz, "Promiscuity and Prostitution in Urbanized Indian Communities," *Mental Hygiene* 54 (1970): 79–91; Morris A. Forslund and Ralph E. Meyers, "Delinquency among Wind River Indian Reservation Youth," *Criminology* 12 (1974): 97–106; Morris A. Forslund and Virginia A. Cranston, "A Self-Report Comparison of Indian and Anglo Delinquency in Wyoming," *Criminology* 13 (1975): 193–97.

19. Stewart, "Questions Regarding American Indian Criminality"; Reasons, "Crime and the American Indian"; Flowers, "Native American Crime"; Peak and Spencer, "Crime in Indian Country."

20. Peak and Spencer, "Crime in Indian Country."

21. Ibid., 485.

22. Travis Hirschi and Michael Gottfredson, "Age and the Explanation of Crime," *American Journal of Sociology* 89 (1983): 552–84; David Greenberg, "Age, Crime and Social Explanation," *American Journal of Sociology* 91 (1985): 1–21; Alfred Blumstein et al., *Criminal Careers and "Career Criminals"* (Washington, DC: National Academy Press, 1986); Lawrence Cohen and Kenneth Land, "Age and Crime: Symmetry vs. Asymmetry, and the Projection of Crime Rates through the 1990's," *American Sociological Review* 52 (1987): 170–83; Gottfredson and Hirschi, "The Methodological Adequacy of Longitudinal Research on Crime," *Criminology* 25 (1987): 581–614.

23. Williams, Chadwick, and Bahr, "Antecedents of Self-Reported Arrest."

24. Mhyra S. Minnis, "The Relationship of the Social Structure of an Indian Community to Adult and Juvenile Delinquency," *Social Forces* 41 (1963): 395–403.

25. Again, however, methodological problems associated with these studies in many ways compromise the generalizability of these findings, particularly in comparison to the standards being applied to current criminological research on both individual and structural determinants of crime with non-Indian populations. See Green, "American Indian Criminality." For example, even though their refusal rate was a mere 7 percent, Williams's and his colleagues' best efforts to obtain a representative group of Seattle Indians generated only 28 percent of their original sample of respondents. On the other hand, Minnis's research is based on inferences drawn primarily from univariate statistics on selected structural indicators of the community and adult and juvenile law violations, with only one bivariate cross-tabulation presented between the variables of degree of crowding and percentage of households with any reported arrests (adults or juveniles).

26. Joane Nagel and C. Matthew Snipp, "American Indian Tribal Identification and Federal Indian Policy: The Reflection of History in the 1980 Census" (Paper presented at the American Sociological Association annual meetings, August 1987); C. Matthew Snipp, *American Indians: The First of This Land* (New York: Russell Sage Foundation, 1989).

27. Ibid.

28. Nagel and Snipp, "American Indian Tribal Identification."

29. Ibid.

30. Ibid.

31. Ibid. For example, according to data presented by Nagel and Snipp, and the Bureau of the Census, between 1960 and 1970, the American Indian population increased by 51.1 percent; between 1970 and 1980, it increased by 72.2 percent; and between 1980 and 1990, it increased by 37.9 percent. Also U. S. Department of Commerce News, Economic and Statistics Administration, Bureau of the Census, "Census Bureau Completes Distribution of 1990 Redistricting Tabulations to States," table 1 (Washington, DC: 11 March 1991).

32. Jeffrey S. Passel, "Provisional Evaluation of the 1970 Census Count of American Indians," *Demography* 13 (1976): 397–409; Snipp, "American Indians," 26–61.

33. Jeffrey S. Passel and Patricia A. Berman, "The Quality of 1980 Census Data for American Indians," *Social Biology* 33 (1986): 163–82; Snipp, "American Indians," and Nagel and Snipp, "American Indian Tribal Identification."

34. While previous studies of American Indian crime patterns have focused on a number of different indicators of criminality, the present discussion will focus, for a number of reasons, on aggregate-level studies that have utilized Uniform Crime Reports (UCR) of arrest figures and U. S. census data to assess Native American involvement in illegal behavior. These two forms of information are perhaps the most consistently reported, widely available, and frequently cited sources of data on United States criminal and general populations. Employed together, they have provided criminologists with the ability to assess the influence of a host of theoretically derived sociodemographic characteristics and social indicators of the population on rates of arrests at national, state, county, and local levels of analysis. In addition to their amenability to studies on the etiology of crime, they also represent society's official reaction to crime in the form of the number of official arrests for crimes known to reporting police agencies throughout the United States, and allow researchers to assess the frequently hypothesized relationship between race and criminal justice processes.

35. See note 17.

36. Ibid. Also see Biderman and Lynch, *Understanding Crime Incidence Statistics.*

37. Von Hentig, "The Delinquency of the American Indian."

38. Stewart, "Questions Regarding American Indian Criminality."

39. Flowers, "Native American Crime."

40. Peck and Spencer, "Crime in Indian Country."

41. Nagel and Snipp, "American Indian Tribal Identification." In these instances, however, improved recording techniques no doubt played an important role in the observed increases.

42. Ibid. For example, Nagel and Snipp report the following census figures for American Indians: 1960, 524,000; 1970, 764,000; 1980, 1,357,000.

43. See "The Crime Wave, *Time Magazine,*" in *Crime in America*, ed. Bruce J. Cohen (Itasca, IL: F. E. Peacock Publishers, Inc., 1977), 6–22.

44. Richard Quinney, *The Social Reality of Crime* (Boston: Little, Brown, 1970).

45. Edwin Lemert, *Human Deviance, Social Problems, and Social Control.* 2d ed. (Englewood Cliffs, NJ: Prentice Hall, 1972); Howard S. Becker, *Outsiders* (New York: Free Press, 1963).

46. Passel, "Provisional Evaluation of the 1970 Census Count"; Passel and Berman, "The Quality of 1980 Census Data"; and Snipp, "American Indians." These three sources provided the estimated natural increase figures for the American Indian population used to compute the arrests rates presented in table 2. According to these estimates, the 1970

census data indicated an "overcount" of American Indians of approximately 8 percent, while the 1980 census reported an "overcount" of American Indians of approximately 26 percent.

47. Actual estimates of the natural increase currently are not available for the 1990 figures. However, utilizing trend data on the natural increase in the American Indian population presented by Passel, Passel and Berman, and Snipp, a conservative estimate of the 1990 "overcount" for American Indians (approximately 20 percent) was employed to derive the 1990 arrest rates based on the natural increase in the American Indian population. Passel, "Provisional Evaluation of the 1970 Census Count"; Passel and Berman, "The Quality of 1980 Census Data"; and Snipp, "American Indians," 70.

48. Gary D. Sandefur and Trudy McKinnell "American Indian Intermarriage," *Social Science Research* 15 (1986): 347–71; Gary D. Sandefur and Arthur Sakamoto, "American Indian Household Structure and Income," *Demography* 25 (1988): 71–80.

49. Ibid. The nineteen so-called Indian states identified by Sandefur and his colleagues are Alaska, Arizona, Idaho, Michigan, Minnesota, Montana, Nebraska, Nevada, New Mexico, New York, North Carolina, North Dakota, Oklahoma, Oregon, South Dakota, Utah, Washington, Wisconsin, and Wyoming.

50. Judith R. Blau and Peter M. Blau, "The Costs of Inequality: Metropolitan Structure and Violent Crime," *American Sociological Review* 47 (1982): 114–29; Peter M. Blau and Reid M. Golden, "Metropolitan Structure and Criminal Violence," *Sociological Quarterly* 27 (1986): 15–26; Robert Parker Nash, "Poverty, Subculture of Violence, and Type of Homicide," *Social Forces* 67 (1989): 983–1007.

51. This resolution does not address two additional problems that have the potential to introduce measurement error in analyses of American Indian criminality. First, it has been noted by Harring (1982) that UCR data does not include Bureau of Indian Affairs (BIA) crime reports from federal reservation lands. Second, we have no evidence to date that assesses the degree to which self-identification problems plague police reports of American Indian criminality. That is, we do not know the extent to which police arrest/crime figures include those individuals who may not be perceived as American Indian but who self-identify with the racial group on census reports, or visa versa.

52. Based on the data presented here, the extent to which this population measurement issue affects rates of American Indian arrests may be decreasing over time. According to census data, the American Indian population increase appears to have peaked in 1980, with a 72 percent increase over the previous decade. The most recent census figures for 1990 indicate that the Indian population increased by only 37.9 percent over the previous 1980 figures. However, even if this problem is ultimately limited to a three- or four-decade period when changing patterns of self-identification among Americans with American Indian ancestry were most pronounced, the problem remains an issue for those who examine arrests rates among this racial group during these years, and correction factors still may be warranted to assess rates during periods in which this "overcount" was particularly problematic.

53. T. Biolosi, "The American Indian and the Problem of Culture," *American Indian Quarterly* 12 (1989): 261–69.

54. Snipp, "American Indians."

55. Ibid.

56. Travis Hirschi, *Causes of Delinquency* (Berkeley, CA:University of California Press, 1969).

57. Susan P. Robbins, "Anglo Concepts and Indian Delinquency: A Study of Juvenile Delinquency," *Social Casework* 65: 4 (April 1984): 235–41; Susan P. Robbins, "Commit-

ment, Belief and Native American Delinquency," *Human Organization* 44:1 (Spring 1985): 57–62.

58. In regard to the concept of Indian identity, a recent study of academic success among Indian students at a state university in the Midwest included measures of attachment to American Indian culture such as attendance at powwows and belonging to Indian organizations. The study found that these involvements were significantly inversely related to academic achievement. Wilbur J. Scott, "Attachment to Indian Culture," *Youth and Society* 17 (June 1986): 392–94.

59. Williams, Chadwick, and Bahr, "Antecedents of Self-Reported Arrest."

8

Public Law 280 and the Problem of "Lawlessness" in California Indian Country

Carole Goldberg

 THIS IS A STORY OF LAW GONE AWRY. Long ago, as far back as the 1830s, principles of federal Indian law established that states had no civil or criminal jurisdiction over Indians on reservations.[1] Tribal and federal authority alone prevailed. With this doctrine in place, tribal sovereignty and federal primacy in Indian affairs largely protected reservation Indians from formal state jurisdiction.

Courts have affirmed, however, that Congress may, in the exercise of its power over Indian affairs, authorize states to exercise jurisdiction that states would not otherwise possess.[2] During the first half of this century, Congress enacted laws instituting state jurisdiction on several individual reservations in different states and over all the reservations in New York.[3] The affected tribes neither solicited these legislative actions nor consented to them. Congress was responding to state initiatives and seeking to lighten the federal government's jurisdictional burden.

Then in 1953, at the height of its post-World War II assimilationist impulse, Congress established a more comprehensive regime for empowering states on reservations. The new law, known as Public Law 280,[4] withdrew federal criminal jurisdiction on reservations in six designated states,[5] including California, and authorized those same states to assume criminal jurisdiction and to hear civil cases against Indians arising in Indian Country. For all other states, Public Law 280 established a mechanism for the future assumption of the same type of criminal and civil jurisdiction. This second group of states had to enact affirmative legislation accepting authority over reservation Indians; and in states that had disclaimers of Indian jurisdiction in their constitutions, constitutional amendments were provided for as well. As was the case with the pre-1953 laws, tribes neither requested nor approved states' Public Law 280 jurisdiction. It was imposed upon them in order to relieve federal financial obligations and to address perceived "lawlessness" on reservations.[6]

From the very beginning, the absence of a tribal consent provision in Public Law 280 raised moral concerns, and not only among the affected tribes.

Carole Goldberg, professor of Law, directs the joint graduate degree program in law and American Indian Studies at UCLA. She is the author of *Planting Tail Feathers: Tribal Survival and Public Law 280*.

Many tribes actively opposed passage of the law, at least to the extent their meager funds could support travel to congressional hearings.[7] And in signing the bill into law, President Eisenhower indicated that the lack of such a provision left him with "grave doubts."[8] For a nation that grounds political legitimacy on "consent of the governed," such qualms were quite proper. While early treaties offer a model for understanding tribal consent to some federal jurisdiction, there are no comparable documents or models for tribal consent to state jurisdiction. Indeed, in treaties with some of the affected tribes, the federal government had promised that reservations would be set aside for their sole and exclusive use and occupancy. Those words have been interpreted to exclude the possibility of most state jurisdiction on the reservations.[9] Even tribes without treaties, which includes most California tribes, had been guaranteed freedom from state jurisdiction on their reservations through Supreme Court decisions resting on tribal sovereignty and the Indian Commerce Clause of the United States Constitution.[10] Furthermore, at the time these states entered the Union, Indians were considered noncitizens—outside the political community of the states.[11] Thus Public Law 280 unilaterally abrogated treaty provisions and legitimate tribal expectations.

Fifteen years and many expressions of outrage after the enactment of Public Law 280, Congress finally amended the law to require tribal consent, via referendum, before states could assume jurisdiction.[12] By this time, nine states (in addition to the six named in the statute) had claimed some or all of the jurisdiction that Public Law 280 allowed.[13] Remarkably, the 1968 amendments did not apply to the areas of Indian Country that had already become subject to state jurisdiction under the original act. Only future extensions of state jurisdiction were covered. To no one's surprise, not a single tribe has consented to state jurisdiction since 1968. But what of the tribes in the six "mandatory" states and the others that had already been forced to bear the weight of state jurisdiction? The 1968 amendments offered no mechanism for tribes to initiate "retrocessions" of jurisdiction back to the federal government—a striking lack of parallelism with the provisions allowing states to initiate such a process.[14]

Serious attention to the principle of "consent of the governed" would have required reopening the jurisdictional arrangements for tribes already affected by Public Law 280. Congress's failure to provide such flexibility leaves Public Law 280 seriously flawed. Courts have ameliorated the situation by interpreting Public Law 280 in a highly restrictive fashion, narrowing the scope of state jurisdiction.[15] As the discussion below will demonstrate, however, these interpretations have eased or shifted, but not removed, the burden of Public Law 280 on affected tribes.

Why did Congress not use the 1968 amendments to rectify its earlier disregard of tribal consent? Ongoing concern with "lawlessness" on reservations was a widely professed reason. Bureau of Indian Affairs (BIA) Commissioner Dillon S. Myer (who had overseen the internment of Japanese-Americans during World War II) had argued in the 1952 congressional hearings on Public Law 280 that many tribal law-and-order systems were so deficient that the tribes should be given no choice about state jurisdiction. And the legislative history of Public Law 280 is laden with references to the problem of "lawlessness" on reservations.[16] Traditional tribal justice systems were described as weakened and ineffectual, and federal mechanisms were considered too limited in their jurisdiction and too costly to expand. Reservations were described as places of rampant crime and disorder. Public Law 280 was supposed to provide the solution to this problem of "lawlessness" by empowering state civil and criminal courts to do what the tribal and federal systems supposedly could not.[17]

Whether anything properly describable as "lawlessness" actually prevailed on reservations is a debatable point.[18] Yet surely a Congress disturbed by the lack of consent could have conceived a way to achieve law and order without violating tribal consent. In hindsight, support for the development of tribal justice systems should have been an obvious alternative to the maintenance of state jurisdiction under Public Law 280, especially since the Supreme Court had very recently rendered an important decision, *William* v. *Lee*,[19] that upheld the authority of tribal courts. That was not, however, the road that Congress chose. Perhaps because the era of federal support for tribal self-determination was more than a decade away, Congress opted instead to impose state authority on unwilling tribes. Brute force rather than negotiations among governments was the model for Public Law 280.

One could base a critique of Public Law 280 solely on the absence of consent and make a powerful statement. This story, however, focuses instead on the official rationale for Public Law 280—"lawlessness"—and questions whether Public Law 280 can be justified on its own terms. Inevitably, this inquiry leads into the meaning of the term lawlessness to non-Indian members of Congress, to tribal members, and to scholars examining the nature and impact of federal Indian law. One purpose of this chapter is to reveal how much the concept of lawlessness is a social construction, reflecting cultural differences and arrangements of power. A second purpose is to expose Public Law 280 as a source of lawlessness (at least according to one understanding) rather than its remedy.

PERCEPTIONS OF "LAWLESSNESS" IN CALIFORNIA INDIAN COUNTRY: 1850–1950

California tribes have no ratified treaties with the United States government. Although eighteen separate treaties were negotiated and signed during the early 1850s, the Senate bowed to pressure from the California delegation and withheld ratification. Many of the tribal signatories to these treaties believed them to be valid and moved from their ancestral lands to the approximately seven million acres that had been promised them. When they arrived, they found that the federal government viewed the promised lands as public domain subject to homesteading. Return to the ancestral lands was impossible, since those lands had been declared public domain as well.[20] Tribes were left landless and without means of support, adding starvation to disease and vigilantism as causes of population decline.[21]

Beginning in 1870, civilian reservations established by federal statute and executive order replaced the five military reservations first set aside for California Indians. Maintenance of law and order and resolution of disputes on these new civilian reservations were, in keeping with standard principles of federal Indian law, federal and tribal—not state—responsibilities. The tribes, however, were not well positioned to discharge this responsibility through the early decades of the twentieth century. Years of population loss and dislocation had disrupted tribal social and political organization. To make matters worse, the Indian Service (predecessor to the Bureau of Indian Affairs) undermined traditional or popularly elected leaders by appointing more compliant individuals to speak for the tribes and to serve as links for the distribution of meager federal benefits. Just as new social and economic conditions engendered new types of conflicts, both among tribal members and with outsiders, tribal institutions were hampered in their capacity to respond.

Under these conditions, non-Indians were prepared to view the tribes as inherently incapable of maintaining a system of laws, rather than being hobbled by federal interference or undergoing an adjustment to new social and economic arrangements. Since the earliest years of European contact, non-Indian commentaries on tribal life have abounded in misconceptions about the existence and nature of tribal legal systems. Because tribal systems look so different and function so differently from non-Indian systems, the outsiders often concluded there was no law at all.[22] In California, for example, the Supreme Court described a group of Indians residing in central California as having

> no tribal laws or regulations, and no organization or means of enforcing any such laws or regulations. The only sort of communal organization or semblance of political autonomy it has consists of the fact that one of them has the title of "Captain," and is treated as their leader or spokesman and receives some deference and respect on that account. But he has no authority. Disputes are sometimes submitted to him for settlement, but his decisions are considered wholly advisory. Each party accepts or rejects them as he chooses, and there is neither enforcement nor means of enforcement thereof.[23]

This account suffers from an ethnocentric conception of law as entailing specific forms of state coercion. Modern-day legal anthropologists, either of the functionalist or the interpretivist sort, have cautioned against such rigid understandings of law.[24] Historians and anthropologists have also demonstrated how, in precontact times, tribal political/legal institutions throughout North America functioned effectively without the use of incarceration or execution of judgments via levies on members' property.[25] Instead, clans and extended families, as well as religious leaders, worked to adjust disputes and restore breaches within the community, providing assurances that resolutions would be carried through. Some institutions of this type, such as the Navajo Peacemaker Court, have resurfaced in recent years, operating side-by-side with non-Indian-style tribal courts.[26] However, for most of the postcontact period, traditional tribal legal processes "went underground" in response to non-Indian hostilities, functioning outside the knowledge of state officials.[27]

Given the nineteenth-century non-Indian understanding of tribes as "lawless," and the exclusive federal responsibility for Indian affairs, one might expect the federal government to have stepped in to supply the needs of law enforcement and dispute resolution in California Indian Country. In fact, in the century preceding Public Law 280, the federal government neither bolstered tribal institutions nor provided an effective legal system for tribal members.

In theory, Bureau of Indian Affairs Indian police and "special officers" were responsible for policing California reservations. Also, the federal government could supply criminal courts and civil dispute resolution through Courts of Indian Offenses, which were established by Interior Department regulations and enforced a code promulgated by the department rather than by Congress.[28] The reality was far different, however. Too few Indian and special officers were assigned to the California reservations to provide meaningful law enforcement. And Courts of Indian Offenses, which existed on reservations elsewhere in the country, could not be found in California through the middle of the twentieth century.[29] Indian agent Charles Porter wrote from California in 1883, for example, that the Hoopa Reservation in Northern California was filled with internal dissension, making it impossible to organize either Indian police or Courts of Indian Offenses.[30] In a 1941 memorandum to California BIA Superintendent John Rockwell, the bureau's chief special officer related the problems of reservation law enforcement to the absence of Courts of Indian Offenses. In his view, the absence of such courts made it impossible for officers to make legal arrests, other than for the ten major crimes identified by Congress in 1886 and for violation of special Indian liquor laws.[31] This limitation existed because officers were authorized by law only to make arrests for the purpose of sending wrongdoers to court. At that time, the law enforcement personnel for all of California Indian Country consisted of only two special officers and roughly eleven Indian police officers. The chief special officer pointed out that unless courts of competent jurisdiction were provided, it was futile to increase enforcement personnel. Meanwhile, the assaults, batteries, attempted rapes, and other offenses falling outside the scope of the Major Crimes Act and liquor laws continued to plague Indians who had no federal protection or legal recourse.[32]

In the area of civil dispute resolution, the federal government was of no greater service to California tribes and their members. Problems with outsiders who trampled upon Indian rights were particularly acute. Non-Indians trespassed on Indian lands, cut their timber, and diverted their water with relative impunity, almost daring the United States as trustee to take action.[33] Rarely was any federal response forthcoming. In the case of Round Valley, for example, political pressure from non-Indians caused the United States attorney to withdraw federal actions against non-Indian trespassers.[34] Disputes among tribal members also had no recourse before the federal government. Indeed, it was a dispute over land rights on the Hoopa Reservation in California that led to the homicide prosecuted by the federal government in the landmark Indian law case of *U.S. v. Kagama*.[35] Kagama and Lyouse were Klamath Indians who had been relocated onto the Hoopa Reservation. Kagama wanted to build a house on the reservation, but Lyouse laid claim to the same site. Kagama requested clarification from the reservation Indian agent, who in turn directed the request to Washington. The bureau did not respond, and the dispute between the two Klamaths escalated into homicide.[36] Lack of federal assistance in this case proved fatal.

Toward the end of the second decade of the twentieth century, members of several Southern California tribes concluded that the federal government would never offer adequate services in the areas of law enforcement and dispute resolution. So they formed the Mission Indian Federation, an association of tribal members and non-Indian allies that lobbied against the BIA and organized its own police force and judiciary to challenge the bureau's authority.[37] A similar organization, the California Federated Indians, formed in Northern California. Until the 1950s, many Southern California reservations had two organizations: an elected spokesperson and councils, opposed by a Mission Indian Federation group, generally direct descendants of traditional leaders followed by traditional families. The Mission Indian Federation has a controversial legacy, because its leaders lent strong support to Public Law 280 and state jurisdiction, while forcefully opposing allotment. Sometimes tribal members perceived as friendly to the bureau or to allotment received harsh treatment from federation police; and some Indians found the federation police to be as abusive as officers from the bureau.[38] Although the organization faded away in the 1950s as Public Law 280 took hold in California, it offered some indication of the potential for Indian self-determination in the area of dispute resolution and law enforcement, belying claims of "lawlessness."

The contention that California reservations suffered from lawlessness, so crucial to the case for Public Law 280, reflected two sorts of blindness. To some degree, non-Indians suffered from enthnocentric blindness to functioning tribal legal institutions. At the same time, advocates for Public Law 280 failed to see that the combination of federal domination and neglect was stunting the adaptive processes of tribal legal systems. If federal interference had been lifted, tribes might well have restored or modified the institutions that had been suppressed.

INSTALLING "LAWLESSNESS" THROUGH PUBLIC LAW 280

Public Law 280 has had both direct and indirect effects on the legal regime within the Indian Country to which it applies. Both types of consequences have implications for the problem of "lawlessness."

In the absence of Public Law 280, the federal government has authority over most crimes committed by Indians against non-Indians (or vice versa), and certain major crimes committed by Indians against other Indians; tribes have jurisdiction over crimes committed by Indians, subject to limits on punishment imposed by the 1968 Indian Civil Rights Act; and the states lack civil and criminal jurisdiction over Indian defendants for matters arising on reservations.[39] (See chart 1.)

Table 1
States without Public Law 280

	Criminal Jurisdiction on Reservation	Civil Jurisdiction on Reservation
Tribal	Over Indians, subject to limits on punishment in Indian Civil Rights Act	Over Indians and non-Indians
Federal	Over offenses committed by Indians against non-Indians or vice versa; over major crimes committed by Indians; over special liquor, gaming, and other offenses; otherwise, same as off-reservation	Same as off-reservation (diversity of citizenship, federal question, etc.)
State	Over crimes committed by non-Indians against other non-Indians	None, except some suits with non-Indian defendants

The direct effects of Public Law 280 were twofold: First, it extended state criminal jurisdiction and civil judicial jurisdiction over reservation Indians in certain states; second, it eliminated special federal criminal jurisdiction over reservation areas in the states specifically named in the law. Thus, the law substituted state legal authority for federal on all the designated reservations. No mention was made of tribal authority.[40] (See chart 2.) Historically, states resented the special rights and status of tribes under federal law, and the federal government often intervened to protect the tribes.[41] Public Law 280 did not strip the tribes of most of these rights and did not erase the trust status of their lands. Indeed, there were several exceptions to state jurisdiction built into the law to protect tribal land, water, hunting, and fishing rights. But by giving the states additional authority on reservations, it empowered an often hostile force.

Table 2
States Designated in Public Law 280

	Criminal Jurisdiction on Reservation	Civil Jurisdiction on Reservation
Tribal	Over Indians, subject to limits on punishment in Indian Civil Rights Act	Over Indians and non-Indians
Federal	Same as off-reservation	Same as off-reservation (diversity of citizenship, federal question, etc.)
State	Over Indians and non-Indians, with exceptions found in Public Law 280	Over suits involving Indians or non-Indians, with exceptions found in Public Law 280

In view of the fact that federal courts were not authorized to hear many civil and criminal disputes arising on reservations in the pre-Public Law 280 era,42 Public Law 280 also expanded the realm of non-Indian control over reservation activities. State courts could suddenly hear reservation-based civil disputes and criminal cases that federal courts would not have entertained in the past and that tribes would have treated as within their sole purview.

The direct effects of Public Law 280 were not the only effects, however. Although this law addressed only the question of which governments had power to resolve criminal and civil disputes on reservations, its passage signaled a change in the philosophy shaping federal Indian policy. No longer would the federal government profess (if not discharge) responsibility for the welfare of tribes and tribal members.[43] Instead, states would be asked to assume that responsibility, just as they were assuming responsibility for the education, welfare, and health care of needy non-Indians. Public Law 280 was just a small step toward the realization of that vision. But the federal Indian bureaucracy—the Bureau of Indian Affairs—used it as an excuse for redirecting federal support on a wholesale basis away from tribes in the "Public Law 280 states" and toward all other tribes.[44]

Nowhere was this reallocation of funds more evident than in California, where the Congress also singled out forty-one small reservations (out of more than one hundred in the state) for termination—meaning that these tribes would no longer be recognized by the federal government, and lands would no longer enjoy federal trust protection. Together, termination and Public Law 280 formed a toxic brew, eating away at the funds authorized by federal law for Indian welfare, education, and health care in California. Moreover, for California, the advent of Public Law 280 meant that tribes were never "dealt in" to many of the new federal Indian programs that Congress and the Bureau of Indian Affairs instituted in the 1960s and 1970s, largely in response to social movements of that period.

The most striking illustration of this phenomenon is funding for tribal law enforcement and tribal courts. Until the middle of this century, federal Courts of Indian Offenses handled dispute resolution on many reservations, ruthlessly imposing non-Indian norms on tribal members. In the 1960s, tribes in the non-Public Law 280 states began to form their own judicial and law enforcement systems, partly to fend off state jurisdiction and partly to express their own sovereignty. Federal funding for tribal courts and police escalated sharply outside of California, fueled by a growing number of United States Supreme Court decisions affirming exclusive tribal jurisdiction over reservation-based disputes. In California, however, the bureau refused to support tribal justice systems, on the ground that Public Law 280 made tribal jurisdiction unnecessary and perhaps even eliminated such tribal authority.[45] In fact, courts, attorneys general, and federal administrators have affirmed that tribal legal authority survived Public Law 280.[46] But legal authority requires infrastructure and institutions, and Public Law 280 stood in their way.

Even if one accepts the claim that many reservations were "lawless" at the time Public Law 280 was enacted, a tragic irony is inescapable. Taking account of the direct and indirect effects described above, Public Law 280 has itself become the source of lawlessness on reservations. Two different and distinct varieties of lawlessness are discernable. First, jurisdictional vacuums or gaps have been created, often precipitating the use of self-help remedies that border on or erupt into violence. Sometimes these gaps exist because no government has authority. Sometimes they arise because the government(s) that may have authority in theory have no institutional support or incentive for the exercise of that authority. I will call this kind of lawlessness the "legal vacuum" type. Second, where state law enforcement does intervene, gross abuses of authority are not uncommon. In other words, power is uncabined by the law that is supposed to constrain it. I will call this kind of lawlessness the "abuse of authority" type.

What explains this phenomenon of lawlessness spawned by a statute designed specifically to combat lawlessness? The capacity to contrast Public Law 280 states with all others offers a kind of natural (somewhat controlled) experiment. Three recent incidents in California Indian Country, and implicit comparisons with what would have happened in non-Public Law 280 states, set the stage for an explanation.

Incident 1:
Sludge Dumping at Torres-Martinez

Located in California's Coachella Valley near the desert town of Indio, the Torres-Martinez Reservation[47] is about half tribally owned and half allotted. In 1989, a tribal member leased her family's 120-acre allotment to a company that proposed to use the site to dump, dry, and compost human waste from treatment plants in San Diego, Orange, and Los Angeles counties. Complaints soon surfaced from tribal members living nearby. The sludge pile stank. It attracted legions of flies. It fouled the local water supply with bacteria and heavy metals. As it dried and was hauled away, it formed great clouds of dust, which choked nearby residents and coated surrounding homes. Meanwhile, the allottee who had leased the land moved off the reservation.

What could the complaining tribal members do to get rid of the sludge? The four-hundred-person Torres-Martinez tribe was not asked to and had not approved the lease. This failure to seek prior permission is not surprising, given the structure and operation of the tribal government. Although the tribe has a five-member tribal council headed by a tribal chair, it has no constitution. Neither does it have codes or ordinances prescribing the conditions for approval of leases or imposing restrictions on activities that might harm the environment. There is no tribal law enforcement agency, and no tribal court or other form of justice system. When disputes arise within the tribe, the only recourse available is to the tribal council, which ordinarily refers the matter to the next meeting of the general council—all the members of the tribe convened together. The criteria applied at such meetings are not specified in advance, but a spokesperson for the tribal council described the unwritten tribal policy as "you can do what you want on your property as long as it doesn't bother other people or the environment."[48] At another point, a spokesperson stated, "She doesn't need our permission for a little business, but the tribe has to decide whether something this big is OK."[49]

Eventually, in February 1994, the general council adopted a resolution that the dumping facility should be closed. But the allottee and the dumping companies disputed the council's authority over allotted land, especially given the absence of a tribal code provision or constitution; and there was no court or other form of justice system available to enforce the council's resolution. The dumping just went on.

Internal conflicts within the Torres-Martinez tribe partly account for the lack of legal infrastructure. There are divisions among allottees and nonallottees, as well as among traditional family groups, leading many to have qualms about creating a powerful tribal government. But part of the responsibility lies at the feet of Public Law 280, which, as described above, prevented tribal justice systems from sprouting in California Indian Country the way they did elsewhere in the United States.

State law could not help the complaining tribal members either, even with the powers the state acquired from Public Law 280. Provisions in Public Law 280 itself preclude states from exercising any authority, civil or criminal, that would affect the status or use of trust land.[50] This exception to state jurisdiction was included in Public Law 280 because the federal government was not relinquishing its trust responsibility over Indian lands, even in states covered by this law. It was merely inserting state justice systems onto the reservations, not terminating the tribes altogether. (Of course, Congress did terminate some reservations in separate legislation enacted soon afterward.) In other words, Public Law 280 was intended to be a point on the path toward termination, but not termination itself.

This exception language in Public Law 280 was enough to prevent state jurisdiction over the sludge dumping at Torres-Martinez, but there were other obstacles to state authority as well. In 1976, the United States Supreme Court interpreted Public Law 280's grant of state civil jurisdiction in a highly restrictive manner.[51] According to the Court, states only acquired the authority to hear civil lawsuits against reservation-based Indian defendants, not to apply state civil regulatory statutes, such as health codes and animal control laws, on reservations. Indeed, even if criminal penalties formed some part of these regulatory codes, code enforcement was outside state authority. If the complaining tribal members had sought to invoke California's solid waste disposal laws, they would have run into the argument that these laws are regulatory and therefore inapplicable to the reservation. Moreover, county zoning laws could not be employed against the dump, because other court decisions have limited the jurisdiction conferred by Public Law 280 to state laws; city and county laws are outside Public Law 280 because they are local rather than statewide in scope.[52] And even though federal environmental laws offer states authority over dumping if certain conditions are satisfied, these same federal laws draw limits on state authority at reservation boundaries.

In the early 1990s, the California legislature doggedly sought to pass legislation allowing the state to control reservation dumping. Legislators pursued this course even in the face of legal opinions from the Department of the Interior, the Environmental Protection Agency, and California's own legislative analyst maintaining that the state had no such authority under Public Law 280 or any other federal law. Eventually California's governor bowed under the weight of legal reasoning and vetoed the bill. The legislature then substituted a statute that would facilitate agreements between tribes and the state over control of dumping, a recognition of the tribes' sovereign status.[53] This struggle over dumping legislation only underscores, however, the powerlessness of the state to aid the complaining tribal members at Torres-Martinez. The complaining members may have resisted the idea of state assistance on grounds of tribal sovereignty anyway; but even had they been willing to set those compunctions aside, they would have been confronted with the absence of state power to do anything about their problem.

Because the sludge situation at Torres-Martinez involved leasing and use of trust land, the federal government ought to have been available as a source of redress. As trustee of the allotment in question, its approval was required before the lease could be valid. Responsibility for determining whether to approve such leases rests with the Bureau of Indian Affairs. The National Environmental Policy Act also requires the bureau to conduct an environmental assessment before approving any leases. Thus, if there was no federal approval, the bureau should have been able to void the lease and stop the lessee's use of the property. As trustee for the remaining tribal land, the federal government was also obliged to take legal action against threats to the land, such as pollution of ground water or general nuisance. Thus, if the sludge pile was creating environmental hazards, the federal government had authority to sue to enjoin it.

In practice, however, the federal government played a passive role at Torres-Martinez. In 1990, the superintendent for the local Bureau of Indian Affairs agency issued a cease and desist order against the dumpers. Bureau officials made no effort to enforce the order, however. Following the general council's resolution in early 1994, the tribal council again requested action from the bureau. Another cease and desist order was issued, but again the dumpers ignored it, and no enforcement action followed. By the summer of 1994 the bureau received a proposed new lease for the dumpsite and referred it to the White House Council on Environmental Quality for guidance about whether the lease could be approved before an environmental assessment was completed. Relying on their perception that the tribal members were divided about the dump site, bureau officials did nothing to expedite a decision.

Public Law 280 did not mandate this passive federal role, but it did enfeeble the federal bureaucracy in California to the point where it could not effectively discharge its trust responsibilities. As such, Public Law 280 amplified a pattern of federal bias against California Indians that dates back to the 1850s, when Congress refused to ratify treaties negotiated with California tribes. Studies conducted as long ago as the 1920s document that California Indians have not received a proportionate share of funding from the Bureau of Indian Affairs.[54] The absence of treaties offers part of the explanation, but so does the decimation of tribal populations during the latter nineteenth and early twentieth centuries. California Native peoples were slaughtered, displaced, and starved; their social/political structures were disrupted; and their numbers targeted for extinction. When it became evident that they would not disappear, many were settled on small, undesirable reservations or rancherias scattered about the state, with the individuals at each such locale labeled a "tribe." It should come as no surprise that such a large number of diverse tribes, totaling more than one hundred, was not well situated to sway the federal bureaucracy to provide funds and services. Mobilization of each individual tribe was hindered by the patchwork of tribal peoples that had been roughly stitched together at each site. Coordinating multiple tribes was nearly impossible without strong organization at the tribal level. And with so many tribes, the transaction costs of such coordinated action were just too high. A single tribe with the same number of members as the many tribes in California would have had far more influence.

With the passage of Public Law 280, the situation worsened. Entire federal Indian programs in areas such as welfare, health, education, and law enforcement were withdrawn from California.[55] As a consequence, California has a much smaller federal Indian bureaucracy in relation to its budget and population served than other parts of the United States. Only three agency offices serve the entire state and its more than one hundred tribes, making lack of communication and responsiveness major obstacles to effective action. In contrast, most significant tribes across the country have their own agencies of the bureau. The Sacramento Area Office, which services the entire state, is also understaffed by comparison with area offices elsewhere in the country.[56] Thus diminished in California, the bureau was ill equipped to investigate the problem at Torres-Martinez or to seek legal action from the United States Attorney in San Diego. And dealing with the remote and overworked bureau staff was not an effective outlet for tribal grievances.

With the tribe, the state, and the federal government all hobbled by Public Law 280, the eruption of lawlessness was predictable. Tribal members at Torres-Martinez organized a protest group and began hounding the bureau and the EPA with complaints. After the group organized a one-day blockade of the dump site in August 1994, the house of a prominent group member was sprayed by bullets from an automatic weapon. Despite calls to the local sheriff, there was no state law enforcement response. Two months later, the protesters, now joined by more than one hundred environmental activists, members from other tribes, and local members of the United Farm Workers Union, piled old tires, railroad ties, chain-link fencing, and empty barrels at the entrance, bringing the one-thousand-tons-per-day sludge deliveries to a halt. A tent encampment also materialized on the site, the protesters signaling their determination to resist the smelly invasion. As rumors circulated of attack by the allottees and their tribal allies, protesters fortified the encampment and prepared for confrontation. County sheriffs cruised the area but held back from arresting the protesters. At one point, trucks carrying the allottees and some sludge executives tried to break the blockade. After almost two dozen sheriff's deputies moved in, the blockaders stepped aside to allow the truck entrance. Then the blockade resumed.

At last, the federal government roused itself to action. At the request of the BIA, the United States Attorney for the Southern District of California filed suit to enjoin the dumping, claiming it was being conducted without federal lease approval and that it constituted a nuisance. Within two weeks of the start of the protest, a federal judge issued a temporary restraining order. A preliminary injunction followed six weeks after that. In the meantime, allies of the allottee seized the tribal hall during a meeting to nominate candidates for the next Torres-Martinez election and locked out the current chair, a sludge opponent. Notwithstanding this disruption, the current chair won reelection.

Lawlessness of the "legal gap" type is both the central current of this story and several of its tributaries. The chief instance of lawlessness, of course, is the blockade, itself a response to the legal vacuum that had been created on the reservation. Had legal authority been more fully realized in the tribal or federal government, the blockade—a self-help action fraught with possibilities of lawless violence—probably could have been avoided. If, for example, the tribe had developed a leasing code, an environmental review process, and some kind of dispute resolution system, a decision could have been made to allow or not to allow the dump; and that decision would have benefited from community acceptance of the process. Alternatively, if the federal government had provided greater support for the bureau officials in California so they could enforce the laws of trespass and nuisance, the complaining tribal members might not have become so frustrated with federal inaction.

Yet this dominant tale of lawlessness should not be allowed to obscure the subplots. Lawlessness is also evident when members of the group opposing the dump were subjected to threats and intimidation, with no response from local law enforcement authorities. Even a spray of bullets across the home of Marina Ortega, the opposition leader, could not evoke a police presence. And as rumors of attack darkened the protesters' camp, they prepared fortifications rather than bother calling the sheriff.

Unfortunately, such stories are common on reservations in Public Law 280 states such as California. John Mazetti, vice chair of the Rincon tribe, testified in 1989 before the Senate Select Committee on Indian Affairs:

> [T]he County Sheriff's Office response to criminal activity is almost non-existent. When the Sheriff's Office receives a call regarding gunfire and someone being shot, it often takes them more than one hour to respond to the incident, if at all. With criminal activities of a lesser degree, often the County Sheriff does not respond at all, leaving the reservation with little or no protection.
>
> The San Diego County Sheriff has stated officially that he does not like to provide services to Indian Tribes. . . . Perhaps the reason for this is due to the reservation not having a taxable base to draw funds from in order to defer the cost of providing law enforcement.[57]

Many tribes suggest that uncertainty about the reach of state jurisdiction under Public Law 280 is the source of sheriffs' reluctance to enter reservations. In fact, Public Law 280 creates a large gray area where state jurisdiction is doubtful, largely where a criminal law is part of a broader state regulatory scheme. This ambiguity in the law is not incidental or merely a drafting problem, however; it is a direct consequence of Congress's attempt in Public Law 280 to steer a middle course between terminating tribes and preserving tribal sovereignty. The problem of unresponsive county sheriffs, as understood in this way, is inherent in Public Law 280.

Mazetti's statement suggests another diagnosis for the problem of unresponsive county officers, however. By empowering the state only partially—giving it law enforcement responsibility but not regulatory or taxing authority—Public Law 280 bred resentment and neglect among state and local authorities. As Mazetti points out, they had costly duties (especially where reservations were remote from county centers), but no means to fund them. Moreover, because the reservations in Public Law 280 states stood apart from state regulatory policy, state and local officials did not view tribal members as part of their political community. This lack of communality seems to have rendered local officials less inclined to protect citizens on reservations. When this absence of fellow feeling combined with the traditional hostility between local communities and tribal Indians, regardless of Public Law 280, the product was a void in county law enforcement.

It is true that tribes in non-Public Law 280 states complain about the nonresponsiveness of federal law enforcement, suggesting that Public Law 280 did not worsen the situation on reservations. But in non-Public Law 280 states, the tribes at least retain criminal jurisdiction over Indian offenders, so long as the penalty imposed is no greater than one year in prison and a $5,000 fine.[58] With the support the federal government has provided for tribal law enforcement and courts, the tribes are not so dependent on outside authority to maintain public peace. In the more serious cases, tribes may still need to rely on the federal government. But although federal agents, prosecutors, and courts are often located further from reservations than their state counterparts, federal authorities have often established cross-deputization agreements with tribal police, enabling the tribe to ensure greater responsiveness. Furthermore, the federal budgeting process and trust responsibility open the way for tribes to put effective pressure on federal officials to provide proper services. Substituting state for federal criminal jurisdiction thus weakened criminal law enforcement as a whole.

A final instance of lawlessness is manifest in the dispute over the Torres-Martinez tribal election, which led to one faction locking the other out of a tribal meeting. Violence was simmering, near to a boil. Close tribal observers note that economic forces have led to destabilization of the Torres-Martinez. Allottees and other tribal members are at odds over whether the tribe should be able to control activities on the allotments. These sharp differences may simply be an amplification of traditions of decentralization and kin group autonomy that long existed among many Southern California tribal groups. Nonetheless, in their current form, these divisions spill over into tribal elections, where members are tempted to use force because they perceive there is no legal authority to restrain corruption, chicanery, or failure to follow tribal rules.

Following contemporary tribal self-determination policy, the federal government generally stands aside from tribal election disputes, unless the outcome warrants withdrawal of federal recognition. Public Law 280 states have no say in such matters, unless they explode into violence. Thus the burden of supplying law fell to the tribe. Had California tribes benefited from the kind of government infrastructure support that tribes in non-Public Law 280 states received, there might have been election codes and justice systems in place to help resolve such conflicts.

Codes would have established a political balance among competing interests in advance of a particular dispute. A justice system would have offered a less political method of dispute resolution once the conflict erupted over the election. Torres-Martinez had none of these.

Public Law 280 is largely to blame for this legal vacuum. It led the federal government to take California tribes less seriously as governments, denying them money to develop codes and courts. For example, in most years California receives not a single dollar of the $10,000,000 allocated annually by the Department of the Interior for Indian judicial services. Less than 1 percent of the national BIA law enforcement budget is allocated to California, which has at least 6 percent of the total Indian service population. As one tribe recently complained, Public Law 280 "has hampered our protection from the local police and developing our own police."

At this point, according to close tribal observers, the Torres-Martinez tribe is so deeply divided that members are actually fearful that a tribal justice system will concentrate too much power in the tribal government. It is possible, of course, that traditions of decentralization and family autonomy within the tribe may have made the tribal members wary of a centralized justice system even without the dumping conflict and lack of federal support. But such traditions prevail among many tribes; and those traditions have not stood in the way of tribal court development in non-Public Law 280 states. The majority of tribes in non-Public Law 280 states have seen the advantages of tribal justice systems as institutions that protect tribal sovereignty and promote a more orderly community.[59] If the federal government had supported California tribes the way it supports tribes in non-Public Law 280 states, it is likely that groups such as Torres-Martinez would have come to the same conclusion.

Incident 2:
Evicting Undesirables at Coyote Valley

The name Polly Klaas is indelibly linked with parental fears.[60] In late 1993, this young girl was abducted from her bedroom while her terrified girl friends looked on and her mother slept in a nearby room. After a two-month search that mobilized the local community and evoked national attention, her dead and mutilated body was found. Soon afterward, a career criminal named Richard Davis was arrested for the crime on the Coyote Valley Reservation, near Ukiah, California, home to about two hundred Pomo Indians. Davis, a non-Indian, was staying at his sister's house.

Davis's sister and her family had been living on the reservation for several years, renting a home from a tribal member. Concerns soon developed within the tribe about her drug dealing and other misbehavior, and the tribe began trying to evict her. Yet in a striking parallel to the situation at Torres-Martinez, legal recourse was unavailable, and Public Law 280 was largely to blame.

The tribe, the state, and the federal government were all effectively disabled by Public Law 280 from helping the Coyote Valley people. The tribe lacked a justice system or police arm that could carry out an eviction, in no small part because Public Law 280 served as an excuse to deny federal support for such institutions. A state court eviction proceeding could not be pursued because trust land was involved, and, as described above, Public Law 280 specifically denies states authority over such lands.[61] State police possessed the power to arrest and prosecute Ms. Davis for the underlying drug violations, but, following a familiar pattern in California Indian Country, no police response was forthcoming when tribal members complained. The BIA superintendent for Northern California acknowledged that "under Public Law 280 jurisdiction is local, but 280 has eroded over the years. Local law enforcement is reluctant to come onto reservations because of cultural differences."[62] As at Torres-Martinez, the federal government did theoretically hold power to grant relief.[63] The Coyote Valley tribe could have brought an eviction action in the nearest federal court. But forcing simple evictions into federal court is like requiring a college degree for a low-wage job. It is too costly, time-consuming, and rigorous to justify the ultimate benefit.

Art Bunce of the All Mission Indian Housing Authority in Escondido, California, testified before the Senate Select Committee on Indian Affairs in 1989, complaining of the unauthorized influx of illegal drug manufacturers onto San Diego-area reservations. Even though some of these operations were in HUD-financed homes, the housing authority could not effectively evict them. As Bunce stated,

> [T]he eviction procedure when actually used in earnest is extremely cumbersome. . . .The Federal courts are overworked, understaffed, and the few cases the housing authority has brought for evictions in drug related cases are taking about 9 months so far and we haven't even gotten to the state of pre-trial conference yet. If that continues . . . the community will continue to have to endure the danger posed by drug operations, some operating in brazen openness on the reservation.[64]

Bunce recommended an amendment to Public Law 280, or at least a revision of the procedural rules for federal courts that would allow summary or expedited eviction proceedings of the sort routinely conducted in California municipal courts. Absent such an amendment, Public Law 280 had left the tribes with no competent means of effecting evictions.

Bunce's plaintive plea forecast the problem at Coyote Valley, where the tribe tried in vain for two years to stop the drug-related activity of Davis's sister. In another parallel to Torres-Martinez, the lack of effective legal redress at Coyote Valley (that is, the condition of lawlessness on the reservation) gave rise to self-help bordering on violence. At the time of Davis's arrest, the FBI removed Davis's sister and her family from their home for questioning and so that a search could take place. Afterwards, the FBI attempted to return the family to the reservation. But during the period while she was in police custody, the tribe had mobilized. One dozen armed deputies of the Coyote Valley Tribal Council, hastily empowered for the occasion, positioned themselves at the entrance of the reservation, limiting access only to tribal members. For more than an hour, these deputies faced approximately sixty armed law enforcement personnel at the roadblock before tensions eased and the family was taken away. Tribal members recall fearing an exchange of fire. Within a week, the tribe reached an agreement with federal and local authorities that Davis's sister and her family would not be resettled on the reservation. Violence was narrowly averted.

The roadblock at Coyote Valley had another purpose besides excluding the sister of Richard Davis. Tribal members wanted to register their outrage over the manner in which Davis had been arrested. Local law enforcement and FBI officers had swooped down on his sister's house without so much as notice to the tribal leaders. This disregard for the welfare of the tribal community and disrespect for tribal sovereignty seriously distressed the tribal members.

The same motifs of "legal vacuum" lawlessness that sounded at Torres-Martinez echo at Coyote Valley. There is the jurisdictional gap created when no governmental authority has effective control over evictions. There is also the absence of local law enforcement response when the tribal community is threatened, as by the alleged drug dealing by Davis's sister. Finally, there is the inevitable sequence of self-help and tense confrontation when the frustrated community can no longer tolerate its vulnerability. As explained above, Public Law 280 plays a significant part in creating each of these problems.

Coyote Valley also experienced the abuse of authority form of lawlessness when local law enforcement stormed into the reservation without notifying the tribe. Even though Davis was a notorious and violent offender, tribal leaders could have been alerted to this invasion of their territory. But Public Law 280 made such acts of comity less likely. First, the absence of a tribal police force meant there was no partner on the reservation for the federal and local police. Second, Public Law 280 diminished the stature of the tribe in the eyes of federal and local police, making them less attentive to the interests of the tribe. As a result, tribal members may have been endangered, and antagonism between the tribe and surrounding non-Indian community members increased.

Incident 3:
Confrontations with Police at Round Valley

Round Valley,[65] about 150 miles north of San Francisco, is one of the earliest and largest reservations established in California, dating back to the 1850s. Indians from several different groups—Yuki, Wailacki, Pomo, Concow, Nomlacki, and Pit River—settled there, some of them brought on a deadly forced march, others refugees from the war of extermination waged by non-Indians during the 1850s and 1860s. Today, approximately twelve hundred Indians reside at Round Valley. In the spring of 1995, three homicides shook the community and exposed the enormous obstacles impeding effective law enforcement on California reservations.

To understand these homicides and their relationship to reservation law enforcement, it is necessary to view reservation life in historical perspective. In the nearly 150 years after Round Valley was established, the community fractured. Traditionalists, many of them educated members who had returned to the community, were on one side. They wanted to preserve and restore traditional cultures, assert tribal sovereignty, and achieve greater economic independence. On the other side were more assimilated members, connected with the Christian Church as a result of missionary activity and integrated into the local non-Indian economy. A deep divide, coursing with animosity, came to separate these two groups and ultimately implicated the local non-Indian population. In particular, traditionalists perceived that the local non-Indians, who opposed the return to traditionalism, favored the more assimilated group, particularly when it came to law enforcement.

The first homicide at Round Valley in 1995 involved a victim from one of these two Round Valley groups and accuseds from another. Teen-age boys of the traditionalist Peters family had been contending with teen-age boys of the more assimilated Britton family. According to the Peters family, one of their boys, Byron, had been jumped and severely beaten by several members of the Britton family a month before the killing. Byron's father contacted the local sheriff's office by telephone on several occasions, asking for a deputy to come out to take their complaint. The Peters family claims the deputies never arrived at the appointed times. As the harassment continued, Byron retaliated on his own, shooting at a truck driven by members of the Britton family. As a result, he was sent to juvenile hall. Although no one was hurt, this incident galvanized older men of the families to become involved. Complaints continued against members of the Britton family and their allies, including several incidents where shots were reportedly fired and threats yelled outside the Peters family home. The sheriff's department made no arrests and merely told the Britton group to stop.

On the day of the killing, Byron's father, Leonard Peters, got into a fistfight with Neil Britton, one of the boys most often accused of causing trouble. Leonard's nose was bloodied, and he left with his friend Bear Lincoln, member of another traditionalist family. Leonard's brother, Arylis, heard of the incident while engaged in some heavy drinking. He went looking for Neil Britton and instead encountered Neil's father, Gene, in the high school parking lot. After a heated confrontation, Gene Britton climbed into his car and Arylis shot him through the car's back window. Whether it was self-defense (because Gene Britton was grabbing for a gun in his car) or murder is contested.[66]

Mendocino County sheriff's deputies could not find Arylis immediately to arrest him. While two deputies searched on the reservation, they encountered Leonard Peters and Bear Lincoln on a dark and remote mountain road. Gunfire ensued, leaving both Peters and one of the deputies dead. Police accounts of these killings differ dramatically from those offered by family and community members. According to the surviving deputy, Peters was killed by the police acting in self-defense, and the deputy was killed when Bear Lincoln ambushed them from the side of the road. According to the Peters family and its allies, who had examined the crime scene, the police must have killed Peters when they took his walking stick for a gun; the deputy died when he was hit by his partner's fire, and the accusation of Bear Lincoln was a coverup. Relying on their own account, the police launched a massive manhunt for Bear Lincoln.

Immediately, Mendocino County police, federal agents, and California Highway Patrol officers descended on the Round Valley Reservation in force. Round Valley tribal members described themselves as "living in a state of terror given the severe and illegal harassment" suffered at the hands of these officers. According to their press release of 20 April 1995, the incidents of police misconduct included

(1) pulling the Lincoln family from a pickup truck and placing guns at their heads, including a five-year-old child, a three-year-old, and two infants;

(2) throwing the sixty-five-year-old crippled mother of Bear Lincoln to the ground and verbally and physically abusing her, leaving her severely bruised;

(3) knocking out the windows of the home of Bear Lincoln's mother and discharging firearms in her home, hitting the cradleboard of one of the infant grandchildren;

(4) entering at least fifty homes without warrants or consent, with guns cocked, searching each room;

(5) pointing a machine gun at a ninety-nine-year-old elder as the police searched her house and her young grandchildren watched in horror;

(6) pulling a ninety-five-year-old man out of his truck at gunpoint and roughing him up for no reason;

(7) stopping countless vehicles at gunpoint;

(8) interrogating minors in their homes while their parents were away at a press conference;

(9) searching homes while only minors were present, with guns pointed at the minor children;

(10) taking minors into custody without their parents' knowledge;

(11) throwing a mentally disabled man to the ground and harassing him.

More than fifty complaints were filed with the sheriff's department. To protect their children from this police activity, many tribal parents evacuated them from the reservation.

Whether these incidents occurred at all and, if so, whether they occurred because the victims were reservation Indians are pertinent questions in assessing Public Law 280. A pending civil rights class action on behalf of the Round Valley residents and a Justice Department investigation will help answer the first question. With respect to the second question, there is reason to believe that police harassed reservation residents more than they would have harassed others. When the Round Valley residents protested police practices to the local board of supervisors, one member stated, "This wouldn't have been handled like this if it happened in Mendocino or Point Arena [non-Indian communities]. It's because it's Covelo [on the Round Valley Reservation]."[67]

The current Mendocino County sheriff claims that the department now responds equally to calls on and off the reservation. But even he concedes that the department has a long history of problems with the Indians at Round Valley, including ones where the deputies were found to have engaged in excessive force and to have been drunk on duty. In May 1987, for example, resentment against police abuse sparked a riot, as one hundred reservation residents smashed windows in the small downtown area of the reservation town of Covelo. A few weeks after the riot, a violent encounter between a tribal member and a deputy left the deputy stabbed and the tribal member severely beaten. The tribal member was acquitted of attempted murder, the jury finding that the deputy had been drunk and had provoked the entire incident. When the jurors insisted on a grand jury investigation of the sheriff's department, the sheriff retaliated by withdrawing officers from the area altogether.

Four months after the police began their intense hunt for Bear Lincoln, he turned himself in to the San Francisco Police Department, all the while insisting on his innocence. He is currently awaiting trial.

The experience at Round Valley illustrates both the "legal vacuum" and the abuse of authority forms of lawlessness. The gap in legal authority was evident when local law enforcement failed to respond to conflicts building up on the reservation. Repeating the complaints of John Mazetti quoted above, the Round Valley residents, particularly the traditionalists, could not count on protection from the police when they were physically threatened and abused. Public Law 280 gave local police the power to act in criminal matters, but rightfully balked at handing states the kind of all-purpose authority that would lead them to view the Indians as fully part of their community. The upshot, following a familiar pattern, was self-help and violence. In this case, the pattern unfortunately elaborated into homicide. When the Brittons were not effectively restrained from bothering Peters family members, one of the Peterses fired his gun at a truck, and another killed a man.

The abuse of authority type of lawlessness is evident in the police response to the death of one of their members. California tribal members have often complained that when police do attend to tribal problems, they lack cultural sensitivity, they are disrespectful of tribal sovereignty, and they employ excessive force.[68] Typically this form of lawlessness arises because the holders of power do not see themselves as accountable to reservation communities, either because these communities are a small political minority or because they do not contribute to the local property tax base. Another possible explanation for such lawlessness is that state officials do not view themselves as part of the same political community as tribal members, who owe allegiance to their tribal governments and, under federal statutes, often receive special exemptions from state laws such as those involving environmental regulation, gaming, and child welfare. When that political separateness is coupled with cultural differences, it is predictable that police will treat the Indians as outsiders, and hence more harshly.

Public Law 280 set up just such a situation. It exempts reservation Indians from property taxes, leaves tribal governments intact (if underfunded), and excludes tribes from considerable amounts of state regulatory law. And the separation between tribes and surrounding communities has been exaggerated by federal court decisions and legislation that have come about since Public Law 280's enactment. Forty years ago, the present extensive regime of special federal statutes regulating Indian affairs did not exist. Indians did not enjoy congressionally blessed freedom from state laws relating to gaming, waste disposal, or adoptive placement, as they now do. No one predicted, at the time Public Law 280 was enacted, that tribal sovereignty would receive the doctrinal support it does under current law, support that is available to tribes in Public Law 280 states along with others. What they envisioned was a relatively rapid assimilation of tribes in Public Law 280 states into the state culture, economy, and polity. Several dozen California tribes were terminated soon after Public Law 280 was enacted, and the expectation was that other tribes would follow within decades.

Those expectations were not realized, largely because most tribes in America were not covered by Public Law 280, and the successful political movements and legal victories led by those tribes swept up the tribes in Public Law 280 states with all others. Thus, most of the terminated tribes in California have been unterminated (reinstated) through successful litigation and legislative efforts spearheaded by federally funded Indian legal services.[69] Tribes in Public Law 280 states have been strengthened by national legal decisions, both legislative and judicial, affirming tribal sovereignty. With enhanced sovereignty has come economic independence through activities such as gaming. And there has been a powerful revival of Native cultures through federal education, language renewal, and repatriation legislation, to name just a few. Leaving tribes to the care of local officials does not make sense under present circumstances. It is too likely that police who feel less political, cultural, and economic affinity with tribal members will treat them disrespectfully when tensions arise, as they did at Round Valley. A state police force that is thwarted by federal courts from seizing tribal gambling machines may feel too greatly tempted to assert its authority in those areas where it still has the power to do so.

CONFIRMING STORIES: RESEARCH SPONSORED BY THE ADVISORY COUNCIL ON CALIFORNIA INDIAN POLICY

In 1992, Congress created the Advisory Council on California Indian Policy, charged with investigating the special problems of California tribes and recommending appropriate federal policy changes.[70] As consultants to the council, the author and Duane Champagne, professor of sociology at UCLA, distributed a questionnaire to all California tribes, requesting information regarding legal problems and dispute resolution systems on their reservations. In addition, we had access to notes of the many hearings that the advisory council held to solicit concerns of tribal members throughout the state. From the questionnaires and hearings come stories that corroborate the account of Public Law 280 as a source of lawlessness.

Responses to the questionnaire reveal concern about both types of lawlessness discussed in this chapter—the legal vacuum type and the abuse of authority type. Of the nineteen tribes that responded, all but two complained of serious gaps in protection from county law enforcement. An oft-repeated theme is that sheriffs fail to respond when they are called, or respond hours after the incident, when it is far too late to intercept the wrongdoer. Calls for help with vandalism, assaults, drunk driving, and drug dealing often go unanswered. In one incident where fighting broke out at a HUD house, the sheriffs called back thirty minutes after a complaint was filed, to ask whether any guns were involved. By the time the deputies arrived, the assailants were gone. Only when non-Indians are involved or the financial interests of the county are at stake (as with enforcement of truancy laws) do county law enforcement officers seem to show sufficient interest.

The abuse of authority type of lawlessness takes two rather distinct forms: disregard for tribal sovereignty and culture, and police harassment. One-third of the tribes complained that county officials fail to respect tribal culture and sovereignty. Some protested trespassing by sheriff's deputies, often in patrol cars going at high speeds. Others noted a pattern of state intrusion on tribal sovereignty, as when local officials seek to enforce county building, sign, or animal control ordinances that are regulatory in nature and hence outside the scope of state authority under Public Law 280. Repeated litigation was necessary to fend off these incursions. Finally, some tribes mentioned that local law enforcement officials fail to respect the judgment of tribal members or leaders when questions arise about the necessity or means of making arrests for minor crimes. There are times when an understanding of tribal social structures and traditions is required in order to ascertain whether an offense has really occurred. Due to a lack of funding and incentive, state and local law enforcement officials rarely have the training that would enable them to appreciate tribal culture. One tribe reported that the local tribal chairmen's association had held several workshops on Public Law 280 in the past four years, but the county officials who were invited usually failed to attend.

Tribal concerns about police harassment also surface in the questionnaires, albeit in more muted form. One-quarter of the nineteen responding tribes complained of unauthorized searches, questioning of children in the absence of adults, excessive force, and general intimidation of Indians both on reservations and in town.

None of the responding tribes operates a tribal court system. According to the responses received, disputes outside the jurisdiction of state or federal courts (or ignored by those systems) are sometimes referred to tribal councils, which usually attempt to mediate while enlisting the advice of Elders. This method of conflict resolution is only partially satisfactory for the tribes. Some tribes report that disputants are willing to abide by the decisions, others find less compliance. Some say the system works well only for certain types of disputes.

More than two-thirds of the responding tribes articulate a need for tribal justice systems. Some are concerned that they lack the funds, expertise, or critical size to establish such systems at this time. Even these tribes, however, would like to see conditions change and cooperative arrangements devised—with other tribes or with the state—so that tribal justice systems can become feasible. Without some form of tribal justice system, tribes fear that problems of alcoholism, drug use, election disputes, trespassing, domestic violence, public disturbances, child welfare, employee discipline, housing conditions, land assignments, and speeding on reservations will never receive proper attention.[71] Furthermore, tribal traditions, such as a preference for rehabilitation over punishment, cannot be given effect without a distinctly tribal justice system. Several tribes report working on the development of tribal or consortium-based court systems, usually with some project-specific federal financial support. A few are in the process of establishing memoranda of understanding with local officials to allow for cross-deputization of tribal and local law enforcement personnel.

Hearings before the advisory council, held between July 1994 and May 1995, offer much the same information as the questionnaires and reinforce their validity. With respect to the legal vacuum, a witness from the Morongo Reservation stated, "A fund for tribal law enforcement needs to be created to allow the tribes to protect themselves when the state fails to do so." Members from the Coyote Valley and other tribes complained that drug trafficking laws, among others, are not enforced on the reservation, either because the sheriff fails to respond at all or waits on the outskirts of the reservation while local community members apply self-help. This story was repeated by a criminal investigator from the BIA, who noted that because the state receives no federal funds for reservation law enforcement, there is no incentive to enforce the drug laws or other criminal provisions. Not only are state law enforcement services inadequate, but the development of tribal justice systems has been hampered by the funding consequences of Public Law 280. One tribal member captured this concern when he said, "Most tribal governments and Indian organizations cannot effectively establish or administer the tribal operation, due to the insufficient allocations of funding to allow the proper administration on a continuing basis."

The hearings also include several statements decrying local officials' disrespect for tribal sovereignty, as well as their harassment of tribal members. As one tribal member stated, "The state tries to control us. And Public Law 280 has a lot to do with it, too." Because some of the hearings occurred soon after the Round Valley incident described above, numerous speakers leveled charges of police abuse. A witness from Coyote Valley, for example, asserted, "It is not acceptable to place an entire community under siege in vengeance." This same witness complained that a disproportionate percentage of tribal members, as opposed to other county residents, was being arrested for drug- and alcohol-related offenses, leading to a "permanent scarring" of the Indian community.

One constructive suggestion that appeared in the hearings was the creation of a series of regional "drug courts" throughout the state, which would exercise tribal jurisdiction, have governing boards appointed by tribal councils, and receive federal funding through special drug-related programs. To enforce the laws administered by the drug courts, tribal police forces would be established and their members cross-deputized with state officials to facilitate cooperative actions.

Another positive recommendation brought out in the hearings was the creation of consortium courts to hear child welfare matters, such as adoptions, foster care placements, and proceedings to terminate parental rights. The intersection of the Indian Child Welfare Act (ICWA) and Public Law 280 has generated considerable confusion, particularly with respect to categories of cases that ICWA assigns to exclusive tribal court jurisdiction.[72] Does ICWA override the state jurisdiction conferred by Public Law 280? There is no simple answer to this question, especially since ICWA provides a federal petitioning process for tribes in Public Law 280 states to "reassume" jurisdiction. Arguably, tribes do not need to reassume child welfare jurisdiction at all, because Public Law 280 never withdrew tribal jurisdiction, and because many types of child welfare proceedings (such as termination of parental rights) never came within the state's jurisdiction under Public Law 280 because they are regulatory in nature.[73] Whether or not the California tribes choose to take the path of "reassumption," they cannot assert child welfare jurisdiction unless they have some form of justice system. Thus, consortium courts are one means of effectively asserting sovereignty in a system where state courts have taken control of Indian children.

CONCLUSION

Tribes in Public Law 280 states are at a disadvantage compared with tribes elsewhere in the United States.[74] They suffer from lower levels of federal support and an absence of compensating state support. They are subject to abuses of power and gaps in legal authority. In California in particular, they have been broken up into such small and heterogeneous groups that forming effective justice systems is usually not feasible at the tribal level. There is indeed a crisis of lawlessness, even greater and more genuine than the one perceived by the Congress in 1953. A federal response is sorely needed.

One possibility, of course, would be for Congress to broaden the scope of state jurisdiction by eliminating the gaps in Public Law 280. If it were possible to ensure that states would fulfill the responsibilities associated with this jurisdiction, then problems of lawlessness might abate. But this solution to the problem of lawlessness would come at a high price, and not only in state law enforcement costs. Tribes would suffer another blow to their sovereignty, and treaty rights would be sacrificed. The principle of "consent of the governed" would be cast aside, just as it was in the original enactment of Public Law 280.

There is another alternative, one more in keeping with current federal Indian policy. The federal government should negotiate a solution to the lawlessness problem with tribal leaders, not impose a solution against their wishes. Any federal response should recognize that so long as tribes remain separate polities, exempt from much state law, the solution of state jurisdiction will likely fail unless mutual and cooperative arrangements are established between tribes and states. And it should acknowledge a federal obligation to make up for the retarded development of tribal institutions in Public Law 280 states, including assistance in the formation of consortia or coalitions whenever tribes deem that desirable.

Many outcomes are possible under these conditions. Retrocession of states' Public Law 280 jurisdiction back to the federal government, upon tribal initiative, is one possibility, and several tribes supported this course of action in their answers to the questionnaire. Tribally initiated retrocession is far from the only possibility, however. Some tribes may prefer to receive federal help to develop tribal law enforcement and dispute resolution institutions, which would operate concurrently and cooperatively with state entities. Other tribes may want to contract with state or local law enforcement to conduct activities that would be too expensive to duplicate. Many such cooperative relationships between states and tribes have been developed in areas such as environmental regulation and child welfare, outside the framework of Public Law 280. Some may want to assert authority over some types of matters, such as child welfare or hunting and fishing, and leave remaining matters to state or federal authorities, at least initially. Once the force of Public Law 280 is lifted, similar creativity can be unleashed, including efforts to develop justice systems that are more consistent with tribal traditions and multitribal consortia that take advantage of economies of scale.[75] But the federal government will have to be a supportive partner in this effort, both financially and as an honest broker between tribes and state governments. When tribes, federal officials, and state governments work together in this fashion, we will see the equivalent of a planting of tail feathers—the revitalization of tribal governance in Public Law 280 states.

Notes

1. *Worcester v. Georgia*, 31 U.S. (6 Pet.) 515 (1832). *Worcester* actually rejected state authority over a non-Indian on the reservation. The reasoning in the case, however, applies a fortiori to state jurisdiction over reservation Indians. And the holding as applied to non-Indians has been modified over time.

2. See *Felix Cohen's Handbook of Federal Indian Law* (1982 ed.) at 361–80.

3. Ibid., 372–76.

4. For the text of Public Law 280, see appendix A, in Carole Goldberg-Ambrose, *Planting Tail Feathers: Tribal Survival and Public Law 280* (Los Angeles: American Indian Studies Center, UCLA, 1998). For a detailed analysis of the statute, see chapter 2.

5. The designated states are Alaska, California, Minnesota, Nebraska, Oregon, and Wisconsin.

6. The Supreme Court's interpretation is that "[t]he primary concern of Congress in enacting Pub.L. 280 that emerges from its sparse legislative history was with the problem of lawlessness on certain Indian reservations, and the absence of adequate tribal institutions for law enforcement." *Bryan v. Itasca County*, 426 U.S. 373, 379–80 (1976).

7. See M. Mazetti, *Historical Overview of PL-280 in California* (Sacramento, CA: Office of Criminal Justice Planning, Indian Justice Program, 1980).

8. For further discussion of the problem of lack of consent, see chapter 2, in Goldberg-Ambrose, *Painting Tail Feathers*, 51–56.

9. See *Worcester v. Georgia*, 31 U.S. (6 Pet.) 515 (1832).

10. See *California* v. *Cabazon Band of Mission Indians*, 480 U.S. 202 (1987).

11. See *Elk* v. *Wilkins*, 112 U.S. 94 (1884). Indians were not declared U.S. citizens until 1924. Citizenship Act of 1924, 43 Stat. 253, 8 U.S.C. sec. 1401(a)(2).

12. 25 U.S.C. sec. 1326.

13. For a list of the states that assumed such jurisdiction, see Appendix B, in Goldberg-Ambrose, *Planting Tail Feathers*.

14. Ibid., chapter 2, 60–64.

15. Ibid., chapter 3.

16. Ibid., chapter 2, 48–49.

17. Of course, state jurisdiction was not the only possible solution to these problems. Tribal institutions could have been strengthened with federal support, the tribes could have been encouraged to enter into cooperative relationships with states, or the federal government could have assumed greater responsibility.

18. See discussion above, pp. 199–202.

19. 358 U.S. 217 (1959).

20. This history is documented in Flushman and Barbieri, "Aboriginal Title: The Special Case of California," *Pacific Law Journal* 17 (1986): 39.

21. The California Indian population has been estimated at 300,000 as of 1750. By 1900, the number of Indians had declined to 15,000. S. Cook, *The Population of the California Indians, 1769–1970* (1976).

22. Several such observations are quoted in R. Strickland, *Fire and the Spirits* (1975), 10.

23. *Anderson* v. *Mathews*, 174 Cal. 537 (1917).

24. See L. Nader and F. Todd, eds., *The Disputing Process: Law in Ten Societies* (1978); C. Geertz, *Local Knowledge: Further Essays in Interpretive Anthropology* (1983).

25. See, e.g., K. Llewellyn and E. A. Hoebel, *The Cheyenne Way* (1941); J. Reid, *A Law of Blood* (1975); R. Strickland, *Fire and the Spirits* (1976); W. Smith and J. Roberts, *Zuni Law* (1954).

26. See Austin, "Freedom, Responsibility and Duty: Alternative Dispute Resolution and the Navajo Peacemaker Court," *Judges Journal* 32 (1993): 8; Zion, "The Navajo Peacemaker Court: Deference to the Old and Accommodation to the New," *American Indian Law Review* 11 (1983): 89.

27. See S. Harring, *Crow Dog's Case: American Indian Sovereignty, Tribal Law, and United States Law in the Nineteenth Century* (1994), 57–141.

28. 25 C.F.R. Part 11.

29. The absence of these Courts of Indian Offenses in California was a mixed blessing. In other parts of the country, these courts often served to suppress Indian culture and to override traditional Indian dispute resolution systems. W. Hagan, *Indian Police and Judges: Experiments in Acculturation and Control* (1966). Sometime after the passage of Public Law 280 in 1953, a Court of Indian Offenses was established on the Hoopa Reservation in California exclusively for the purpose of prosecuting fish and game violations, which were outside state jurisdiction under the act.

30. Annual Report of the Commissioner of Indian Affairs, 1883, "Reports of Agents in California,"13.

31. In addition to the Major Crimes Act, there are federal statutes penalizing a variety of offenses when committed within "Indian Country," but only when the perpetrator is non-Indian and the victim is Indian or vice versa. 18 U.S.C. sec. 1152.

32. Proposed Report of H.R. 2841, included in letter from J.R. Venning, Chief, Law and Order Section, United States Department of the Interior, Office of Indian Affairs to

John G. Rockwell, Superintendent, Sacramento Indian Agency, 3 July 1943.

33. 1872 Report of Commissioner of Indian Affairs, quoted in H. H. Jackson, *A Century of Dishonor* (1885), 456; Report of Special Agent C. E. Kelsey to the Commissioner of Indian Affairs, commissioned by 33 Stat. 1058 (1905) (copy in possession of author).

34. 1872 Report of the Commissioner of Indian Affairs, quoted in H.H. Jackson, *A Century of Dishonor* .

35. 118 U.S. 375 (1886).

36. An account of this case can be found in S. Harring, *Crow Dog's Case*,144–45.

37. E. Castillo, "Twentieth-Century Secular Movements," in *Handbook of North American Indians: California* (1978), 715.

38. Letter from Max Mazetti (former chair, Rincon tribe) to Pauline Girvin (Executive Director, Advisory Council on California Indian Policy), 17 June 1995.

39. See Clinton, "Criminal Jurisdiction over Indian Lands: A Journey Through a Jurisdictional Maze," *Arizona Law Review* 18 (1976): 503.

40. For a discussion of the continuation of tribal jurisdiction, see chapter 4, in Goldberg-Ambrose, *Planting Tail Feathers*.

41. See *United States* v. *Kagama*, 118 U.S. 375 (1886). The Court declared, "Indian tribes are the wards of the nation. . . . Because of local ill feeling, the people of the States where they are found are often their deadliest enemies."

42. There was no special federal statute authorizing federal civil jurisdiction over reservation-based disputes. Thus, unless diversity of citizenship or a federal question were involved, a federal court would not hear a tort or contract action arising on the reservation. The federal criminal statutes applicable on reservations did not reach minor crimes where both perpetrators and victims were Indian.

43. In fact, the federal government had never effectively carried out its responsibilities to California tribes. Studies dating back to 1883 document federal neglect of the health, welfare, law enforcement, and educational needs of California tribes. See, e.g., "Report on the Condition and Needs of the Mission Indians of California, Made by Special Agents Helen Jackson and Abbot Kinney, to the Commissioner of Indian Affairs," reprinted in H. H. Jackson, *A Century of Dishonor*, appendix 15; C. Goodrich, "The Legal Status of the California Indian," *California Law Review* 14 (1926): 83; The Status of the Indian in California Today, A Report by John G. Rockwell, Superintendent of the Sacramento Agency to the Commissioner of Indian Affairs (1944).

44. F. Shipek, "History of Southern California Mission Indians," in *Handbook of North American Indians: California*, 614.

45. See C. Goldberg-Ambrose and D. Champagne, "A Second Century of Dishonor: Federal Inequities and California Tribes" (report prepared for the Advisory Council on California Indian Policy, 26 March 1996), 47–59.

46. See chapter 4, in Goldberg-Ambrose, *Planting Tail Feathers*.

47. This account is drawn from information supplied by tribal members, newspaper stories, and R. Russell, "Moving Mountains," *Amicus Journal* 16 (1995): 39.

48. T. Gorman, "Neighbors Blockade Sludge Mountain," *Los Angeles Times*, 21 October 1994.

49. Ibid.

50. See chapter 2, Goldberg-Ambrose, *Planting Tail Feathers*, 82–86.

51. *Bryan* v. *Itasca County*, 426 U.S. 373 (1976).

52. *Santa Rosa Band of Indians* v. *Kings County*, 532 F.2d 655 (9th Cir. 1975).

53. California Public Resources Code secs. 44201–44210.

54. See C. Goldberg-Ambrose and D. Champagne, "A Second Century of Dishonor:

Federal Inequities and California Tribes," 9–14.

55. Ibid.

56. Ibid.

57. "Issues of Concern to Southern California Tribes," Hearing before the Select Committee on Indian Affairs, United States Senate, 101st Cong., 1st sess., 122 (1989). Statements to similar effect span the entire period since enactment of Public Law 280. A 1991 *Los Angeles Times* article points out that the La Jolla Reservation in San Diego County has been overrun with drugs and violence, with six young tribal members murdered during a period of several months in the late 1980s. According to a past tribal chair, when members called the sheriff's department to report a murder, it was usually an hour before a deputy arrived. Anything short of homicide, and the wait for a sheriff's response was at least three days. Sometimes no response came at all. Even representatives of the sheriff's department acknowledged that the remoteness of the reservations, the cultural differences between the police and tribal members, and the uncertainties of jurisdiction law discouraged police responsiveness. A. Wallace, "No More No-Man's Land," *Los Angeles Times*, 17 June 1991. In 1966, a U.S. Senate Subcommittee found that "Public Law 280 . . . [has] resulted in a breakdown in the administration of justice to such a degree that Indians are being denied due process and equal protection of the law." "Public Law 280: Legislative History," Committee on Interior and Insular Affairs, United States Senate, 94th Congress, 1st sess., 29–30 (1975). The 1976 American Indian Policy Review Commission reached the same conclusion based on its own investigations.

58. This limit is imposed by the Indian Civil Rights Act, 25 U.S.C. sec. 1302.

59. More than 150 tribes nationwide have tribal courts.

60. This account is based on newspaper articles, interviews with individuals involved in the incident, and testimony given before the Advisory Council on California Indian Policy.

61. 25 U.S.C. sec. 1360(b): "[Nothing in the grant of civil jurisdiction to states in Public Law 280] shall confer jurisdiction upon the State to adjudicate . . . the ownership or right to possession of [property of any Indian tribe held in trust by the United States]. . . ." In *All Mission Indian Housing Authority v. Silvas*, 680 F. Supp. 330 (C.D. Ca. 1987), U.S. District Judge Tashima interpreted this language to deny state jurisdiction over an eviction action brought by a federally funded Indian housing authority. At the same time, the judge upheld a federal common law action for eviction, reasoning in part from the absence of a state forum. Judge Tashima's analysis was rejected in *Round Valley Indian Housing Authority v. Hunter*, 907 F. Supp. 1343 (N.D. Ca. 1995), which found against federal common law as the basis for eviction actions by Indian housing authorities and affirmed the existence of state jurisdiction. Writing in the Round Valley case, U.S. District Judge Brennan began by asserting, "Because landlord-tenant disputes are matters of state law, an action for eviction cannot be the basis for federal question jurisdiction." 907 F. Supp. at 1345. He then distinguished cases that had upheld federal common law claims involving possessory interests in trust land, on the ground that these earlier cases had involved tribal claims to possession, rather than the claims of separate entities such as housing authorities. In denying state jurisdiction, the *All Mission Indian Housing Authority* case seems to present the stronger case. It takes the language of 25 U.S.C. sec. 1360(b), quoted above, seriously; in contrast, *Round Valley* effectively ignores that express prohibition against state adjudication of possessory interests in trust land. Furthermore, there is no long historical support for the view that landlord-tenant matters are entirely outside the bounds of federal jurisdiction, in the same way that certain domestic relations matters are. See *Ankenbrandt v. Richards*, 504 U.S. 689 (1992).

62. B. Mandel, "No Proof of a Fate Worse Than Death," *San Francisco Examiner*, 5 December 1993.

63. This proposition seemed widely accepted until the decision in *Round Valley Indian Housing Authority* v. *Hunter*, 907 F. Supp. 1343 (N.D. Ca. 1995) rejected federal jurisdiction in cases where the tribe itself was not suing for possession. For the reasons discussed in note 61, the Round Valley decision seems highly questionable. Nonetheless, it is understandable that federal judges would prefer not to embark on responsibility for routine "unlawful detainer" actions, which are often the responsibility of state municipal courts.

64. "Issues of Concern to Southern California Tribes," Hearing before the Senate Select Committee on Indian Affairs, United States Senate, 101st Congress, 1st sess., 40 (1989).

65. This account is drawn from newspaper stories, postings on the computer bulletin board known as "Nativenet," features from an internet newspaper called the *Albion Monitor*, testimony given to the Advisory Council on California Indian Policy, and information supplied by the tribe.

66. Arylis was convicted of murder based on a guilty plea, although his public defender tried to withdraw the plea and substitute self-defense. The judge refused to allow withdrawal of the plea, and the matter is on appeal while Arylis serves a twenty-one-years-to-life sentence.

67. N. Wilson, "What Really Happened?" *Albion Monitor*.

68. See Southern California Indians for Tribal Sovereignty, "Statement on Public Law 280 and Law Enforcement," delivered at Bureau of Indian Affairs Indian Priority System Budget Meeting, Riverside, California, 11 September 1991 (on file at UCLA American Indian Studies Center), detailing abuses on the Pechanga, Barona, and Viejas reservations.

69. See, e.g., *Hardwick* v. *United States*, No. C-79-1710 SW (U.S. Dist. Ct., N.D. Ca., 20 July 1983); *Big Sandy* v. *Watt*, No. C-80-3787 MHP (U.S. Dist. Ct., N.D. Ca.); *Smith* v. *United States*, 515 F.Supp. 56 (N.D. Ca. 1978); *Duncan* v. *Andrus*, 517 F. Supp. 1 (N.D. Ca. 1977); *Table Bluff Bend* v. *Watt*, 432 F. Supp. 255 (N.D. Ca. 1981); Public Law 103-434; Public Law 103-454.

70. Public Law 102-416.

71. In response to a question asking about the major types of conflicts that come before the community or tribal organization, the following received the highest ratings: substandard housing conditions; trespass; constitutional or article bylaws interpretations; election and enrollment procedures; land use conflicts relating to assignments or allotments; and vandalism. This list obviously does not include conflicts that are routed to state or federal courts.

72. These are cases where the Indian child is domiciled or resides on the reservation.

73. See chapter 4, in Goldberg-Ambrose, *Planting Tail Feathers*, 180–82.

74. Answers to the tribal questionnaire reveal that California tribes also believe themselves to be at a disadvantage.

75. These consortia also offer the feature (sometimes viewed positively, sometimes negatively) of providing decision-makers who come from outside the small community within which the dispute arose. For further discussion of consortium courts, see chapter 4, in Goldberg-Ambrose, *Planting Tail Feathers*, 202–203.

PART V

REPATRIATION

On November 16, 1990, as the result of intense lobbying efforts by individual Native American tribes and national and local Indian organizations, Congress enacted the Native American Graves Protection and Repatriation Act (NAGPRA). The act provides for the protection of American Indian burial sites and creates a process for the repatriation of Native American human remains, funerary objects, and objects of cultural patrimony to federally recognized Native American tribes. NAGPRA mandated a new and ongoing dialogue that included the recognition of tribal sovereignty and tribes' control of their past and future. Thus, NAGPRA changed the basic relationship between Native American people and those people who, in the past, had "studied" Indian people.

NAGPRA stated that by November 1993, any federal agency, museum, and/or any institution of higher learning who received federal funds and held Native American artifacts was required to prepare a summary of their collections for distribution to culturally affiliated tribes. By November 1995, the universities and museums were required to prepare detailed inventories of their Native American collections, also to be made available to culturally affiliated tribes. Unfortunately, no provisions in NAGPRA requires notification of, or return of, collections to nonfederally recognized tribes. This includes most of the California Native tribes.

The passage of NAGPRA corrected generations of neglect and disrespect for Native American people and the sacred remains of their ancestors. Since European contact, explorers, settlers, and private entrepreneurs (pot hunters and grave robbers) have excavated ancient and contemporary Indian gravesites and the removed Native American skeletal remains, sacred objects, and cultural artifacts. Much of this has been done under the name of science (anthropology). In some instances this desecration was done simply out of curiosity, and in other instances it was nothing short of cultural theft.

While there is a long history of Indian efforts to force the return of these remains and artifacts, successful reacquisition began only in the1980s. The recognition of Native American tribal sovereignty and the self-determination legislation and programs of the Nixon Administration are in part responsible. Perhaps most symbolic of the shift in acceptable practices was the 1989 decision by the Smithsonian Institution, after several years of negotiation, to return the skeletal remains and funerary artifacts of hundreds of Native people to their modern descendants. Other groups followed the Smithsonian example. The state of New York agreed to return twelve wampum belts to the Onondaga Nation and, in 1990, Zuni war gods in museums around the country were returned to their New Mexico homelands.

Authors Peregoy and Goldberg provide two essays that address important NAGPRA issues: cross-cultural conflict and resolution and the ongoing claims of nonfederally recognized tribes in California for inclusion in the repatriation process.

Robert M. Peregoy brings to this discussion "Nebraska's Landmark Repatriation Law: A Study of Cross-Cultural Conflict and Resolution." In this article, he explores cross-cultural conflicts between Indian tribes, museums, and archaeological communities in Nebraska during the 1980s and early 1990s. Background for this case study provides an overview of the competing interests of these parties and interrogates the legal foundation of Nebraska repatriation. Then the author places all of the above in the context of the attempts to repatriate and rebury Pawnee Indian human remains, providing an overview of the Nebraska statutory law and the common law rights of the Pawnee people. As a result of the conflicts of the Nebraska statutory law and the common law rights of the Pawnee people, in 1989, Nebraska enacted a new reburial law. Peregoy provides an excellent summary of the "precedent-setting reburial act," that calls for "the return and reburial of all human skeletal remains and associated burial offerings that can be reasonably linked to a modern Indian tribe or tribes based on a preponderance of evidence." The author also discusses the issue of protection of unmarked burial sites in Nebraska and dispute resolution and enforcement. In summation, the author states that "Nebraska's landmark repatriation legislation represents the triumph of human rights, religious freedom, and common decency."

The second chapter in this section addresses the issues of nonfederally recognized Native American tribes. Carole Goldberg focuses on the "access of unacknowledged or unrecognized [nonfederally recognized] tribes, especially those in California, to legal rights of repatriation. . . ." The author explains how, beginning in 1870, federal government actions resulted in many historic California Indian tribes loosing their land claims and ultimately their federal recognition and protections. The author also answers the question: How does a tribe become acknowledged or regain their recognition? Goldberg's discussion is set in the tenor of the applicability or in-applicability of NAGPRA. The question is, does NAGPRA apply to these tribes that have been, through no fault of their own, denied federal recognition? The author states that "one should not assume that the NAGPRA eligibility rules apply. They apparently do not."

9

Nebraska's Landmark Repatriation Law: A Study of Cross-Cultural Conflict and Resolution

Robert M. Peregoy

 THIS ARTICLE EXPLORES the cross-cultural repatriation conflict between Indian tribes and the museum and archaeological communities in Nebraska during the 1980s and early 1990s. It seeks to provide an understanding of the issues (and nonissues) surrounding the enactment of the nation's first general statute requiring public museums to repatriate Indian skeletal remains and burial offerings to Indian tribes for reburial. The focus is a case study of the bitter, widely publicized dispute between the Nebraska State Historical Society (NSHS) and the Pawnee Tribe of Oklahoma, an indigenous Nebraska tribe. The first part of the article is an overview of the competing interests of Indian tribes and the museum and archaeological communities, as manifested in the cross-cultural conflict. The second part delineates the legal foundation of tribal repatriation efforts and Nebraska's landmark repatriation legislation. The third part presents an overview of the processes and politics that led to the enactment of the human rights law designed to resolve the cross-cultural conflict. The fourth part summarizes the provisions of the watershed legislation. The last part focuses on the implementation of the repatriation provisions of the statute in the context of the Pawnee Tribe of Oklahoma and the Nebraska State Historical Society.

THE BATTLE LINES OF THE CLASSIC CROSS-CULTURAL CONFLICT

> When Our people die and go on to the spirit world, sacred rituals and ceremonies are performed. We believe that if the body is disturbed, the spirit becomes restless and cannot be at peace. Why do you impose your values on us when we do not impose our values on you? All we want is reburial of the remains of our ancestors and to let them finally rest in peace, and for all people in Nebraska to refrain from, forever, any excavation of any Native American graves or burial sites.[1]

Robert M. Peregoy, a Flathead Indian, is a part-time appellate court judge of the Confederated Salish and Kootenai tribes and a senior staff attorney of the Native American Rights Fund, Boulder, Colorado.

With this simple, yet eloquent plea in March 1988, chairman Lawrence Goodfox, Jr. of the Pawnee Tribe of Oklahoma issued the first of several requests to the Nebraska State Historical Society (NSHS) for the repatriation of the remains and burial offerings of untold hundreds of deceased Pawnee individuals long held by the NSHS.[2] Led by executive director James Hanson, the NSHS, a powerful state agency, steadfastly refused to respond to the tribe's repeated requests to rebury deceased Pawnee ancestors and their burial offerings in accordance with tribal religious beliefs and mortuary practices. As a result, a protracted, nationally visible battle ensued between the Pawnee Tribe and the NSHS.

As succinctly captured by Chairman Goodfox in his opening plea to the NSHS, the bitter controversy amounted to a classic cross-cultural conflict. This conflict pitted the religious freedom and equal protection rights of Indian peoples against the avowed interests of racial biology in curating and studying dead Indian bodies in the name of science. It also directly implicated the interests and practices of museums and historical societies that retain and exhibit sacrosanct Native American burial offerings for public viewing.

Briefly stated, Pawnee burial ceremonies constitute religious practices that are part of both the historical and contemporary greater tribal belief system.[3] These time-honored beliefs hold that, if remains or burial offerings are disturbed or separated, the spirits of the deceased will wander restlessly and never be at peace. Pawnee tradition further teaches that adverse spiritual and physical consequences, even death, may be visited upon the living relatives of the deceased or anyone involved with the disturbance of dead Pawnee bodies or associated burial offerings. Thus, notwithstanding the motive for disinterring Pawnee burials, such sacrilegious activity causes emotional distress and spiritual sickness among the living. This was precisely what happened in 1988 when the Pawnee tribal government and people first learned that the NSHS had plundered hundreds of Pawnee graves in Nebraska during the first half of this century.[4]

Throughout this cross-cultural conflict, the NSHS refused to recognize or honor the religious-based mortuary traditions, practices, and rights of the Pawnee people. Consistently focusing on the interests of science and history, the NSHS executive director opposed reburial on the basis of the perceived value of Pawnee remains and burial offerings to "discovering how people lived" in Nebraska's past.[5] Framing the issue as a "science versus religion" dispute, Hanson disparagingly equated dead Pawnee bodies with books and argued that "a bone is like a book . . . and I don't believe in burning books."[6] The state official further insinuated that the Pawnee people had ceased to practice their traditional mortuary ceremonies, requiring that the dead remain undisturbed in their final places of rest.[7] At one point, Hanson publicly challenged the Pawnee to "prove their religion is being affected by our possession of these things."[8] Other NSHS officials, in a further attempt to retain certain peace medals buried with deceased Pawnee, alleged that such burial offerings "are not religious objects like crucifixes, rosaries and bibles."[9]

The battle lines of this classic cross-cultural conflict were thus drawn. The insensitivity of NSHS officials and the misinformation they disseminated made it clear that remedial relief would not be forthcoming until cross-cultural education and sensitization occurred. This need was particularly compelling considering that NSHS policymakers were all non-Indian and that the overwhelming majority had ignored or misrepresented the religious values and traditions of the Pawnee and other tribes throughout the controversy.

In light of the relentless resistance of the NSHS to reburial, the Pawnee Tribe realized that a satisfactory remedy at the administrative level of state government was simply not available. Accordingly, the tribe joined forces with Nebraska tribes to seek legislation that would force the recalcitrant agency to repatriate the Indian dead and their burial offerings. This coalition ultimately led to the 1989 enactment of the nation's first general repatriation statute, the Unmarked Human Burial Sites and Skeletal Remains Protection Act, commonly known as LB 340.[10]

The landmark law was the first in the country to require public museums to return all tribally identifiable skeletal remains and burial offerings to Indian tribes that requested them for reburial. The Nebraska legislation has been widely recognized as a model that has led to the enactment of similar laws in Arizona, Hawaii, and other states, and to the enactment of two federal repatriation statutes,[11] the National Museum of the American Indian Act[12] and the Native American Graves Protection and Repatriation Act.[13]

Nebraska's law was the result of a prolonged struggle by indigenous and present-day Nebraska tribes to secure equal protection and treatment of the Indian dead. The repatriation battle between the NSHS and the Pawnee Tribe ultimately was fought in all three branches of state government as well as in the federal bureaucracy. The legislative battle and debates on LB 340 constituted, by all accounts, one of the most controversial, hard-fought, and emotional issues to come before the Nebraska legislature in years. Reburial opponents, led by the NSHS, waged a carefully orchestrated grassroots campaign of misinformation, sensationalism, half-truths, and outright lies in an attempt to derail the historic human rights legislation. Under color and authority of state law, the NSHS raised every conceivable obstacle to prevent reburial of the Pawnee dead in accordance with tribal religious beliefs and practices. At one point, the Nebraska State Historical Society even instigated the active involvement of the United States government in an attempt to defeat the Pawnee Tribe's quest to rebury its dead ancestors.

Yet the Indian tribes and peoples prevailed. In the final analysis, the courageous vision of enlightened Nebraska lawmakers firmly committed to the principles of fairness, equality, and human dignity won the day for a traditionally oppressed minority group, many of whom could not even vote for the lawmakers who carried the banner of justice on their behalf.[14] The strong support for Indian tribes and peoples manifested by Nebraskans in this historic action is sound testimony to their commitment to the American system of justice.

Although the tribes prevailed at the legislative level, the bitter dispute between the NSHS and the Pawnee Tribe continued to rage throughout the implementation phase of the law. These post-LB 340 disputes resulted from the NSHS's open defiance of the mandates of the legislature and the tribe's reburial claims and rights. The disputes found their way to the state attorney general, the state ombudsman, and the state court. The Pawnee Tribe prevailed in each instance.

The Legal Foundation of Tribal Repatriation Efforts and Nebraska's Reburial Statute

While the nation's legal system and social policy have largely failed to protect the sepulcher of the American Indian dead, applicable law amply supports the repatriation of dead Indian bodies and funerary objects held by institutions such as the NSHS. Indeed, the sources of law underlying the Nebraska Unmarked Human Burial Sites and Skeletal Remains Protection Act include the common law, precursor state statutes, constitutional law, and federal Indian law.

Pre-LB 340 Nebraska Statutory Law and Common Law Rights to Rebury Pawnee Dead

During the initial attempt to prevent the repatriation and reburial of Pawnee dead bodies,[15] the NSHS claimed that it legally owned or had title to all human skeletal remains in its possession.[16] However, under American common law, there is no property interest or ownership right to a dead body.[17] The remains of any race are not chattels that may be bought, sold, or traded in the marketplace. Ownership of the burial land does not affect this rule. Landowners have only technical possession of graves and simply hold them in trust for the relatives or descendants of the deceased.[18] Thus, because landowners cannot convey any title, the NSHS or any other institution may not own or have title to Indian remains, even if obtained with the permission of landowners.

Once duly interred, a dead body is in the custody of the law and may be removed only pursuant to proper legal authority.[19] The common law has a strong presumption against the removal of a dead body, even for reinterment to another place.[20] This presumption is logically stronger where no reinterment is contemplated, as when the NSHS removed hundreds of dead Pawnee bodies from tribal cemeteries.[21]

State statutes also may regulate the exhumation or removal of the dead.[22] For a court to construe a statute permitting disinterment of a dead body, "it must be clear in its intent."[23] In the absence of such specific statutory or constitutional provisions, common law remains in effect.[24]

Nebraska statutory law makes it a misdemeanor to dig up, disinter, remove, or carry away "any dead human body or the remains thereof" from "its place of deposit or burial."[25] This criminal statute grants three narrow exemptions in (1) lawfully authorized dissection of bodies; (2) change of sepulcher by cemetery officials;[26] and (3) change of sepulcher by relatives or intimate friends.[27]

Nebraska, like most other states, has specific statutory procedures for the disinterment of human bodies.[28] State law requires that only the next of kin[29] or a county attorney[30] may apply for and obtain a disinterment permit from the Bureau of Vital Statistics. A licensed funeral director[31] must directly supervise the disinterment. A party attempting to disinter more than one human body must submit "an order from a Court of competent jurisdiction" to the Bureau of Vital Statistics with the permit application.[32] The required court order must specify "the place for reinterment, and the reason for disinterment."[33] The statute thus contemplates a requirement that the party exhuming human remains shall reinter them. This statutory scheme enacted in 1921 provides no exemption for NSHS disinterment or retention of Pawnee remains removed from Pawnee burials. Thus, the NSHS would have had to comply with these statutory requirements for the state agency to colorably claim a superior right to tribal skeletal remains acquired after 1921.[34]

The NSHS must also meet the applicable common law requirements for a non-tribal entity to have a right of disposition superior to an Indian tribe. Under common law, NSHS's or any other party's disturbance and removal of skeletal remains is "subject to the control and direction of a court of equity."[35] In Nebraska, the courts have held that the consent of judicial authority is essential to allow disinterment for even the next of kin.[36] Significantly, common law considers an allegation that a given tribal human remain may be of historic or scientific interest insufficient grounds to allow disinterment without court or other approval.[37]

Nebraska statutory law also specifies the persons who have the right to control the disposition of a deceased's remains.[38] Under the law of descent and distribution, where there is no surviving competent spouse, adult child, parent, or sibling, an adult next of kin is vested with this right.[39] Where a tribal government represents all living members and therefore all descendant tribal members, common law presumes that the tribe is the nearest "next of kin."[40] The tribe need not prove specific blood ties between the unknown decedents and specific living kin to obtain its rights to control the remains.[41] Additionally, under Nebraska statutory law, skeletal remains do not escheat to the state unless there are no next of kin takers.[42] Therefore, in situations such as the Pawnee case, a tribal right to control disposition of Indian remains takes statutory preference over that of a state agency or institution, if exercised on behalf of its entire membership.

Without this type of statutory scheme, the common law applies notice to and consent of the nearest next of kin as critical factors in determining whether removal of the skeletal remains was proper. Courts typically allow disinterment with the consent of a relative only when meeting controlling authority's narrowly prescribed circumstances and only where reinterment is contemplated.[43] Next of kin may maintain an action for a deprivation of the right of sepulcher or for mutilation of the body.[44] Courts universally hold liability for damages to arise for disinterment done[45] without the knowledge of the nearest next of kin.[46] The judiciary considers notice to parties who have a right to object (1) to ensure that final sepulcher is not disturbed against their will;[47] (2) to provide an opportunity to assure themselves that the exhumation is done with dignity; and (3) to document the reburial and its location.[48] This duty of notice pertains even if the next of kin do not own the burial land.[49]

Any agency seeking to withhold Indian remains from reburial holds the burden of proof to show proper legal authority to disinter the dead and to control the disposition of the dead.[50] In the Pawnee repatriation dispute, the NSHS failed to produce a single regulatory permit or court order authorizing it to disinter any deceased Pawnee.[51] Moreover, the NSHS was unable to produce any colorable evidence that it had sought or obtained the Pawnee tribal government's consent to disinter any of the Pawnee graves.[52] Finally, no Nebraska statute expressly authorizes the NSHS to disinter dead bodies as a matter of course or right.[53] The NSHS therefore failed to show any legal right or authority to disinter, procure, possess, or withhold the Pawnee dead from reburial. Because the NSHS's disinterment and removal of Pawnee dead bodies from Pawnee cemeteries was not authorized by law, it constituted unlawful and *ultra vires* conduct. Thus, under applicable statutory and common law, the right to control the disposition and reburial of Pawnee dead bodies is vested in the Pawnee Tribe, not the NSHS.[54]

Common Law Rights of Possession to Pawnee Funerary Objects

American common law has long held that disinterred funerary objects are the property of the person or persons who furnished the grave or their known descendants.[55] This rule applies even if the specific identities of the deceased individuals are unknown[56] and even if the rightful owner does not own the land where the graves are located.[57] More specifically, landowners where graves are located have only technical possession of the burial objects, holding them in trust for the donors or their descendants.[58] Thus, a landowner or anyone who disinters burial goods with a landowner's permission does not have and therefore cannot convey title to burial goods in instances where, as in the case of the NSHS, the landowners or gravediggers are strangers to the decedent or his or her descendants. The length of time a body has been buried is irrelevant.[59]

A court applied these common law rules in a dispute over the ownership of Indian burial offerings in *Charrier* v. *Bell*, 496 So. 2d 601 (La. App.), *cert. denied*, 498 So. 2d 753 (La. 1986). The facts of *Charrier* are substantially analogous to the Pawnee situation in Nebraska. *Charrier* was an action to quit title to two-and-one-half tons of Tunica Indian burial goods unearthed by an amateur archaeologist. The burial goods came from 150 Indian graves about 250 years old, located on private land that bore no resemblance to a cemetery when the goods were unearthed. The court held that the Tunica Tribe was the lawful owner of the grave goods, even though the specific identities of the deceased individuals were unknown. The court stated,

> They were burial goods then and they remain burial goods today, whether they are referred to as artifacts, funerary offerings or the "Tunica Treasure.". . . [We] cannot agree that ownership of such objects may be acquired by reducing them to possession and over the objections of the descendants of the persons with whom the objects were buried. Reason dictates that these objects, when and if removed, rightfully belong to the descendants if they be known and for such disposition as the descendants may deem proper. We hold accordingly. Charrier v. Bell, No. 5,552, slip op. at 11-13 (20th Jud. Dist., La. Mar. 18,1985), aff'd, 496 So. 2d 601 (La. App. Cir.1 1986), cert. denied, 498 So. 2d 753 (1986).

Significantly, the court ruled in the tribe's favor despite the claimed historic or scientific value of the grave goods. The court noted,

In some quarters, Charrier's discovery is viewed as an archaeological find of considerable significance. To others it is viewed as the systematic despolia- tion of ... [the Tunica's ancestral burial grounds. While we can fully appreci- ate the former view, it cannot override the equally considerable merit we find in the latter view. Id. at 14.

Finding that the deceased Tunica Indians were interred "with their earthly possessions for use in the spiritual hereafter," the *Charrier* court further ruled that the common law doctrine of abandonment does not apply to burial offer- ings. The Court outlined its reasoning as follows:

The fact that the. . . fellow tribesmen of the deceased Tunica Indians resolved, for some customary, religious or spiritual belief, to bury certain items along with the bodies of the deceased, does not result in a conclusion that the goods were abandoned. While the relinquishment of immediate possession may have been proved, an objective viewing of the circum- stances and intent of the relinquishment does not result in a finding of abandonment. Objects may be buried with a decedent for any number of reasons. The relinquishment of possession normally serves some spiritual, moral, or religious purpose of the descendant/owner, but it is not intended as a means of relinquishing ownership to a stranger. [Charrier's] argument carried to its logical conclusion would render a grave subject to despoliation either immediately after interment or indefinitely after removal of the descendants of the deceased from the neighborhood of the cemetery. Char- rier v. Bell, supra, 496 So. 2d at 604-05 (1986).

No Nebraska statute altered these long-standing rules of common law prior to general codification in the state's 1989 landmark reburial law. Similarly, it is unlikely that other states have statutorily or otherwise altered these rules. Thus, the common law provides ample support for Native Americans and their tribes seeking to repatriate Indian grave offerings for reburial or other appropriate dis- position. Further, this long-standing body of American law serves as a solid legal basis for the enactment of legislation mandating the relinquishment of improperly obtained Indian burial offerings.

Constitutional and Federal Law Claims Available to Repatriate Pawnee Dead and Burial Offerings

Where disputes over the repatriation of Indian remains and funerary objects involve state officials acting under color and authority of state law, con- stitutional and federal statutory causes of action are available to tribes and their members. Because questions of race, religion, and property are directly impli- cated by the inherent nature of these disputes, there are cognizable constitu- tional claims under the First and Fourteenth amendments to the United States Constitution.

The Fourteenth Amendment forbids invidious discrimination based on race.[60] The Supreme Court has strongly intimated that racially motivated state action resulting in denial of sepulcher to the Indian dead raises serious ques- tions "concerning a denial of the equal protection of the laws guaranteed by the

Fourteenth Amendment."[61] The facts in the Pawnee repatriation controversy establish that the NSHS, acting under color and authority of state law, conducted a systematic effort to unearth hundreds of Pawnee dead bodies and engaged in a carefully orchestrated campaign to prohibit their reburial. The NSHS has not subjected any other race or Indian tribe to such mistreatment. Thus, the Pawnee Tribe and its members have a colorable equal protection claim to challenge this state action by the NSHS.

The Fourteenth Amendment also prohibits a state from taking property in violation of due process of law. Because the property right in disinterred grave goods vests in the descendants of the decedent, a state may have obtained this property in violation of due process of law and without just compensation.[62]

Further, state action that interferes with religious mortuary practices may violate the First Amendment Free Exercise Clause.[63] The NSHS's disinterment and withholding of Pawnee dead from reburial unequivocally infringes on fundamental Pawnee religious beliefs and mortuary traditions.[64] Accordingly, the Pawnee people have a colorable constitutional claim for state interference with their religious rights and practices. Under this same rationale, Nebraska attorney general Robert Spire concluded in 1988 that a court would rule in favor of the Pawnee Tribe and its members and order the repatriation and reburial of all Pawnee dead bodies and burial offerings held by the NSHS.[65]

Although untested in a repatriation context, these constitutional safeguards remain available in most repatriation situations, notwithstanding the Supreme Court's recent decision in *Employment Division* v. *Smith*, 494 U. S.___, 108 L. Ed. 2d 876, 110 S. Ct. 1595 (1990). While that decision narrowed the protective scope of the Free Exercise Clause of the First Amendment, the Pawnee repatriation issue, and perhaps others, can be distinguished from the facts and holding of *Employment Division* v. *Smith*.[66] In any event, the Supreme Court has indicated that the legislature is the proper forum for balancing society's competing interests implicating the First Amendment's Free Exercise Clause.[67] Therefore, legislation such as the Nebraska repatriation statute would likely survive a court challenge.[68]

Federal Indian Law Recognizes the Pawnee Tribe's Inherent Sovereign Right and Authority to Repatriate Pawnee Dead and Burial Offerings Disinterred on Historic Pawnee Lands

Beyond state, common, and constitutional law, the Pawnee Tribe's repatriation claim and the Nebraska statute are strongly grounded in established principles of federal law governing Indian treaties and tribal sovereignty. These federal and tribal political rights provide an additional legal basis for the Pawnee and other tribes to repatriate their deceased relatives and burial offerings held by nontribal entities.

Indian treaty construction is governed by the principle that "the treaty is not a grant of rights to the Indians but a grant of rights from them—a reservation of those [rights] not granted."[69] Under this Supreme Court rule, any right not ceded by a tribe to the United States in a treaty is implied to be reserved by the tribe.[70] In addition to land, the term *reservation* of rights includes other valuable rights not relinquished when Indians conveyed their aboriginal title to the United States.[71] Another principle governing treaty construction states that a treaty must be interpreted as the Pawnee would have understood it,[72] given the practices and customs of the tribe at the time the treaty was negotiated.[73]

The Pawnee Tribe and the federal government entered into several treaties beginning in 1833. Pursuant to these treaties, the tribe ceded certain lands in Nebraska to the United States.[74] Consistent with these rules of treaty construction, the Pawnee Tribe's land cession cannot fairly be construed to encompass a relinquishment of tribal authority and control over Pawnee burials in Nebraska. Given the fundamental importance of the tribe's religious-based mortuary traditions, customs, and practices of sepulcher,[75] the only logical and fair inference is that the Pawnee Tribe reserved this right and authority.

While treaties may be interpreted by federal agents' representations,[76] the canons of Indian treaty construction bar imputing an illegal intent to the United States as trustee for Indian tribes.[77] Thus, the federal government could not have intended to obtain Pawnee lands to disinter dead Pawnee bodies or to condone such, because grave robbing was a well-established common law crime by the time the Pawnee treaties were negotiated.

The Supremacy Clause of the United States Constitution is applicable to international and Indian treaties alike.[78] It prohibits a state from enacting or enforcing any state statute or regulation that conflicts with treaties between Indian tribes and the United States.[79] The Supremacy Clause further precludes a state from applying its law to Indians located outside the geographical boundaries of an Indian reservation when its application interferes with a tribe's reserved treaty rights.[80] Thus, even though the Pawnee Tribe retains no reservation lands in Nebraska, regulatory or policy actions by the NSHS, an agency of Nebraska, prohibiting the repatriation of the Pawnee dead are null and void under superseding federal treaty law.

In addition to reserved treaty rights, Indian tribes, as sovereign governments, retain the right to govern the internal affairs of their members.[81] The power to govern the domestic relationship between the living and the dead comprises a fundamental attribute of the Pawnee tribal government.[82] State or federal governments may not encumber this sovereign right unless expressly allowed by Congress.[83]

Beginning in 1988, the Pawnee Tribe initiated official action to repatriate all dead Pawnee Indians and their burial offerings held by the state of Nebraska under the auspices of the NSHS.[84] Since that time, under color and authority of state law, the NSHS has acted systematically to prevent the Pawnee Tribe from reburying all of its dead held by the state agency. Congress has never authorized this interference, and therefore it probably would not withstand judicial scrutiny.[85]

The forgoing rules of law formed the legal basis of the Pawnee Tribe's repatriation claims against the NSHS. These legal principles are also available to other tribes seeking repatriation of their dead and burial offerings. Nebraska's landmark repatriation statute enacted in 1989 codified the majority of the rules. They can further serve to form the legal foundation of repatriation in other states.

THE PROCESSES AND POLITICAL RESOLUTION OF THE CROSS-CULTURAL CONFLICT

Nebraska's 1989 reburial statute is the product of protracted tribal negotiations and lobbying in both the administrative and legislative arenas of Nebraska state government. An examination of the issues, processes, and hurdles that the tribes confronted and overcame in seeking legislation to remedy the disparate treatment accorded the Indian dead in Nebraska facilitates an understanding and appreciation of the precedent-setting law.

Nebraska Reburial Movement: 1971–87

Tribal efforts to have legislation passed to protect the Native dead in Nebraska date at least to 1971. In November of that year, the Nebraska Indian Commission, a state agency, called for the enactment of legislation to stop the uncontrolled digging and desecration of Indian graves in the state.[86] However, the commission's 1971 plea went unanswered.

Between 1981 and 1986, the Omaha and Winnebago tribes worked to preserve, protect, and salvage unmarked burial sites in Nebraska from archaeological excavations grave robbing, and construction projects. Their efforts met with little success.[87] Undaunted, the tribes and the state Indian commission pushed ahead and drafted a proposal for consideration by the state legislature during the 1987 session.[88]

In January 1987, Senator James Pappas introduced LB 612, which initially proposed the adoption of the Nebraska Unmarked Human Burial Sites and Skeletal Remains Protection Act.[89] The bill was designed to protect unmarked burial sites from unauthorized disturbance and to require the repatriation of human skeletal remains and burial offerings held by public institutions and other entities in the state.[90] The bill received extensive media attention, spawned primarily by the Nebraska State Historical Society which bitterly opposed the bill on the basis that it allegedly would "cripple" forensic research and the "science of archaeology" and would force the NSHS to lose "more than 10,000 irreplaceable artifacts."[91] The society's core concern with the bill, according to executive director James Hanson, rested with the fact that the legislation required the NSHS to return coveted peace medals that it had removed from Pawnee burials.[92]

The society waged a successful media campaign against LB 612 and called on its members, numbering in excess of four thousand persons throughout the state, to lobby their senators.[93] Perhaps the most effective tool employed by the NSHS was a "legislative alert" sent to its membership. Using unfounded scare tactics, NSHS director Hanson warned, "If LB 612 becomes law, you could go to jail for a year and be fined up to $1,000 for giving an arrowhead, a piece of pottery, or a chip of flint to a child, a friend, or even a Nebraska museum!"[94] Labeling the bill a "raid" on the NSHS's "collection" of human skeletal remains and burial offerings,[95] Hanson called on the politically powerful NSHS membership to oppose the bill.[96] The record reflects that Hanson's legislative alert generated numerous letters to state senators in opposition to LB 612.[97] The legislature took no action on LB 612, which accordingly died at the end of the 1988 legislative session.[98]

In the final analysis, the grass-roots political organization and power of the NSHS killed LB 612.[99] The Nebraska tribes simply were not financially capable or adequately staffed to effectively join the battle waged by a powerful state agency with extensive media and political contacts, a staff of over one hundred people, and an annual budget approaching $4 million. The NSHS had enormous, unparalleled resources at its immediate disposal to be devoted at will to the campaign to defeat the tribal reburial movement and thereby to frustrate the legitimate human and religious rights and interests that the Indian tribes of Nebraska sought to vindicate.

Pre-LB 340 Politics: 1988 Negotiations with the NSHS to Establish a Repatriation Policy at the Administrative Level of State Government and to Draft Unmarked Grave Protection Legislation

In early 1988, the Pawnee Tribe of Oklahoma learned from representatives of the Nebraska tribes that the Nebraska State Historical Society had custody of an unspecified number of Pawnee dead bodies and burial offerings.[100] Desiring to accomplish a dignified reburial of their ancestors, the Pawnee Tribe, represented by the Native American Rights Fund (NARF), joined ranks with the Nebraska tribes to try to establish a statewide repatriation policy. The entry of the Pawnee Tribe of Oklahoma and NARF into the Nebraska repatriation movement proved to be a strategically and pivotal move, shifting the balance of power from the museum and archaeological communities to the tribes. This ultimately led to the enactment of Nebraska's landmark burial legislation. However, the process culminating in the new law was long and costly and often was characterized by bad faith, deception, and unlawful conduct by the NSHS.

The goal of the new tribal coalition was to bring all interested parties together and begin the negotiation process anew. The LB 612 experience demonstrated at least one major issue on which the tribes and museum community apparently could agree: the need to protect unmarked burials throughout the state from unauthorized disturbance.[101] Concomitantly, the interested parties remained unable to agree on the real issue in the controversy—the repatriation and reburial of dead bodies and burial offerings held by museums in the state.

The tribes devised a two-pronged approach to the burial issue: First, as to protecting unmarked burials, tribal advocates recommended the establishment of a writing committee consisting of representatives of the tribes and museum and archaeological communities to draft legislation for introduction in the 1989 legislature. Second, as to repatriating Indian skeletal remains and burial offerings, the tribes, led by the Pawnee, focused on negotiating with the NSHS for the establishment of an effective repatriation policy at the administrative level of state government.[102]

NSHS's attempts to undermine the legislation drafting process. In March 1988, the writing committee, consisting of representatives of the NSHS, the University of

Nebraska, the Nebraska Indian Commission, and the Native American Rights Fund on behalf of the Pawnee Tribe began work.[103] After a seven-month process and three drafts, the committee developed what tribal representatives believed was a consensus legislative proposal designed to protect unmarked graves throughout the state.

However, on 9 September 1988, the president of the NSHS executive board informed tribal representatives that the NSHS staff had drafted a separate bill. The NSHS, a state government agency that had declared itself committed to work openly with tribal representatives to develop the consensus bill, had drafted its own self-serving bill in the back room.[104] The tribes were shocked and outraged by this secret, deceptive conduct.

Finding that the secret bill failed to protect Indian rights and interests, the tribes requested the opportunity to provide input into the NSHS legislation.[105] The NSHS denied this request. Then, as a stopgap measure, the tribes asked the NSHS executive board to refrain from introducing the secret NSHS bill and to continue working with Indian representatives on the consensus bill. At its 17 December 1988 meeting, the NSHS board granted the tribes' request, declaring its desire "to develop a legislative bill acceptable to all."[106]

Disregarding the NSHS executive board's clear directive, the NSHS staff refused to work with the writing committee on the consensus bill. Instead, NSHS director Hanson proceeded unilaterally, convincing two senators to introduce the secret bill during the first session of the ninety-first legislature. After a committee hearing in March 1989, the legislature resoundingly killed LB 691 because of the secret drafting process and because the bill competed with the more comprehensive, protective consensus bill, LB 340. The legislature noted that, with the exception of the repatriation provisions, all interested parties represented on the writing committee had developed LB 340.[107]

In retrospect, the failure of LB 691 and the concomitant enactment of LB 340 exemplified the commitment of the Government, Military, and Veterans' Affairs Committee and the Ninety-First Nebraska Legislature to fairness and due process. In this instance, Nebraska lawmakers held the NSHS, a state government agency, accountable to itself and to the Indian tribes it had treated in an underhanded manner.

Tribal attempts to seek repatriation at the administrative level of state government. To establish an effective repatriation policy leading to the reburial of its ancestors and burial offerings held by Nebraska museums, the Pawnee Tribe first negotiated with the Nebraska State Historical Society for several reasons. First, the state agency possessed the skeletal remains and burial offerings of untold hundreds of deceased Pawnee, erroneously claiming it owned them.[108] Equally important, the NSHS took the lead role in opposing repatriation and reburial and was a proven powerful political force. Finally, the Pawnee Tribe considered negotiation necessary to exhaust its administrative remedies and thereby protect its option to appeal to other forums of government for relief. Accordingly, the Pawnee Tribe had two primary objectives in negotiating with the NSHS: (1) the establishment of a model repatriation policy at the administrative level of state government, and (2) pursuant to such policy, the timely return and reburial of all reasonably identifiable Pawnee dead bodies and burial offerings held by the NSHS.

As part of their repatriation request, the Pawnee and other tribes proposed that the NSHS adopt a repatriation policy requiring the return of all tribally identifiable skeletal remains and burial offerings to requesting tribes for reburial.[109] To support its proposed repatriation policy, the Pawnee Tribe provided NSHS policymakers with extensive information on the historical and contemporary religious-based mortuary traditions and practices of the Pawnee and other Indian peoples.[110] Also, in response to the president of the NSHS executive board, the tribe furnished a comprehensive legal memorandum supporting, if not mandating, repatriation in light of governing law.[111]

Hanson responded by proposing a competing policy that strictly limited repatriation to any remains disinterred in the future.[112] Thus, the NSHS staff proposal circumvented the basic question of the repatriation of remains and burial goods already disinterred and held by the state agency.

It soon became apparent that the NSHS executive board had no intention of conducting a fair hearing process and that it was predisposed to reject both the Pawnee repatriation claim and the proposed policy. The tribe's primary concern centered on the fact that the policymaking body intended to limit its solicitation of external comments to one or two carefully selected representatives of the scientific community who opposed reburial. Specifically, the board indicated it would not make a policy decision until it had the benefit of the testimony of a Smithsonian Institution scientist conducting studies on the precise Pawnee skeletal remains at issue.[113] Moreover, the Smithsonian scientist was officially on record as opposed to the reburial mandates of LB 612.[114] Thus, the primary "expert" that the NSHS intended to and did call had a classic conflict of interest and simply corroborated Hanson's antireburial position. The tribe's efforts to facilitate a fair hearing proved futile, because the NSHS executive board ultimately rejected the Pawnee Tribe's proposed policy and repatriation request.

Beyond this administrative gamesmanship, the NSHS further hampered the tribe's request with unlawful conduct. Specifically, NSHS director Hanson denied Pawnee tribal researchers access to NSHS burial records documenting the Pawnee disinterments. Pursuant to the state's public records law, the tribe successfully petitioned the state attorney general.[115] On 6 October 1988, the attorney general ordered the NSHS to disclose the withheld records. He concluded, *inter alia*, that the NSHS was a state agency or other public body subject to the public records law and that the information sought constituted public records that were not exempt from the disclosure requirements of the statute.[116] Two days later, the NSHS executive board unanimously voted to comply with the order of the attorney general.[117]

Even with this clear directive, Hanson continued to refuse to disclose a significant portion of the disputed records.[118] His actions necessitated a second directive from the attorney general.[119] Finally, Hanson granted access to NSHS burial records. However, the six-month delay severely stymied the tribe's research project and repatriation negotiations.

Resolution of the burial records dispute did not thwart the relentless campaign of NSHS officials to prevent reburial of the Pawnee dead. Hanson, a non-lawyer, resorted to nonexistent or inapplicable federal law in an attempt to justify his position. Specifically, he erroneously advised the policymaking body that a federal regulation conferred ownership of the Pawnee collection in the United States government[120] and that the NSHS therefore could not lawfully return the Pawnee skeletal remains or burial offerings to the tribe.[121] Although the alleged federal regulation never existed,[122] Hanson's legal cite played a key role in the board's decision to take no action on the tribe's repatriation request at the October 1988 meeting.[123]

Later conceding that the federal regulation did not exist, the NSHS director then turned to inapplicable federal authority to defend his position.[124] Specifically, he claimed that reburial of the Pawnee collection would violate the 1906 federal Antiquities Act and other unspecified federal law allegedly prohibiting reburial, because funds provided by the defunct Works Progress Administration (WPA) were utilized to disinter Pawnee burials.[125] Further, Hanson enlisted the assistance of the National Park Service (NPS), a powerful federal agency.[126]

The federal government's entrance into the dispute further complicated the already protracted conflict. In November 1988, the Midwest Archaeological Center of the National Park Service threatened confiscation of the Pawnee collection of skeletal remains and burial offerings if the NSHS board took action in favor of reburial.[127] The NPS based its threat on the 1906 federal Antiquities Act.[128] However, after the Pawnee Tribe established that the Antiquities Act was inapplicable,[129] the NPS withdrew its confiscation threat.[130]

Notwithstanding this withdrawal, the NPS central office in Washington, D. C., continued to allege that the federal government "may" have an unspecified "interest" in the NSHS collection because of NSHS's use of federal WPA funds.[131] The NPS advised the NSHS not to take any action on the Pawnee repatriation request until the NPS could determine the exact nature of the alleged interest.[132] However, the NPS again failed to provide any authority to support its claim. In contrast, the Pawnee Tribe provided both the NPS and the NSHS with controlling legal authority establishing that the federal government had no legal interest in or control over the Pawnee collection because of WPA funds, or otherwise.[133]

The collusive action of the federal and state governments to concoct a federal ownership claim or interest in the Pawnee collection further delayed state agency action on the tribe's repatriation claim.[134] On 14 December 1988, Nebraska's attorney general issued a legal opinion concluding that a court would rule in favor of the Pawnee Tribe and order the return of all Pawnee skeletal remains and burial offerings for reburial.[135] Even with the great weight of legal authority supporting repatriation and the absence of any colorable federal ownership claim or interest, the NSHS executive board voted overwhelmingly to reject the Pawnee Tribe's repatriation request.[136]

The decision of the state agency was a great disappointment to the Pawnee Tribe and its many supporters.[137] On 20 December 1988, the United States Department of the Interior officially waived any interest the federal government may have had in the Pawnee collection.[138] On this basis, the Pawnee Tribe formally appealed to the NSHS to reconsider its adverse decision.[139] Without presenting the request to the board or responding directly, Frederick Wefso, then the NSHS executive board's recently elected president, announced publicly that the NSHS would take no further administrative action on the matter.[140]

Thus, the Pawnee Tribe realized that any further effort to negotiate with the NSHS would prove futile and that all administrative remedies had been exhausted. The tribe then turned to the legislative branch of Nebraska state government to force the recalcitrant state agency to repatriate deceased Pawnee ancestors and their burial offerings for a dignified reburial.

1989 Enactment of the Nebraska Reburial Law

The convention of the Ninety-First Nebraska Legislature in 1989 was marked by a definite shift in the balance of political power from reburial opponents to the tribes. This transition was the product of two years of intense media coverage, public education, tribal lobbying,[141] and growing public disgust with the NSHS treatment of the Pawnee Tribe. Nevertheless, the repatriation question remained at the forefront of controversy.

Senator Ernie Chambers, the only black member of the Nebraska legislature and a longtime advocate of the rights of the oppressed, introduced the reburial bill, LB 340, in January 1989.[142] After a public hearing by the Government, Military, and Veterans' Affairs Committee, a majority of the committee members favored the *reburial of skeletal remains and burial offerings to be disinterred in future, as well as the reburial of Indian skeletal remains previously disinterred and held by public institutions.*[143] However, the senators were divided on the provision of the bill requiring these entities to return for reburial *all previously disinterred funerary objects identifiable to a specific tribe or tribes, notwithstanding whether such objects could be linked with a specific set of tribal skeletal remains.* To move the bill out of committee, the tribes agreed to an amendment limiting the definition of burial goods to grave offerings that "can be traced with a reasonable degree of certainty to the specific human skeletal remains" with which they were buried.[144]

After the committee approved the bill, the NSHS executive director vowed publicly to support LB 340. His commitment was intended to defuse the controversy and thereby minimize the intense pressure exerted on senators by lobbyists and the pubic.[145] The NSHS executive board then voted to Support LB 340, contingent upon an amendment allowing the NSHS to retain burial offerings "important to telling the state's history."[146] Not unexpectedly, Hanson reneged on his promise to support LB 340, causing senators Baack and Chambers to charge publicly that he had acted in bad faith.[147] Senator Baack subsequently proclaimed on the floor of the legislature that the NSHS director's actions "give more meaning than before to the old saying 'White Man speaks with a forked tongue.'"[148]

This development served to erode the NSHS's credibility even further in the eyes of the legislature and the public. In mid-February 1989, the *Omaha World-Herald*, the only Nebraska newspaper with a statewide circulation, published the results of its scientifically based public opinion poll. This poll revealed that nearly seven of ten (69 percent) Nebraskans surveyed supported the reburial of Indian skeletal remains and burial goods held by the NSHS.[149]

In response to public opinion and rising legislative support, NSHS officials and other reburial opponents accelerated their campaign in an attempt to derail the repatriation legislation. Their tactics degenerated from the absurd to the outrageous. Hanson publicly claimed that if the NSHS repatriated Pawnee dead bodies, Nebraska would risk the loss of "hundreds of millions" of federal dollars allocated to highway construction projects, the Farmers Home Administration, the Soil Conservation Service, and the NSHS's historic preservation programs.[150] Hanson further announced that the Pawnee Tribe would place its deceased ancestors and burial offerings in an Oklahoma museum, rather than reburying them. Attempting to rally the support of the University of Nebraska's "Big Red" football fans, the NSHS director further suggested that "[f]rankly, I think we get beat bad enough in football by Oklahoma that we shouldn't have to turn our museum over to Oklahoma."[151]

Most egregious was the attack of reburial opponents on Pawnee religious beliefs and practices. Frederick Wefso, NSHS executive board president, and F. A. Calabrese, head of the Midwest Archaeological Center of the National Park Service, publicly leveled charges that the Pawnee Tribe sought repatriation to sell its ancestors' remains and their burial offerings on the open market.[152] Hanson and his staff further made erroneous charges, discussed above, impugning the sincerity of Pawnee religious beliefs.

These unfounded attacks on the Pawnee people were designed to generate an amendment to LB 340 allowing the NSHS to retain "precious" Pawnee burial goods alleged to be "priceless" or "worth millions."[153] At the core were three peace medals,[154] which officials claimed were worth up to $1 million each.[155] Hanson admitted, on the basis of "good [NSHS] recordkeeping,"[156] that LB 340 would require the agency to relinquish the three medals.[157]

Against this backdrop, the Nebraska legislature began floor debate on LB 340 in early March 1989. Senator Chambers eloquently and persuasively characterized the bill as long overdue religious freedom and human rights legislation. He stated,

> What we are talking about with this bill is nothing less than human dignity, and what we are asking for is common decency: the same concern accorded to those that we identify as Native Americans accorded routinely to every other group on this planet and certainly in this country. It should not be necessary for a group who were wronged in the first instance to be required to bring out their religion and have it pass muster before those who may have wronged them in the first instance. They should not be required to prove every tenet of their creed, or their doctrine, or their dogma as no other member of any religion is required to do before he or she is allowed to say that I revere and respect my dead and I want the same respect from you. We must be able to conceive of the idea that to Native American people there can be as much concern on their part for their ancestors who are departed as we have for ours. We must be able to conceive that to the same

way a blessed rosary has a special significance when buried with a departed
Catholic that the burial goods placed with our Native American brothers
and sisters would have the same consecrated significance for them. . . .
Everybody on this floor understands very well what it is I am talking about
and were it not for a group that has traditionally been despised, abused,
spat upon, who are few in numbers, impoverished . . . if we were not talking about such a group as that, this bill would not even be necessary. We
didn't need a bill like this to protect the ancestors of white people or any
other group, and I think the very fact that we have to do it in this fashion is
a shame upon all of us, but we can rectify a long existing wrong as much
lies within our power. . . .[158]

LB 340 ultimately passed the three required rounds of floor debate and
action. Proponents defeated all hostile amendments, including several designed
to strike burial goods from the scope of the legislation. Ultimately heeding the
advice of Senator Baack that the "right thing to do" in this "moral and religious"
issue was to rebury "these captives that we have kept in the historical society
and finally let the spirits go,"[159] the unicameral adopted the historic measure on
19 May 1989.[160] Governor Kay Orr signed the precedent-setting human rights
legislation into law on 23 May 1989. Thus, Nebraska's Unmarked Human Burial Sites and Skeletal Remains Protection Act became the first general repatriation statute in the nation.[161]

THE PROVISIONS OF NEBRASKA'S PRECEDENT-SETTING REBURIAL ACT [162]

The primary purpose of Nebraska's Unmarked Human Burial Sites and Skeletal
Remains Protection Act is to "assure that all human burials are accorded equal
treatment and respect for human dignity without reference to ethnic origins,
cultural backgrounds, or religious affiliations. . . ."[163] To carry out this intent,
the statute regulates two areas: (1) the reburial of tribally identifiable dead bodies and associated grave offerings held by public entities in the state;[164] and (2)
the protection of unmarked burials throughout Nebraska.[165] In effect, the
Nebraska Reburial Act codifies longstanding, relevant rules of common law,
constitutional law, and federal Indian law.

Repatriation

The repatriation provisions of LB 340 require state-sponsored or state-
recognized public bodies in possession or control of "reasonably identifiable"
disinterred human skeletal remains and associated "burial goods" of American
Indian origin to return such to a relative or Indian tribe or tribes for reburial
within one year of the receipt of a request.[166] The one-year period affords institutions holding such the opportunity to initiate, conduct, or complete study in
the interest of science or history.[167] The act thus strikes a reasonable balance
between the competing interests of the mortuary beliefs of the Indian tribes and
the concerns of the scientific community.[168]

The two key terms in the legislation are *reasonably identifiable* and *burial goods*. The reburial statute defines *reasonably identifiable* as "identifiable, by a preponderance of the evidence, as to familial or tribal origin based on any available archaeological, historical, ethnological, or other direct or circumstantial evidence or expert opinion."[169] Under this definition, the act requires the return and reburial of *all* human skeletal remains and associated burial offerings that can be reasonably linked to a modern Indian tribe or tribes based on a preponderance of evidence.[170] The antiquity or age of the skeletal remains is not a relevant consideration, as long as they are "reasonably identifiable" to a specific tribe or tribes. The definition of *reasonably identifiable* also provides for the submission of tribal ethno-historical accounts, including oral histories, in determining tribal affiliation of dead Indian bodies and burial offerings held by state entities.[171]

The repatriation statute defines *burial goods* as "any item or items reasonably believed to have been intentionally placed with an individual at the time of burial which can be traced with a reasonable degree of certainty to the specific skeletal remains with which it or they were buried."[172] The legislature's intent was to limit the application of "burial goods" to those funerary objects that can be reasonably linked to a specific set of human skeletal remains.[173] The reburial statute does not require that funerary objects be linked to actual, available human skeletal remains in order to fall within the statutory definition.[174] Colorable documentation or other reasonable means establishing that the funerary object is somehow associated with a specific set of human skeletal remains is sufficient.[175] Upon such a showing, the funerary object constitutes a "burial good" within the meaning of the statute and is therefore subject to reburial.[176] In the absence of such a showing, a funerary object is not a "burial good" under the act, even when reasonably identified with a specific Indian tribe.[177]

The act requires public bodies subject to a repatriation claim to provide the requesting relative or Indian tribe with an itemized inventory of all human skeletal remains and burial goods subject to repatriation ninety days prior to the date of such return.[178] The act further requires the transferring entity and the party receiving the remains and burial offerings to sign, at the time of actual repatriation, a transfer document specifically identifying each transferred human skeletal remain and burial good by inventory number and description.[179] Thus, the statute contemplates that tribes shall have access to burial records created and maintained by affected public entities. This access allows tribal representatives to advance their repatriation claims and sign the statutorily mandated transfer documents with full knowledge and information.[180] The legislature intended tribes to have access to such agency records, in part because the agencies are the sole source of records documenting the specifics of the disinterments.[181]

Protection of Unmarked Burial Sites in Nebraska

The Unmarked Human Burial Sites and Skeletal Remains Protection Act provides extensive protections for unmarked burials and cemeteries throughout the state.[182] The act requires any person who encounters or discovers human skeletal remains or burial offerings associated with an unmarked grave to cease immediately any activity causing further disturbance of the burial.[183] Such person is then required to report the presence and location to local law enforcement officials,[184] who in turn are required to notify the landowner, the county attorney, and the Nebraska State Historical Society.[185] If the county attorney determines criminal activity is implicated, the official is authorized to retain custody of the remains until the matter is resolved.[186] In any event, the act requires reburial in conformity with its provisions.[187]

The statute authorizes the NSHS to assist in the examination of human skeletal remains and burial offerings disinterred from unmarked cemeteries to attempt to determine their identity or origin.[188] If the human remains or burial offerings are determined to be of non-American Indian origin, the NSHS is required to notify the county attorney. This official then is required to cause the reinterment of the remains in compliance with existing state statutes.[189]

If the NSHS determines that the discovered remains or burial offerings are of American Indian origin, the society is required to promptly notify the Nebraska Indian Commission and any known relatives.[190] If no relatives are known, the NSHS is required to notify Indian tribes that it identifies as linked or related to the human remains.[191] In all cases, the statute requires the NSHS to comply with the decision of the relative or Indian tribe regarding reburial or other disposition.[192]

The act further prohibits public agencies from displaying human skeletal remains that are reasonably identifiable as to next of kin or tribal origin.[193] It does authorize the curation of human skeletal remains and burial offerings of unknown familial or tribal origin but only where such are "clearly found to be of extremely important, irreplaceable, and intrinsic scientific value."[194] Notwithstanding this limited authorization, the act contemplates that all human remains and burial offerings will be reinterred.[195]

Dispute Resolution and Enforcement

The statute provides an administrative procedure for the resolution of disputes arising under the act.[196] This provision requires an aggrieved party seeking relief to submit documentation to the adverse party, describing the nature of the grievance. The parties then are required to meet within sixty days to determine if they can resolve the dispute. If they cannot, the act further requires the two adverse parties to designate a third party to assist in resolution of the dispute. Such designation must occur within fifteen days after the initial meeting of the adverse parties. If the disputants cannot agree on a third party within the prescribed period, the state public counsel ombudsman is automatically designated to serve in that capacity.[197]

Following the designation of a third party, the aggrieved party is authorized to submit a petition and supporting documentation to the third party, describing the nature of the grievance. The act requires the aggrieved party simultaneously to serve the adverse party, which then has thirty days to respond by submitting documentation to the other two parties. Thereafter, the third party is required to review the petition, the response, all supporting documentation, and other relevant information. Following such review and within ninety days of the filing of the petition, the three parties are required to resolve the dispute by majority vote.[198]

This dispute resolution procedure is the exclusive remedy available to an aggrieved party under the act. The statute prohibits lawsuits prior to exhaustion of the mandated administrative remedy. Thereafter, either the aggrieved or the adverse party may apply for judicial relief.[199]

The repatriation statute further authorizes "any person, Indian tribe, or tribal member" to bring a civil cause of action "against any person alleged to have intentionally violated" the Unmarked Human Burial Sites and Skeletal Remains Protection Act.[200] The statute of limitations on these causes of action is two years from the discovery of the alleged violation.[201] If the plaintiff prevails, courts may award actual damages for each violation.[202] A court may also award injunctive and equitable relief to a prevailing plaintiff, including forfeiture and reinterment of any human skeletal remains or burial offerings held in violation of the act.[203] The statute further provides for the forfeiture of equipment used in violation of the act.[204] Courts may also award reasonable attorney fees to the prevailing party in civil actions.[205]

By adding burial offerings to the prohibition, the act amended an earlier statute prohibiting the disinterment or removal of skeletal remains.[206] Under the act, it is now a crime to aid, incite, assist, encourage, or procure the disinterment or removal of burial goods from the place of burial.[207] Trafficking, throwing away, or abandoning human remains and burial offerings known or reasonably known to have been disinterred is likewise prohibited.[208] Violation of these statutory prohibitions constitutes a Class I misdemeanor.[209]

IMPLEMENTATION OF NEBRASKA'S UNMARKED HUMAN BURIAL SITES AND SKELETAL REMAINS PROTECTION ACT

The NSHS bitterly resisted implementation of Nebraska's landmark human rights legislation. Its resistance stands in contrast to the University of Nebraska's cooperative and dignified repatriation of human skeletal remains and funerary objects of the Omaha Tribe. The NSHS's continued defiance of the law illustrates the importance of including adequate procedural safeguards and remedies governing the implementation of repatriation legislation.

NSHS's Continuing Campaign to Resist Reburial

The NSHS continued its campaign to frustrate Pawnee repatriation efforts. In June 1989, NSHS director Hanson refused to grant tribal researchers access to NSHS burial records for the third time in less than a year. This was despite two standing orders of the Nebraska attorney general directing the NSHS to disclose its records. Because the NSHS is the sole source of such information, this unlawful denial further frustrated the tribe's attempt to compile an independent tribal inventory of Pawnee remains and burial offerings subject to repatriation under the act.[210]

The Pawnee Tribe again appealed to the state attorney general to order the NSHS to disclose its burial records.[211] In response, the attorney general admonished NSHS director Hanson to "quit horsing around" and ordered the state agency to comply with both the open records law and the repatriation statute.[212] Both the attorney general and the Pawnee Tribe vowed to sue the NSHS it did not disclose the requested information.[213] Thereafter, the NSHS capitulated and granted the tribe access to burial records. This was the NSHS executive board's second policy decision in less than a year to comply with the public records law.[214]

Notwithstanding, the NSHS continued to defy both the public records and repatriation statutes. In the fall of 1989, Hanson publicly criticized the legislature for enacting LB 340, labeling the new law "censorship" and characterizing the legislative action as "dictatorial."[215] Additionally, an NSHS employee represented that their statutorily mandated inventory would include only "historic" Pawnee skeletal remains dating from 1750 A.D., rather than all the "reasonably identifiable" Pawnee remains required by the new law.[216] The Pawnee Tribe wrote a series of letters to the NSHS to determine if this was the official position of the NSHS and to ascertain how the agency interpreted the tribe's repatriation claim and the scope of the reburial law.[217] However, Hanson steadfastly refused to respond to these inquiries.

Finally, in January 1990, the Pawnee Tribe requested the withheld information under the state's open records law.[218] In response, Hanson, without authorization from the executive board, filed suit against the Pawnee Tribe in state court.[219] In its suit, the NSHS claimed that it was not a state agency but rather a private, nonprofit corporation and therefore was not subject to the state's open records law. In the alternative, the NSHS contended that the documents the tribe sought were not public records or were exempt from the disclosure requirements of the law. The NSHS also alleged that the Pawnee Tribe was not a "person" within the meaning of the open records law and therefore was not entitled to examine the records.[220] The NSHS further claimed that the repatriation statute, not the open records law, governed the records dispute and that the repatriation statute did not require disclosure of the information. The tribe counterclaimed, alleging that the opposite of the NSHS claims was true and that the NSHS was violating the open records law. Shortly thereafter, the attorney general of Nebraska intervened in the lawsuit on the side of the Pawnee Tribe.

After extensive discovery and a five-day trial, the court ruled in favor of the Pawnee Tribe and the state of Nebraska on all issues.[221] In short, the court stopped the NSHS from denying it is a state agency, ruled it had violated the open records law, and ordered it to produce all of the disputed documents in its possession.[222]

The NSHS executive board ultimately voted to appeal all issues in the case, including a subsequent court order awarding the Pawnee Tribe over $61,000 in attorney fees and costs as the prevailing party under Nebraska's public records law.[223] The society's decision to appeal caused a public outcry and was labeled a "BIG mistake" in an editorial in the *Lincoln Journal-Star*.[224] The editorial posited that a reversal, although described as "unlikely," of the district court's ruling that the NSHS is a state agency and not a private corporation could result in the legislature's terminating its annual appropriation to the NSHS in excess of $3 million—an action that would destroy the state's historical society.[225] In effect, the editorial characterized the NSHS judicial appeal as a "no win" situation.[226] Appellate briefing is scheduled for early 1992, with a decision anticipated in late 1992 or early 1993.

Also in January 1990, two state senators opposed to LB 340 sponsored a bill designed to remove burial goods from the reach of the repatriation statute.[227] The senators introduced this bill at the approximate time the NSHS filed its open records lawsuit against the Pawnee Tribe. Attempting to retain the coveted Pawnee peace medals held by the NSHS, society member Ron Hunter lobbied vigorously in support of the proposed legislation.[228] However, the landmark law that had been enacted the previous year was not undone.[229] In response to the sentiments of enlightened senators, a sympathetic public, and well-organized tribal opposition, Nebraska lawmakers killed the bill in committee after its hearing in February 1990.[230] However, this action did not stop the NSHS's relentless campaign to prevent the reinterment of Pawnee burial goods coveted by the agency.

NSHS Attempts to Resist Pawnee Repatriation Claims Filed under the Statute: The Pawnee Tribe's Invocation of Statutory Grievance Procedures

The NSHS continued to resist Pawnee repatriation efforts during its inventory of Pawnee skeletal remains and burial goods. In June 1990, the NSHS produced the inventory mandated pursuant to the repatriation law.[231] However, the document was limited to "historic Pawnee" and "Lower Loup" cultures. Based on tribal research completed by archives expert Dr. Anne Diffendal, a comparison of the NSHS inventory with the tribe's research of NSHS records revealed that the state's inventory omitted the skeletal remains and burial offerings of hundreds of "prehistoric" individuals documented by the Pawnee Tribe to be "reasonably identifiable" as Pawnee relatives or ancestors.[232] Thus, the inventory discrepancies confirmed that the NSHS did not intend to comply with the requirements of the reburial law. They also substantiated Pawnee tribal conclusions that the NSHS filed the open records lawsuit to prevent the tribe from examining records that might have revealed that the NSHS was defying the reburial law.

In accordance with the act, the Pawnee Tribe submitted a grievance and supporting documentation to the NSHS in an attempt secure a two-party resolution of the dispute.[233] The tribe's grievance included three parts.

First, it challenged the NSHS's refusal to return specific burial offerings admitted to be interred with and traceable to specific Pawnee skeletal remains. The NSHS claimed that, although it once had possession of the skeletal remains of these fourteen individuals, they had since been discarded or were now inexplicably missing. The NSHS based its refusal on an erroneous interpretation of the reburial statute: The society alleged that the statute required the physical presence of a bone fragment in order for the funerary object to be considered a "burial good" subject to return under the law.[234]

Among these specific burial goods was the George III peace medal, which the NSHS had fought to retain as "important to Nebraska's past." Prior to LB 340, Hanson represented publicly that the legislation would force the NSHS to return the George III medal to the Pawnee Tribe.[235] The prospect of relinquishing the peace medals was a primary basis of Hanson's vociferous, widely publicized opposition to the repatriation legislation.[236] Further, the initial inventory produced by the NSHS in June 1990 established that the NSHS was then in possession of numerous human bone fragments associated with the George III medal. However, the NSHS staff later suspiciously amended this portion of its inventory, alleging that these bone fragments were somehow missing.[237] Thus, the NSHS's reasons for refusing to return the medal it coveted became highly questionable.

Because of these suspicious circumstances, the Pawnee Tribe requested the opportunity to examine the George III peace medal. Not surprisingly, the NSHS refused.[238] However, after three state senators informed Hanson that they would accompany tribal representatives and a numismatic expert to the NSHS museum to inspect and authenticate the medal, the agency ultimately capitulated.[239] During this inspection and authentication, the NSHS inadvertently disclosed that it recently had purchased a second George III medal[240] for under $4,000—a far cry from its previous representations that peace medals were worth $1 million each.[241]

The second prong of the tribe's grievance focused on the NSHS's refusal to repatriate the skeletal remains and associated burial offerings of more than one hundred individuals disinterred from burial sites associated with the prehistoric Loup River/Itskari phase of Nebraska history. The NSHS refused even though John Ludwickson, an NSHS archaeologist, had concluded in 1978 that these deceased individuals were the lineal ancestors of the present-day Pawnee.[242] The NSHS based its refusal on an erroneous interpretation of the scope of the reburial law. Ignoring the plain language of the statute, the NSHS alleged that the legislature did not intend LB 340 to require the repatriation of "materials older than 1700 A.D.," i.e., those identified as "prehistoric."[243]

The third prong of the Pawnee Tribe's grievance challenged the refusal of the NSHS to repatriate the skeletal remains and burial offerings of an unspecified number of individuals disinterred from burials associated with the Central Plains Tradition of Nebraska history.[244] The Pawnee Tribe asserted this repatriation claim jointly with the Arikara and Wichita tribes, because the three tribes descended from Northern Caddoan groups occupying Central Plains Tradition sites in Nebraska.[245] The NSHS rejected this claim, alleging that the repatriation statute does not provide for multiple tribal claims. Further, the NSHS's opposition was a reversal of its interpretation of Central Plains archaeology, which it had embraced prior to the repatriation controversy. That interpretation, evidenced by published and unpublished statements of NSHS archaeologists as recently as 1985, recognized the existence of the requisite relationship between the Pawnee and groups of the Central Plains Tradition.[246] Significantly, but not surprisingly, NSHS staff archaeologists were not able to cite or produce any evidence that would serve as a basis for the society's eleventh hour change in position.[247]

According to archaeologist Larry Zimmerman, professor of anthropology and chairperson of the Department of Social Behavior of the University of South Dakota, the Nebraska State Historical Society's new archaeological view demanded a level of proof and data that, by definition, is virtually impossible to attain in the, field of archaeology.[248] In effect, the NSHS rejected the repatriation act's standard of "reasonably identifiable by a preponderance of the available evidence" and replaced it with a standard of certainty.[249] Not only was the NSHS's self-serving standard contrary to controlling law, it constituted an aberration in the world of archaeology.[250]

In compliance with the Nebraska repatriation law, the Pawnee Tribe presented its grievance to NSHS officials on 21 September 1990 in an effort to settle the dispute informally. However, the meeting did not resolve the fundamental disagreements forming the tribe's grievances. At the meeting, the parties submitted the names of respective nominees for the third party required by the act. Because the NSHS and the tribe could not agree on the third party,[251] the act automatically designated the public counsel/ ombudsman of the state of Nebraska to serve.[252]

Following the administrative grievance procedure, the Pawnee Tribe filed a formal grievance and supporting documentation with the public counsel on 11 December 1990.[253] The NSHS responded with its position and documentation in January 1991.[254] Thereafter, the Pawnee Tribe submitted its rebuttal.[255]

In March 1991, the public counsel ruled for the Pawnee Tribe.[256] The public counsel ruled that the law does not require the physical presence of a bone linked with a funerary object in order for a burial offering to constitute a "burial good" within the meaning of the act.[257] Rather, documentary evidence that "reasonable traces of a burial offering to a specific set of human remains is sufficient under the law."[258] Thus, even though some remains were somehow missing, the public counsel ordered the NSHS to return to the Pawnee Tribe for reburial *all* burial goods in the NSHS's possession that are reasonably identifiable as Pawnee.[259]

The public counsel also ruled that the Pawnee Tribe had established, by a preponderance of the evidence, that all of the human skeletal remains and burial goods from the prehistoric Itskari phase were reasonably identifiable as ancestors to the Pawnee.[260] The public counsel rejected the NSHS's most recent opinion that the skeletal remains from the Itskari phase were not identifiable as Pawnee; the counsel found that the NSHS had submitted no documentation to support its claim.[261] Accordingly, the public counsel ordered the NSHS to repatriate all such Pawnee skeletal remains and burial of offerings held by the state agency.[262]

The third issue required the public counsel to decide whether all of the skeletal remains and burial goods of the Central Plains Tradition peoples were reasonably identifiable as Pawnee, Arikara, or Wichita in origin.[263] Although the public counsel found that the evidence suggested that *some* of the peoples of the Central Plains Tradition may be ancestral to the Pawnee and Arikara tribes, he concluded that the evidence would not support a finding that *all* such peoples were collectively identifiable as the ancestors of one or more of the three petitioning tribes.[264] Accordingly, the public counsel invited submission of a revised joint tribal petition addressing constituent parts of the Central Plains Tradition that might be reasonably identifiable as ancestral to the petitioning tribes.[265] Most significant was his ruling that multiple tribal claims[266] are authorized under the act.

Repatriations Effectuated Pursuant to Nebraska's Law

In September 1990, the NSHS returned the skeletal remains and burial goods of nearly four hundred Pawnee individuals whom the agency had listed on its inventory as Pawnee.[267] During the transfer, the tribe and the NSHS conducted a meticulous verification process to ensure that all skeletal remains and burial goods listed on the NSHS inventory were returned.[268] This process culminated with the signing of hundreds of transfer documents by tribal and NSHS officials. Thereafter, the Pawnee delegation transported the caskets holding the remains of their ancestors in a dignified funeral procession, led by officers of the Lincoln Police Department and the Nebraska State Patrol, to Genoa, Nebraska. The tribe reburied the individuals in accordance with Pawnee tribal mortuary traditions.[269]

This repatriation constituted the first return and reburial in the United States of dead Indian bodies and burial goods under a general repatriation statute. Further, in late September 1991, in accordance with the Nebraska public counsel award, the NSHS repatriated over one hundred deceased Pawnee Indians and their burial goods from the Loup River/Itskari phase of Nebraska history. These individuals were reinterred in a mass grave in southwestern Nebraska.[270]

On 28 October 1991, the public counsel of Nebraska held an evidentiary hearing pursuant to a formal grievance filed by the tribe regarding the lawful ownership and disposition of the George III medal. On 5 November 1991, prior to a ruling, the NSHS capitulated and returned the medal to the Pawnee Tribe.[271] The tribe plans to reinter this burial good at an undisclosed site.

In November 1991, in response to the prospect of another statutory grievance to be filed by the Pawnee Tribe, the NSHS executive board voted to repatriate all Indian skeletal remains and associated burial goods left in the society's collection, with board president Dennis Mihelich announcing publicly that "we are out of the bones business."[272] These human remains and burial goods are from prehistoric people, including ancestors of the Pawnee who inhabited Nebraska from approximately 1000 A.D. to 1500 A.D. They include the Nebraska Phase, Upper Republican, St. Helena, and Central Plains cultures.[273] When this repatriation is completed, over one thousand Pawnee ancestors and tens of thousands of their burial offerings disinterred by the NSHS will have been reburied by the tribe according to religious-based tribal mortuary traditions and practices.

In addition to these Pawnee repatriations, the University of Nebraska returned the skeletal remains and burial offerings of nearly one hundred Omaha tribal ancestors.[274] The Omaha Tribe reburied the individuals in Nebraska on 3 October 1991.[275]

The Omaha repatriation situation has been characterized by genuine, good faith cooperation and negotiations between the two parties and accordingly has precluded invocation of the grievance procedures under Nebraska's repatriation law. The University of Nebraska's willing cooperation with the Omaha Tribe stands in stark contrast to the obstinate and often unlawful conduct of the Nebraska State Historical Society. Indeed, the University of Nebraska's dignified, forthright, and lawful treatment of the Omaha Tribe exemplifies the conduct all public officials should emulate when responding to repatriation claims of Indian tribes and their members.[276]

CONCLUSION

Nebraska's landmark repatriation legislation represents the triumph of human rights, religious freedom, and common decency. By enacting the historic measure, Nebraska lawmakers sent a loud and clear message that the state will no longer tolerate the disparate, sacrilegious treatment of the Indian dead, whether in the name of science, history, or otherwise. Senator Baack, now the speaker of the Nebraska Unicameral Legislature, succinctly personified the underlying sentiments that ultimately generated the precedent-setting legislation. Senator Baack stated,

> The way I look at it, we will be burying a part of our history, but we probably didn't have the right to dig up the Native American history to start with. I became convinced that the artifacts are such a part of their religious beliefs that we have no right to keep them. Their religious beliefs are also part of our history. By putting them back, we are honoring part of our history, rather than reburying it.[277]

Equally important, the Nebraska legislation clearly establishes that state lawmakers will not condone the mistreatment of Native Americans by a state agency when tribal governments seek to rebury their dead in accordance with Indian religious traditions and practices. Without question the Nebraska State Historical Society's arrogant and insensitive conduct toward the Pawnee Tribe shocked the conscience of legislators and the public alike. It thus served to underscore the dire need for state legislation to remedy the cross-cultural conflict. Similarly, the NSHS's abhorrent conduct shocked the national museum community and served to enlighten Congress about the compelling need for national grave protection and repatriation legislation to preclude the occurrence of another "worst case scenario" like that in Nebraska.[278]

Acknowledgments

The author gratefully acknowledges NARF co-counsel Walter Echo-Hawk, attorney James Botsford, chairman Louis LaRose of the Winnebago Tribe of Nebraska, and Roger Echo-Hawk, a student of Pawnee tribal history, for their helpful comments in reviewing drafts of this article and, more importantly, for their dedicated work leading to the enactment of Nebraska's landmark reburial act.

Notes

1. Statement of chairman Lawrence Goodfox, Jr. of the Pawnee Tribe of Oklahoma, Nebraska State Historical Society, Executive Board Meeting, Lincoln, Nebraska (25 March 1988) (available from NARF).

2. See Orlan Svingen, "The Pawnee of Nebraska: Twice Removed," *American Indian Culture and Research Journal* 16:2 (1992).

3. See Roger Echo-Hawk, "Preface," *American Indian Culture and Research Journal* 16:2 (1992).

4. See Svingen, "The Pawnee of Nebraska: Twice Removed."

5. See Margaret Reist, "Tribal chairman requests return of skeletal remains," *Lincoln Journal*, 25 June 1988.

6. Ibid.

7. See, e.g., Minutes, Nebraska State Historical Society Executive Board Meeting, 17 December 1988 (available from the NSHS).

8. See David Schwartzlander, "Board approves plan for remains," *Lincoln Journal*, 18 December 1988.

9. See Statement of Citizens to Save Nebraska's History, February 1989 (available from NARF).

10. Neb. Rev. Stat. secs. 12-1201 through 12-1212 (Supp. 1990); sec. 28-1301 (Supp. 1990).

11. See, e.g., Bob Reeves, "State ancestral remains law said 'landmark' bill for nation," *Lincoln Journal-Star*, 9 March 1991.

12. 20 U. S. C. sec. 80q-9 (1989).

13. 25 U. S. C. sec. 3005 (1990).

14. The Pawnee people have largely resided in Oklahoma since the 1870s, when they were forced to leave Nebraska and establish a new homeland. Accordingly, Oklahoma Pawnee are not eligible to vote in Nebraska elections.

15. The term *dead body* in a legal sense means human skeletal remains, including pieces or particles of bones that are "distinguishable from the soil in which they were placed, i.e., that have not decomposed." Thus, under the law, one bone or particle thereof constitutes a dead body.

16. See letter from James Hanson, NSHS executive director, to Walter Echo-Hawk, 26 August 1988 (available from NARF and the NSHS). The NSHS claimed that it held title to a certain number of Pawnee dead bodies and burial offerings on the basis of a bill of sale from A. T. Hill to the NSHS, dated 17 April 1942 (available from the NSHS). The state agency also claimed it obtained permission from landowners to disinter and remove Pawnee burials in its possession.

17. See 22A Am. Jur. 2d, *Dead Bodies* sec. 2 (1988); 25A C. J. S. *Dead Bodies* sec, 2 (1966); Jackson, *The Law of Cadavers and of Burials and Burial Places*, 129–34 (2d ed., 1950); accord, Op. Cal. Att'y Gen. (21 May 1990); 88 Op. Ks. Att'y Gen. 73 (1988).

18. See, e.g., *Traveler's Insurance Co. v. Welch*, 82 F. 2d 799, 801 (5th Cir. 1936); *Busler v. State*, 184 S. W. 2d 24, 27 (Tenn. 1944).

19. 22A Am. Jur. 2d, secs. 18–21, 23, 25; 25A C. J. S., sec. 4; see also *Stastny v. Tachovsky*, 178 Neb. 109, 132 N.W. 2d 317 (1964). Although not favored, a state district court has authority to order exhumation where good and substantial reason is shown.

20. 25A C. J. S., sec. 9, 523, n. 75.

21. See, e.g., *State v. Johnson*. 50 P. 907 (1897) (unexplained possession of a dead body illegally removed is prima facie evidence of wrongful possession); *State v. Schaffer*, 95 Iowa

379, 64 N.W. 276 (1895). (Burden is on defendant to show he had lawful authority to disinter a dead body.)

22. *King v. City of Shelby*, 40 Ohio App. 195, 178 N.E. 22 (1931).

23. Jackson, *The Law of Cadavers*, 108.

24. See, e.g., *Matter of Morehead*, 10 Kan. App. 2d 625 706 P. 2d 480 (1985); *Bd. of County Commissioners v. Central Air Conditioning*, 235 Kan. 977, 683 P. 2d 1282 (1984); *Gonzales v. Atchison*, 189 Kan. 689, 371 P. 2d 193 (1962).

25. Neb. Rev. Stat. sec. 28-1301(1) (a)-(c) (1989).

26. Neb. Rev. Stat. sec. 71-605 (1989).

27. Neb. Rev. Stat. sec. 71-605, 28-1301(2) (1989).

28. Neb. Rev. Stat. sec. 71-605(5), (6) (1921) (reissue 1989).

29. Neb. Rev. Stat. sec. 71-605(5) (1989); see also Neb. Rev. Stat. sec. 71-1339 (1990).

30. Neb. Rev. Stat. sec. 71-605(5) (1989).

31. Ibid.

32. Neb. Rev. Stat. sec. 71-605(6) (1989).

33. Ibid.

34. See, Neb. Rev. Stat. sec. 71-1339(5) (1990). The vast majority of the Pawnee dead bodies disinterred and held by the NSHS were disinterred from Pawnee cemeteries after 1921. See letter from James Hanson to Walter Echo-Hawk, 26 August 1988 (available from NSHS and NARF).

35. 25A C. J. S., 496. See also Jackson, 101–122.

36. *McEntee v. Banacum*, 66 Neb. 651, 92 N.W. 633 (1902).

37. In fact, the earliest common law prosecutions against body snatchers explicitly rejected the "Dr. Frankenstein defense" that a "specimen" for dissection and anatomical studies motivated and justified the disinterment. See 21 ALR 2d, *Corpse and Removal*, sec. 3 *The English Background*, 479 (1952).

38. Neb. Rev. Stat. sec. 71-1339 (1990).

39. Neb. Rev. Stat. sec. 71-1339(5) (1990); Neb. Rev. Stat. sec. 30-2303(5) (1989). *Black's Law Dictionary* (5th ed., 1979) defines *next of kin* as follows: "In the law of descent and distribution, this term properly denotes the person's nearest of kindred to the deceased, that is, those who are most nearly related to him by blood; but it is sometimes construed to mean only those who are entitled to take under some statute of distribution, and sometimes to include other persons" (citation omitted).

40. *Charrier v. Bell*, 496 SO. 2d 601, 604 (La. App.) *cert. denied*, 498 So. 2d 753 (La., 1986). See also Op. Neb. Att'y Gen. (14 December 1988).

41. Ibid.

42. See Neb. Rev. Stat. secs. 30-2303, 30-2305 (1989).

43. *Traveler's Insurance Co. v. Welch*. (Relative who is beneficiary of life insurance policy of deceased may consent to delay of interment or disinterment for purpose of autopsy for promotion of truth and justice.)

44. Ibid. A wide variety of other common law causes of action are available to Indian tribes seeking the repatriation of their dead held by institutions such as the NSHS. Withholding a dead body from those with a right to burial gives rise to a cause of action in tort. See 25A C. J. S., sec. 8(3), 512. It is no defense that the withholding entity is a public, charitable institution or that disinterment without notice to relatives was done "in good faith." See *Howard v. Children's Hospital*, 37 Ohio App. 144, 174 N.E. 166 (1930); see also 25A C. J. S., sec. 9, 521. The next of kin may maintain damages actions based upon trespass and wrongful disinterment, even though the next of kin have no legal interest in the land containing the human remains. Ibid., sec. 8(5), 516. Common law causes of action for breach

of trust duties against institutions withholding the Indian dead from reburial also are available to tribes. These trust duties can be created in three different ways. First, one in possession of a dead body cannot "own" the body but merely holds the same "in trust" for those who have the right to possession for purposes of burial. Hence, the common law imposes a trust upon those in possession of dead bodies. That it may be a state who is the party in possession makes no difference because the "public has a vital interest in the proper disposition of the bodies of its deceased members. Ibid., sec. 5, 507. Commentators describe this trust as being "on the nature of a sacred trust for the benefit of all." Ibid., sec. 3, 491. Second, owners of lands containing graves may have technical possession of the burials, but they merely hold this possession under the common law as trustees for the rightful owners. If the landowner breached that trust duty by allowing the human remains or burial offerings of a tribe to expropriated, and an institution reaped the benefit from such breach of trust, then equity deems that institution to be a "quasi trustee" accountable to the rightful owners. See Jackson, 142, 157. Third, in instances where institutions such as the NSHS wrongfully obtained or are in wrongful possession of dead Indian bodies or funerary objects in breach of a legal duty owed to the tribe or in violation of equity, then equity will create a "resulting trust" or a "constructive trust" in favor of the tribe. Failure to return such remains or burial offerings to the beneficiaries of the trust upon request may constitute an actionable breach of trust or repudiation of the trust.

45. *Ferguson v. Utilities Elkhorn Coal Co.*, 313 S.W. 2d 395 (Ky. 1958); *Louisville Cemetery Ass'n v. Downs*, 241 Ky. 773, 45 S.W. 2d 5 (1931).

46. See. e.g., *Block v. Har Nebo Cemetery Co.*, 14 Pa. D&C 237 (1930); *McDonald v. Butler*, 10 Ga. App. 845, 74 S.E. 573 (1912); *Jacobus v. Congregation of Children of Israel*, 107 Ga. 518, 33 S.E. 853 (1899).

47. *Gardener v. Swann Point Cemetery*, 20 R.I. 646, 40 A. 871 (1898).

48. *Louisville Cemetery Ass'n v. Downs*, 241 Ky. 773, 45 S.W. 2d 5 (1931).

49. *Hamilton v. Individual Mausoleum Co.*, 149 Kan. 216, 86 P. 2d 501 (1939); *North East Coal Co. v. Pickelsimer*, 253 Ky. 11, 68 S.W. 2d 760 (1934); *North East Coal Co. v. Delong*, 254 Ky. 22, 70 S.W. 2d 972 (1934); *Louisville Cemetery Ass'n v. Downs*, 241 Ky. 773, 45 S.W. 2d 5 (1931).

50. See Neb. Rev. Stat. sec. 71-1339(5) (1990). This showing is required even if the withholding agency did not itself disinter the remains, because a state institution, as a donee or purchaser, can acquire no better right than the doctor or seller could convey. See, e.g., Walter R. Echohawk, "Museum Rights vs. Indian Rights: Guidelines for Assessing Competing Legal Interests in Native Cultural Resources," *N. Y. U. Review of Legal and Social Change* 14 (1986): 437, 441 n. 18 and accompanying text. Moreover, the law requires institutions in Nebraska, such as the NSHS, in possession of "any dead human body or the remains thereof" to make a showing of proof to overcome N.R. S. sec. 28-1302(1) (c) (1989), which makes such possession illegal in all but the most limited, enumerated circumstances. See also *State v. Schaffer*, 95 Iowa 379, 64 N.W. 2d 276 (1895). (Burden is on defendant to show he had lawful authority to disinter a dead body.)

51. The NSHS cited only one "source" to support its long-standing exhumation of Pawnee dead bodies—an erroneous, antiquated, one-half page, unsigned opinion of the Nebraska attorney general—issued in 1958—some twenty to thirty-five years after the NSHS had disinterred the vast majority of Pawnee bodies. See *Historical Newsletter*, Nebraska State Historical Society, February 1989. The 1958 opinion stated that "[t]he law appears to be well established that the term 'dead body' does not include remains that have long since decomposed, such as would be the case with the remains of Indians who inhabited Nebraska before the advent of the white settlers here." P. Neb. Att'y Gen. (1958). The

258 / Robert M. Peregoy

opinion concluded that it therefore was lawful for the NSHS to exhume "the skeletal remains of ancient Indians" without obtaining permission from any public official. Ibid. However, "well established law" holds that "dead human body" includes any "visible and indentifiable portion of a human body," including "bones or pieces and particles of bones" that exist in a condition where they are distinguishable from the soil in which they were placed, i.e., which are not "decomposed." See letter from Robert Peregoy to Frederick Wefso, 18 November 1988, pp. 4–8 (available from NARF and NSHS). The irony, if not the absurdity, of the 1958 opinion on which the NSHS relied rests with the fact that the state agency withheld the Pawnee skeletal remains from reburial in order to prevent decomposition in the first place. Further, the NSHS continued to base its refusal to repatriate the Pawnee dead bodies on this erroneous, *post hoc* opinion despite the fact that, in 1989, the Nebraska attorney general issued an opinion concluding that the Pawnee Tribe had a superior legal right to repatriation and reburial of dead Pawnee ancestors held by the NSHS. See Op. Neb. Att'y Gen. (14 December 1988) (Spire to White Shirt).

52. See Svingen, "The Pawnee of Nebraska: Twice Removed."

53. For example, nothing, in the plain language of Neb. Rev. Stat. sec. 82-101 (1987), originally enacted in 1883, can be construed to grant the Nebraska State Historical Society authority to exhume dead bodies in any manner, especially when done in violation of common law or of Neb. Rev. Stat. secs. 71-605(5)–(6) (1989), 71-1339 (1990), and 28-1301 (1989). The 1883 statute that made the NSHS a state agency provides that the NSHS museum is to be used for "the preservation, care and exhibition of documents, books, newspapers, weapons, tools, pictures, relics, scientific specimens, farm and factory products, and all other collections pertaining to the history of the world, particular to that of Nebraska and the West." The terms *preservation, care, and exhibition* do not include exhumation or disinterment. Nor do any of the objects specified expressly include dead bodies or portions thereof, or grave goods that may have been removed by illegal or dubious means. Nor does Neb. Rev. Stat. sec. 39-1363 (1987), enacted in 1959, confer any express right on the NSHS to exhume or retain dead bodies. It merely authorizes state agencies to enter into agreements with the Nebraska Department of Roads to remove and preserve "historical, archaeological, and paleontological remains" disturbed during highway construction projects after 1959. Because the statute does not expressly authorize the removal of dead bodies, it cannot be facially construed as authorizing the removal or preservation thereof. The American common law, which strongly disfavors such activity, was well established in the United States when these statutes were enacted. Any significant departures from the moral sensibilities protected by the common law would have to have been expressly stated by the legislature before any such intent could be imputed to that body. Importantly, the society may own or dispose of property only "with the consent of the Legislature." Neb. Rev. Stat. sec. 82-101 (1987). The Nebraska legislature subsequently vested the right of disposition of human remains to other persons with an enumerated statutory preference. Neb. Rev. Stat. sec. 71-1339 (1990). Hence, even assuming *arguendo* that intent can somehow be imputed to the legislature to consent to the acquisition and possession of dead bodies by the NSHS in 1883, such consent was revoked in 1954 with the enactment of Neb. Rev. Stat. sec. 71-12339 (1990).

54. Aside from these considerations, where a state agency seeks permanently to retain the bodies of dead persons from burial, problems of lawful storage immediately arise under other provisions of Nebraska statutory law. Neb. Rev. Stat. sec. 12-606 (1987) appears to prohibit the retention of dead bodies in public structures except "within the confines of an established cemetery." See also Neb. Rev. Stat. secs. 12-607–12-618 (1987). (Other statutory requirements must be met before above-the-ground structures may be used to contain

the body of any dead person.)

55. *Charrier* v. *Bell*, No. 5,552, slip op. (20th Jud. Dist., La. 18 March 1985), *aff'd* 496 So. 2d 601, 605–604 (La. App. Civ. 1 1986), *cert. denied*, 498 So. 2d 753 (1986); *Busler* v. *State*, 184 S.W. 2d 24 (Tenn. 1944) (even if a coffin may have become part of the realty, it becomes the personal property of heirs of deceased when removed and may be the subject matter of larceny); *Ware* v. *State*, 121 S.E. 251 (Ga. App. 1924); *Maddox* v. *State*, 121 S.E. 251 (Ga. App. 1924); *State* v. *Doepke*, 68 Mo. 208 (1878) (coffin and burial offerings are property of the person who buried the deceased); *Tennant* v. *Boudreau*, 6 Rob. 488 (La. 1844) (jewels removed from tomb by thief convicted of larceny belong to heir of deceased for whatever disposition desired); *Wonson* v. *Sayward*, 13 Pick. 402 (Mass. 1832).

56. See *Charrier* v. *Bell*, 496 So. 2d, 604 (La. App. 1 1986).

57. *Busler* v. *State*, 184 S.W. 2d 24 (Tenn. 1944).

58. Ibid.

59. *Charrier* v. *Bell*, no. 5,552 slip op., 11–13 (20th Jud. Dist. La. March 18, 1985), *aff'd* 496 So. 2d 601 (La. App. Civ. 1 1986), *cert. denied*, 498 So. 2d 753 (1986).

60. See *Rice* v. *Sioux City Cemetery*, 349 U.S. 70, 80 (1955) (Black, J., dissenting); see also *Washington* v. *Davis*, 426 U.S. 229 (1976); *Regents* v. *Baake*, 438 U.S. 265 (1978). Further, the Ninth Amendment may also be pertinent, since the disputes affect deeply ingrained and universally held values and rights regarding the sanctity of the dead. The Ninth Amendment to the United States Constitution provides that "the enumeration in the Constitution, of certain rights, shall not be construed to deny or disparage others retained by the people."

61. See Rice, 349 U.S., 80 (Black, J., dissenting) (deceased Winnebago Indian denied sepulcher in all-white cemetery pursuant to racially restrictive covenant; equal protection issue not decided as a result of intervening state law banning such restrictive covenant).

62. See *Charrier* v. *Bell*, 496 S. 2d 601, 605 (La. App. Cov. 1 1986), *cert. denied*, 498 So. 2d 753 (La. 1986).

63. See, e.g., *Fuller* v. *Marx*, 724 F. 2d 717 (8th Cir. 1984); Walter Echo-Hawk, "Tribal Efforts to Protect Against Mistreatment of the Dead: The Quest for Equal Protection of the Laws," *Native American Rights Fund Legal Review* 3 (1988): 14.

64. See Roger Echo-Hawk, "Preface."

65. Op. Neb. Att'y Gen., 8–9 (14 December 1988) (Spire to White Shirt).

66. In *Employment Division* v. *Smith*, the Supreme Court ruled that the compelling state interest test is no longer applicable where a general, religion-neutral law burdens the free exercise of religion of a particular group. Ibid., 890–92. However, the Pawnee repatriation matter did not involve a facially neutral rule of general applicability. rather, the administrative policy or regulation promulgated by the NSHS, an agency of state government, was expressly limited to prohibiting the repatriation and reburial of hundreds of Pawnee dead and their burial offerings. See Minutes, Nebraska State Historical Society Executive Board, 17 December 1988, 2. Thus, the Pawnee fact situation falls outside the scope of the holdings of *Employment Division* v. *Smith* and its progeny. The constitutional protections guaranteed to the Pawnee people by the Bill of Rights survive that line of decisions. See, e.g., *Hunafu* v. *Murphy*, 907 F. 2d 46, 48 (7th Cir. 1990) (practice of serving pork to inmates is equivalent to a general, secular regulation applicable to all inmates and does not violate First Amendment rights, even if offensive to Jews and Muslims); *Yang* v. *Sturner*, 750 F. Supp. 558, 559 (D. R. I. 1990) (autopsy conducted by state's chief medical examiner pursuant to facially neutral autopsy statute of general applicability held under *Smith* not to violate First Amendment rights of decedent's family, even though the autopsy was offensive to their religious beliefs).

67. See *Employment Division* v. *Smith*, 494 U.S.___, 108 L. Ed. 2d, 893 (1990); *Lying* v.

N.W. Indian Cemetery Protection Assoc., 485 U.S. 439, 452 (1988).

68. In addition to these constitutional protections, federal statutory law may protect the interests and rights of Indian tribes in repatriation disputes. Title 6 of the Civil Rights Act, 42 U.S. C. sec. 2000d (1964), forbids racial discrimination or denial of benefits by any federally funded program. Further, 18 U.S. C. sec. 1163 (1956) prohibits theft, conversion, or possession of "any . . . property belonging to any Indian tribal organization." A federal cause of action to redress deprivation of federally protected rights under color of state law, custom, or usage is also available under 42 U.S. C. sec. 1983 (1979).

69. *United States v. Winans*, 198 U.S. 371. 381 (1905).

70. Ibid.

71. *United States v. Michigan*, 471 G. Supp. 192, 254 (W.D. Mich. 1979), *stay denied*, 505 F. Supp. 467, 623 F. 2d. 488, 89 F. R. D. 307, 653 F. 2d 277, 520 F. Supp. 207 (W. D. Mich. 1981), *cert. denied*, 454 U. S. 1124 (1981).

72. See *Choctaw Nation v. Oklahoma*, 397 U.S. 620, 621 (1970).

73. *Kimball v. Callahan*, 493 F. 2d 564, 566 n. 7 (9th Cir. 1974).

74. See, e.g., Treaty, 9 October 1833, U.S.–Pawnee Tribe, 7 Stat. 488.

75. See Roger Echo-Hawk, "Preface."

76. See *United States v. Oneida Nation of New York*, 576 F. 2d 870 (N. Y. Ct. Cl. 1978).

77. See F. Cohen, "Limitations on Federal Power," in *Handbook on Federal Indian Law* (Charlottesvile, VA: Michie Bobbs-Merrill, 1982), 217–28.

78. *United States v. Michigan*, 471 F. Supp. 192, 265 (W.D. Mich.), cert. denied, 454 U.S. 1124 (1981).

79. Ibid.

80. Ibid.

81. See, e.g., *United States v. Quiver*, 241 U.S. 605, 606 (1910).

82. Ibid.

83. Ibid.

84. See discussion above, pp. 229–32.

85. See *Mexican v. Circle Bear*, 370 N.W. 2d 737 (S. D. 1985). (Under principles of federal Indian law, state court granted comity to tribal court order disposing of the body of dead Indian, although relevant state and tribal law differed.)

86. *Lincoln Star*, 18 November 1971; see also *Chronology of Events Leading to the Introduction of LB 340*, March 1989 (hereinunder LB 340 *Chronology*) (available from NARF).

87. See LB 340 Chronology, 1.

88. Ibid. Tribal representatives primarily responsible for organizing and launching the Nebraska reburial movement and for drafting and advancing LB 612 included attorney James Botsford; Louis LaRose, chairman of the Winnebago Tribe of Nebraska; Dennis Hasting, historian of the Omaha Tribe; and Reba White Shirt, executive director of the Nebraska Indian Commission. These leaders were subsequently joined by Daniel Denney, chairman of the Santee Sioux Tribe of Nebraska.

89. LB 612, 90th Neb. Legis., 1st sess. (1987).

90. See Nebraska Legislative Council, *The Nebraska State Historical Society-Interim Study LR 409 Final Report*, (1988),17–18 (hereafter *LR 409 Final Report on NSHS*).

91. Fred Thomas, "Hanson Blasts Bill on Indian Burial Sites," *Omaha World-Herald*, 10 February 1988.

92. Ibid.

93. Throughout this process, the society received favorable press coverage from the *Omaha World-Herald*, whose publisher was then a member of the executive board of the NSHS. In addition to favorable news articles, the *World-Herald* printed at least one editor-

ial in opposition to LB 612, charging that it would be "crazy" to repatriate burial offerings. See "Graves Protection Proposal Raises Legitimate Concern," *Omaha World-Herald*, editorial, 9 March 1988. Reflecting NSHS treatment of the tribes, the editorial focused solely on the interests of science and history in retaining Pawnee burial offerings, while completely ignoring the cultural and religious interests of the tribes in reburying their dead. See also Fred Thomas, "Hanson Blasts Bill on Indian Burial Sites," *Omaha World-Herald*, 10 February 1988; Fred Thomas, "Society Head's Opposition to Bill Called Proper," *Omaha World-Herald*, 9 March 1988.

94. Letter from James A. Hanson, director, Nebraska State Historical Society, to society members, 2 February 1988 (available from NSHS). Reba White Shirt, executive director of the Nebraska Indian Commission, labeled such tactics "alarmist and unfounded." Nebraska senator Ernie Chambers charged that "Mr. Hanson is being dishonest in much of his wild, misleading exhalations." See Thomas, "Society Head's Opposition to Bill Called Proper." NSHS executive board member Roger Welsch, then a professor at the University of Nebraska, charged that opponents to the bill were being "hysterical." See J. L. Schmidt, "Opponents of grave-protection bill labeled hysterical by its supporters," *Lincoln Journal*, 15 February 1988. These unfounded scare tactics ultimately caused many people to refer to the NSHS as the "Nebraska State Hysterical Society." See, e.g., Paul Fell, "Two Famous Indian Fighters Meet," *Lincoln Journal*, 30 July 1991 (editorial cartoon).

95. See Schmidt, "Opponents of grave-protection bill labeled hysterical."

96. Among the NSHS membership are doctors, lawyers, judges, professors, bankers, newspaper publishers, state senators, and members of Congress.

97. See, e.g., files of Senator Dennis Baack, chairman of the Government, Military and Veterans' Affairs Committee, Ninetieth Nebraska Legislature (1987–8).

99. Roger Welsch, a professor at the University of Nebraska and a former NSHS executive board member who supported the reburial initiatives of the tribes, stated, "[A]n enormous, expensive campaign has been launched against [LB 612], primarily by the 'diggers'—the very people who got us in this mess to begin with." See Schmidt, "Opponents of grave-protection bill labeled hysterical."

100. During the LB 612 controversy throughout 1987 and early 1988, the NSHS represented to Nebraska tribal representatives that the only identifiable tribal remains it held were Pawnee. The NSHS director accordingly chided the Nebraska tribes for having no interest or standing before the NSHS. Telephone interview with James Botsford, Esq., attorney representing the Winnebago Tribe of Nebraska (13 August 1991). In response, Nebraska tribal representatives contacted the Pawnee Tribe to inform its governing officials that the NSHS had custody of an untold number of deceased Pawnee individuals and their burial offerings. Ibid. At this juncture, the Pawnee Tribe entered the controversy and began to seek the return and reburial of Pawnee relatives or ancestors held by the NSHS.

101. The issue of unmarked burials protection was not in controversy, because the NSHS and other archaeologists had ceased proactive digging of Indian graves sometime in the late 1960s or early 1970s. Apparently, after that time the NSHS became involved with digging Indian graves only in conjunction with state highway construction projects where Indian burial grounds were inadvertently disturbed.

102. The Pawnee Tribe was the logical tribal party to lead the negotiations with the NSHS, because the NSHS claimed that the only identifiable dead bodies in its collection were Pawnee. Thus, a genuine, ripe controversy existed in the repatriation context between the Pawnee Tribe of Oklahoma and the NSHS.

103. See LB 340 *Chronology*, 1.

104. See, e.g., Al Laukaitis, "Decision delayed on Indian remains," *Lincoln Star-Journal*, 9

October 1988; see also Minutes, Nebraska State Historical Society Executive Board Meeting, 8 October 1988, 1–2 (available from the NSHS).

105. A brief comparative analysis of LB 691 and LB 340 reveals that LB 601, the NSHS staff bill, provided for little or no tribal role in the decision-making process regarding the disposition of human skeletal remains and burial offerings. See LB 691, secs. 2 and 3, 91st Neb. Leg., 1st sess. (1989). Instead, it conferred near absolute power on the NSHS to make such decisions, requiring the NSHS to "consult" with tribes only when such consultation was "possible." Ibid., sec. 2. In stark contrast, LB 340 provided a significant role for tribes in determining the disposition of Indian remains and burial offerings. Further, LB 340 proposed more stringent protections of unmarked burials, including the confiscation of equipment used by persons convicted of robbing unmarked graves. Finally, LB 340 established a policy requiring equal treatment of the dead—a key provision absent from the unsuccessful LB 619. Ibid., sec. 3.

106. Minutes, Nebraska State Historical Society Executive Board Meeting, 17 December 1988, 2 (available from the NSHS).

107. See, e.g., "Committee Kills Burial Site Measure," Omaha-World Herald, 17 March 1989.

108. At the outset of the Pawnee negotiations with the NSHS in March 1988, the tribe did not know how many Pawnee dead bodies or burial offerings the NSHS held. Apparently, neither did the NSHS. Executive director Hanson had initially claimed that the NSHS possessed the skeletal remains of approximately five hundred deceased Native American individuals, one hundred of whom were identifiable as Pawnee and the rest unidentifiable as to tribe. See Fred Thomas, "Indian Tribes Request Remains for Reburial," Omaha World-Herald, 26 March 1988; see also letter from James A. Hanson to Walter Echo-Hawk, 26 August 1988 (available from the NSHS). However, tribal research discovered that the NSHS retained in excess of five hundred Pawnee dead bodies.

109. See letter from Lawrence Goodfox, Jr. to Walter Huber, president of the NSHS executive board, 23 June 1988, 5 (available from NARF and the NSHS).

110. See Roger Echo-Hawk, "Preface"; letters from Lawrence Goodfox, Jr. to NSHS executive board (23 March, 23 June 1988); letter from Robert Peregoy to Walter Huber (6 July 1988) (available from NARF).

111. See "Legal Memorandum in Support of the Pawnee Tribe's Request for the Return of Pawnee Decedents and Associated Burial Goods Expropriated, Procured and Controlled by the Nebraska State Historical Society," from Walter Echo-Hawk and Robert M. Peregoy, attorneys for the Pawnee Tribe of Oklahoma, to Walter Huber, president, Nebraska State Historical Society, and NSHS board members, 30 September 1988 (hereafter "Legal Memorandum of the Pawnee Tribe") (available from NARF and NSHS). The legal authority delineated in the 1988 memorandum is summarized in this chapter.

112. See Minutes, NSHS Executive Board Meeting, 24 June 1988, 1 (available from NSHS).

113. The scientist was Douglas Owlsley, an osteologist. The NSHS had entered into an agreement with Dr. Owlsley in 1984 to study Pawnee remains in the custody of the NSHS. During 1988–90 the NSHS transferred the Pawnee skeletal remains to the Smithsonian Institution under the study of Dr. Owlsley. Against the Pawnee Tribe's stated wishes, his study included destructive analysis of the Pawnee remains.

114. See letter from Robert Peregoy to Walter Huber, 6 July 1988, 16–17.

115. Petition to Review Records Being Withheld by the Nebraska State Historical Society from Inspection by the Pawnee and Winnebago Tribes Pursuant to R. S. N. Sec. 84-712.03(2), 23 September 1988 (available from NARF). The cited provision of the public records law provides

for several remedies available to an aggrieved party. Under the law, an aggrieved party may either file suit or petition the attorney general to review and act on the grievance. The Pawnee Tribe elected the latter remedy, in part to avoid costly, protracted litigation. Hanson evinced his reluctance to disclose NSHS burial records to Indian representatives prior to the public records controversy with the Pawnee Tribe. On 29 February 1988, he stated to Reba White Shirt, executive director of the Nebraska Indian Commission—a sister state agency—that his reluctance was based on the fact that the Indian Commission "is supporting legislation which would confiscate [NSHS] collection material, while this agency opposes it." See letter from James Hanson director, NSHS, to Reba White Shirt, director, Nebraska Indian Commission (29 February 1988) (on file with author).

116. Letter from attorney general Robert Spire and assistant attorney general Charles Lowe to Walter Echo-Hawk and Robert Peregoy with copy to James Hanson, 6 October 1988 (available from NARF).

117. See Minutes, NSHS Executive Board Meeting, 8 October 1988, 3 (available from the NSHS).

118. See David Swartzlander, "Indian leaders get access to records," *Lincoln Journal*, 7 October 1988; letter from Robert Peregoy to Attorney General Spire, 12 October 1988 (available from NARF).

119. Letter from attorney general Robert Spire and assistant attorney general Charles Lowe to Robert M. Peregoy, 21 October 1988, 1 (available from NARF). The specific information that the executive director attempted to withhold concerned archaeological site files that describe the exact location of Pawnee burial grounds in the state. Hanson withheld the information and later demanded confidential treatment, alleging that he was concerned that public access "would have devastating effects on the security of the collections and of archeological materials *in situ.*" See Spire and Lowe letter, 6 October 1988, note 116 (emphasis in original). The Pawnee Tribe subsequently learned that the NSHS had published numerous studies over the years that describe the precise location of virtually all known Pawnee burial grounds in the state. Most of these publications have been available in public libraries for years. The author has chosen not to cite these studies in the interest of protecting the security of the sites.

120. Thus, the NSHS director reversed his earlier, unsubstantiated claim that the NSHS "owns or has title to all of the human skeletal remains in its possession." See letter from James Hanson to Walter Echo-Hawk, 26 August 1988, 3.

121. See David Swartzlander, "Rule cited in reburial case doesn't exist," *Lincoln Journal*, 26 October 1988; letter from Robert Peregoy to Frederick Wefso, president, Nebraska State Historical Society, 13 October 1988, 2–6 (available from NARF and the NSHS); Fred Thomas, "Argument on Skeletons May Flare," *Omaha World-Herald*, 3 October 1988.

122. See letter from Robert Peregoy to Frederick Wefso, 13 October 1988, 2–6. Tribal research revealed that the NSHS executive director's "legal cite" was apparently based on a rule that was *proposed* by the National Park Service in 1977 but was never promulgated into law and therefore was void and of no effect. Ibid., 3 (citing 42 Fed. Reg. 1977, pp. 5375–85). The proposed rule read by Hanson to the executive board at the October 1988 meeting provided that "[d]ata recovered from lands not under the control or jurisdiction of a federal agency but as a condition of a federal license, permit or other entitlement are recovered on behalf of the people of the United States and thus are the properties of the United States government." Ibid.

123. See Al Laukaitis, "Decision delayed on Indian remains," *Lincoln Journal-Star*, 9 October 1988.

124. See Swartzlander, "Rule cited in reburial case."

125. See Thomas, "Argument on Skeletons May Flare."

126. See Thomas, "Indians Hire Lobbyists in Bid for Items," *Omaha World-Herald*, 16 November 1988; Thomas, "Foes Prepare Arguments in Burial-Goods Dispute," *Omaha World-Herald*, 13 December 1988; see also letter from Bennie Keel, departmental consulting archaeologist, National Park Service, to James Hanson, 16 October 1988 (available from the National Park Service and NSHS); letter from Walter Echo-Hawk to F. A. Calabrese, Midwest Archaeological Center, National Park Service, 28 November 1988 (available from NARF); letter from Walter Echo-Hawk to Bennie Keel, 29 November 1988 (available from NARF and National Park Service). The NSHS director also sought the support of the Smithsonian Institution in his efforts to block Pawnee reburial. See letter from James Hanson to Lauryn Guttenplan Grant, assistant general counsel, Smithsonian Institution, 13 January 1989 (available from the NSHS). However, the Smithsonian Institution refused involvement in the dispute. See letter from Lauryn Guttenplan Grant to James Hanson, 23 March 1989 (available from the NSHS).

127. Telephone conference between F. A. Calabrese and Robert M. Peregoy, 16 November 1988 (*Statement of F. A. Calabrese*); personal conference between attorneys for the Pawnee Tribe, Robert M. Peregoy, and Walter Echo-Hawk, together with attorney James Botsford and F. A. Calabrese, held at the Midwest Archaeological Center, Lincoln, Nebraska, 17 November 1988. See also letter from Walter Echo-Hawk to F. A. Calabrese, 28 November 1988 (available from the National Park Service and NARF).

128. Ibid.

129. See *Additional Legal Authorities in Support of the Proposed Repatriation Policy and Request of the Pawnee Tribe*, October 1988 (citing Antiquities Act. 16 U. S. C. secs. 431, 433) (available from NARF); letter from Robert Peregoy to Frederick Wefso, 14 November 1988, 1–3 (available from NARF and the NSHS). Specifically, tribal attorneys pointed out that the NSHS executive director had admitted several months earlier that the Pawnee dead bodies and burial offerings held by the agency were disinterred from private or state lands. See letter from James Hanson to Walter Echo-Hawk, 26 August 1988, 2 (available from NARF and the NSHS). Accordingly, the tribe asserted that the Antiquities Act did not provide any basis for the federal government's threatened "ownership" claim, because the federal law is expressly limited to regulating "archaeological resources" acquired exclusively from federal lands. The Native American Graves Protection and repatriation Act, 25 U. S. C. sec. 3005 (1990), forecloses any such future threat from the NPS or any other federal agency.

130. See letter from F. A. Calabrese, NPS, to Walter Echo-Hawk, 5 December 1988 (available from the NPS and the NARF).

131. See letter from Bennie Keel, NPS, to James Hanson, 16 November 1988 (available from NARF and the NSHS).

132. Ibid.

133. See, e.g., letter from Robert Peregoy to Frederick Wefso, 15 December 1988, 3–6 (citing *United States* v. *City of Columbus*, 54 F. Supp. 37, 40 [D. N. D. 1943])(holding that the federal government has no legal interest or control over WPA projects once they are completed and turned over to the sponsoring entity).

134. A special meeting of the NSHS executive board scheduled for mid-November 1988 was canceled when the NPS intervened in the dispute, alleging that the federal government "may" have an "interest" in the Pawnee skeletal remains and burial offerings.

135. Letter from Robert Spire, attorney general of Nebraska, to Reba White Shirt, executive director, Nebraska Indian Commission, 14 December 1988, 9–10 (available from NARF).

136. See Minutes, Nebraska State Historical Society Executive Board Meeting, 17 Decem-

ber 1988, 1–2 (available from the NSHS). This action *sub silento* constituted a rejection of the policy proposed by the tribes. Not surprisingly, the negative vote was based in large part on the advice of the NSHS director that the federal government "owned" the Pawnee collection and that federal "officials are standing by their opinion that the society cannot release skeletal remains or artifacts since [the NSHS] agreed to preserve them as a condition of receiving federal funds." Ibid. During the meeting, the NSHS board did vote to return a limited number of Pawnee remains and burial offerings, subject to certain conditions. The Pawnee Tribe had previously rejected these conditions as arbitrary and repugnant to tribal traditions and religious beliefs. See letter from Walter Echo-Hawk to Frederick C. Luebke, NSHS board member, 2 December 1988 (available from NARF and the NSHS). The Pawnee Tribe rejected the NSHS proposal on the basis that the NSHS (1) refused to repatriate any burial offerings; (2) would not repatriate any of the hundreds of deceased Pawnees who lived before the year 1750 A.D.; and (3) demanded that all repatriated dead bodies be placed in a waterproof burial vault that would prevent decomposition. This latter demand was particularly repugnant to tribal religious and mortuary practices, because it would allow for future disturbances of the deceased and would preclude the deceased from going from "dust to dust" as required by tribal practices. Ibid.

137. See Fred Thomas, "Foes Prepare Arguments in Burial-Goods Dispute," *Omaha World-Herald*, 13 December 1988; see Minutes, Nebraska State Historical Society Executive Board Meeting, 17 December 1988, 1 (available from the NSHS).

138. See letter from Ross O. Swimmer, assistant secretary of the Department of the Interior, to Walter Echo-Hawk, 20 December 1988 (available from NARF).

139. See letter from Walter Echo-Hawk to Frederick Wefso, 3 January 1989 (available from NARF and the NSHS).

140. See David Swartzlander, "Society asked to reconsider action on remains," *Lincoln Journal*, 5 January 1989.

141. The Pawnee and Nebraska tribes conducted an intensive lobbying effort in the Nebraska legislature's 1989 session in an effort to enlighten senators as to the religious practices and human rights vindicated through the grave protection and repatriation legislation. As a key part of this effort, NARF, on behalf of the Pawnee and Winnebago tribes, disseminated a comprehensive scientific bases of the legislation and provided a brief background on Pawnee religious beliefs and disinterments by the NSHS. See "Briefing Document: LB 340—Nebraska Unmarked Human Burial Sites and Skeletal Remains Protection Act," Native American Rights Fund, January 1989 (available from NARF). In addition to this comprehensive document, tribal lobbyists furnished senators with numerous analysis of hostile amendments proposed by senators opposing LB 340.

142. Senator James Pappas, the sponsor of the reburial legislation (LB 612) in the two previous sessions of the legislature, lost his 1988 bid for reelection. Senator Chambers also introduced a bill, LB 151, in the 1989 legislature to reorganize the NSHS to bring the agency and its executive director under the direct control of the governor. As currently organized, the NSHS executive board, largely elected by the NSHS membership, has hiring and firing authority over the executive director. LB 151 was designed to statutorily impose accountability on the state agency, particularly in light of NSHS mistreatment of the tribes throughout the repatriation controversy. LB 151 was killed in committee. See transcripts of hearing on LB 151, 91st Neb. Leg., 1st sess. (1989), 1–83. Notwithstanding, key senators are committed to the prospective enactment of such a measure.

143. See transcripts of hearing on LB 340, Government, Military and Veterans' Affairs Committee, 91st Neb. Leg., 1st sess. (25 January 1989) 83–190.

144. See Neb. Rev. Stat, sec. 1201204(1) (Supp. 1990). Funerary objects outside the

statutory definition of burial goods include those removed from burials without the dead bodies and those with no documentation or other reasonable means to trace to the skeletal remains. The tribal governments reluctantly agreed to this restrictive statutory definition of burial goods, recognizing that various common law causes of action remained available to tribes seeking the return of tribally identifiable funerary objects outside the scope of the act.

145. See "Historical Society chief backed bill to return Indian remains," *Lincoln Star*, 31 January 1989. The NSHS executive director made his promise in front of the media immediately following a two-hour negotiation session with Senator Baack and Robert Peregoy, representing the Pawnee Tribe. Committee chairman Baack called the meeting to craft an agreement to eliminate "bloodshed" on the legislative floor. After this meeting, the bill was sent to the floor of the legislature. In addition to this meeting, the speaker of the legislature, Senator William Barrett, now a member of Congress, subsequently held two lengthy sessions attended by key senators and NSHS and tribal representatives for the same purpose.

146. Martha Stoddard, "Historical Society board backs LB 340 if amended," *Lincoln Journal*, 4 February 1989. The policymaking body of the state agency sought to include the following additional conditions in amendments to LB 340: (1) the allowance of three years' study time for all collections to be returned for reburial, rather than one year; (2) a requirement that reburial take place in Nebraska; (3) a provision that museums not be restricted in what they exhibit or how they label exhibits; and (4) the establishment of a committee for dispute resolution. Ibid.

147. See Ed Howard, J. L. Schmidt, "Hanson 'reneged' on remains bills," *Lincoln Journal*, 7 February 1989.

148. Floor debate on LB 340, 91st Neb. Leg., 1st sess., 2862–63 (daily ed., 27 March 1989) (statement of Senator Baack).

149. "Most Favored Giving Remains to Tribes," *Omaha World-Herald*, 16 February 1989. The poll indicated only 19 percent of those polled were opposed to such repatriation, while 11 percent were undecided.

150. Interview with James Hanson by radio station KFOR, "Lincoln Live," 20 January 1989, Lincoln, Nebraska (transcripts and tapes available from NARF).

151. Ibid.

152. See Thomas, "Tribal Lawyer Criticizes Board President," *Omaha World-Herald*, 11 January 1989. To counter this self-serving misinformation, the Pawnee Tribe held a press conference with tribal chairman Lawrence Goodfox, Jr. to dispel these myths publicly. See John Share, "Pawnee Leader Says Burial Goods Wouldn't Be Sold," *Omaha World-Herald*, 22 February 1989.

153. See Vicki Quade, "Who Owns the Past?" *Barrister* (Spring, 1990): 30.

154. See Thomas, "3 Medals Are Part of Burial Sites Controversy," *Omaha World-Herald*, 22 February 1989.

155. See Thomas, "3 Medals"; Share, "Warner: Give Up Bones, Nothing Else," *Omaha World-Herald*, 11 February 1989. In 1990, the NSHS purchased a comparable copy of the George III peace medal disinterred from a Pawnee burial. LB 340 opponents alleged during the 1989 legislative session that this type medal was worth up to $1 million. The 1990 purchase price of the second medal was under $4,000. See, e.g., "Not only does peace medal exist—it has a twin," *Lincoln Star*, 11 September 1990. See also "Pawnees to get George III medal back," *Lincoln Journal-Star*, 2 November 1991.

156. See Thomas, "Hanson Says Bill Should Exclude Non-Tribal Items," *Omaha World-Herald*, 11 February 1989.

157. See Thomas, "3 Medals Are Part of Burial Sites Controversy." The NSHS ultimately refused to return the George III medal to the Pawnee Tribe after LB 340 was enacted into

law on the basis, in part, of attempting to impeach the accuracy of it own burial record-keeping system.

158. Floor debate on LB 340, 1700–1701 (daily ed., 1 March 1989) (statement of Senator Chambers).

159. Floor debate on LB 340, 2866 (daily ed., 27 March 1989) (statement of Senator Baack).

160. The third round vote was 30–16 to enact LB 340 into law. See floor debate on LB 340, 7402 (daily ed., 19 May 1989). A simple majority of twenty-five votes of the forty-nine senators is required on each of three separate votes to pass a bill in the nation's only unicameral legislature. Accordingly, LB 340 passed by a comfortable margin.

161. Throughout the LB 340 process, the tribes garnered the support of many non-Indian individuals, religious groups, and political, educational, and human rights organizations. This broad-based support was crucial in the enactment of LB 340 into law.

162. Neb. Rev. Stat. secs. 12-1201 through 12-1212 (Supp. 1990); Neb. Rev. Stat. sec. 28-1301 (Supp. 1990).

163. Neb. Rev. Stat. sec. 12-1203(1) (Supp. 1990).

164. Neb. Rev. Stat. secs. 12-1209–12-1211 (Supp. 1990).

165. Neb. Rev. Stat. secs. 12-1205–12-1208 (Supp. 1990).

166. Neb. Rev. Stat. sec. 12-1209 (Supp. 1990). Although section12-1209 facially requires repatriation to a qualifying Indian tribe, Nebraska's public counsel interpreted the intent of the legislature to require repatriation to multiple tribes where such human remains and burial offerings can be linked to more than one tribe but not to one alone. See "Arbitration Award in the Matter of the Pawnee Tribe of Oklahoma, et. al., and the Nebraska State Historical Society," Office of the Public Counsel/Ombudsman, state of Nebraska, 12 March 1991, 52–53 (hereafter "First Arbitration Award") (available from NARF). Thus, the act contemplated the possibility of joint claims by two or more Indian tribes in order to repatriate the skeletal remains and burial offerings of common ancestors. The term *Indian tribe* is defined as "any federally recognized or state recognized Indian tribe, band or community." Neb. Rev. Stat. sec. 1201204(4) (Supp. 1990). The repatriation provisions of the act focus on the return and reburial of dead Indian bodies and associated burial offerings held by Nebraska institutions, precisely because such entities never targeted the dead of other races on a systematic, massive scale for exhumation, curation, study, or display.

167. See floor debate on LB 340, 1706–1707 (daily ed., 1 March 1989) (statement of Senator Landis). The one-year study period was also included to enable institutions such as the NSHS to "duplicate" burial offerings deemed important to history and education prior to reburial.

168. The legislature considered the fact that the NSHS has retained possession of the Pawnee dead bodies and burial offerings at issue for at least fifty years when it provided for a one-year study period. Ibid., 2862.

169. Neb. Rev. Stat. sec. 12-1204(6) (Supp. 1990).

170. This provision was unanimously adopted by the legislature as a floor amendment to LB 340 in order to clarify the extent of human skeletal remains and burial offerings subject to repatriation and reburial under the act. See floor debate on LB 340, 2815–16 (daily ed., 23 March 1989) (statement of Senator Bernard-Stevens). Thus, it removed any question that repatriation was limited to "historic" skeletal remains and burial offerings dating from 1700 A.D. in Nebraska, as was the understanding of one senator three weeks prior to the adoption of the clarifying amendment. Ibid., 1969. See also, "First Arbitration Award," 31–61.

171. See, e.g., Roger Echo-Hawk, "Preface."

172. Neb. Rev. Stat. sec. 12-1204(1) (Supp. 1990).

173. See floor debate on LB 340, 1695–97 (daily ed., 1 March 1990).

174. Ibid.

175. Ibid.

176. Ibid. See "First Amendment Award," 19–27, 61.

177. Funerary objects that fall outside the statutory definition of *burial goods* include those that were disinterred from burials where the dead bodies were not removed from the graves or where there is no documentation or other reasonable means to trace such burial offerings to the specific human skeletal remains with which they were originally buried. In the original version of LB 340, all funerary objects that were identifiable to a specific Indian tribe were defined as burial goods subject to reburial. However, in order to move the bill out of committee to the floor, it was necessary for the tribes to compromise and support a committee amendment that restricted the statutory scope of *burial goods*. See floor debate on LB 340, 1966–98 (daily ed., 1 March 1989). Notwithstanding this restricted statutory definition, various causes of action under the common law remain available to Indian tribes seeking the repatriation of tribally identifiable burial offerings that fall outside the scope of the act. Moreover, the 1990 federal Native American Graves Protection and Repatriation Act requires museums receiving federal funds, such as the NSHS, to return such "unassociated" tribally identifiable burial offerings to requesting Indian tribes that establish cultural affiliation by a preponderance of the evidence. See 25 U. S. C. sec. 3005(a)(4) (1990).

178. Neb. Rev. Stat. sec. 12-1210 (Supp. 1990).

179. Ibid. The legislature enacted this requirement to provide assurances to the parties, in particular Indian tribes, that all items listed on the statutory inventory would in fact be repatriated and reburied. The legislature was particularly sensitive to unfounded allegations by the NSHS and the National Park Service that the Pawnee Tribe sought repatriation in order to sell tribal burial offerings on the antiquities market, rather than for purposes of reburial in accordance with Pawnee mortuary traditions and practices. The signature requirement serves to preclude agencies such as the NSHS from withholding items listed on the inventory and from subsequent allegations that the tribe sold its burial offerings, should any be found on the antiquities market.

180. See floor debate on LB 340, 2810–11 (daily ed., 23 March 1989) (statement of Senator Conway). In any event, records held by public institutions or agencies in Nebraska are public records subject to disclosure under the state's Public Records Act. Neb. Rev. Stat. secs. 84-712 et. seq. (1987). See also Ops. Neb. Att'y Gen (6 October 1988, Spire and Lowe to Echohawk and Peregoy; 21 October 1988, Spire and Lowe to Peregoy; 28 June 1989, Spire to Peregoy and Hanson); Order, *Nebraska State Historical Society* v. *Pawnee Tribe of Oklahoma et. al.* v. *State of Nebraska*, docket 448, p. 217, District Court of Lancaster County, Nebraska, 31 May 1991, 10–14.

181. See, e.g, floor debate on LB 340, 2812 (daily ed., 23 March 1989) (statement of Senator Conway).

182. See Neb. Rev. Stat. secs. 12-1205–12-1208 (Supp. 1990).

183. Neb. Rev. Stat. sec. 12-1205(1) (Supp. 1990). Subsection 2 of sec. 12-1205 contains similar requirements for the state Department of Roads when it encounters unmarked burials in the course of highway construction projects. This provision authorizes the removal of such burials following examination by appropriate agencies pursuant to Neb. Rev. Stat. sec. 39-1363 (reissue 1988) and compliance with applicable federal requirements. However, such human skeletal remains and burial offerings are required to be treated and reburied in accordance with the requirements of secs. 12-1207 and 12-1208 of the Unmarked Human Burial Sites and Skeletal Remains Protection Act.

184. Failure to make such a report is a misdemeanor under sec. 12-1205.

185. Neb. Rev. Stat. sec. 12-1206 (Supp. 1990).

186. Neb. Rev. Stat. sec. 12-1207 (Supp. 1990).

187. Ibid.

188. Neb. Rev. Stat. sec. 12-1208 (Supp. 1990).

189. Ibid. The "pre-existing state statutes" primarily include Neb. Rev. Stat. sec. 71-1339 (1959), which lists the next of kin vested with the right to rebury the dead body of a relative. Under sec. 12-1208(2) (Supp. 1990), if the next of kin are known, they are responsible for paying for the reburial. If there are no known relatives, reburial is at the expense of the county in which the remains are interred.

190. Neb. Rev. Stat. sec. 12-1208(3) (Supp. 1990).

191. Ibid.

192. Ibid. This subsection requires reburial at the expense of a known relative or affected Indian tribe. In cases where reasonably identifiable Indian skeletal remains or burial offerings are unclaimed by a known relative, reburial is required pursuant to sec. 12-1208(2).

193. Neb. Rev. Stat. sec. 12-1208(2) (Supp. 1990).

194. Ibid. While this provision authorizes the "curation" of such human skeletal remains and burial offerings, it does not authorize their display.

195. Ibid.

196. Neb. Rev. Stat. sec. 12-1211 (Supp. 1990).

197. Ibid.

198. Ibid.

199. Ibid.

200. Neb. Rev. Stat. sec. 12-1212(1) (Supp. 1990).

201. Ibid.

202. Neb. Rev. Stat. sec. 12-1212(2)(b) (Supp. 1990).

203. Neb. Rev. Stat. sec. 12-1212(2)(a) (Supp. 1990).

204. Ibid.

205. Neb. Rev. Stat. sec. 12-1212(2)(a), (3) (Supp. 1990).

206. Neb. Rev. Stat. sec. 28-1301(2) (Supp. 1990).

207. Neb. Rev. Stat. sec. 28-1301(2)(a) (Supp. 1990).

208. Neb. Rev. Stat. sec. 28-1301(2)(b) and (c) (Supp. 1990).

209. Neb. Rev. Stat. sec. 28-1301(2)(a) (Supp. 1990). In addition to reenacting prior statute exemptions to sec. 28-1301 concerning disinterment and reinterment of dead bodies—i.e., authorized dissections of dead bodies, reinterment by cemetery pursuant to permit, reinterment by relative or intimate friend pursuant to lawful authority and permit—the act subjects burial offerings to the statutory permit requirement when cemetery officials or a friend or relative intends to disinter and reinter a dead body and associated burial offerings. The act further exempts the following from its criminal prohibitions: (1) a professional archaeologist engaged in an otherwise lawful and scholarly excavation of a *nonburial* site, who unintentionally encounters human skeletal remains or associated burial goods, if the archaeologist complies with the notice requirement of the act; and (2) any archaeological investigation by the Nebraska State Historical Society, if any human skeletal remains or associated burial offerings discovered during such investigation are lawfully disposed of pursuant to sec. 12-1208 of the act. See Neb. Rev. Stat. sec. 28-1301(3) (Supp. 1990).

210. Neb. Rev. Stat. sec. 12-1210 (Supp. 1990).

211. See letters from Robert Spire to Walter Echo-Hawk and Robert M. Peregoy, Native American Rights Fund, 6, 21 October 1988.

212. See letter from Robert Spire, attorney general of Nebraska, to Robert M. Peregoy and

James Hanson, 28 June 1989 (available from NARF).

213. See "Spire, Attorney Vow to Sue for Records," *Omaha World-Herald*, 17 June 1989.

214. See Minutes, Nebraska State Historical Society Executive Board, 23 June 1989, 3. See also Robert Reeves, "Board makes records available to Indians," *Lincoln Star*, 24 June 1989.

215. See David Swartzlander, "Hanson criticizes state on Indian remains issue," *Lincoln Journal*, 24 September 1989.

216. See Reeves, "Indians say director won't cooperate," *Lincoln Star*, 5 January 1990.

217. See letters from Steven C. Moore to James Hanson, 14 October 1989; 21 November 1989; 14 December 1989; 10 January 1990 (available from NARF and the NSHS).

218. See letters from Steve Moore to James Hanson, 10 January 1990 (available from NARF and the NSHS).

219. See Order, *Nebraska State Historical Society v. Pawnee Tribe of Oklahoma et.al. v. State of Nebraska*, docket 488, p. 217, District Court of Lancaster County, Nebraska, filed 23 January 1990.

220. At the pretrial conference in September 1990, the NSHS stipulated that the Pawnee Tribe is a "person" within the meaning of the open records law.

221. See Order, *Nebraska State Historical Society v. Pawnee Tribe of Oklahoma et.al. v. State of Nebraska*, 31 May 1991, 9–11. The evidence established that the NSHS's executive director filed the lawsuit without receiving authorization or approval from the executive board, the agency's policy-making body. The court listed extensive evidence showing that the NSHS is a state agency, including (1) a 108-year-old statutory scheme expressly establishing the NSHS as a state agency; (2) legislative appropriations exceeding $21 million since 1980, accounting for over 75 percent of the agency's annual operating budget; and (3) numerous express representations of the NSHS to the state and federal government that the NSHS is a state agency. Ibid, 6. The court rejected the society's claim that the 1883 statute making the NSHS a state agency was unconstitutional. Ibid., 4–5. The court further found that the NSHS had never complied with the reporting requirements for a private nonprofit corporation. Ibid., 6–7.

222. Ibid. On 30 October 1991, the court entered its final order in the public records law case and awarded the Pawnee Tribe of Oklahoma $61,017.79 in attorneys' fees and other litigation costs, pursuant to the attorneys' fees provision of the public records law, Neb. Rev. Stat. sec. 84-712.07 (reissue 1987). The court also overruled the Nebraska State Historical Society's motion for a new trial in the case. See Order, *Nebraska State Historical Society v. Pawnee Tribe of Oklahoma et.al. v. State of Nebraska*, No. 448, p. 217, 3–4 (Lancaster County District Court, 30 October 1991).

223. See Robynn Tysver, "Historical Society to appeal," *Lincoln Journal*, 14 November 1991; see also, "Statement of the Issues to Be Raised on Appeal," *Nebraska State Historical Society v. Pawnee Tribe of Oklahoma et.al. v. State of Nebraska*, docket 448, p.217, Lancaster County District Court, filed 27 November 1991 by the NSHS.

224. See "Court victory could wreck the state's historical society," *Lincoln Journal-Star*, 17 November 1991.

225. Ibid.

226. The society's lawsuit and posture that it is a private corporation has caused the agency additional problems. State auditor John Breslow has taken the position that if the NSHS is a private corporation, as it contends, it owes the auditor's office $48,000 for past state-funded audits of the NSHS. Breslow also withheld the state's audit of federal funds expended by the NSHS, causing the NSHS to claim that more than $600,000 in federal funds are in jeopardy as long as the state audit of NSHS federal funds is withheld. Further, auditor Breslow, citing a Texas situation involving misappropriation of artifacts, called for

an audit of all artifacts in the NSHS collection to "ensure that the society's house is in order." In the midst of all these problems, James Hanson resigned as executive director of the Nebraska State Historical Society, effective 31 January 1992. See Robynn Tysver, "Historical society, auditor toe to toe," *Lincoln Journal*, 10 January 1992.

227. LB 1097, 91st Neb. Leg., 2d sess., 1990. See "Bill Would Reverse Indian-Remains Law," *Omaha World-Herald*, 11 January 1990.

228. See "Historian Says Artifacts Worth More Than $1 Million," *Omaha World-Herald*, 20 January 1990; Hearing on LB 1097, Committee on Government, Military and Veterans' Affairs, 91st Neb. Leg., 2d sess., 22 February 1990, 38–59, 73–75.

229. See "2 senators seek to undo remains law," *Lincoln Journal*, 11 January 1990.

230. See hearing on LB 1907, 75.

231. See Inventory of Human Remains and Burial Goods to Be Repatriated to the Pawnee Tribe, Nebraska State Historical Society, 12 June 1990.

232. Since 1988, the Pawnee Tribe had retained historians and archival experts Orlan Svingen and Anne P. Diffendal to conduct an independent review and analysis of the society's archaeological site files believed to contain information pertaining to Pawnee skeletal remains and burial offerings held by the NSHS. Diffendal was formerly employed by the NSHS for thirteen years, where she served as state archivist. She currently is the executive director of the Society of American Archivists in Chicago. In the tribe's estimation, approximately 25 percent of the data presented in the NSHS inventory was flawed in some way. Diffendal met with NSHS officials four times between June and August 1990 to resolve these discrepencies. While many were resolved, the major omissions concerning "reasonably identifiable" Pawnee skeletal remains and burial offerings were not. See "Petition of the Pawnee Tribe of Oklahoma for Repatriation of Human Remains and Burial Goods from the Nebraska State Historical Society," Office of the Public Counsel, State of Nebraska, 11 December 1990, 3–4 (hereafter "First Pawnee Repatriation Petition").

233. See Neb. Rev. Stat. sec. 12-1211 (Supp. 1990).

234. See "First Pawnee Repatriation Petition," 4; "Rebuttal of the Pawnee Tribe of Oklahoma to the Position of the Nebraska State Historical Society on the Subject of the Repatriation of Human Remains and Associated Burial Goods," Office of the Public Counsel, State of Nebraska, 27 February 1991, 2–15 (hereafter "First Rebuttal of Pawnee Tribe").

235. See "First Rebuttal of the Pawnee Tribe," 14, exhibit G.

236. Thomas, "Hanson Says Bill Should Exclude Non-Tribal Items," *Omaha World-Herald*, 11 February 1989.

237. See "First Pawnee Repatriation Petition," 7–28; "First Rebuttal of Pawnee Tribe," 2–15.

238. See Thomas, "Dispute Arises on Pawnee Artifacts Transfer," *Omaha World-Herald*, 5 September 1990.

239. See Reeves, "Legislators to view 'peace medals' as dispute over Indian artifacts rages on," *Lincoln Star*, 7 September 1990.

240. See Swartzlander, "Remains and artifacts of Pawnees put on truck for burial at Genoa," *Lincoln Journal*, 10 September 1990; "Not only does peace medal exist—it has a twin," *Lincoln Star*, 11 September 1990.

241. See "Pawnees to get George III medal back," *Lincoln Journal-Star*, 2 November 1991.

242. See "First Pawnee Repatriation Petition," 28–41; "First Rebuttal of Pawnee Tribe," 42–51.

243. See "Nebraska State Historical Society Position Statement for Native American Rights Fund Filing of Grievance under LB 340," dated 26 June 1990, as amended dated 13 September 1990 and "Petition Before Public Counsel" dated 11 December 1990 (14 January

272 / **Robert M. Peregoy**

1991), section B, 7–8 (hereafter "NSHS Position Statement") (available from NSHS).

244. See "First Pawnee Repatriation Petition," 41–47; "First Rebuttal of Pawnee Tribe," 15–42.

245. Ibid.

246. See "First Rebuttal of Pawnee Tribe," 30 (statement of Larry Zimmerman).

247. Ibid., 29–30.

248. Ibid., 30. Dr. Zimmerman served as the tribe's primary expert witness in the grievance proceedings.

249. Ibid.; see "NSHS Position Statement," 9–34 (section B, 14 January 1991).

250. See "First Rebuttal of Pawnee Tribe," 30 (statement of Larry Zimmerman).

251. While the society rejected the tribe's nominee, a professor at the University of Nebraska, the tribe did accept one of the NSHS's four nominees, a former chief justice of the Nebraska Supreme Court. However, he declined to serve. The NSHS submitted the names of all four of its nominees without their knowledge or consent.

252. See Neb. Rev. Stat. sec. 12-1211 (Supp. 1990).

253. See "First Petition of Pawnee Tribe." The supporting documentation included an extensive report by Larry Zimmerman, professor of anthropology at the University of South Dakota. In addition, the tribe submitted supporting affidavits and accompanying information by numerous anthropologists and archaeologists and an extensive historical report by tribal member and historian Roger Echo-Hawk.

254. See "NSHS Position Statement." Therein, the NSHS relied on staff archaeologists and the affidavits of external anthropologists and archaeologists.

255. See "First Rebuttal of the Pawnee Tribe." Therein, Zimmerman responded to the archaeological and anthropological assertions of the NSHS.

256. "Arbitration award, in the Matter of the Pawnee Tribe of Oklahoma, et.al., and the Nebraska State Historical Society, Office of the Public Counsel, State of Nebraska, 12 March 1991 (hereafter "First Arbitration Award").

257. Ibid., 25–26.

258. Ibid.

259. Ibid., 61. The public counsel indicated that, in order for the tribe to obtain the return of the burial goods at issue, "there would need to be sufficient independent evidence to establish that the items were, in fact, burial goods within the meaning of the law. Thus, there would need to be independent evidence that the item or items (1) were intentionally placed with the Indian skeletal remains of an individual at the time of burial, and (2) can be traced with a reasonable degree of certainty to the specific skeletal remains with which it or they were buried. There would also need to be sufficient independence to identify the human skeletal remains disinterred in association with the item or items in question as to familial or tribal origin." Ibid., 26. Because the tribe's "First Repatriation Petition" was primarily limited to the legal question of whether such funerary objects constitute "burial goods" under the law, the public counsel did not decide specific fact questions as to the individual burial goods at issue. He left that question open for a follow-up arbitration, without the necessity of going through the preliminary steps of sec. 12-1211, in light of the fact that the tribe raised these specific fact questions with the NSHS during the informal dispute resolution process. Ibid., 30. Importantly, in light of the fact that the evidence necessary to decide these questions of fact is in the sole possession of the NSHS, the public counsel placed the burden of proof on the NSHS. Ibid., 31. This ruling ultimately placed the NSHS in the untenable position of impeaching its own records kept in the normal course of business. As a follow-up to this matter, the Pawnee Tribe filed a second petition seeking an award directing the NSHS to return specific burial goods at issue. See "Petition of Pawnee Tribe of Okla-

homa for Pawnee Burial Goods from the Nebraska State Historical Society," Office of the Public Counsel, State of Nebraska, 9 August 1991.

260. See "First Arbitration Award," 51.

261. Ibid., 50–51.

262. Ibid., 61.

263. Ibid., 60.

264. Ibid., 58–60.

265. Ibid., 60.

266. Ibid., 52–53.

267. See Reeves, "Pawnee remains going 'home' after long wait," *Lincoln Star*, 11 September 1990. These deceased individuals and burial goods were listed on the NSHS inventory, initially produced in June 1990 and amended thereafter.

268. The tribe employed Anne Diffendal and Tom Witty, Kansas state archaeologist, to verify and document the transfer of each dead body and burial good. To protect against previous allegations that the tribe sought the repatriation to sell its burial goods on the antiquities market, the tribe videotaped the contents of the small coffins, nailed each shut, and sealed the top and sides with the tribal seal to prevent reopening. Moreover, the tribe invited NSHS officials to the funeral ceremony to observe burial of the sealed caskets. However, the NSHS declined.

269. The Pawnee Tribe selected Genoa as the site for reburial in recognition of the fact that the area was the last ancestral home of the Pawnee people before they were forced to move to Oklahoma in the 1870s. Reinterment was in the well-lit city cemetery, which is patrolled on a regular basis by local police. The caskets were placed in a mass grave, which was reinforced on the top with a six-inch concrete slab with holes to allow seepage and natural decomposition in the "dust to dust" burial traditions and practices of the tribe. These measures were taken to protect the burials eternally from any further disturbers.

270. The Pawnee Tribe also is preparing other repatriation claims to be filed with other entities in the state affected by Nebraska's repatriation statute. However, the tribe anticipates that these other institutions will readily cooperate with the tribe, thus avoiding the time, expense, and trouble of invoking the act's grievance mechanisms.

271. See "Pawnee to get George III medal back."

272. See Thomas, "Society to Relinquish Remaining Indian Bones," *Omaha World-Herald*, 15 November 1991.

273. Ibid.

274. See Thomas, "University Will Return Remains of Omaha Tribe," *Omaha World-Herald*, 15 August 1989.

275. Telephone interview with Dennis Hastings, historian, Omaha Tribe (1991); telephone interview with Clyde Tyndall, Omaha tribal planner (15 October 1991).

276. In 1986, the Omaha Tribe took official tribal government action, declaring a moratorium on all tribal dealings with the NSHS. To date, the moratorium still stands. Telephone interview with Dennis Hastings, historian of the Omaha Tribe, 9 August 1991.

277. See Vicki Quade, "Who Owns History?" *Barrister* (Spring, 1990): 30.

278. See, e.g, Testimony of Walter Echo-Hawk Before the House Committee on Interior and Insular Affairs, Administration and Public Works and Transportation on the National American Museum Act, H.R. 2688 (20 July 1989) 101st Cong., 1st sess.; Statement of Walter Echo-Hawk Before the Senate Select Committee on Indian Affairs on Native American Museum Claims Commission Act, S. 187 (29 July 1988), 100th Cong., 2d sess., 86–90, 233–315; Statement of Walter Echo-Hawk, Hearing Before the Senate Select Committee on Indian Affairs on the Native American Grave and Burial Protection Act (Preparation), Native

American Repatriation of Cultural Patrimony Act, and Heard Museum Report (14 May 1990), 101st Cong., 2d sess., 50–53, 174–267.

10

Acknowledging the Repatriation Claims of Unacknowledged California Tribes

Carole Goldberg

 THIS CHAPTER FOCUSES on the access of unacknowledged or unrecognized tribes, especially those in California, to legal rights of repatriation—that is, rights founded in statutes or administrative rules that are enforceable through the courts. Some tribes have been able to secure repatriation through negotiation even where legal rights have been uncertain or nonexistent by persuading a state or federal agency to cooperate in the return of skeletal remains or objects. Such negotiations have spared all interested parties the cost and distress of litigation. Often, however, it is difficult for tribes to conduct such negotiations unless they can make at least a colorable claim of legal entitlement to repatriation.

For the many federally unacknowledged tribes in California, therefore, it is important to know whether they can invoke legal rights to repatriation. Initially, it is worth clarifying exactly what it means to be an unacknowledged or unrecognized tribe. I want to underscore that a Native American group does not need to be acknowledged or recognized by the federal government to be a tribe. Federal recognition is merely an affirmative act by the federal government to acknowledge its trust responsibility and its statutory or other obligations to provide services and programs to Indian groups. The fact that the federal government has not provided this recognition or acknowledgment does not mean that an Indian group is not a tribe. But certain consequences flow from this recognition, the most important of them being many of the services and programs in education, health, and welfare that the federal government provides to Indian people.

How does a tribe become acknowledged or recognized? The easiest way is to point to a treaty, statute, or presidential executive order that creates a reservation or indicates the tribe's existence. Outside these easiest cases, however, tribes have no sure guides. For a long time there were court decisions and federal regulations that touched obliquely on what was required to be recognized as an Indian tribe. The whole process became much more systematic in 1978 when the secretary of

Carole Goldberg, professor of law, directs the joint graduate degree program in Law and American Indian Studies at UCLA. She is the author of *Planting Tail Feathers: Tribal Survival and Public Law.*

the interior issued an official list of federally recognized tribes and promulgated regulations that were designed to create a process whereby tribes could apply for recognition or acknowledgment.[1] These regulations made it exceedingly difficult for tribes to satisfy the requirements for acknowledgment if they could not locate a decisive treaty, statute, or executive order.

One of the most serious difficulties created for tribes seeking federal recognition under these regulations is that the regulations require proof of continuity in long historical sequence for Indian groups. Furthermore, Indian groups must show continuity of certain kinds of political organization and authority, and they must demonstrate continuity of general community understanding of the group as a Native American tribe. It has been very difficult for tribes, with limited funds and access to research materials, to establish recognition under this process. The regulations were relaxed a bit a few years ago, but the process is still extraordinarily slow and burdensome.

The burden of these recognition criteria and the process for satisfying them have been particularly onerous for California tribes. The reason goes back to the history of the failure of the federal government to ratify treaties that were made with California tribes in the early 1850s. These eighteen separate treaties were negotiated and signed, and the Indian people thought they meant something. As a consequence, members of California tribes moved from their ancestral lands to what they thought were the eight-million acres of reservation lands that had been set aside for them. In fact, because the treaties were never ratified, these lands were not ever set aside for them, and the lands they had left behind weren't protected either. Congress passed laws demanding that claimants to California lands file their claims through a special process, a process that was unknown to the tribes at that time. Furthermore, the Indians did not think they needed to assert land claims at all because they had been promised reservations. In the end, the tribes not only were unable to secure the reservations named in the treaties, but also lost the ancestral lands they had left behind.[2] So the most established and potent indicators of recognition, a treaty and reservation, were denied to California tribes. What followed from their landless state was dispersion, homelessness, starvation, and, on the part of the non-Indians residing in California at that time, systematic attempts at extermination. It is a horrible and tragic chapter in the history of this state.

Beginning around 1870, the federal government set aside some areas—usually by presidential executive order, sometimes by congressional statute—for what were described as the homeless Indians of California. These areas were often arid, steeply graded, and highly inaccessible. Consequently, large numbers of California Indians chose not to settle on these plots. These areas became rancherias and reservations that did eventually achieve federally recognized status—and there are more than one hundred recognized tribes in California today, more than in any other state. But there were still many bands, groups, and individuals that did not acquire status by occupying these lands because they chose to live elsewhere. Not surprisingly, in California there are larger numbers of unacknowledged Indian people and more groups seeking to apply for federal acknowledgment than in any other part of the United States.[3]

What is especially unsettling about this state of affairs is that many of the individual Indians who belong to these groups seeking acknowledgment have other means of demonstrating very clearly to the federal government, indeed from the federal government, that they are Indian people. In the 1920s and again in the 1940s to 1960s, Congress authorized California Indians to pursue land claims litigation to achieve compensation for the lands that were lost when those eighteen treaties were not ratified by the Congress. This litigation was authorized for the entire group of California Indians as defined by ancestry, not just particular tribal groups. Large sums of money, although not nearly all that was owed, were distributed as a result of these lawsuits. In order to distribute the money, however, lists or rolls had to be prepared of all the individuals who were entitled to receive the proceeds. Individuals had to come forward and demonstrate their descendance from the people who were members of the groups that had entered into the unratified treaties back in the 1850s. Consequently, although there are official federal lists of people who are entitled to these distributions, many of the people on these rolls are not members of tribes that currently receive acknowledgment from the federal government. Here, in other words, is a federal indication that individuals are members of California Indian groups, and yet these same groups may not be able to satisfy the stringent criteria for federal recognition.

A second inexplicable aspect of the lack of recognition for California groups is that quite a few Indian people in the state possess allotments that were carved from the public domain rather than from reservations. These public domain lands were federal property, often forest lands, that were frequently located where reservations were supposed to have been created under the unratified treaties. Remarkably, many of the holders of these public domain allotments are members of groups that have not received federal acknowledgment. In the case of these allottees, the federal government is evidently denying a trust responsibility to them even though the federal government holds their allotments in trust and is responsible for managing their lands.

The existence of judgment fund rolls and the existence of public domain allotments mean that in California you do not have to guess who the Indian people are or put them through some elaborate process to demonstrate that they are genuinely Indian. And yet because they have difficulty proving the kinds of continuity that the federal acknowledgment process demands—precisely because of the history of federal dislocation of California tribal groups—these individuals are not deemed members of federally recognized tribes; and they are denied the benefit of most federal Indian statutes and programs.

Recent developments in the Congress and the courts have given new benefits and new status to these California tribal groups. I will mention two. One is the Indian Health Care Improvement Act of 1988 (IHCIA),[4] which establishes eligibility for federal services provided by the Indian Health Service (IHS). The IHS is part of the Department of Health and Human Services, not the Department of the Interior (which administers the acknowledgment regulations). Importantly, the eligibility standards of the IHCIA for California do not turn on whether a tribe is recognized by the Department of the Interior and placed on the official list maintained by that department. For California Indians in particular, an individual may establish eligibility for Indian Health Service benefits if he or she: (1) is descended from an Indian who was residing in California on June 1, 1852, if that individual lives in California, belongs to a community served by an IHS program, and is viewed as an Indian by the community in which she or he lives; (2) holds a public domain, national forest, or reservation allotment; or (3) is, or is descended from, an Indian who was identified as such pursuant to the termination acts of the 1950s. Thus, almost every California Indian is eligible for IHCIA services according to these standards, regardless of whether his or her tribe is acknowledged by the Department of the Interior. Most significantly, the IHCIA was an amendment to the Snyder Act, the basic federal statute that the secretary of the interior uses as authority to deliver education, welfare, and many other benefits to tribes.

Several other federal statutes of the past fifteen years do not specifically mention California tribes, but more generally include tribes lacking Department of the Interior acknowledgment in classes of federal benefits. For example, the Job Training Partnership Act of 1982 has a subchapter establishing comprehensive training and employment programs for Native American communities. It specifies that its programs "shall be available to federally recognized Indian tribes . . . and to other groups and individuals of Native American descent."[5] Likewise, the Community Services Block Grant Program authorizes diversion of state block grant funds to Indian tribes and defines such tribes as "those tribes, bands, or other organized groups of Indians recognized in the State in which they reside or considered by the Secretary of the Interior to be an Indian tribe or an Indian organization for any purpose."[6] Thus unrecognized California groups that do not appear on the secretary's list are receiving federal benefits and a form of acknowledgment, at least if they are recognized by the state. In 1994, for example, California recognized the Gabrieleno/Tongva Tribe as the aboriginal tribe of the Los Angeles Basin.[7]

In the courts, unrecognized California groups have received noteworthy support. An important case decided by the United States Court of Appeals for the Ninth Circuit in 1994, *Malone v. Bureau of Indian Affairs*,[8] directly involved benefits provided by the Department of the Interior under the Snyder Act. The benefits involved were higher education grants and loans. Under regulations set forth by the department, these benefits were limited to enrolled members of federally recognized tribes. What the Ninth Circuit said when a member of an unacknowledged tribe challenged this restriction was that the Department of the Interior had not followed proper procedures in promulgating the requirement. Furthermore, the department had erred in its interpretation of an earlier Ninth Circuit decision and mistakenly thought it was required to impose an eligibility standard based on tribal recognition. According to the court, the department needed to go back, rethink its regulation, and follow proper procedures. Offering its advice, the court suggested that the department try to adopt criteria "consistent with the broad language of the Snyder Act," which simply says that benefits are available to Indians in the United States. It went on to "encourage the Bureau [of Indian Affairs] to look to eligibility criteria used in other Snyder Act programs such as those set forth in the 1988 Amendments to the Indian Health Care Improvement Act." In other words, the department and bureau were given strong indications that the IHCIA is not limited in its application to health benefits administered by the IHS. As a most recent expression of congressional intent, the IHCIA should be broadly interpreted to allow all benefits for California Indians, such as higher education grants, regardless whether they belong to federally acknowledged tribes.

An even stronger decision for unacknowledged California groups, although one from a lower federal court, is *Laughing Coyote* v. *United States Fish and Wildlife Service*, decided in 1994 in an unpublished opinion.[9] There the United States District Court for the Eastern District of California invalidated a Department of Interior, Fish and Wildlife Service regulation implementing the Eagle Protection Act[10] because it excluded unacknowledged tribes. This particular legislation permitted the taking of eagle parts for the religious purposes of Indian tribes where such activity was consistent with preserving the eagle population. A California Indian, whose descent from aboriginal California tribes was uncontested, was nonetheless denied a permit to take some eagle parts by the Fish and Wildlife Service. The basis for the denial was a regulation requiring that permittees be members of tribes on the Department of the Interior's list of recognized tribes. The federal court found this restriction "arbitrary and capricious" in relation to the language and intent of the Eagle Protection Act and struck it down.

In my view, the federal trust responsibility means that federal statutes are to be interpreted, when they are ambiguous, so as to benefit the Indian people. According to the Native American Graves Protection and Repatriation Act (NAGPRA), an Indian tribe is defined as any group that is recognized as eligible for the special programs and services provided by the United States to Indians because of their status as Indians.[11] In California, it is plain that an individual does not have to be on the Department of the Interior's list of federally acknowledged tribes in order to be eligible for many types of Indian program benefits. So if the NAGPRA regulations restrict repatriation to tribes on the department's list, they misconstrue the statute. Of course, like all implementing regulations, those implementing NAGPRA will be entitled to some deference from the courts. But even that deference did not save the regulation in *Laughing Coyote*. The fact that the NAGPRA regulations exclude unacknowledged tribes does not make them right—and will not save them from litigation.

In thinking about eligibility to make claims for repatriation, it is important not to view NAGPRA as the only governing law. It is not. For example, the University of California system and UCLA have both established rules according to which Indian groups are entitled to seek repatriation if they are recognized by the federal government, but also if they are recognized by the state of California for any purpose. What does that mean?

The state of California does not have an official process, like the one the federal government administers, in which a tribal group applies to a federal agency or is placed on an official list of recognized tribes. There are some states on the East Coast that actually have state reservations, but California has none of these either. However, there are state laws that grant rights and benefits to tribes because of their status as Indians, and some of these are not restricted to federally acknowledged groups. For example, the Public Resources Code creates within the state government the Native American Heritage Commission, at least five of whose members are to be "elders, traditional people, or spiritual leaders of California Native American tribes, nominated by Native American organizations, tribes, or groups within the state." There is no limiting language at all restricting participation to federally recognized tribes. Furthermore, if one examines the process that occurs under the California Environmental Quality Act, in which Indian groups must monitor and review excavations in their ancestral territories, it becomes apparent that the tribes need not be federally recognized in order to participate.

Based on this survey of state law, it seems that in dealing with the University of California, one should not assume that the NAGPRA eligibility rules apply. They apparently do not. And there may be other agencies and operations besides the University of California where that is true as well. It is important for unrecognized groups to test the limits and legitimacy of any restrictive practices.

In the meantime, the Advisory Council on California Indian Policy, established by Congress in 1992, is recommending new federal legislation that will make it easier for California tribes to establish federally recognized status. The change in Congress since then has made prospects for enactment of this legislation dim. Nevertheless, one of the most gratifying things I've seen working with the Advisory Council is that recognized and unrecognized tribes are beginning to work together more effectively. With combined efforts, they may find they can successfully challenge the limiting language of the NAGPRA regulations.

Notes

1. See 25 C.F.R. Part 83.
2. See Bruce S. Flushman and Joe Barbieri, "Aboriginal Title: The Special Case of California," *Pacific Law Journal* 17 (1986): 291.
3. See Carole Goldberg-Ambrose and Duane Champagne, *A Second Century of Dishonor: Federal Iniquities and California Tribes* (Report prepared for the Advisory Council on California Indian Policy, 1995).
4. 25 U.S.C. sec. 1679(b).
5. 25 U.S.C. sec 1671.
6. 42 U.S.C. sec. 9903(d)(5).
7. California Assembly Joint Resolution No. 96, adopted August 31, 1994, resolution Chapter 146.
8. 38 F.3d 433 (9th Cir. 1994).
9. A copy is on file with the author.
10. 16 U.S.C. secs. 668 et seq., implementing regulation at 50 C.F.R. secs 22.1 et seq.
11. 25 U.S.C. sec. 3001(7).

PART VI

ACTIVISM

Many of the federal government's legislative changes and much of the contemporary awareness of Native American issues have their roots in the American Indian activism of the 1950s, 1960s, and 1970s. Identified by names such as the American Indian Youth Council, United Native Americans, Indians of All Tribes, Women Of All Red Nations, and the American Indian Movement, these groups, made up primarily of young Native Americans, protested against treaty violations, termination, urban relocation, reservation unemployment and violence, and attempts at detribalization and assaults on the remaining Indian land base. These acts of protest demanded recognition of treaty rights, protection of fishing and hunting rights, protection of religious freedoms, and a new demand for recognition of Indian self-determination and tribal sovereignty.

American Indian activists built upon the larger social conditions present in America at that time. The 1960s and early 1970s were times of urban unrest across the United States. The civil rights movement, Black Power, the rise of LaRaza, the stirring of the new feminism, the rise of the New Left Generation, and the Third World strikes, were sweeping the nation, particularly college campuses. Sit-ins, sleep-ins, teach-ins, lock-outs, and boycotts became everyday occurrences at colleges and universities. Young Native Americans, who had come to the urban areas through the relocation program, were now enrolled in colleges and universities where they watched and learned.

This unrest, however, was not the cause of Indian activism. Instead, Indian activism was more a manifestation of centuries of mistreatment of Indian people, the *latest being the government relocation program of the 1950s. This program relocated more than 100,000 Indian people to urban areas and promised vocational training, assistance in finding jobs, adequate housing, and financial assistance. Many of these, however, became broken promises, resulting in frustration and protest.*

Authors Johnson, Champagne, and Nagel, provide a historical background of the Native American activism period beginning in the 1950s and culminating with the July 1978 Longest Walk on Washington. They state that, following 1978, the strategy of property seizures fell out of favor, and activist leaders instead pursued other avenues such as seeking recognition from the United Nations for treaty, national, and humanitarian rights. The authors state that the activism of the sixties and seventies achieved many of its goals. More Indian students were attending college, and, by the 1980s, there were over one hundred Native American/American Indian studies programs on U.S. campuses. In summary, the authors feel that perhaps the most profound effect of the contemporary Native American protest period was to educate and change the consciousness of people in the United States and around the world. "In the end," they say, "the Alcatraz–Red Power Movement may have strengthened and diversified U. S. society and made it a more tolerant place for all."

11

American Indian Activism and Transformation: Lessons from Alcatraz

Troy Johnson, Duane Champagne, and Joane Nagel

 THE OCCUPATION OF ALCATRAZ ISLAND in 1969–71 initiated a unique nine-year period of Red Power protest that culminated in the transformation of national consciousness about American Indians and engendered a more open and confident sense of identity among people of Indian descent. Between 20 November 1969 and the Longest Walk in 1978, there were more than seventy property takeovers by Indian activists.[1] This series of collective actions is referred to as the Alcatraz-Red Power Movement (ARPM) because it started with—and was modeled after—the Alcatraz takeover. Certainly, many individual Indian people were politically active before and after this period, but what made the movement so powerful were the large numbers of organized demonstrations and the property seizures aimed at airing national and local Indian grievances.

The ARPM was predominantly a struggle to secure redress for overwhelming conditions of political, cultural, and economic disadvantage that mirrored the long history of Indian poverty, not only on reservations, but more recently in urban environments. Current theories of social movements focus on situations of group repression or disadvantage while emphasizing elements of individual and group choice, such as active leaders, effectively organized groups, formation of common group and individual interests, and the development of group ideology.[2] Both repressive and voluntarist elements must be analyzed to understand the rise, development, and decline of social movements. Voluntarist elements within the ARPM include charismatic leaders, the legacy of historical Indian resistance and social movements, the tactic of property seizure, a pan-Indian identity, formation of a national activist organization—in this case, the American Indian Movement (AIM)—and a common national agenda of self-determination for Indian people and communities. Other structural and voluntarist elements are situational and have to be understood within the specific historical context. Some of these situational events are the civil rights movement, the Vietnam War

Troy Johnson is an associate professor of American Indian Studies and U. S. History at California State University, Long Beach. Duane Champagne is a professor in Department of Sociology and director of the American Indian Studies Center at UCLA, and editor of the *American Indian Culture and Research Journal*. Joane Nagel is a professor and chair of the Department of Sociology at the University of Kansas.

protests, widespread student activism, the rise of radical ethnic groups, the reluctance of the federal government to overtly repress social movements during the late 1960s and early 1970s, and the mass media attention heaped on many Indian takeovers, including Alcatraz Island.

Despite its influence, the occupation of Alcatraz Island has largely been overlooked by those who write or speak today of American Indian activism. Much has been written about the battles fought by Indian people for their rights to hunting and fishing areas reserved by treaties in the states of Washington, Oregon, Wisconsin, and Minnesota, as well as about Six Nations efforts to secure guaranteed treaty rights in the northeastern United States and Indian actions protesting the demeaning use of Native American mascots by athletic teams. The 1972 takeover of the Bureau of Indian Affairs (BIA) headquarters in Washington, D.C., and the 1973 occupation of Wounded Knee are also well known, as is the killing of the young Coeur d'Alene Indian Joseph Stuntz, and also the deaths of two FBI agents on the Pine Ridge Reservation in 1975, which resulted in the imprisonment of Leonard Peltier. Yet it was the occupation of Alcatraz Island that launched the greatest wave of modern-day American Indian activism. In the pages that follow, we will describe and analyze the rise, organization, fall, and legacy of the Alcatraz–Red Power Movement.

THE LEGACY OF NATIVE AMERICAN ACTIVISM

The ARPM protests were not unusual in that they were part of a long line of rebellions and social movements among Native Americans as means to resist colonial and U.S. control over their livelihood, culture, government, and resources. To better understand the ARPM, we will compare it with some of the major types of Indian movements occurring throughout history, pointing out similarities, differences, and important continuities.

Religious revitalization movements, numerous in Native American history, have provided spiritual solutions to the conditions of economic marginalization, political repression, and major losses of territory, as well as the ability to carry on traditional life. The more notable movements of this type include the Delaware Prophet (1760–63), the Shawnee Prophet (1805–11), the Winnebago Prophet (1830), the Ghost Dance of 1870, and the Ghost Dance of 1890, but there are also many local and lesser-known movements. In each of these, a prophet relied on ritual knowledge and power to gather a pan-Indian following either to fight against European invaders or to pray for a cataclysmic event that would restore the Indian Nations to the peace, plenty, and life they had known before American or European intrusions.[3] Most of these movements were either militarily repressed, or the followers abandoned them when the predicted events did not come to pass. In some cases, small groups continued in the religion, but there were no pan-Indian churches or enduring community change. Similar to the ARPM, the religious revitalization movements formed a multitribal gathering of adherents, and both movements were reactions to severe conditions of economic, political, and cultural deprivation. But the ARPM was secular, relying on physical tactics rather than spiritual solutions; and while the ARPM depended on charismatic leaders, it did not focus on prophets or the formation of new religious beliefs.

Social revitalization movements, most of which led to reformed religions with present-day practicing adherents, also served to establish modified forms of community organization designed to better accommodate American-style agriculture, reservation land, and political restrictions. These movements include Handsome Lake Church (1799–present), the Delaware Big House Religion (1760–1910), the Kickapoo Prophet (1830–51), the Shaker Church (1881–present), and the Native American Church (1800–present). Multiple tribal groups gathered for the Kickapoo Prophet, Shaker Church, and Native American Church, while the Delaware Big House Religion and Handsome Lake Church were exclusively tribal in nature.[4] Unlike these social revitalization movements, the ARPM was not concerned directly with reconstituting Indian communities as a solution to poverty or with political marginalization. Rather, ARPM protests were aimed at getting the attention of U.S. officials and agencies to gain access to material resources to alleviate poverty and redress cultural and political repression. Building Indian colleges, creating Indian studies programs, and preserving Indian cultures through federally funded cultural centers and museums were goals that could be achieved while working within U.S. institutions. The ARPM did not require major institutional change within Indian or reservation societies but rather sought fairer treatment, the honoring of treaty obligations, and financial assistance from the federal government.

While the eighteenth and nineteenth centuries were studded with the rise of Indian religious movements, secular Indian movements have characterized much of the twentieth century. Early national Indian reform movements, led by organizations such as the Society of American Indians (SAI), were composed of well-educated Indian professionals who favored assimilation of Indian people into mainstream American society as the solution to the poverty and misery of reservation life. They formed national organizations and were involved in the Indian policy issues of the 1920s and 1930s.[5] Like the ARPM, the SAI worked within the larger U.S. societal framework, but the SAI's assimilationist stance generated much internal debate. The ARPM sought not assimilation but the preservation of Indian identity and culture. The SAI, however, sowed the seed for a national Indian policy and a lobbying force in American politics, which came to fruition with the formation of the National Congress of American Indians (NCAI) in 1944.

In the 1950s, the Six Nations peoples[6] used passive resistance and militant protests to block various New York State projects. For example, the Tuscarora and Mohawk demonstrated in opposition to the building of the Kinzua Dam in upstate New York, which required the displacement of Indians and the flooding of Indian land. Activism began to build in the 1950s, as more than twenty major demonstrations or nonviolent protests were orchestrated by Indian people. These demonstrations were aimed at ending further reductions of the Indian land base, stopping the termination of Indian tribes, and halting brutality and insensitivity toward Indian people. This rise in Indian activism was largely tribal in nature, however; very little, if any, pan-Indian or supratribal activity occurred. The militancy was primarily a phenomenon of traditional people typified by the participation of Elders, medicine people, and entire communities, not the forging of alliances outside tribal boundaries, such as would later occur during the Alcatraz occupation and which characterized the Alcatraz–Red Power Movement.

A major example of tribally based activism was the dispute over state taxes in New York in the late 1950s. In 1957, Wallace "Mad Bear" Anderson, a Tuscarora Indian, helped the Mohawk fend off a New York State income tax on the grounds of Indian sovereignty on Indian reservations. Anderson led a protest group of several hundred Indians from the St. Regis Reservation to the Massena, New York, courthouse, where they tore up summonses for nonpayment of state taxes.[7] In April 1958, Anderson led a stand against land seizures, a move that ultimately brought armed troops onto Indian land. The New York Power Authority, directed by its chairman, Robert Moses, planned to expropriate 1,383 acres of Tuscarora land for the building of a reservoir and the back-flooding of Indian lands. Anderson and others practiced such harassment tactics as standing in the way of surveyors' transits and deflating vehicle tires. When Power Authority workers tapped the Indian leaders' telephones, Tuscaroras switched to speaking in their tribal language. When the Tuscaroras refused to accept the state's offer to purchase the land, one hundred armed state troopers and police invaded Tuscarora lands. They were met by a nonviolent front of 150 men, women, and children, led by Anderson, who blocked the road by lying down or standing in front of government trucks. At the same time, Seneca and Mohawk Indian people set up camps on the disputed land, challenging the state to remove them. Anderson and other leaders were arrested, but the media attention forced the Power Authority to back down. The Federal Power Commission ruled that the Indians did not have to sell the land, and the tribe did not sell. The *Buffalo Courier Express* reported that Mad Bear Anderson, more than anyone else, was responsible for the tribe's decision.[8]

Following the Six Nations' success in New York State, the Miccosukee Indian Nation of Florida summoned Anderson to help fight the federal government's attempt to take tribal land as part of the Everglades Reclamation Project. In 1959, several hundred Indian people marched on BIA headquarters in Washington, D.C., to protest the government policy of termination of Indian tribes, and they attempted a citizen's arrest of the Indian commissioner. In California, Nevada, and Utah, the Pit River Indians, led by Chief Ray Johnson, refused $29.1 million of claims case money awarded by the government and demanded return of their traditional lands. The Pit River Indian people carried on their battle until 1972, at which time they reached a negotiated settlement for partial restoration of land and a monetary payment.

During the 1950s and 1960s, Indian resistance to U.S. policies was galvanized by the common threat of termination of reservation and tribal status. Termination policy sought to detribalize and liquidate Indian land, directly abrogating federal treaties and agreements. The NCAI was joined by organizations such as the Indian Rights Association and the American Friends Services

Committee in their fight against termination. Today, the NCAI, composed of tribal representatives—each with one vote—works within the political system as a national lobbying group for tribal-reservation (but not urban Indian) interests. It presents legislation to Congress, serves as a legislative guardian over Indian issues, and organizes Indian support or opposition to congressional actions. By contrast, the ARPM used social protest rather than established political procedures, and it represented the interests and concerns of urban Indians as well as disfranchised reservation Indians, who often were unfriendly to the established tribal governments and their leaders. These differences in approach created tensions between the more established NCAI and certain ARPM organizations, such as AIM, during the 1960s and 1970s.

The federal government's policy of termination led to interest among Indians in strengthening Indian policy, and numerous Indian rights and protest organizations emerged in the early 1960s, most notably the National Indian Youth Council (NIYC). The NIYC was organized by young college-educated Indians following the American Indian Charter Convention held in Chicago in 1961. They adopted some of the ideas of the civil rights movement and staged numerous fish-ins in the Pacific Northwest, where Washington State was attempting to use state laws to restrict Indian fishing rights guaranteed by federal treaties.[9] The NIYC encouraged greater tribal self-sufficiency and autonomy and was therefore critical of federal and BIA policy. Although the group was active throughout the 1960s, it never got the media attention that the ARPM did in the 1970s, nor did it engage in the same protest tactics.

The rhetoric of Indian self-determination can be traced to the early 1960s, when Melvin Thom, a Paiute Indian from Walker River, Nevada, and the cofounder and president of the NIYC, recognized the need to alleviate the poverty, unemployment, and degrading lifestyles experienced by urban and reservation Indians. Thom realized that it was essential that Indian people, Indian tribes, and Indian sovereign rights not be compromised in the search for solutions to various problems. He said, "Our recognition as Indian people and Indian tribes is very dear to us. We cannot work to destroy our lives as Indian people."[10] He understood that family, tribalism, and sovereignty had sustained Indian people through the many government programs designed to destroy them as a people and to nationalize their traditional lands. The official government policy, dating back to 1953, was termination of the relationship between the federal government and Indian communities, meaning that Indian tribes would eventually lose any special relationships they had under federal law—for example, the tax-exempt status of their lands and federal responsibility for Indian economic and social well-being. In other words, Indian tribes themselves would be effectively destroyed. Thom described the termination policy as a "cold war" that was being fought against Indian people:

> The opposition to Indians is a monstrosity which cannot be beaten by
> any single action, unless we as Indian people could literally rise up, in
> unison, and take what is ours by force. . . . We know the odds are against

us, but we also realize that we are fighting for the lives of future Indian generations. . . . We are convinced, more than ever, that this is a real war. No people in this world ever has been exterminated without putting up a last resistance. The Indians are gathering.[11]

Indian people wanted self-determination rather than termination. This included the right to assume control of their own lives independent of federal control, the creation of conditions for a new era in which the Indian future would be determined by Indian acts and Indian decisions, and the assurance that Indian people would not be separated involuntarily from their tribal groups.

The 1960s witnessed a continuation of localized Indian protest actions such as the brief Indian occupation of Alcatraz Island in 1964. Preceding this event, however, were the fish-ins along the rivers of Washington State. The fish-in movement began when tribal members and their supporters fished in waters protected by federal treaty rights but were restricted by state and local law enforcement. When Isaac Stevens was appointed governor of the new Washington Territory in 1853, he concluded the Medicine Creek (1854) and Point Elliott (1855) treaties, which guaranteed Indian rights to fish both on and off the reservation and to take fish at usual and accustomed grounds and stations. In the mid-1950s, state authorities tried to control Indian fishing in off-reservation areas on the Puyallup River. The Indians protested, arguing that these were "usual and accustomed grounds and stations" within the meaning of the 1854 and 1855 treaties. In 1963, the U.S. Court of Appeals upheld the rights of Indian people to fish in accordance with these treaties. In 1964, in defiance of the Supreme Court decision in United States v. Winons (1905), the state courts in Washington closed the Nisqually River to Indian fishermen in areas off the Nisqually Reservation. In the same year, the Survival of American Indians Association (SAIA) was formed as a protest organization to assert and preserve off-reservation fishing rights. Fish-ins were organized by SAIA and held at Frank's Landing on the Nisqually River. A large number of state and local law enforcement officers raided Frank's Landing in 1965, smashing boats and fishing gear, slashing nets, and attacking Indian people, including women and children. Seven Indians were arrested. Dangerous though they might be, the fish-ins nonetheless provided the Indian youth of Washington with an opportunity to express their disillusionment and dissatisfaction with U.S. society and also to protest actively the social conditions endured by their people. Celebrities such as Marlon Brando lent their names to bring national media coverage of these protest actions. The Indian people who participated in the fish-ins would later provide assistance to the occupiers on Alcatraz Island.

In March 1966, President Lyndon Johnson attempted to quiet the fears of Indian people. In a speech before the Senate, he proposed a "new goal for our Indian programs; a goal that ends the old debate about termination of Indian programs and stresses self-determination; a goal that erases old attitudes of paternalism and promotes partnership and self-help."[12] In October 1966, Senator George McGovern from South Dakota introduced a resolution that highlighted the increased desire of Indian people to be allowed to participate in decisions concerning their development. The frustration resulting from years of BIA paternalism and the new Indian awareness of their powerlessness resulting from years of neglect, poverty, and discrimination had finally attracted the attention of the bureaucracy in Washington, D.C.

In the summer of 1968, United Native Americans (UNA) was founded in the San Francisco Bay Area. Many of the Indian occupiers of Alcatraz Island were, or had been, members of UNA, many more were strongly influenced by the organization. UNA had a pan-Indian focus. It sought to unify all persons of Indian blood throughout the Americas and to develop itself as a democratic, grassroots organization. Its goal was to promote self-determination through Indian control of Indian affairs at every level. Lehman Brightman, a Sioux Indian, was the first president of UNA.

The year 1968 closed with a confrontation between Canada, the United States, and members of the Iroquois League. Canada had been restricting the free movement of Mohawk Indians (members of the Iroquois League) between the United States and Canada, demanding that the Mohawk pay tolls to use the bridge and pay customs on goods brought back from the United States. Members of the Iroquois League felt that this was an infringement of their treaty rights granted by Great Britain, and members of the Mohawk tribe confronted Canadian officials as a means of forcing the issues of tolls and customs collections on the Cornwall International Bridge (the St. Lawrence Seaway International Bridge) between the two countries. The protest was specifically over Canadian failure to honor the Jay Treaty of 1794 between Canada and the United States.[13]

A number of Mohawk Indians were arrested for blockading the Cornwall Bridge on 18 December 1968, but when they pressed for presentation of their case in the court system, the Canadian government dismissed the charges. This protest action was not without precedent. In 1928, the Indian Defense League, founded in 1926, had argued that unrestricted rights for Indians to trade and travel across the U.S.–Canadian border existed based on the Jay Treaty of 1794 and the Treaty of Ghent in 1814. It was not until the 1969 concession, however, that the Canadian government formally recognized these rights, under article 3 of the treaty, and allowed Indians to exchange goods across the border, duty-free, and permitted unrestricted travel between the countries.[14]

The 1968–69 Cornwall Bridge confrontation also brought about the creation of *Akwesasne Notes*, an Indian newspaper, which began as an effort to bring news to Indian people regarding the crisis by reprinting articles from diverse newspapers. Edited by Jerry Gambill, a non-Indian employed by the Canadian Department of Indian Affairs, *Akwesasne Notes* developed into a national Indian newspaper with a circulation of nearly fifty thousand. As a result of coverage in *Akwesasne Notes*, Cornwall Bridge became a prominent discussion topic for Indians across the nation. Later, the Alcatraz occupation would find an Indian media voice in *Akwesasne Notes*.

In addition to his newspaper work, Jerry Gambill assisted Ernest Benedict, a Mohawk Indian, in establishing the North American Indian Traveling College and the White Roots of Peace. The White Roots of Peace harked back to an earlier

Mohawk group, the Akwesasne Counselor Organization, founded by Ray Fadden, a Mohawk Indian, in the mid-1930s. The counselor organization had "traveled far and wide inculcating Indian pride among Mohawk youth . . . hoping to influence a group of young Mohawk to take up leadership roles in the Mohawk Longhouse."[15] This was largely an attempt by Fadden and other Mohawk to preserve and revive Iroquois lifeways. Seeing the spiritual crisis caused by the death of key Elders and noting that many young Indians were moving away from the faith, Benedict and Gambill founded the White Roots of Peace, which was committed to the preservation of tradition by bringing back the Great Binding Law through speaking engagements to Indian and non-Indian communities and school audiences.

As part of this increase in Indian activism in the 1960s, the Taos Pueblo Indians of New Mexico reasserted their claims to ancestral lands. In 1906, the U.S. government had appropriated the Taos Blue Lake area, a sacred site belonging to the Taos Pueblos, and incorporated it into part of the Carson National Forest.[16] In 1926, the tribe, in reply to a compensation offer made by the government, waived the award, seeking return of Blue Lake instead. As a result, they got neither the compensation nor Blue Lake. On 31 May 1933, the Senate Indian Affairs Committee recommended that the Taos Pueblo Indians be issued a permit to use Blue Lake for religious purposes. The permit was finally issued in 1940. On 13 August 1951, the tribe filed a suit before the Indian Claims Commission seeking judicial support for the validity of their title to the lake. On 8 September 1965, the Indian Claims Commission affirmed that the U.S. government had taken the area from its rightful owners. On 15 March 1966, legislation was introduced to return Blue Lake to the Taos Pueblo Indians; however, the bill died without action in the Senate Interior and Insular Affairs Subcommittee. On 10 May 1968, House Bill 3306 was introduced to restore the sacred area to the tribe. Although it was passed unanimously in the House of Representatives, it once again died in the Senate Interior and Insular Affairs Subcommittee.[17]

The return of Taos Blue Lake became the centerpiece of Indian policy for the administration of Richard Nixon, the incoming president. Two other significant events also had a strong effect on Nixon's developing policy of Indian self-determination. First was the receipt of a study of the BIA by Alvin M. Josephy, Jr., entitled *The American Indian and the Bureau of Indian Affairs, 1969.*[18] In his report, completed on 24 February 1969, Josephy chastised the federal government for its ineptitude in the handling of Indian affairs. Specifically, he condemned the failure of various presidents to effect any change in the multilayered, bureaucratically inept BIA, the failure of the government's Indian education policy, and the high rates of unemployment, disease, and death on Indian reservations. Second was the publication in 1969 of Edgar S. Cahn's *Our Brother's Keeper: The Indian in White America*, a study of the ineptitude of the BIA and an indictment of the BIA for its failure to carry out its responsibilities to the American Indian people.[19] Cahn high-lighted the numerous studies of Indian people, all except one conducted by non-Indians, and stated that "recommendations have come to have a special non-meaning for Indians. They are part of a tradition in which policy and programs are dictated by non-Indians, even when dialogue and consultation have been promised."[20]

Other movements, such as the Alaska Native Claims Movement of 1960–71, raged on. This particular movement consisted of regional coalitions of over two hundred Alaska Native villages joined in a statewide land claims protest. A large land claims settlement was finally negotiated in 1971 whereby the Alaska Natives retained 44 million acres of land and received $962 million and other benefits.[21] The Alaska Native Claims Settlement Act (ANCSA) of 1971 became a model for many struggling indigenous movements around the world.

Indian protests for assertion of treaty-based fishing rights continued throughout the 1960s and early 1970s and were often associated with arrests and violence. In a 1970 protest over treaty fishing rights at Frank's Landing in Washington State, sixty Indians were arrested. SAIA members, led by Janet McCloud, a Tulalip Indian, gathered in Seattle and marched in protest at the federal courthouse. In January 1971, Hank Adams, a former member of NIYC and now a member of SALA who had participated in a decade of fish-ins, was shot in the stomach by two white sport fishermen as he slept in his pick-up truck. Adams had been tending a set of fish nets for a friend on the Puyallup River. He survived the shooting, but the police, who sympathized with the non-Indian sport fishermen, disputed his account of the incident and did not search for his attackers. In February 1974, a federal judge, George Boldt, ruled in *United States* v. *Washington* to uphold the treaty rights of the Indian people to fish at their usual and accustomed grounds and stations off reservation and "in common with" other citizens.[22]

Self-determination formed the logic for much tribally based litigation, lobbying, and protest action. The outlines of the Indian self-determination policy were formed during the late 1960s, when Zuni Pueblo took advantage of a little-known law to contract BIA services. The Zuni wanted to minimize BIA interference in their community, preferring to manage their own affairs. The success of the Zuni contracting of BIA programs came to the attention of Nixon administration officials, and the new self-determination policy announced in 1970 was based on contracting of federal and BIA services directly to tribal governments. However, the contracting mechanisms for enabling tribal governments to take advantage of the self-determination policy were not worked out until passage of the Indian Self-Determination and Education Act of 1975. Nevertheless, the new policy of self-determination was designed to give Indian people greater control over their communities, tribal governments, and reservation institutions, all of which had been managed by BIA officials since late in the nineteenth century. Although ultimately the effects of the self-determination policy were limited, most Indian communities strongly favored the new policy.

By the late 1960s and early 1970s, Native Americans thus had a rich and long legacy of social movements. Most were tribally centered around treaty or land issues. Others were multitribal, led by groups such as the NCAI and composed of loose coalitions of tribal groups or members allied temporarily to struggle against a common external threat, such as termination. Most Indian social movements revolved around issues of injustice, deprivation, or suppression, something they shared with the Alcatraz–Red Power Movement. The fact that the ARPM relied on a history of past incidents to inform and organize its members and leadership also was not unusual. The ARPM drew selectively on many elements of Indian history, especially symbols of resistance. Geronimo, the Apache leader who fought against U.S. control over reservation communities in the 1880s, was one such symbol for the Alcatraz Island occupiers. Custer's defeat in 1876 was used to symbolize Indian victory and defiance, and the Wounded Knee Massacre in 1890 became a major symbol of Indian repression during the Wounded Knee seizure in 1973.

The ARPM was very different from earlier and contemporary Indian social movements. Its members sought change and inclusion in U.S. institutions while preferring to retain Indian cultural identity. This was a form of nonassimilative inclusion that was not well understood at the time but later helped form the contemporary vision of a multicultural society. The defining characteristics of the ARPM were its emphasis on a supratribal identity and the tactic of property seizure, which was used only sparingly by other Indian social movements. Since most Indian people were repressed and marginalized throughout the 1960s, there was much activism, but nothing of the scale or significance of the Alcatraz–Red Power Movement in terms of tactics, new identity formation, visibility in U.S. society, and bringing attention to Indian issues. So we must look to other issues beyond the legacy of Indian social movements for explaining the rise of the ARPM, its goals, pattern of organization, and tactics, as well as its legacy.

CHANGE AND PROTEST IN AMERICAN SOCIETY

The occupation of Alcatraz Island occurred at the height of considerable urban unrest in the United States. To understand both the causes of the occupation and its consequences for American Indian activism, individual ethnic consciousness, and Native American community survival, it is important to recall the atmosphere of the 1960s and the changes underway in U.S. social and political life at the time.

The United States was deeply involved in an unpopular war in Vietnam. The new feminism was stirring, and the civil rights movement, Black Power, LaRaza, the Latino movement, the New Left, and Third World strikes were sweeping the nation, particularly its college campuses. While U.S. armed forces were involved in the clandestine invasion and bombing of Cambodia, the 1969 announcement of the massacre of innocent civilians in a hamlet in My Lai, Vietnam, burned across the front pages of American newspapers.[23] Ubiquitous campus demonstrations raised the level of consciousness of college students. People of all ages were becoming sensitized to the unrest among emerging minority and gender groups who were staging demonstrations and proclaiming their points of view, many of which were incorporated by student activists. Sit-ins, sleep-ins, teach-ins, lock-outs, and boycotts became everyday occurrences.

The occupation of Alcatraz Island was part of the much larger movement for social change, which had its roots in the 1950s and 1960s and was now being promoted by people of many colors, genders, and ages. The 1960s witnessed a marked upsurge in political awareness and activity sparked by events in the national arena such as the civil rights movement. The Student Non-Violent Coordinating Committee (SNCC), founded in April 1960, was made up of black-led, nonviolent sit-in activists. It combined with Students for a Democratic Society (SDS), founded in 1962, to form what came to be called the "New Left." Young black Americans were hearing an angrier and more militant voice, a voice coming from former members of SNCC and participants in the civil rights movement. Between 1964 and 1967, more than a hundred major riots and scores of minor disruptions occurred in cities across the country. By the end of 1968, racial upheavals had resulted in more than two hundred deaths and property destruction valued at approximately $800 million. It was during this time that the Black Panther Party (BPP) was born.[24]

The activist movements of the 1960s were marked by a variety of racial, class, and gender groups: young college students were joined by Vietnam veterans, gay rights activists, women's liberation activists, urban American Indian people, Mexican American farm workers, and members of LaRaza, the newly emerging Chicano/Chicana empowerment movement. These disparate groups came together in an era marked by dynamic personal change, cultural awareness, and political confrontation. Meanwhile, many Indian activists observed the civil rights movements and contemplated how this activity could be brought to bear on Indian issues.[25]

The Vietnam War came to be defined in the minds of many Indian men and women as a war fought to defend a freedom that they themselves had never experienced. While Indian people may have been the forgotten Americans in the minds of many politicians and bureaucrats during peacetime, this was not the case in time of war or national emergency. American Indians were required to serve and did so honorably: 1,000 in World War I; 44,500 in World War II; and 29,700 during the Korean conflict. The Vietnam War proved no exception, with a total of 61,100 Indians serving during this era.[26] Beginning with the commitment of troops to Vietnam in 1963, Indians either volunteered or were drafted into military service for this undeclared war against a people some Indian servicemen considered to be as much of an oppressed minority as American Indians themselves were. Mad Bear Anderson, the Tuscarora activist, visited Vietnam seven times and stated, "When I walk down the streets of Saigon those people look like my brothers and sisters."[27] Robert Thomas, a Cherokee anthropologist, commented that Indian people understood the war in Vietnam better than his university colleagues did: "The conflict in Vietnam was tribal in origin, and the Vietnamese were tired of the war machine flattening their crops."[28]

American Indians coming back from Vietnam faced difficult choices. Those who returned, or attempted to return, to life on the reservation found high unemployment rates, poor health facilities, and substandard housing conditions—as did Indian veterans coming back from World War II service. Those who elected to relocate or settle in urban areas encountered what can best be described as "double discrimination." First, they were faced with the continuing discrimination against Indian people that resulted in high unemployment, police brutality, and, very often, alcoholism and death. Second, they experienced the discrimination felt by other Vietnam veterans viewed as participants in an unpopular war; rather than being hailed as heroes or shown some measure of respect for their sacrifices, they were considered third-rate citizens and treated as outcasts. In an attempt to retreat for a period of time, to adjust to a changing society, or perhaps simply to acquire skills for future employment, many of the returning Indian veterans utilized their GI bill educational benefits and enrolled in colleges in the San Francisco Bay Area. Indian students from these colleges, many of them Vietnam veterans, filled the ranks of the rising Indian activism movement now emerging as Red Power.

ORGANIZATION AND PROTEST IN THE URBAN ENVIRONMENT

In 1990, more than 50 percent of American Indians lived in cities. This trend toward urbanization began during World War II as a result of wartime industrial job opportunities, federal policies of relocation (in tandem with the termination of tribal rights and the forced assimilation of Indians into non-Indian society), and the urbanization of the U.S. population as a whole. Many Native Americans migrated to the Bay Area during this time to work in defense industries; thousands of others were relocated there by the federal government. In the Bay Area, which was one of the largest of more than a dozen relocation sites, the newly urban Indians formed their own organizations to provide the support that the government had promised but had failed to deliver. While some groups were known by tribal names such as the Sioux Club and the Navajo Club, there were also a variety of intertribal organizations, including sports clubs, dance clubs, and the very early urban powwow clubs. Eventually, some thirty Bay Area social clubs were formed to meet the needs of the urban Indians and their children— children who would, in the 1960s, want the opportunity to go to college and better themselves.[29]

Many of these organizationally connected urban Indians were dissatisfied with conditions in the cities and on reservation homelands—specifically, with the lack of self-determination in both communities and with federal policies concerning Indian affairs. They represented a population that was poised on the brink of activism: disillusioned Indian youth from reservations, urban centers, and universities who called for Red Power in their crusade to reform the conditions of their people. Native American scholar Vine Deloria, Jr., in *Behind the Trail of Broken Treaties*, states: "The power movements which had sprung up after 1966 now began to affect Indians, and the center of action was the urban areas on the West Coast, where there was a large Indian population."[30]

These Red Power groups strongly advocated a policy of Indian self-determination, with the NIYC in particular emphasizing the psychological impact of powerlessness on Indian youth. This powerlessness and lack of self-determination was explained by Clyde Warrior, a Ponca Indian and cofounder of NIYC, when he told government officials in Washington, D.C., in 1967: "We are not allowed to make those basic human choices and decisions about our personal life and about the destiny of our communities which is the mark of free mature people. We sit on our front porch or in our yards, and the world and our lives in it pass us by without our desires or aspirations having any effect."[31] An article in *Warpath*, the first militant, pan-Indian newspaper in the United States, established in 1968 by UNA, summed up the attitude of the Bay Area Indian community:

> The "Stoic, Silent Redman" of the past who turned the other cheek to white injustice is dead. (He died of frustration and heartbreak.) And in his place is an angry group of Indians who dare to speak up and voice their dissatisfaction at the world around them. Hate and despair have taken their toll and only action can quiet this smoldering anger that has fused this new Indian movement into being.[32]

On 11 April 1969, the National Council on Indian Opportunity (NCIO), established by President Lyndon Johnson by Executive Order 11399, conducted a public forum in San Francisco before the Committee on Urban Indians. The purpose of the forum was to gain as much information as possible on the condition of Indian people living in the area so as to help find solutions to their problems and ease the tensions that were rising among young urban Indians. The hearings began with a scathing rebuke by the Reverend Tony Calaman, founder of Freedom for Adoptive Children. Reverend Calaman attacked the San Francisco Police Department, the California Department of Social Welfare, and the Indian child placement system, stating that the non-Indian system emasculated Indian people. When asked to explain, he said: "it is a dirty, rotten, stinkin' term [emasculation], and the social workers are doing it and the police officers are doing it when they club you on the head. It is a racist institution, just pure racism—and you all know what racism is, and you all know what racists are. Look in the mirror, and you will see a racist."[33]

Earl Livermore, director of the San Francisco American Indian Center, appeared next and concentrated his testimony on problems Indian people face in adjusting to urban living, particularly Indian students faced with unfavorable conditions in the public school system. Those conditions ranged from lack of understanding by school officials to false or misleading statements in school textbooks. Livermore pointed out that many of the textbooks in use damaged the Indian child's sense of identity and personal worth. His testimony also addressed urban Indian health problems, which often were the result of Indian people not being properly oriented to urban living and the frustration and depression that often followed. Lack of education, according to Livermore, resulted in unemployment, which in turn led to depression, which led Indian people deeper into the depths of despair. Alcoholism, poor nutrition, and inadequate housing were also highlighted as major problems.[34]

A total of thirty-seven Indian people took advantage of the opportunity to appear at the public forum to highlight the problems and frustrations felt by urban American Indians. Twenty-five of them would be among the occupiers of Alcatraz Island seven months later. Dennis Turner, a Luiseño Indian, testified before the committee about his personal frustrations resulting from the relocation program and about the inadequacy of the educational system to meet Indian needs. He also highlighted problems of inadequate housing and lack of counselors for Indian people newly relocated to the urban areas. More directly, Turner addressed the problem of governmental agencies such as the NCIO conducting hearings and making promises, and the frustration of seeing no change as a result of hearings such as the one before which he was presently testifying. Addressing LaDonna Harris, a Comanche Indian and chairperson of the Committee on Urban Indians, Turner stated: "After it's [the hearing] over with, you're going to wonder what is going to happen? Is something going to come off or not? The Indian is still hoping. If he keeps on hoping, he's going to die of frustration."[35]

In response to a press query, "Are you going to have some militant Indians?" Harris replied, "Heavens, I hope we will."[36] Her statement was, in fact, a look into the future, to plans not yet formalized but soon to capture the attention of Americans throughout the nation and to be played out as a nineteen-month drama on Alcatraz Island. But her premonition was not without precedent. In a 1969 meeting at the San Francisco Indian Center, Richard McKenzie, a Sioux Indian who was one of the members of a shortlived 1964 Alcatraz occupation party, recognized the uniqueness of the Indian situation as opposed to the civil rights movement. He said, "Kneel-Ins, Sit-Ins, Sleep- Ins, Eat-Ins, Pray-Ins like the Negroes do, wouldn't help us. We would have to occupy the government buildings before things would change."[37]

The rise of Indian activism was also prophesied by Walter Wetzel, the leader of the Blackfeet of Montana and former president of the National Congress of American Indians: "We Indians have been struggling unsuccessfully with the problems of maintaining home and family and Indian ownership of the land. We must strike."[38] Mad Bear Anderson, who had turned back the bulldozers when a dam was planned on Iroquois land, declared: "Our people were murdered in this country. And they are still being murdered. . . . There is an Indian nationalist movement in the country. I am one of the founders. We are not going to pull any punches from here on in."[39]

President Nixon's self-determination policy would be tested in California, particularly the Bay Area, which had become the hotbed for the newly developing Indian activism. Jack Forbes, a Powhatan/Lenape Indian and professor of Native American studies and anthropology at the University of California, Davis, became an advisor and mentor to many of the new Indian students. In the spring of 1969, Forbes drafted a proposal for a College of Native American Studies on one of the California campuses. American Indian or Native American studies programs were already being formed, for example, at UC Berkeley, UCLA, and San Francisco State College. These programs grew out of the Third World strikes in progress on the various campuses and included Indian students who would soon be intimately involved in the Alcatraz occupation: Richard Oakes, Ross Harden, Joe Bill, Dennis Turner, LaNada Boyer, and Horace Spencer.[40]

On 30 June 1969, the California legislature endorsed Forbes's proposal for the creation of a separate Indian-controlled university. Forbes wrote to John G. Veneman, assistant secretary of Health, Education, and Welfare, and requested that Veneman look into the availability of a 650-acre site between Winter, California, and Davis. Additionally, in 1969, the Native American Student Union (NASU) was formed in California, bringing together a new pan-Indian alliance between the emerging Native American studies programs on the various campuses. In San Francisco, members of NASU prepared to test President Nixon's commitment to his stated policy of self-determination before a national audience by occupying Alcatraz Island. For Indian people of the Bay Area, the social movements of the 1960s not only had come to full maturity but would now include Indian people. In November 1969, American Indians moved onto the national scene of ethnic unrest as active participants in a war of their own. Alcatraz Island was the battlefield.[41]

THE ALCATRAZ OCCUPATIONS

In actuality, there were three separate occupations of Alcatraz Island.[42] The first was a brief, four-hour occupation on 9 March 1964 by five Sioux Indians representing the urban Indians of the Bay Area. The event was planned by Belva Cottier, the wife of one of the occupiers. The federal penitentiary on the island had been closed in 1963, and the government was in the process of transferring the island to the city of San Francisco for development purposes. But Belva Cottier and her Sioux cousin had plans of their own. They recalled having heard of a provision in the 1868 Sioux treaty with the federal government that stated that ownership of all abandoned federal lands that once belonged to the Sioux reverted to the Sioux people.[43] Using this interpretation of the treaty, they encouraged five Sioux men to occupy Alcatraz Island and issued press releases claiming the island in accordance with the treaty and demanding better treatment for urban Indians. Richard McKenzie, the most outspoken of the group, pressed the claim for title to the island through the court system, only to have the courts rule against him. More important, however, the Indians of the Bay Area were becoming vocal and united in their efforts to improve their lives.

The 1964 occupation of Alcatraz Island foreshadowed the unrest that was fomenting, quietly but surely, among the urban Indian population. Prior to the occupation, Bay Area newspapers contained a large number of articles about the federal government's abandonment of the urban Indian and the refusal of state and local governments to meet Indian people's needs. The Indian social clubs that had been formed for support became meeting places at which to discuss discrimination in schools, housing, employment, and health care. Indian people also talked about the police, who, like law officers in other areas of the country, would wait outside Indian bars at closing time to harass, beat up, and arrest Indian patrons. Indian centers began to appear in all the urban relocation areas and became nesting grounds for new pan-Indian, and eventually activist, organizations.[44]

The second Alcatraz occupation had its beginning on Bay Area and other California college and university campuses when young, educated Indian students joined with other minority groups during the 1969 Third World Liberation Front Strike and began demanding courses relevant to Indian students. Indian history written and taught by non-Indian instructors was no longer acceptable to these students, awakened as they were to the possibility of social protest to bring attention to the shameful treatment of Indian people. Anthropologist Luis S. Kemnitzer has described the establishment of the country's first Native American Studies Program at San Francisco State College in 1969—the spring before the occupation. The students involved in this program went on to plan the Alcatraz occupation:

> . . . a non-Indian graduate student in social science at San Francisco State who was tutoring young Indian children in the Mission District came to know a group of young Indians who . . . all had some contact with college and had come to San Francisco either on vocational training, relocation, or on their own. . . . Conversation with the student tutor led them to become interested in the strike and in exploring the possibility of working toward a Native American studies department. . . .
>
> [T]he university and the Third World Liberation Front had started negotiations, and there was limited room for movement. . . . [LaRaza] agreed to represent the Indians in negotiations, and there was close collaboration between representatives of LaRaza and the future Native American studies students. I was one of the faculty members on strike, and, although I was not involved in the negotiations with the university administration, I was informally recruited by other striking faculty to help plan and negotiate with LaRaza.[45]

Richard Oakes was one of the students in the program. He came from the St. Regis Reservation, had worked on high steel in New York, and had traveled across the United States, visiting various Indian reservations. He eventually wound up in California, where he married a Kashia Pomo woman, Anne Marufo, who had five children from a previous marriage. Oakes worked in an Indian bar in Oakland for a period of time and eventually was admitted to San Francisco State College. In September 1969, he and several other Indian students began discussing the possibility of occupying Alcatraz Island as a symbolic protest, a call for Indian self-determination. Preliminary plans were made for the summer of 1970, but other events led to an earlier takeover. During the fall term, Oakes and his fellow Indian students and friends caught the attention of a nation already engrossed in the escalating protest and conflict of the civil rights movement as they set out across the San Francisco Bay for Alcatraz Island.[46]

The catalyst for the occupation was the destruction of the San Francisco Indian Center by fire in late October 1969. The center had become the meeting place for the Bay Area Indian organizations and the newly formed United Bay Area Indian Council, which had brought the thirty private clubs together into one large council headed by Adam Nordwall (later to be known as Adam Fortunate Eagle). The destruction of the center united the council and the American Indian student organizations as never before. The council needed a new meeting place, and the students needed a forum for their new activist voice. The date for the second occupation of Alcatraz Island was thus moved up to 9 November 1969. Oakes and the other students, along with a group of people from the San Francisco Indian Center, chartered a boat and headed for Alcatraz Island. Since many different tribes were represented, the occupiers called themselves Indians of All Tribes.[47]

The initial plan was to circle the island and symbolically claim it for all Indian people. During the circling maneuver, however, Oakes and four others jumped from the boat and swam to the island. They claimed Alcatraz in the name of Indians of All Tribes and then left the island at the request of the caretaker. Later that evening, Oakes and fourteen others returned to the island with sleeping bags and food sufficient for two or three days but left the next morning, again without incident, when asked to do so.[48]

In meetings following the 9 November occupation, Oakes and his fellow students realized that a prolonged occupation was possible. It was clear that the federal government had only a token force on the island and that so far no physical harm had come to anyone involved. A new plan began to emerge. Oakes traveled to UCLA, where he met with Ray Spang and Edward Castillo and asked for their assistance in recruiting Indian students for what would become the longest Indian occupation of any federal facility. Spang, Castillo, and Oakes met in UCLA's Campbell Hall, now the home of the American Indian Studies Center and the editorial offices of the *American Indian Culture and Research Journal*, in private homes, and in Indian bars in Los Angeles. When the third takeover of Alcatraz Island began, seventy of the eighty-nine Indian occupiers were students from UCLA .[49]

In the early morning hours of 20 November 1969, eighty-nine American Indians landed on Alcatraz Island in San Francisco Bay. These Indians of All Tribes claimed the island by "right of discovery" and by the terms of the 1868 Treaty of Fort Laramie, which gave Indians the right to unused federal property that had previously been Indian land. Except for a small caretaker staff, the island had been abandoned by the federal government since 1963, when the federal penitentiary was closed. In a press statement, Indians of All Tribes set the tone of the occupation and the agenda for negotiations during the next nineteen months:

> We, the native Americans, reclaim the land known as Alcatraz Island in the name of all American Indians. . . . [W]e plan to develop on this island several Indian institutions: 1. A CENTER FOR NATIVE AMERICAN STUDIES . . . 2. AN AMERICAN INDIAN SPIRITUAL CENTER . . . 3. AN INDIAN CENTER OF ECOLOGY . . . 4. A GREAT INDIAN TRAINING SCHOOL . . . [and] an AMERICAN INDIAN MUSEUM . . . In the name of all Indians, therefore, we reclaim this island for our Indian nations. . . . We feel this claim is just and proper, and that this land should rightfully be granted to us for as long as the rivers shall run and the sun shall shine. Signed, INDIANS OF ALL TRIBES.[50]

The occupiers quickly set about organizing themselves. An elected council was put into place, and everyone was assigned a job: security, sanitation, day-care, housing, cooking, laundry. All decisions were made by unanimous consent of the people. Sometimes meetings were held five, six, or seven times per day to discuss the rapidly developing events. It is important to remember that, while the urban Indian population supported the concept of an occupation and provided the logistical support, the Alcatraz occupation force itself was made up initially of young, urban Indian students from UCLA, UC Santa Cruz, San Francisco State College, and UC Berkeley.[51]

The most inspiring person, if not the recognized leader, was Richard Oakes, described as handsome, charismatic, a talented orator, and a natural leader. The casting of Oakes as the person in charge, a title he himself never claimed, quickly created a problem. Not all the students knew Oakes, and, in keeping with the concepts underlying the occupation, many wanted an egalitarian society on the island, with no one as their leader. Although this may have been a workable form of organization on the island, it was not comprehensible to the non-Indian media. Newspapers, magazines, and television and radio stations across the nation sent reporters to the island to interview the people in charge. They wanted to know who the leaders were. Oakes was the most knowledgeable about the landing and the most often sought out, and he was therefore identified as the leader, the "chief," the "mayor of Alcatraz." He was strongly influenced by the White Roots of Peace, which had been revitalized by Ray Fadden, and Mad Bear Anderson. Before the Alcatraz occupation, in the autumn of 1969, Jerry Gambill, a counselor for the White Roots of Peace, had visited the campus of San Francisco State and inspired many of the students, none more than Oakes.[52]

By the end of 1969, the Indian organization on the island began to change, and two Indian groups rose in opposition to Oakes. When many of the Native American students left the island to return to school, they were replaced by Indian people from urban areas and reservations who had not been involved in the initial planning. Where Oakes and the other students claimed title to the island by right of discovery, the new arrivals harked back to the rhetoric of the 1964 occupation and the Sioux treaty, a claim that had been pressed through the court system by Richard McKenzie and had been found invalid. Additionally, some non-Indians took up residence on the island, many of them from the San Francisco hippie and drug culture. Drugs and liquor had been banned from the island by the original occupiers, but they now became commonplace.[53]

The final blow to the nascent student occupation occurred on 5 January 1970 when Oakes's thirteen-year-old stepdaughter, Yvonne, who was apparently playing unsupervised with some other children, slipped and fell three floors to her death down an open stairwell. The Oakes family left the island, and the two groups began maneuvering for leadership roles. Despite these changes, the demands of the occupiers remained consistent: title to Alcatraz Island, the development of an Indian university, and the construction of a museum and cultural center that would display for and teach non-Indian society the valuable contributions of Indian people.[54]

In the months that followed, thousands of protesters and visitors spent time on Alcatraz Island. They came from a large number of Indian tribes, including the Sioux, Navajo, Cherokee, Mohawk, Puyallup, Yakima, Hoopa, and Omaha. The months of occupation were marked by proclamations, news conferences, powwows, celebrations, "assaults" with arrows on passing vessels, and negotiations with federal officials. In the beginning months, workers from the San Francisco Indian Center gathered food and supplies on the mainland and transported them to Alcatraz. However, as time went by, the occupying force, which fluctuated but generally numbered around one hundred, confronted increasing hardships as federal officials interfered with delivery boats and cut off the supply of water and electricity to the island. Tensions on the island grew.[55]

The federal government, for its part, insisted that the Indian people leave, and it placed an ineffective Coast Guard barricade around the island. Eventually, the government agreed to the Indian council's demands for formal negotiations. But, from the Indian people's side, the demands were nonnegotiable. They wanted the deed to the island; they wanted to establish an Indian university, a cultural center, and a museum; and they wanted the necessary federal funding to meet their goals. Negotiations collapsed for good when the government turned down these demands and insisted that the Indians of All Tribes leave the island. Alcatraz Island would never be developed in accordance with the goals of the Indian protesters.[56]

In time, the attention of the federal government shifted from negotiations with the island occupants to restoration of navigational aids that had been discontinued as the result of a fire that shut down the Alcatraz lighthouse. The government's inability to restore these navigational aids brought criticism from the Coast Guard, the Bay Area Pilot's Association, and local newspapers. The federal government became impatient, and on 11 June 1971, the message went out to end the occupation of Alcatraz Island. The dozen or so remaining protesters were removed by federal marshals, more than a year and a half after the island was first occupied.[57] Some members of Indians of All Tribes moved their protest to an abandoned Nike missile base in the Beverly Hills, overlooking San Francisco Bay. While that occupation lasted only three days, it set in motion a pattern of similar occupations over the next several years.

The events that took place on Alcatraz Island represented a watershed moment in Native American protest and caught the attention of the entire country, providing a forum for airing long-standing Indian grievances and for expressing Indian pride. Vine Deloria noted the importance of Alcatraz, referring to the occupation as a "master stroke of Indian activism." He also recognized the impact of Alcatraz and other occupations on Indian ethnic self-awareness and identity: "Indian[n]ess was judged on whether or not one was present at Alcatraz, Fort Lawson, Mt. Rushmore, Detroit, Sheep Mountain, Plymouth Rock, or Pitt River. . . . The activists controlled the language, the issues, and the attention."[58] In 1993, Deloria reflected on the longer-term impact of the Red Power movement:

> This era will probably always be dominated by the images and slogans of
> the AIM people. The real accomplishments in land restoration, however,

were made by quiet determined tribal leaders. . . . In reviewing the period we should understand the frenzy of the time and link it to the definite accomplishments made by tribal governments.[59]

The Alcatraz occupation and the activism that followed offer firm evidence to counter commonly held views of Indians as powerless in the face of history, as weakened remnants of disappearing cultures and communities. Countless events fueled American Indian ethnic pride and strengthened Indian people's sense of personal empowerment and community membership. Wilma Mankiller, now principal chief of the Cherokee Nation of Oklahoma, visited Alcatraz many times during the months of occupation. She described it as an awakening that "ultimately changed the course of my life."[60] This was a recurrent theme in our interviews with Native Americans who participated in or observed the protests of that period:

GEORGE HORSE CAPTURE: In World War II, the marines were island-hopping; they'd do the groundwork, and then the army and the civilians would come in and build things. Without the first wave, nothing would happen. Alcatraz and the militants were like that. They put themselves at risk, could be arrested or killed. You have to give them their due. We were in the second wave. In the regular Indian world, we're very complacent; it takes leadership to get things moving. But scratch a real Indian since then, and you're going to find a militant. Alcatraz tapped into something. It was the lance that burst the boil.[61]

JOHN ECHOHAWK: Alcatraz just seemed to be kind of another event—what a lot of people had been thinking, wanting to do. We were studying Indian law for the first time. We had a lot of frustration and anger. People were fed up with the status quo. That's just what we were thinking. Starting in 1967 at the University of New Mexico Law School, we read treaties, Indian legal history. It was just astounding how unfair it was, how wrong it was. It [Alcatraz] was the kind of thing we needed.[62]

LEONARD PELTIER: I was in Seattle when Alcatraz happened. It was the first event that received such publicity. In Seattle, we were in solidarity with the demands of Alcatraz. We were inspired and encouraged by Alcatraz. I realized their goals were mine. The Indian organizations I was working with shared the same needs: an Indian college to keep students from dropping out, a cultural center to keep Indian traditions. We were all really encouraged, not only those who were active, but those who were not active as well.[63]

FRANCES WISE: The Alcatraz takeover had an enormous impact. I was living in Waco, Texas, at the time. I would see little blurbs on TV. I thought, These Indians are really doing something at Alcatraz. . . . And when they called for the land back, I realized that, finally, what Indian people have gone through is finally being recognized. . . . It affected how I think of myself. If someone asks me who I am, I say, well, I have a name, but Waco/Caddo—that's who I am. I have a good feeling about who I am now. And you need this in the presence of all this negative stuff, for example, celebrating the Oklahoma Land Run.[64]

ROSALIE McKAY-WANT: In the final analysis, however, the occupation of this small territory could be considered a victory for the cause of Indian activism and one of the most noteworthy expressions of patriotism and self-determination by Indian people in the twentieth century.[65]

GRACE THORPE: Alcatraz was the catalyst and the most important event in the Indian movement to date. It made me put my furniture into storage and spend my life savings.[66]

These voices speak to the central importance of the Alcatraz occupation as the symbol of long-standing Indian grievances and increasing impatience with a political system slow to respond to native rights. They also express the feelings of empowerment that witnessing and participating in protest can foster. Loretta Flores, an Indian woman, did not become an activist herself until several years after the events on Alcatraz, but she has eloquently described the sense of self and community that activism can produce:

The night before the protest, I was talking to a younger person who had never been in a march before. I told her, 'Tomorrow when we get through with this march, you're going to have a feeling like you've never had before. It's going to change your life.' Those kids from Haskell (Indian Nations University) will never forget this. The spirits of our ancestors were looking down on us smiling.[67]

THE ALCATRAZ–RED POWER MOVEMENT: A NINE-YEAR ODYSSEY

The success or failure of the Indian occupation of Alcatraz Island should not be judged by whether the demands for title to the island and the establishment of educational and cultural institutions were realized. If one were to make such a judgment, the only possible conclusion would be that the occupation was a failure. Such is not the case, however. The underlying goals of the Indians on Alcatraz were to awaken the American public to the reality of their situation and to assert the need for Indian self-determination. In this they succeeded. Additionally, the occupation of Alcatraz Island was a springboard for Indian activism, inspiring the large number of takeovers and demonstrations that began shortly after the 20 November 1969 landing and continued into the late 1970s. These included the Trail of Broken Treaties, the BIA headquarters takeover in 1972, and Wounded Knee II in 1973.

304 / Troy Johnson, Duane Champagne, and Joane Nagel

Many of the approximately seventy-four occupations that followed Alcatraz were either planned by or included people who had been involved in the Alcatraz occupation or who certainly had gained their strength from the new "Indianness" that grew out of that movement. For example, on 3 November 1970, in Davis, California,

> scores of Indians scaled a barbed wire fence and seized an old Army communications center . . . unimpeded by four soldiers whose job it was to guard the facility. Raising a big white tepee on the surplus Government property, 75 Indians occupied it for use in development of an Indian cultural center. Several veterans of the successful Indian invasion of Alcatraz Island a year ago took part in [the] assault.[68]

Most occupations were short lived, lasting only a few days or weeks, such as those that occurred during 1970–71 at Fort Lawton and Fort Lewis in Washington, at Ellis Island in New York, at the Twin Cities Naval Air Station in Minneapolis, at former Nike missile sites on Lake Michigan near Chicago and at Argonne, Illinois, and at an abandoned Coast Guard lifeboat station in Milwaukee.

A number of protest camps were established during the early 1970s, including those at Mount Rushmore and the Badlands National Monument. During the same years, government buildings also became the sites of protests, including regional Bureau of Indian Affairs offices in Cleveland and Denver, as well as the main headquarters in Washington, D.C. Many of these occupations took on a festive air as celebrations of Indian culture and ethnic renewal, while others represented efforts to provide educational or social services to urban Indians. The September 1971 attempted "invasion" of BIA headquarters was described as follows:

> A band of militant young Indians sought to make a citizens' arrest of a Federal official today and wound up in a noisy clash with Government guards at the Bureau of Indian Affairs. . . . [T]hey sought a conference with bureau officials on their contention that Indians were being denied basic rights. Some of the Indians . . . barricaded themselves in two rooms of the public information office on the first floor and others occupied Mr. Crow's [deputy commissioner of Indian affairs) office on the second floor. . . . The invasion of the bureau was directed by the American Indian Movement and the National Indian Youth Council.[69]

As Indian activism in the 1970s progressed, some events were characterized by a more serious, sometimes violent tone, revealing the depth of grievances and difficulty of solutions to the problems confronting Native Americans after nearly five centuries of Euro-American contact. An example was the November 1972 week-long occupation of BIA headquarters. This unplanned takeover occurred at the end of the Trail of Broken Treaties, a protest event involving caravans that traveled across the United States to convene in Washington, D.C., the purpose being to dramatize and present Indian concerns at a national level. The inability of an advance party to secure accommodations in private homes and churches for several hundred exhausted Indians led to the occupation of BIA offices. Angry participants, many of whom mistakenly thought the federal government had agreed to provide housing and then reneged, literally destroyed the inside of BIA headquarters. They barricaded the doors with furniture and office equipment, soaking each pile with gasoline so it could be quickly ignited in the event of forced removal. They smashed plumbing fixtures and windows, covered the walls with graffiti, and gathered up BIA files and Indian artifacts to take back to their reservations. The protest ended a week later after a series of negotiations with federal officials. Damage to the building was estimated at $2.2 million.

During this period, the ARPM protest strategy began to shift from Alcatraz-style takeovers to different forms and terrains of contention linked to the organizational underpinning of supratribal collective action and its urban population base. Researchers and journalists generally reported that participants in activist events in 1970 and 1971 were Indians of varied tribal backgrounds who mainly lived in urban areas and were associated with the NIYC or some other supratribal organization—or else with AIM, the primary organization of the Red Power movement.[70] Before Alcatraz, AIM was essentially an Indian rights organization concerned with monitoring law enforcement treatment of Native people in American cities. However, the occupation of Alcatraz captured the imagination of AIM as well as the rest of the country, and as a result, AIM embarked on a historic journey into Indian protest activism.[71]

The American Indian Movement, founded in Minneapolis in 1968, quickly established chapters in several U.S. cities. AIM's membership was drawn mostly from urban Indian communities, and its leadership and membership both tended to come from the ranks of younger, more progressive and better educated urban Indians.[72] Although not involved in the initial takeover of Alcatraz Island, AIM played an important role in the spread of supratribal protest action during the 1970s and in shaping the Red Power agenda, tactics, and strategies for drawing attention to Indian people's grievances. Ward Churchill and James Vander Wall have noted that

> the 19-month occupation [of Alcatraz] . . . demonstrated beyond all
> doubt that strong actions by Indians could result not only in broad pub-
> lic exposure of the issues and substantial national/international support
> for Indian rights, but could potentially force significant concessions from
> the federal government as well. . . . The lessons of this were not lost on
> the AIM leadership.[73]

The American Indian Movement was enormously influential, but its role in orchestrating Red Power protest events must not be overstated. While many collective event participants claimed AIM membership, the more common thread was education, urban ties, and Indian ethnic identification. AIM and its visible leadership provided a symbolic as well as an actual organizational point of entry for these potential participants in Red Power. Networks of urban Indian centers, Indian churches, and Indian charitable organizations helped plan and support collective actions by AIM.[74] Protest activities and strategies moved through

Indian communities via Indian social and kin networks and by way of the "pow-wow circuit," which passed information along to Indian families who traveled between the cities and the reservations.[75] However, the most important factor contributing to AIM's influence on Red Power protest was probably its ability to use the news media—newspapers, radio, magazines, and television—to drama- tize Indian problems and protests.

After visiting the Indians on Alcatraz Island and realizing the possibilities available through demonstration and seizure of federal facilities, AIM embarked on a national activist role. Its leaders recognized the opportunities when they met with the Indian people on the island during the summer of 1970 and were caught up in the momentum of the occupation. AIM leaders had seen firsthand that the bureaucracy inherent in the federal government had resulted in immobility: No punitive action had been taken thus far on the island. This provided an additional impetus for AIM's kind of national Indian activism and was congruent with the rising tide of national unrest, particularly among young college students.

AIM's first attempt at a national protest action came on Thanksgiving Day 1970 when its members seized the Mayflower II in Plymouth, Massachusetts, to challenge a celebration of colonial expansion into what had mistakenly been con- sidered a "new world." During this action, AIM leaders acknowledged the occu- pation of Alcatraz Island as the symbol of a newly awakened desire among Indians for unity and authority in a white world. In his 1995 autobiography, *Where White Men Fear to Tread*, former AIM leader Russell Means has stated:

> [A]bout every admirable quality that remains in today's Indian people is
> the result of the American Indian Movement's flint striking the white man's
> steel. In the 1970s and 1980s, we lit a fire across Indian country. We
> fought for changes in school curricula to eliminate racist lies, and we are
> winning. We fought for community control of police, and on a few reserva-
> tions it's now a reality. We fought to instill pride in our songs and in our
> language, in our cultural wisdom, inspiring a small renaissance in the
> teaching of our languages. . . . Thanks to AIM, for the first time in this cen-
> tury, Indian people stand at the threshold of freedom and responsibility.[76]

It was on Alcatraz, however, that the flint first met the steel; it was on Alca- traz that young Indian college students stood toe to toe with the federal govern- ment and did not step back.

After 1972, the involvement of urban Indian individuals and groups, such as AIM, in ARPM protests revealed tensions inside the Indian communities them- selves—between urban and reservation Indians, between AIM and tribal gov- ernments, and between different age cohorts—often arising out of political divisions on the reservations. The tone of protest became less celebratory, less other directed, and more harsh, more inward, and sometimes more violent. No single event of the Alcatraz–Red Power Movement more clearly illustrates the combination of Indian grievances and community tensions than the events on the Pine Ridge Reservation in South Dakota in the spring of 1973, a ten-week siege that came to be known as Wounded Knee II.[77]

The conflict at Wounded Knee, a small town on the reservation, involved a dispute within Pine Ridge's Oglala Lakota (Sioux) tribe over its controversial tribal chairman, Richard Wilson. Wilson was viewed as a corrupt puppet of the BIA by some segments of the tribe, including those associated with AIM. An effort to impeach him resulted in a division of the tribe into opposing camps. The two camps eventually armed themselves and began a two-and-a-half month siege that involved tribal police and government, AIM, reservation residents, federal law enforcement officials, the BIA, local citizens, nationally prominent entertainment figures, national philanthropic, religious, and legal organizations, and the national news media.[78]

The siege began with the arrival of a caravan of approximately 250 AIM supporters, led by Dennis Banks and Russell Means, on the evening of 27 February 1973. Although the armed conflict that followed AIM's arrival is generally characterized as a stand-off between AIM and its supporters and the Wilson government and its supporters, the siege at Wounded Knee was really only one incident in what had been a long history of political instability and factional conflict on the Pine Ridge Reservation.[79] The next weeks were filled with shootouts, roadblocks, negotiations, visiting delegations, and the movement of refugees out of various fire zones. There were also moments of high drama. For example, on 11 March "the occupiers, together with a delegation of Sioux traditionals who had entered Wounded Knee during a truce, proclaimed the new Independent Oglala Nation, . . . announced its intention to send a delegation to the United Nations. . . . [and] on March 16, 349 people were sworn in as citizens."[80]

When the siege ended on 9 May, after protracted negotiations between Leonard Garment, representing President Nixon, and AIM leaders Dennis Banks and Carter Camp, two Indians and one FBI agent were dead and an unknown number on both sides had been wounded. Wilson remained in office (though he was challenged at the next election), and many of the AIM members involved in the siege spent the next few years in litigation, in exile, and in prison.[81]

Although the action at Wounded Knee was inconclusive in terms of upsetting the balance of power in the Oglala Lakota tribal council,[82] the siege became an important component of the ARPM repertoire of contention. In the next few years, there ensued a number of both long- and short-term occupations. Many, but not all, of these occupations were similar to Wounded Knee in that they occurred on reservations and involved tribal factions associated with AIM or urban tribal members. These events included the six-month occupation of a former girls' camp on state-owned land at Moss Lake, New York, in 1974; the five-week armed occupation of a vacant Alexian Brothers novitiate by the Menominee Warrior Society near the Menominee reservation in Wisconsin in 1975; the eight-day takeover of a tribally owned Fairchild electronics assembly plant on the Navajo reservation in New Mexico in 1975; a three-day, followed by a one-day (several weeks later), occupation of the Yankton Sioux Industries plant on the reservation near Wagner, South Dakota, in 1975; and the week-long occupation of a juvenile detention center by members of the Puyallup tribe in Washington State in 1976.[83]

Red Power protests in the mid- to late-1970s were increasingly enacted in an atmosphere of heightened confrontation. The following, which took place in 1976, illustrates the tension of later activism:

> With little pomp, unobtrusive but heavy security and an impromptu Indian victory dance, the Federal Government today commemorated the 100th anniversary of the battle of Little Bighorn.. . . .Today on a wind-buffeted hill covered with buffalo grass, yellow clover and sage, in south-eastern Montana where George Armstrong Custer made his last stand, about 150 Indians from various tribes danced joyously around the monument to the Seventh Cavalry dead. Meanwhile at an official National Park Service ceremony about 100 yards away, an Army band played. . . . just as the ceremony got underway a caravan of Sioux, Cheyenne and other Indians led by Russell Means, the American Indian Movement leader, strode to the platform to the pounding of a drum.[84]

The last major event of the Alcatraz–Red Power Movement occurred in July 1978 when several hundred Native Americans marched into Washington, D.C., at the end of the Longest Walk, a protest march that had begun five months earlier in San Francisco. The Longest Walk was intended to symbolize the forced removal of American Indians from their homelands and to draw attention to the continuing problems of Indian people and their communities. The event was also intended to expose and challenge the backlash movement against Indian treaty rights that was gaining strength around the country and in Congress. This backlash could be seen in the growing number of bills before Congress to abrogate Indian treaties and restrict Indian rights.[85] Unlike many of the protest events of the mid-1970s, the Longest Walk was a peaceful event that included tribal spiritual leaders and Elders among its participants. It ended without violence. Thus, Red Power protest had come fill circle, from the festive Alcatraz days, through a cycle of confrontations between Indian activists and the federal government, to the traditional quest for spiritual unity that marked the end of the Longest Walk.

The decline of the Alcatraz–Red Power Movement is generally attributed to FBI suppression. That is probably only part of the story. AIM leaders were jailed, brought to trial, and many AIM members were found dead.[86] Internal debates in AIM underscored a long-standing split in the movement between those who preferred to work for the benefit of the urban Indian community using conventional methods of federal funding and community service and those who favored the activist national/supratribal agenda. The activist leadership began to withdraw from AIM: some moved on to other issues; some were kept busy fighting legal battles or serving jail time; and others were excommunicated from AIM by those who preferred more conventional tactics. Some leaders, disillusioned with the possibilities of attaining recognition of Native rights within the United States, sought recognition of treaty, national, and humanitarian rights within international forums such as UNESCO. After 1978, AIM leaders pursued many of the same goals as ARPM leaders, but the tactic of property seizures—the defining characteristic of the ARPM—fell out of favor, signaling the end of a formative period of Red Power activism.[87]

In some sense, the ARPM was no longer needed. It had laid the foundation of Indian activism and achieved many of its goals, mostly by conventional means. More Indian students were attending college, by the early 1980s there were over a hundred Indian studies programs in the United States, many tribal museums had opened, the National Museum of the American Indian was being planned, and an international indigenous rights movement has been recognized by the United Nations. However, throughout the 1980s and into the 1990s, AIM remained a force in American Indian activism and consciousness, organizing and participating in protests in the Black Hills (Camp Yellow Thunder);[88] continuing the battle over land and grazing rights in Navajo and Hopi territory; protesting athletic team Indian mascots, gestures, logos, and slogans; and working for the repatriation of Indian burial remains, funerary items, and sacred objects.

Social scientists have written extensively on the consequences of activism for the individuals and communities involved in protest movements, which can be life-transforming events.[89] Doug McAdam has found, for example, that the lives of participants in the 1964 Freedom Summer voter registration campaign in the South were altered such that these activists remained ever different from their uninvolved contemporaries, and, furthermore, the effects of these changes extended well into their adulthoods.[90] In his study of labor actions and strikes, Rick Fantasia has found that the participants in such activism redefine themselves and others in terms of their awareness of class distinctions and power relations. He has also pointed out that the community divisions arising out of sustained protest can be long lived and sometimes bitter.[91]

Sometimes, individual communities are strengthened by their members coming together in protest action. For example, Annette Kuhlmann, Richard White, and Carol Ward have all found that many Native American communities have benefited from the involvement of former activists, whether as museum curators, newspaper editors, community or legal service providers, or tribal leaders.[92] Joane Nagel has argued that the activist period of the 1970s contributed to the cultural renaissance currently underway in many Indian communities in the form of tribal museum development, tribal language instruction, cultural preservation and apprenticeship programs, tribal history projects, and the preservation and reinstitution of ceremonial and spiritual practices.[93]

Perhaps the most profound effect of the Alcatraz–Red Power Movement was to educate and change the consciousness of people in the United States and around the world. By the 1980s, more Americans were familiar with Indian issues as a result of the attention brought to bear by ARPM activism. While Americans have generally demanded assimilation from Indians, the ARPM made the point that Indians have cultures, traditions, history, and communities that they want to preserve—but that they also want equal justice, economic opportunity, access to education, and more accurate portrayal of Indians in the media and in history books. Along with other ethnic group movements, the ARPM contributed to the debate over multiculturalism within the U.S. national community.

In the end, the Alcatraz–Red Power Movement may have strengthened and diversified U.S. society and made it a more tolerant place for all.

Notes

1. Stephen Cornell, *The Return of the Native* (New York: Oxford University Press, 1988), 180.

2. See R. H. Turner, "Collective Behavior and Resource Mobilization as Approaches to Social Movements," *Research in Social Movements, Conflict and Change* 4 (1981): 1–24; Charles Tilley, *From Mobilization to Revolution* (Reading, MA: Addison-Wesley); Doug McAdam, *The Political Process and the Development of Black Insurgency, 1930–1970* (Chicago: University of Chicago Press, 1982).

3. Michael Hittman, *Wovoka and the Ghost Dance* (Carson City, NV: Grace Danberg Foundation, 1990), 63–64, 182–94.

4. For a discussion of spiritual and social revitalization movements, see Duane Champagne, "Transocietal Cultural Exchange within the World Economic and Political System," in *The Dynamics of Social Systems*, ed. Paul Colomy (Newbury Park, CA: Sage, 1992), 120–53.

5. H. W. Hertzberg, *The Search for an American Indian Identity* (Syracuse, NY: Syracuse University Press, 1971), 6.

6. Six Nations peoples consist of the Mohawk, Oneida, Onondaga, Cayuga, Seneca, and Tuscarora Indian tribes of the northeastern United States.

7. Guy B. Senese, *Self-Determination and the Social Education of Native Americans* (New York: Praeger, 1991), 146.

8. Ibid., 147.

9. Fay G. Cohen, *Treaties on Trial: The Continuing Controversy over Northwest Indian Fishing Rights* (Seattle: University of Washington Press, 1986), 69.

10. Quoted in Senese, *Self-Determination*, 145.

11. Ibid., 148.

12. Ibid., 144.

13. Troy R. Johnson, "Part 3: Native North American History, 1960–94," in *Chronology of Native American History*, ed. Duane Champagne (Detroit, MI: Gale Research, 1994), 355.

14. Ibid., 361–62.

15. Quoted in Senese, *Self-Determination*, 224.

16. Robert Hecht, "Taos Pueblo and the Struggle for Blue Lake," *American Indian Culture and Research Journal* 13:1 (1989): 55.

17. R. C. Gordon-McCutchan, *The Taos Indians and the Battle for Blue Lake* (Santa Fe, NM: Red Crane Books, 1991), xvi–xvii. This book recounts the story of the government taking of Blue Lake and the Taos Indians' successful campaign to recover it.

18. Alvin Josephy, "The American Indian and the Bureau of Indian Affairs, 1969: A Study with Recommendations," 24 February 1969. Report commissioned by President Richard M. Nixon.

19. Edgar S. Cahn, "Postscript," in *Our Brother's Keeper: The Indian in White America*, ed. Edgar S. Cahn (New York: New Community Press, 1969), 187–90.

20. Ibid.

21. R. D. Arnold, *Alaska Native Land Claims* (Anchorage: Alaska Native Foundation, 1978).

22. Cohen, *Treaties on Trial*, 82–83.

23. The Nixon presidential archives make no mention of the invasion of Cambodia, since it was largely a secret operation (though poorly kept) at the time. President Nixon and his staff make direct analogies among the Indian people on Alcatraz, the events of My Lai, and the shootings at Kent State. It was agreed that the American people would not stand by and see Indian people massacred and taken off Alcatraz in body bags.

24. Judith Clavir Albert and Stewart Edward Albert, *The Sixties Papers: Documents of a Rebellious Decade* (New York: Praeger, 1984), 18.

25. Wub-e-ke-niew, *We Have a Right to Exist* (New York: Black Thistle Press, 1995), xxxix.

26. Veterans Administration Statistical Brief, "Native American Veterans," SB 70-85-3 (October 1985), Washington, DC.

27. Quoted in Stan Steiner, *The New Indians* (New York: Harper & Row, 1968), 282.

28. Ibid.

29. Joan Albion, "Relocated American Indians in the San Francisco Bay Area: Social Interaction and Indian Identity," *Human Organization* 23 (Winter 1964): 297.

30. Vine Deloria, Jr., *Behind the Trail of Broken Treaties: And Indian Declaration of Independence* (Austin: University of Texas Press, 1985), 34.

31. Quoted in Alvin M. Josephy, Jr., *The American Indian Fight for Freedom* (New Have, CT: Yale University Press, 1978), 84. Clyde Warrior is often referred to as the founder of the Red Power movement.

32. Quoted in Jack D. Forbes, *Native Americans and Nixon: Presidential Politics and Minority Self-Determination, 1969–1972* (Los Angeles: American Indian Studies Center, University of California, 1981), 28. Brightman founded and began publication of *Warpath* in 1968, providing a voice for rising urban Indian youth groups.

33. Quoted in National Council on Indian Opportunity, "Public Forum before the Committee of Urban Indians, San Francisco, Calif.," 11–12 April 1969, 3 (hereafter NCIO, "Public Forum"). In the possession of Adam Fortunate Eagle, Fallon Indian Reservation, Fallon NV.

34. Ablon, "Relocated Indians in the San Francisco Bay Area," 296–304.

35. NCIO, "Public Forum," 39.

36. Ibid., 41.

37. Quoted in Steiner, *New Indians*, 45.

38. Ibid.

39. Ibid.

40. Johnson, "Part 3," 355–57.

41. During this period, the University of California, Davis, was attempting to acquire the same site for its own use. It was the occupation of the intended site by Indian youth, some of which had been involved in the Alcatraz occupation, that ultimately led to success for the Indian-controlled university. In April 1971, the federal government turned this land over to the trustees of Deganawida-Quetzalcoatl (D-Q) University, a joint American Indian and Chicano university. One of the demands of the Alcatraz occupiers, in 1964 and again in 1969, was the establishment of an Indian university on Alcatraz island. While this never occurred, the establishment of D-Q University was seen by many as the fulfillment of that demand.

42. Troy Johnson, *The Occupation of Alcatraz Island: Indian Self-Determination and the Rise of Indian activism* (Urbana: University of Illinois Press, 1996). The occupation took place on 9 March 1964, the night of 9–10 November 1969, and 20 November 1969.

43. Belva Cottier interview with John Garvey, San Francisco, CA, 13 May 1989. Copy in possession of Troy Johnson.

44. NCIO, "Public Forum."

45. Luis S. Kemnitzer, "Personal Memories of Alcatraz, 1969," chapter 7 in *American Indian Activism: Alcatraz to the Longest Walk*, Troy Johnson, Duane Champagne, and Joanne Nagel, eds. (Urbana: University of Illinois Press, 1997), 114–15.

46. Johnson, *Occupation of Alcatraz Island*, 119.

47. Earl Livermore, Blackfoot, interview with John D. Sylvester, 8 April 1970, Doris Duke Oral History Project, University of Utah, Salt Lake City.

48. Johnson, *Occupation of Alcatraz Island*, 48.

49. Ibid.

50. "Unsigned Proclamation," reproduced in *Alcatraz Is Not an Island*, ed. Peter Blue Cloud (Berkeley, CA: Wingbow Press, 1972), 40–42.

51. Johnson, *Occupation of Alcatraz Island*, 71–72.

52. Ibid., 40–41.

53. Ibid., 154–55.

54. Ibid., 206.

55. Ibid., 152, 169.

56. Ibid., 182–83.

57. Ibid., 226.

58. Vine Deloria, Jr., "The Rise of Indian Activism," in *The Social Reality of Ethnic America*, ed. R. Gomez, C. Collingham, R. Endo, and K. Jackson (Lexington, MA: D.C. Heath, 1974), 184–85.

59. Vine Deloria, Jr., correspondence with the authors, 1993.

60. Wilma Mankiller telephone interview with Joane Nagel, Tahlequah, OK, 27 November 1991. Transcript in the authors' files.

61. George Horse Capture telephone interview with Joane Nagel, Fort Belknap, MN, 24 May 1994. Transcript in the author's files. See also George Horse Capture, "An American Indian Perspective," in *Seeds of Change: A Quincentennial Commemoration*, ed. Herman J. Viola and Carolyn Margolis (Washington, DC: Smithsonian Institution Press, 1991).

62. John Echohawk telephone interview with Joane Nagel, Boulder, CO, 9 July 1993. Transcript in the authors' files.

63. Leonard Peltier telephone interview with Joane Nagel, Leavenworth, KS, 1 June 1993. Transcript in the authors' files.

64. Frances Wise telephone interview with Joane Nagel, Oklahoma City, OK, 24 August 1993. Transcript in the authors' files.

65. Quoted in Judith Antell, "American Indian Women Activists" (Ph.D. diss., University of California, Berkeley, 1989), 58.

66. Grace Thorpe interview with John Trudell on "Radio Free Alcatraz," 12 December 1969. Transcript available from Pacifica Radio Archive, 3729 Cahvenga Boulevard, North Hollywood, CA 91604.

67. Loretta Flores telephone interview with Joane Nagel, Lawrence, KS, 12 May 1993. Transcript in the authors' files.

68. "Indians Seize Army Center for Use as Cultural Base," *New York Times*, 4 November 1970, 6. This land later became the site of Deganawida-Quetzacoatl (D-Q) University. See *Akwesasne Notes* (January–February 1971): 17.

69. William M. Blair, "24 Indians Seized in Capital Clash," *New York Times*, 23 September 1971, 49.

70. Ward Churchill and James Vander Wall, *Agents of Repression: The FBI's Secret War against the Black Panther Party and the American Indian Movement* (Boston: South End

Press, 1988), 121; Rex Weyler, *Blood of the Land* (New York: Everett House, 1984) 24, 42–43; Peter Matthiessen, *In the Spirit of Crazy Horse* (New York: Viking, 1991); Alvin M. Josephy, Jr., *Now That the Buffalo's Gone* (New York: Knopf, 1982), 228–31.

71. Johnson, *Occupation of Alcatraz Island*, 219–20; Wub-e-ke-niew, *We Have the Right to Exist*, xl–xlvii.

72. Churchill and Vander Wall, *Agents of Repression*, 121.

73. Ibid. Ironically, several researchers also cite the role of common prison experiences in the formation of the American Indian Movement organization. See Matthiessen, *In the Spirit of Crazy Horse*, 34; Weyler, *Blood of the Land*, 35; Rachel A. Bonney, "Forms of Subtribal Indian Interaction in the United States" (Ph.D. diss., University of Arizona, 1975), 154–55.

74. Fay G. Cohen, "The Indian Patrol in Minneapolis: Social Control and Social Change in an Urban Context" (Ph.D. diss., University of Minnesota, 1973), 52.

75. Ibid., 49–50; Jeanne Guillemin, *Urban Renegades: The Cultural Strategy of American Indians* (New York: Columbia University Press, 1975); Roy Bongartz, "The New Indians," in *Native Americans Today*, ed. H. M. Bahr, B. A. Chadwick, and R.C. Day (New York: Harper & Row, 1968), 495.

76. Russell Means with Marvin J. Wolf, *Where White Men Fear to Tread: The Autobiography of Russell Means* (New York: St. Martin's Press, 1995), 540.

77. Today, most commentators, participants, and observers refer to the 1973 siege at Wounded Knee, South Dakota, as "Wounded Knee." At the time, the press and commentators often called the siege "Wounded Knee II," to distinguish it from the U. S. 7th Cavalry's massacre of Lakotas which took place there in December 1890. See Robert Utley, *The Last Days of the Sioux Nation* (New Haven, CT: Yale University Press, 1963), 110.

78. See Edward Lazarus, *Black Hills, White Justice: The Sioux Nation versus the United States, 1775 to the Present* (New York: HarperCollins, 1991), chap. 12; Matthiessen, *In the Spirit of Crazy Horse*, chap. 3; Churchill and Vander Wall, *Agents of Repression*, chap. 5; Stanley D. Lyman, *Wounded Knee 1973: A Personal Account* (Lincoln: University of Nebraska Press, 1991); Rolland Dewing, *Wounded Knee: The Meaning and Significance of the Second Incident* (New York: Irvington, 1985).

79. For instance, Lazarus reports that, up to a point, the "Pine Ridge Sioux had never reelected a president to a second term" (*Black Hills, White Justice*, 309).

80. Ibid., 307.

81. The most celebrated of the cases involves Leonard Peltier, who was tried and convicted for the deaths of two FBI agents who were shot on the Pine Ridge reservation in 1975. See Matthiessen, *In the Spirit of Crazy Horse*, 162.

82. For instance, Wilson remained in office and was reelected after a challenge by AIM leader Russell Means in 1974. Wilson died in 1990. See Churchill and Vander Wall, *Agents of Repression*, 189; Martin Waldron, "President of the Oglala Sioux Is Re-elected," *New York Times*, 9 February 1974, 23; Matthiessen, *In the Spirit of Crazy Horse*, 581.

83. While several of the post–Wounded Knee occupations were marked by tribal conflict, the Puyallup occupation of the detention center appears to have been undertaken by a unified tribe.

84. Grace Lichtenstein, "Custer's Defeat Commemorated by Entreaties on Peace," *New York Times*, 25 June 1976, II-1.

85. For a general description of anti-Indian backlash groups and activities in the late 1970s, see the series of articles in "Nationwide Backlash against the Indian Tribes," the 18 July 1977 supplement of the *Yakima Nation Review*: Richard La Course, "Anti-Indian

Backlash Growing; Tribes, Groups Form Defense Tactics"; Carole Wright, "What People Have Formed Backlash Groups?"; June Adams, "Three Major 'Backlash Bills' in Congress"; June Adams and Richard La Course, "Backlash Barrage Erupts across U. S." See also, Fay G. Cohen, "Implementing Indian Treaty Fishing Rights: Conflict and Cooperation," in *Critical Issues in Native North America*, vol. 2, ed. W. Churchill (Copenhagen: International Work Group for Indigenous Affairs, 1991), 155–73.

86. Ken Stern, *Loud Hawk: The U. S. versus the American Indian Movement* (Norman: University of Oklahoma Press, 1994), 93–98. The deaths were never investigated, but Indian people suspect the FBI was involved.

87. See, for example, Wub-e-ke-niew, *We Have the Right to Exist*, xlv, 232–33; Josephy, *Now That the Buffalo's Gone*, 254–55.

88. Camp Yellow Thunder was established in the early 1980s to protest federal violations of Sioux treaties and the refusal of the federal government to return the Black Hills. See Lazarus, *Black Hills, White Justice*, 411–12; and Donald Worster, *Under Western Skies: Nature and History in the American West* (New York: Oxford University Press, 1992), chap. 8.

89. See, for example, Leila Rupp and Verta Taylor, *Survival in the Doldrums: The American Women's Rights Movement, 1945 to the 1960s* (New York: Oxford University Press, 1987); Doug McAdam, *Freedom Summer* (New York: Oxford University Press, 1988); Rick Fantasia, *Cultures of Solidarity: Consciousness, Action, and Contemporary American Workers* (Berkeley: University of California Press, 1988); Verta Taylor and Nancy E. Whitier, "Collective Identity in Social Movement Communities: Lesbian Feminist Mobilization," in *Frontiers in Social Movement Theory*, ed. A. D. Morris and C. M. Mueller (New Haven, CT: Yale University Press, 1992), 104–20; Joane Nagel, "American Indian Ethnic Renewal: Politics and the Resurgence of Identity," *American Sociological Review* 60 (1995): 947–65.

90. McAdam, *Freedom Summer*.

91. Fantasia, *Cultures of Solidarity*.

92. Annette Kuhlmann, "Collaborative Research on Biculturalism among the Kickapoo Tribe of Oklahoma" (Ph.D. diss., University of Kansas, 1989); Richard H. White, *Tribal Assets: The Rebirth of Native America* (New York: Henry Holt, 1990), 124; Carol Ward, "The Intersection of Ethnic and Gender Identities: The Role of Northern Cheyenne Women in Cultural Recovery," paper presented at the annual meeting of the Society for the Scientific Study of Religion, Raleigh, NC, October, 1993, 86.

93. Joane Nagel, *American Indian Ethnic Renewal: Red Power and the Resurgence of Identity and Culture* (New York: Oxford University Press, 1996), 195–200.

INDEX

The following typographical conventions used in this index are: f and *t* identify figures and tables, respectively, *n* identifies a note.

315

ACKNOWLEDGMENTS

ANDERS, GARY. INDIAN GAMING: FINANCIAL AND REGULATORY QUESTIONS, FROM ANNALS OF THE AMERICAN ACADEMY OF POLITICAL AND SOCIAL SCIENCE (556), 98-108, © 1998 BY SAGE PUBLICATIONS, INC. REPRINTED BY PERMISSION OF SAGE PUBLICATIONS, INC.

JOHNSON, TROY, DUANE CHAMPAGNE, AND JOANNE NAGEL. AMERICAN INDIAN ACTIVISM AND TRANSFORMATION: LESSONS FROM ALCATRAZ, FROM AMERICAN INDIAN ACTIVISM: ALCATRAZ TO THE LONGEST WALK, © 1997 BY THE BOARD OF TRUSTEES OF THE UNIVERSITY OF ILLINOIS. REPRINTED BY PERMISSION OF UNIVERSITY OF ILLINOIS PRESS

GOLDBERG, CAROLE. PUBLIC LAW 280 AND THE PROBLEM OF LAWLESSNESS IN CALIFORNIA INDIAN COUNTRY, FROM PLANTING TAIL FEATHERS: TRIBAL SURVIVAL AND PUBLIC LAW 280, © 1997 REGENTS OF THE UNIVERSITY OF CALIFORNIA.REPRINTED BY PERMISSION OF THE AMERICAN INDIAN STUDIES CENTER, UCLA

The following articles are reprinted from the *American Indian Culture and Research Journal*, by permission of the American Indian Studies Center, UCLA, © Regents of the University of California:

THE TRAGEDY AND THE TRAVESTY: THE SUBVERSION OF INDIGENOUS SOVEREIGNTY IN NORTH AMERICA. WARD CHURCHILL (22:2, 1998)

THE PAST AS LEGACY AND PROJECT: POSTCOLONIAL CRITICISM IN THE PERSPECTIVE OF INDIGENOUS HISTORICISM. ARIF DRILIK (20:2, 1996)

RECENT UNITED NATIONS INITIATIVES CONCERNING THE RIGHTS OF INDIGENOUS PEOPLES. STEPHEN V. QUESENBERRY. (21:3, 1997)

CLAIMING MEMORY IN BRITISH COLUMBIA: ABORIGINAL RIGHTS AND THE STATE. FAE L. KORSMO (20:4, 1996)

TRADITIONAL AMERICAN INDIAN ECONOMIC POLICY. RONALD TROSPER (19:1, 1995)

THE CONTEXTUAL NATURE OF AMERICAN INDIAN CRIMINALITY. DONALD E. GREEN (17:2, 1993)

NEBRASKA'S LANDMARK REPATRIATION LAW: A STUDY OF CROSS-CULTURAL CONFLICT AND RESOLUTION. ROBERT M. PEREGOY (16:2, 1992)

ACKNOWLEDGING THE REPATRIATION CLAIMS OF UNACKNOWLEDGED CALIFORNIA TRIBES. CAROLE GOLDBERG (21:3, 1997)

About the Editor

TROY R. JOHNSON is an Associate Professor of American Indian Studies and U. S. History at California State University, Long Beach. He is an internationally published author who has conducted extensive research on race and ethnicity. He is author, editor, or associate editor of eleven books and numerous scholarly journal articles and has presented a score of papers at scholarly conferences. His publications include *The Occupation of Alcatraz Island, Indian Self-Determination and the Rise of Indian Activism*; *American Indian Activism, Alcatraz to the Longest Walk*; *We Hold the Rock*; and the forthcoming updated and expanded edition of *Red Power*.